MEN WHO MANAGE

MEN

Fusions of Feeling

One of a series of books from the research program of the

Institute of Industrial Relations, University of California

WHO MANAGE

and Theory in Administration

MELVILLE DALTON

Associate Professor of Sociology
Department of Anthropology and Sociology

Associate Research Sociologist
Institute of Industrial Relations

University of California, Los Angeles

NEW YORK · JOHN WILEY & SONS, INC.

LONDON · CHAPMAN & HALL, LIMITED

Foreword

With this book, the Southern Division of the Institute of Industrial Relations makes its first contribution to a series in industrial relations published by John Wiley and Sons. Professor Dalton is concerned with managers, with the roles they play and with the coexistence of formal and informal systems of organization in the modern business enterprise. Accordingly, his study embraces the sociology of the enterprise in its larger aspect, although he also deals with industrial relations considered as an important part of this larger setting.

From its inception at the University of California at Los Angeles in 1945, the Institute of Industrial Relations has supported a broad and diversified program of research. By avoiding commitment to single all-embracing projects, the Institute has been able to promote a healthy pluralism of specialties and specialists, nonetheless linked together under the common term, industrial relations. Through books, monographs, and articles in professional journals, research sponsored by the Institute has embraced such areas as collective bargaining, the law of labor-management relations, labor history, labor economics, and human relations. Studies are actively continuing in all of these fields and will eventuate in additional publications as they are completed.

The Institute consists of a Northern Division on the Berkeley campus and a Southern Division on the Los Angeles campus. In addition to the support of diversified research in industrial relations, both divisions also conduct continuing community programs for labor and management groups and for the general public. These programs have the dual purpose of bringing the latest results of research to practitioners in the field and of keeping the academic specialists informed regarding problems and practices developed by the practitioners themselves. Overall, the objective of the Institute is to contribute to improved labor-management relations through the development of knowledge and its dissemination to the community.

In a sense Professor Dalton's work breaks new ground, in keeping with his own description of himself as a "marginal researcher," seeking to link academic theories of business organization with what can be observed by direct observation of managers themselves. His purpose is not to draw a contrast between theory and fact, or to substitute description of the concrete for the scientific task of inference and generalization. Quite the contrary. Viewed as an organization, every enterprise confronts certain recurring typical problems: pressure for economy, cooperation of experts with their superiors, development of localized meanings for decisions reached on high, uncertainty regarding methods of advancement through the managerial hierarchy, recognition of superior contributions and differential rewards for them, and those psychological and moral conflicts experienced by every executive in reconciling ends and means. In Professor Dalton's own words, the central theme of his book is "a study of compromises among key individuals and groups in rational organizations, and the human strictures on compromise." Their locus is the conflict between those advocates of routine whose passion is method and procedure, and those pragmatists who resort to adaptation and expedient in order to get the job done. Clearly, this study suggests rich possibilities for further research, particularly for labor-management relations.

GEORGE H. HILDEBRAND
DIRECTOR, SOUTHERN DIVISION
INSTITUTE OF INDUSTRIAL RELATIONS

September, 1958

Preface

This is primarily an analytical record of interplays between compromising situations and compromising managers in commercial and industrial settings. Much of the usual explicit prefatory comment is contained in the Introduction. Here I want only to make some personal asides about aim, method, and intended audience.

An implicit hope of the book is to give academicians and industrialists a sharper picture of each other through the device of *unguarded* managerial plain talk and professorial analyses. Since the professors are always training personnel for the managers, there should be less— or more realistic—name-calling than I find in traveling back and forth between them.

My own compromises in filling interdisciplinary academic posts, and doing research among labor unions, and industrial and civic groups over recent years have of course stamped the book. Prolonged touch-and-go relations of this kind usually bar a man from full acceptance by any of the worlds in which he moves. But with all its shocks, this marginal role offers high excitement. And it forces the tenant to search for connecting links among his erratic and overlapping orbits. The search may tire one at times, and even seem to fail. But the joy of confirmed hunches mixed with jarring surprises keeps one at the task. With the acquisition of different academic viewpoints one also learns the accompanying stereotypes that the disciplines have of each other. One obviously does not accept the challenge to change these stereotypes, but wisely utilizes them in the research.

However, the marginal researcher *does* accept the other and greater challenge to communicate between the extreme academic theorist and the industrial practitioner who moves by pure intuition. Both of course have their stereotypes of the field researcher. The practitioners, for example, often tell me that, as an academician, I generalize irresponsibly —and largely for my colleagues. Some of the academic extremists assure me that my field work is self-defeating because I cannot master the life of enough different firms to warrant generalizations, because I spend so much time in the forest that I never really see it, because I am insufficiently reflective and theoretical.

Moderates from both sides scout these criticisms. They suggest that a report of this kind, with the secondary aim of bringing devisers and doers nearer a common outlook, should be presented in general rather than specialized language. I have largely followed this advice by directing the bulk of the book to a general audience. Yet inasmuch as the specialist is professionally and sentimentally tied to at least a family of disciplines, I have usually reserved the footnotes and references—and certainly the Appendix—for more specialized readers.

MELVILLE DALTON

May, 1959
SANTA MONICA, CALIFORNIA

Acknowledgments

I am greatly indebted to the Institute of Industrial Relations of the University of California at Los Angeles for economic aid and use of facilities over later years of the inquiry; for freedom in choosing and following my research problems, and for support through two summers and part of the regular academic year while I organized and wrote the book. I am grateful to Benjamin Aaron, Associate Director of the Institute, for his suggestions from a critical reading of the manuscript. I am further obliged to Professors Irving R. Weschler and Melvin Rothbaum of the Institute for their work and helpful suggestions as members of a reading committee, and to J. A. C. Grant, Professor of Political Science and Divisional Dean of the Social Sciences, who chaired the committee. Special thanks for many favors in connection with the research are also due members of the Institute Library, particularly Paul Miles, Librarian, Edwin Kaye, Assistant Librarian, Helen Peak, and Walther Liebenow.

During the initial inquiry at the "Milo Fractionating Center" I was aided by a research grant from the Committee on Human Relations in Industry of the University of Chicago. And for over a year, Professor Herbert Blumer, then at Chicago, counseled me on the research at Milo, indicated detours around inherent obstacles in public relations, and critically commented on an early draft of Milo materials. Since then he has encouraged the larger research and, under the stress of final weeks before an academic leave, obligingly read and commented on nine chapters of the manuscript then completed.

A small part of the material in Chapters 3, 4, 5, and 6 appeared earlier as progress reports of a kind. I wish to thank the editors and publishers of the following papers for permission to adapt and republish those parts that have been used.

Chapter 3: "Industrial Controls and Personal Relations," *Social Forces,* 33: 244–249, March, 1955, and "Managing the Managers," *Human Organization,* 14: (3) 4–10, Fall, 1955.

Chapter 4: "Conflicts Between Staff and Line Managerial Officers," *American Sociological Review,* 15: 342–351, June, 1950.

Chapter 5: "Unofficial Union-Management Relations," *American Sociological Review,* 15: 611–619, October, 1950.

Chapter 6: "Informal Factors in Career Achievement," *American Journal of Sociology,* 56: 407–415, March, 1951.

M. D.

Contents

CHAPTER 1

Introduction

This is a study of how business and industrial managers* manage. There is of course endless literature on personnel problems in industry, and a flood of guidebooks for overriding obstacles to the goals of management. This literature has an important place, but according to one high authority[1] many of those who are being advised are unable to keep abreast of these encyclopedias of procedure. And a distinguished administrator has recently declared, "We do not need proof or provable theses so much as we need questions and hypotheses which will stimulate insights among practitioners."[2] Here we shall seek both to raise questions and hypotheses, and to give some supporting evidence for them.

As a study of how managers manage, this is not an effort at muckraking, or an apology, or a guidebook in disguise, or an attempt to belittle bureaucratic operations. Rather the aim is to get as close as possible to the world of managers and to interpret this world and its problems from the inside, as they are seen and felt at various points and levels. Such a project requires attention also to the counter influences between managers and firm, and the consequences for each and for the individual from what occurs in the process. Where relevance

---

* This term is used loosely for all members of management—executives and foremen, staff specialists and supervisors. (Throughout the book, documentary footnotes are indicated by numbers and collected at the end of the chapter; content notes are asterisked and placed at the bottom of the page.)

and data allow, we want to relate this world to the surrounding community. Finally we wish to describe both unique and typical experiences and events as bases for theory that is developed and related to other studies.

The case materials of the study were drawn chiefly from four firms located in or adjacent to Magnesia,* a city of Mobile Acres, a heavily industrialized region of Central United States. Three of the companies are factories: the Milo Fractionating Center, the Fruhling Works, and the Attica Assembly Company; the fourth, Rambeau Mart, is a department store. All are units of corporations with home offices located outside Mobile Acres. The Fruhling firm has a total work force fluctuating around 20,000; Milo, around 8000; Attica, 2600; and Rambeau upwards of 400. Other firms inside and outside Mobile Acres will be referred to in various contexts. I had considerable first-hand experience in two of these firms both before and concurrently with part of the inquiry.† The period of employment, the direct field work, and follow-up visits continued for over a decade.

Here we can only touch the related literature,‡ which can be roughly categorized for our purposes. Some executives, for instance, have theorized from their experiences and observations without giving specific data. Examples are Chester Barnard, who has done this with remarkable insight and detachment in his *Functions of the Executive,* and Lieut.-Col. Lyndall F. Urwick, whose writings are internationally renowned. Other executives have described aspects of their experiences, attacked current trends and practices in industry and business as undemocratic, inefficient, etc., and have recommended many changes. Examples are T. K. Quinn, *Big Business: Threat to Democracy,* and H. Frederick Willkie, *A Rebel Yells.*

A third group of studies are those by various editors and research teams of *Fortune.* Recent examples are *A Guide to Modern Management Methods* (largely by Perrin Stryker), *The Executive Life, Is Anybody Listening?* (chiefly by W. H. Whyte, Jr.), and Whyte's *The Organization Man.* The data of these studies are collected through interviews, questionnaires, and statistical records from apparently a

---

* My indebtedness for trust and aid from dozens of industrial officials—management and union—requires compliance with their wish for anonymity of place, firm, and person. This is regrettable for scientific purposes but the case materials show why it must be. Those executives in other firms of Mobile Acres, and on the West Coast, who initially welcomed my research efforts and then blocked me as I approached the confidential areas reported here, will surely understand my obligation.

† For details of method, see the Appendix.

‡ See the various chapters for bibliographical details and fuller discussion.

great range of firms and industries. These studies give helpful statistics, reveal flashes of insight, raise important questions, and are provocatively presented. Repeatedly we pay our respect by preying on them. However, they frequently do not get close enough to industrial situations to consistently get at covert activities and the meanings assigned to them by participants, and to spell out the consequences, in terms of individual and group actions, for the organization.

Academic studies by specialists in business and in the social and psychological sciences fall into a fourth group. These efforts may have specific departmental flavors or be interdisciplinary. Among the many we will use are Ginzberg, *What Makes an Executive?;* Dimock,* *The Executive in Action;* Zaleznik, *Foreman Training in a Growing Enterprise;* Newcomer, *The Big Business Executive;* the twin reports by Warner and Abegglen, *Occupational Mobility in American Business and Industry,* and *Big Business Leaders in America;* Learned, Ulrich, and Booz, *Executive Action;* Drucker, *The Practice of Management;* Tead, *The Art of Administration;* Dubin, *Human Relations in Administration;* Roethlisberger, *Management and Morale,* etc.; Kruisinga, *The Balance Between Centralization and Decentralization in Managerial Control;* Lombard, *Behavior in a Selling Group;* Scott and Lynton, *Three Studies in Management;* Ronken and Lawrence, *Administering Change;* and so forth.

The place of these studies and others—as theories about the nature of organization, as explanations for the gap between recipe and performance, as records of clash between theorists and decision-makers, as reports on careers, etc.—will be obvious throughout the book.

A participant at Milo and Fruhling, I was repeatedly puzzled by the gap between official and unofficial ways of doing things, and by the emotional splits and name-calling among associates devoted to one general approach or the other. As developed in the Appendix, this experience raised questions that I formulated as a guide for seeking answers. Returns from queries followed at Milo and Fruhling led me to utilize excellent contacts at Rambeau and Attica to look for similar problems there. In some cases I was able to see allied problems more closely, or I found conditions in one plant that stimulated further inquiry in the others.

The general approach to all firms was first to learn the issues and who was involved. Problems of recurring concern were then viewed in terms of their extent and the ramifications of behavior that kept them alive. Since the larger aspect of many problems was officially non-

---

* Dimock has been both an academician and an executive.

existent, the study is heavily concerned with unofficial behavior, though official and unofficial are reciprocal aspects of the same thing. The tug-of-war between these states of organization will be part of every problem cluster in Chapters 3 through 7. Chapter 8 is devoted exclusively to an analysis of the nominal and nebulous poles of organization, the middle ground between them, and the interconnections that enable the paper organization to continue. Organization is seen not as a chiseled entity, but as a shifting set of contained and ongoing counter phases of action.

The recurring problem* areas we will discuss grow out of (1) pressures for economy of operation; (2) "cooperation" of officially powerless experts with their administrative superiors; (3) local meanings found by union and management in the high level work agreements to which they are subject; (4) uncertainty about the route to a place in middle and upper management; and (5) the task of recognizing and rewarding differential contributions. Both as an accompaniment and a residuum of these organizational perturbations are (6) the psychological and moral conflicts of the individual executive who must in some fashion balance the spirit and letter of the firm as he meets the claims of subordinates and associates.

Each of these six problem areas is made the subject of a chapter. There is no pretense that these are the only personnel problems, or that all aspects of each area are explored, or—most lamentable shortcoming of the effort—that the problems were investigated with equal thoroughness in each firm or in any one of the firms, or that all relevant literature has been covered. Obviously the volume of published materials, the size of the companies, and the limitations of a lone researcher forced compromises.

Milo's formal structure and the theories of industrial organization held by its staffs are discussed in Chapter 2. These theories and the functions of staffs typify American industry. The formal chart is limited to Milo because only there could I develop a comparable chart of key managers ranked according to their relative unofficial influence (Chapter 3). Like Milo, Fruhling and Attica were staff-line type organizations under central offices. Fruhling was more complex, and Attica simpler and with fewer staffs, than Milo. Essential details of the structure of both, and of Rambeau, are presented in context.

Dealing with the social repercussions of economic pressures at Milo, Chapter 3 charts the schisms between nominal and exercised authority.

---

* There is no claim that all these problems—and many of the practices we shall see—are peculiar to business and industry, or to our time.

An example of typical clashes between the branches of Operation and Maintenance is presented. Steps are followed in a struggle that led to creation of a formal control to reduce costs and to limit the conflict. Our observation of the control's breakdown and the covert adaptation of one later imposed by the home office, is supplemented with a theory of cliques as the indispensable action centers and preservers of the large complex organization.

Controversies over the sphere of operations and authority of industrial staffs are discussed in Chapter 4. The out-of-role staff practices at Milo; the typical staff and line stereotypes of each other; the internal problems of staffs at Milo, Fruhling, and smaller firms; and the middle and lower line evasion of staff rules as compared with the relative harmony at top levels are typical points of departure. Disharmonies are analyzed in terms of differences in outlook, job opportunity, etc., against the restrictive background of line authority, the concerns of top management, staff need to prove itself, etc.

Chapter 5 focuses on the meaning of broad labor agreements in the local plant. Milo, Fruhling, and Attica supply case materials of local expediencies at all levels of management; and Attica points an instructive case of internal and plant-community compromises involving minority groups. With or against the contract, by adherence to one's official camp or through union-management cliques, surface harmony and deference to the contract are merged with getting the job done. Grievance records are a clue to the compromises which are analyzed in terms of friendships, economic and production pressures, and fear of punishment by unwillingly involved top level chiefs.

Problems related to entry and climb through the hierarchy are the subject of Chapter 6. Official statements of how members rise in the firm may be given freely. But these recitals often conceal more than they reveal—and not always from intent, for spokesmen well-informed on official policy may be ignorant of relevant but more subtle factors in success. The rubbery gauge of "ability" as a measure of fitness can mean anything powerful figures want it to mean. And probably no set of objective factors can be rigorously adhered to in picking and advancing members. In an atmosphere of rivalries, this is due in part to inability of the organization either to recognize officially the out-of-role contributions that are necessarily made by some members or to reward them. Formal education in specialized subject matter is clearly not an open sesame to quick achievement of high place. But variously imparted initial drives toward education, with the attendant experiences of acquiring it, may build more potential for mastering confusion, and skill in the required social mimicry, than do supposedly more important formal factors. That is, promotion may or may not be made on the basis of nominal fitness and contributions. But survival at a given level is likely to correlate with skills not explicitly recognized, or even contrary to those formally accented. Focusing on Milo, this chapter explores official records, unofficial practices and influences, and draws heavily on supplementary literature.

Chapter 7 deals with the problem of unofficially rewarding implicit contributions to the organization, as distinct from the need to prevent misuse of the firm's materials and services. Here the concern is to find a line between recognized theft and the unofficial use of company resources as inducements, rewards, and perquisites; and to show how ineptly used tacit reward can grow to pilfering rights. We note how various informal roles, such as theft intelligencer, faction-broker, etc., serve to carry out essential functions and are implicitly requited. Milo, Rambeau, and various small firms are sources of data that point the social and moral complications of assuming that all necessary contributions can be induced and rewarded by purely official means.

Thus the major recurring social problems of operation, threshed out by some combination of official and unofficial action, move around production costs, the relations of advisory experts and line executives, the priority of local interests over wider fealty in union-management affairs, the routes to careers, and the task of distinguishing requital from theft in compensating exceptional help that cannot be officially recognized or rewarded.

The cumulative effects of these strains on the individual executive is the topic of Chapter 9. No reward or group support can save him from the responsibility of reconciling what some see as commendable with what others see as reprehensible practices. As a pivot in the clash of policy and action, his latitude of choice leads to compromises and moral burdens. Trapped in the cross-claims of associates, he may find the organization's demand for seemly appearances and impersonal action beyond his endowment or any aid he can command. To preserve his formal role he must constantly reinforce or adapt it by taking informal roles, and be sensitive to the same practice by others. Ambiguous situations and varying ingenuity in solving contradictions thus operate to raise or depress the influence of individual managers regardless of formal equalities they share.

The book is thus a study of compromises among key individuals and groups in rational organizations, and the human strictures on compromise. From concessive exchanges among and between vertical and horizontal groups, the study eventually generalizes on compromise between two types of managers who exist at all levels and in all formal divisions and are equally committed to serve top level administrators by specific and dignified means. On the one hand are the systematizers and routinizers to whom method and procedure are paramount. On the other hand are the adapters and reorganizers who stress ends over means. The first cling to the official as their protection. Cloaked in conformity, the second depart and innovate as they think wise—and can. The collaborative struggle of these two types is an ongoing action in which moral convictions are confirmed or outraged, and careers made or broken according to the skill and success of members in forming elastic alliances to protect themselves against unwanted change and aggression as they advance their respective views of policy, method, and personal interests. Both types pay obeisance to the official code but alter it as they submit to the claims of associates and experiment to win ends. For however irregular their conduct, the effective methods they develop in their struggles are ultimately and happily phrased into the expansive book of understood and written proprieties.

DOCUMENTARY NOTES

1. Lyndall F. Urwick, *The Pattern of Management,* University of Minnesota Press, Minneapolis, 1956, p. 14.

2. Gordon R. Clapp, "The Social Scientist and the Administrative Art," in L. D. White, ed., *The State of the Social Sciences,* University of Chicago Press, 1956, p. 396.

CHAPTER **2**

Managers on Paper

Practitioners and students with a general knowledge of the subject may wish to skip this chapter. Other readers may want some detail on the nature of staff activities and the theories of organization held by Milo's top managers.

Milo's buildings and accessories covered over a square mile. Loosely defined, the managers numbered 402, but 176 of these were hourly-paid foremen, or their assistants, or others not on salary who in many cases were only temporarily bearing supervisory titles. This left 226 unequivocal managers, which included all officers in both staff and line who made official decisions for other people, supplied information vital to plant operations, had a voice in hiring or releasing employees or assigning and directing work duties, were paid a monthly salary, and did not punch a time clock. Though the 176 fringe members are not included in the sample, attention will be given to them when they are involved in issues.

Of the 226, 36 were in staff groups as heads, assistants, general supervisors and specialists; 36 were line superintendents of various grades such as divisional, departmental, assistant, or "assistant-to," which will be defined later. Sixty-one were general foremen, that is, the immediate superiors of groups of the lowest ranking or "first-line" foremen. The latter numbered 93.

Milo's formal organization chart (Fig. 1) lumps together the group of 226 with over 100 of the marginal members. The latter are indistinguishable from the 93 salaried first-line foremen with whom they are included at the bottom of the chart.

Every enclosure represents an officer. The legend distinguishes staff from line officers and indicates levels of supervision in the line organization. The chart of course shows the official interconnecting lines of authority, the formal status of each officer, and his area of jurisdiction.

For example, at the top it is seen that Milo was subject to control by a general office which we shall call the Office. Below the Office, managers Finch and Stevens are clearly on the same level of authority, but have different areas of command. Below them each rectangle or circle shows an officer's area of responsibility and the person to whom he answers.

In the upper center of the chart, dropping from the Office, is the top of the line organization headed by Stevens and Hardy. Just below Hardy flowing to the right is a group of *staff* departments, while to the left are the *line* divisions and departments. In the line, or production branch of the firm, there are three divisions, A, B, and C. Below these are the eleven line departments. Discounting the Office, the chart shows in most cases seven levels of supervision in the line branch. From top to bottom these are: plant manager, assistant plant manager, divisional superintendents, departmental superintendents, assistant departmental superintendents, general foremen, and first-line foremen.

The chart shows some anomalies. For example, there are general foremen who have assistants between themselves and the first-line foremen; foremen who report directly to superintendents because there is no office of general foreman; and superintendents without assistants. These cases arise from conditions that will be explained later. At this point we need only say that officially, the members of each ascending level of the managers had greater status, more authority, and wider control.

To follow the chain of command from bottom to top, note the position of Peters in the lower left of the line organization. Below and directly responsible to Peters are twelve first-line foremen, each with his area of control over certain operations and workmen. The vertical from Peters meets a horizontal which joins him with eleven other general foremen in the same department. All twelve share a common rank and authority.

Rising from the horizontal linking these general foremen is a vertical to their departmental chief, superintendent Taylor. To the right of Taylor and with the same rank and title is Dicke. The vertical rising from Taylor and Dicke shows that both are accountable to divisional chief Blanke. The horizontal above Blanke shows that he, Revere, and

Springer have the same rank. Rising from the divisional chiefs is a
vertical ascending through two more levels to the Office. This line
of course indicates that Blanke, Revere, and Springer, and their subordinates, answer to Hardy, he to Stevens, and Stevens to the Office.

Above the level of general foremen, the chart shows offices the in-
cumbents of which lack authority over others. For example, see the
rectangles suspended from those of Revere and Springer. These positions are known as "Assistants-to" the superintendent, rather than
"Assistant Superintendent." This important distinction is not always
clear to lower management and production workers. Though officially
without influence, officers in these posts may and often do have a
power over affairs, which we will discuss later.

The Auditing Department, a staff group directly accountable to the
Office, is represented at the upper left of the chart. Though a total
of only three levels is indicated, each of the eleven subdepartments had
from two to four levels. As a control agency over Milo, Auditing was
entirely an instrument of the Office. The solid line from the Office to
Auditor Finch declares this relation, while the broken horizontal running from Finch to Stevens represents an official communication channel
between them, not an authority relation in either direction. Stevens
did of course have authority over the other six staffs which are represented as flowing to the right of the vertical at a point just below
Hardy. The unbroken connection between these staffs and Hardy shows
that they are controlled by the local line organization. There was
embarrassment about the broken lines rising from the staffs of Production Planning, Engineering, Chemistry, Industrial Relations, and Industrial Engineering. It was vaguely understood that the hyphenated
verticals meant the "right" of the staff in question to communicate
directly with the Office in case of crisis. Staff people inferred privately
that aid would be given by the Office to a staff group in "distress."
While "crisis" was not defined, the lines were reticent admission of
potential staff-line conflict that might require direct but confidential
communication to the Office by a staff. As indicated, the staff of
Inspection had no official channel to the Office, but was entirely under
the control of Milo managers.*

The names (fictitious) of twenty-one officers are given on the chart.
They will be discussed because of their force in plant affairs, or of the
gap that existed in some cases (to be charted) between their nominal
and actual influence in the eyes of associates. Other Milo personalities

---

* In some organizations, Inspection is not regarded as a staff function, but in
Milo all functions are staff or line, and Inspection was considered as an advisory,
not an operative function.

will be considered where they are important in problems, or where they aided the research by showing their own involvements or by revealing some part of obscure arrangements, or in shaping and responding to work directives.

In the Auditing Staff, the subdepartments, "Inventory Control," "Cost Analysis," "Record Storage," etc., are "control" bodies. They prepare reports of what *should* occur, and what *is* occurring and what *has* occurred in terms of operating costs and volume of production. Agencies of this kind precipitate much unofficial activity among those subject to higher interpretations of the reports. Their compilations are built around the hope that market and personnel behavior are relatively amenable to long range planning (which they are, within limits). But great stress on minute control increases evasion and weakens the working assumption that personnel relations are perfectly stable and that controllees are much less ingenious than controllers.

Inventory Control is concerned with keeping an up-to-date record of the materials and supplies, on hand or to be ordered, necessary to assure unbroken production.

The substaff, *Cost Analysis,* works to standardize operating expenses of the various departments. Analyses leading to these ideal estimates are based on overhead budgets and rates, as well as direct labor and material costs. Then, to check the accuracy of an analysis, the expected cost for a given period is compared with the actual costs. For our purposes an important item, officially ignored in cost analysis, is the uncharted activity of executives to keep costs down or to give the *appearance* of having low costs.

Record Storage is of course the firm's central filing system. The interplay between official and unofficial activities around this department merits digression. These archives reflect plant history through thousands of documents dealing with hiring and release of personnel, sales and purchases, production and safety, minutes of meetings, building plans, blueprints of equipment and plant layout, grievance proceedings and events in union-management affairs, etc. What is preserved varies among firms.[1] But current issues build demand for items from the records to justify new plans or support developing departmental policy, etc. In other cases a hard-pressed executive or an ambitious group may wish to search old issues for helpful new meanings.

Records of seniority, employment, and wages are scrutinized by groups eager to extract interpretations to support a line of action.* Staffs under fire to cut back or check their expanding personnel

---

* Discussions of maneuvers are often interlarded with seriocomic saws, such as "Figures don't lie, but liars sure figure."

variously use Record Storage for building appliable generalizations.
For example, data on jobs paid by piece-rate are sometimes collected
and adapted by the staffs concerned so that the pay of future similar
jobs can be determined by fewer staff personnel.

Any class of jobs subject to dispute about the rates for given tasks
at given times may find workers keeping private records of what certain
jobs "paid" them. Ensuing disputes force entry of Record Storage
to settle the issue.

Decisions may thus hinge on a given group's producing a document.
This magnifies the importance of persons in charge of Record Storage.
As filing experts, in a crisis they become custodians of official secrets.
They learn who would like to see certain records "lost" and why.*
Homage is paid to them to gain access and to block entry of others
to the firm's catalog of documents. To the extent that these guardians
exploit the situation, they exercise an influence not foreseen or intended
by planners.

Among staffs directly under control of Stevens, the *Department of
Inspection* was responsible for examining the product at various points
in its course—from raw material through shipment to the customer—to
assure that the goods were meeting requirements. Some members of
the staff also inspect repaired parts of plant equipment before the pieces
may be released from maintenance shops for return to the job site.

Staffs of *Production Planning* prepare, schedule, dispatch, and follow
the course of each order so that the customer can be advised in case
of delay. At Milo this staff is also responsible to a degree for keeping
a supply of maintenance parts on hand. We shall see representatives
of other operations, from the work level to top management, informally
opposing rigid order scheduling by Production Planning.

Members of various *Engineering* staffs are of course in part "idea
men," and inventors, experts in tool design and drafting and in part
advisers to Maintenance. Their role as seen by themselves and line
chiefs will appear repeatedly.

Chemical staffs make routine analyses and do research. At various
stages in its passage through the plant they analyze the product and
its associated gases, solutions, etc. The research may be "pure" or
applied and include methods, improvement of the product, and search

---

* In a case discussed in Chapter 4, the engineer, Haupt, caught between the
union and top management, adjusted the "average pay" of a work group to expedient levels by having the irregular and contradictory items "lost" in Record
Storage. Obviously such action may require unofficial rewards for some participants, and certainly the whole procedure relies on strong unofficial alignments.
See Chapters 7 and 8.

for new products.   Reports and recommendations of these staffs are a practical necessity.   We shall see these reports in social contexts at Milo and Fruhling.

Staffs of *Industrial Relations* have many functions: research; rule-making and rule interpretation in the testing, hiring, and release of employees; and the development of training, safety, welfare, and recreational programs.   But at Milo and Fruhling the emphasis is on the handling of grievances and aid to various managers in translating the contract.   The staff also passes down informal decisions to keep issues from entering formal grievance machinery or, once they do, to settle them at lower levels.

Industrial Engineering has several meanings.   In some firms the phrase is equivalent to "applied mechanical engineering."   In others it refers to "rate-setting," "efficiency organization," and the like.   These meanings are related to those at Milo and Fruhling, but both firms have evaded the malodorous connotations of these phrases by broadly defining the work of Industrial Engineering as *reduction of operating costs*. To accomplish this, they focus on more effective placement of equipment (shop layout) and labor to simplify work by detailed analysis of jobs, and by more economical use of available skills.   And, as a spur to greater effort among workers, the Milo staff, especially, has made time-and-motion studies of hundreds of different jobs.   Findings have been translated into periods of "standard time"[2] for doing the jobs.   These standards, known to workmen, represent a theoretical time to be compared with the actual time required by the workman to complete a job or set of operations.   When the standard time exceeds the actual time, the operator receives "bonus pay" of differing amounts in addition to his guaranteed hourly pay.   The various standards for doing the jobs are combined into wage incentive plans intended to relate the worker's pay as closely as possible to his increased efforts.

Thus each staff is accountable for a working service, or for a body of up-to-date knowledge essential in daily operations and for development of workable theories to guide future action.

Milo's managerial blueprint is incomplete without some comment on the assumptions of staff theorists responsible for the formal chart.   One belabors the obvious to say that administrative organizers try to arrange subordinates in a pattern promoting the firm's purposes.   But one who spurns the obvious may fail to see that model charts also incorporate certain compromises, suggest the points where pressures will mount, indicate what the chart makers consider their place and work to be, and only hint at the degrees of authority and freedom exercised by different officers in the design.

Milo industrial engineers theorized around three models of administrative organization, "straight-line," "functional" and "staff-line."[3] Certain advantages and disadvantages were thought to inhere in the first two. But staff-line organization, Milo's type, was regarded as combining the advantages of the other two without their defects. The sketches below are intended to represent only the theory.

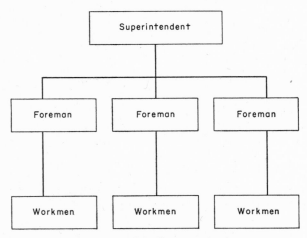

Fig. 2.   Straight-line organization.

Straight-line Organization

Figure 2 is a sketch of the straight-line type in simple form. Where usable, the engineers held, this arrangement enables maximum control of personnel. The executive at the top is in close contact with his supervisors. He knows what they are doing and, aided by the direct communication, he is in a position to know pretty well what they are thinking. Each worker is responsible to one superior only. This foreman, also subject to only one superior, controls all the worker's shop activities and has full authority over the productive behavior of a section of workers. The foreman's intensive interaction with his superiors forces him to plan ahead and allows little escape from their expectations.

Able to work closely with his supervisory subordinates, the top executive coordinates all activities by direct orders and authority. Officers in different departments communicate with each other only through him. He quickly knows who to reward or punish for maximum organizational effectiveness.

However, the requirement that each foreman know and direct all operations in his sector becomes a defect in the straight-line type. Decades ago this was not true. But increasing complexity of equipment, spread of applied science, entry of disturbing variables stemming from union-management conflict, etc., have all made this type obsolete in most cases. New operations call for skills and division of labor that expand the organization unmanageably for the foreman. And even where the firm remains fairly small the burden of knowledge, skills, and communications usually becomes too heavy for foremen in the straight-line organization.

Functional Organization

The "functional" plan of organization (Figure 3) is thought to escape many of these evils by allowing the greatest possible specialization. The foreman and staff specialist (engineer, chemist, cost analyst) each deal

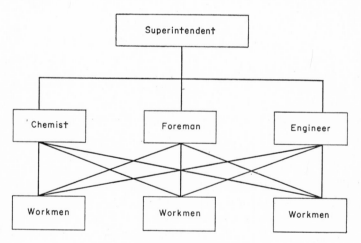

Fig. 3. Functional organization.

with but one phase of operations. Each follows his particular activity wherever it occurs in that part of the plant assigned to him. The relation of his specialty to that of others is of no official concern to him. Theoretically, if every officer can give all his time to one activity he will come to do that one so supremely well that heads of departments or sections will have little to do in coordinating the efforts of their subordinates. Although the functional scheme is logically sound, Milo theorists saw its problems for the coordinator. Usually distant from the work level, he has trouble establishing common action among his subordinates. Communication between levels is more difficult because the specialized subordinates state only a partial view of a given situation. This leads to conflicting reports and increases the coordinator's burden of knowledge. There is also confusion at the production level. Employees receive orders that treat the work process as though it is made up of independent rather than interlocking operations. Again,

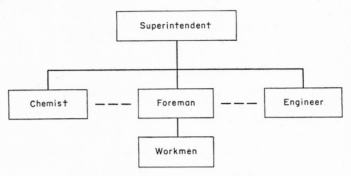

Fig. 4.   Staff and line organization.

as the officers focus on their respective spheres of work, their shared authority overlaps and leads to contradictory orders, evasion of duties, and poor discipline. Hence the problem becomes one of weighing the merits of specialization against impaired communication and control. The choice is usually to blend the functional and straight-line types to form the staff-line type (Figure 4).

Staff-line Organization

In this type the engineer, or another advisory officer, becomes a "staff" person with no direct authority over production or workmen except as line officers may delegate such authority. Middle and lower managers are able to draw on the services of experts at any time. In some instances they can have staff specialists assigned to them, as in the case of Taylor (Figure 1). Thus the burden of detail on higher executives is reduced, as the dependence of middle and lower line officers on a few remote chiefs is lessened.

The relation between foremen and staff is improved. As shown by the broken line between them neither has authority over the other— nor staff over workers. Rather staff and foremen confer, and the foreman acts on advice and information given him by the staff. The staff-line scheme is thus more flexible than the others. Specialists can focus on urgent problems, or abreast of these, they can do "pure" research and study the methods of other firms. In any case, they ease the weight of coordination on higher chiefs by giving technical information at essential levels rather than by mechanically funneling it in at a fixed level, which allows deliberate distortion on the way down.

Among other possible variations, a single staff—say engineering—may semipermanently spread its personnel from the bottom to near the top of the line. In this situation, the engineer assumes responsibility for his specialty at the level where he is stationed, which is similar to the functional type. In nearly any variation at any level, coordination is accomplished by line chiefs at a higher level. Milo planners admitted one possible defect in their staff-line theory: line officers conceivably might lack the skill to translate staff advice into effective working policy. Another weakness still often not appreciated, but demonstrated at Milo and elsewhere, is the assumption that staff offerings will be welcomed by line chiefs. Frequently this is only a hope. As we shall see, many factors complicate cooperation between the two groups.

In Milo, as at Fruhling and elsewhere, the charted blueprint of official relations,[4] with its written and understood rules, is indispensable. Each officer knows (1) those whom he can and cannot officially escape; (2) the official limit beyond which he cannot expect others to share his responsibilities; (3) that he can officially protect himself from undue claims on his time and abilities; (4) that the blueprint is the most tangible working theory of how his associates will line up in emergencies.

With its body of explicit and understood rules, the official map is an excellent point of departure for study of events that escape and reshape its logic.

DOCUMENTARY NOTES

1. See P. Stryker, *A Guide to Modern Management Methods,* McGraw-Hill Book Co., New York, 1954, chap. 10 and especially p. 164.

2. See C. W. Lytle, *Wage Incentive Methods,* The Ronald Press Co., New York, 1942; M. S. Viteles, *Motivation and Morale in Industry,* W. W. Norton and Co., New York, 1954; R. Marriott, *Incentive Payment Systems,* Staples Press Ltd., London, 1957, especially chaps. 2–5 and pp. 210–224.

3. Their thinking was similar to that in much of the literature on industrial organization. See E. S. Roscoe, *Organization for Production,* Richard D. Irwin, Homewood, Ill., 1955; L. Gulick and L. Urwick, eds., *Papers on the Science of Administration,* Institute of Public Administration, Columbia University, New York, 1937; Lawrence L. Bethel et al., *Industrial Organization and Management,* McGraw-Hill Book Co., New York, 1945; H. S. Person, ed., *Scientific Management in American Industry,* Harper and Brothers, New York, 1929.

4. In terms of our research, the most realistic assessment of bureaucratic status systems is that made by C. I. Barnard. See his "Functions and Pathology of Status Systems in Formal Organizations," in W. F. Whyte, ed., *Industry and Society,* McGraw-Hill Book Co., New York, 1946, pp. 207–243.

CHAPTER 3

Power Struggles in the Line

FORMAL CHARTS AND AUTHORITY

An official map such as we have described is really a chart of expectations.[1] All the things it reflects, authority implied by title and rank, detailed planning, systems of detection and control, etc., do not quite hold individuals to routine activity and assured compliance.

The optimistic charts are regularly cursed but never damned systematically, for they always reflect *some* relations that occur. In terms of daily working relations a given chart seldom reflects less than what is possible or more than an existing tendency.

This inevitable distortion was the picture at Milo and at other firms we will discuss. Some of the managers did not fill their offices whereas others exceeded them, thus creating gaps between authority granted or understood and authority exercised;[2] and of course creating gaps between the formal chart and a series of more accurate ones that could have been made. Conditions in the rise of these gaps, with the individuals and groups inseparable from them, is our chapter subject.

One can think of variances in exercise of authority by persons on the same level as arising "naturally" from differences in ability to do what is needed, from preoccupation with rivalries, or from disputes about goals and methods. These concerns may be confined to individuals. But dominant and responsible individuals obviously have followers. Thus there are unofficial group identities and actions that usually sweep along those who might choose to act in the isolation indicated by a chart. The existence and action of these groups is obvious to all responsible persons in a firm, but a world of rapid change and action based largely on impressions has created hypersensitivity about public relations and a demand to hide internal disputes. Hence management consultants and other students often feel the obligation to ignore conflict over issues or to clothe them with euphemistic terms.[3] Other students freely refer to these tensions as "power struggles." Because one cannot talk of organizational factions without giving offense, I shall use this familiar term rather specifically. It will apply to conditions in which individuals or groups are seeking to loosen controls on themselves and tighten them on others. It will not imply violence or attempt to destroy. The phrase will cover the behavior of executives seeking to advance their departments, to answer the claims of competing subordinates, to "protect" their departments against the "aggressions" of other departments as all compete to maintain low operating costs, set production records, prevent accidents—and escape responsibility for them, get credit for ideas contributed and service given, and to "get along and keep out of trouble" with each other and with production workers. These are common expectations of top directors in business and industry. Spurs to achievement and punishments for failure are many and are both formalized and unofficial.

Call these clashes what we will, the accumulated consequences in terms of authority exercised by individuals cannot be reflected by an official map because the actions are too fluid and the map could not be kept up-to-date.[4] But knowledge of how persons behave in critical situations, and judgments by observers and participants as to who "won" or "lost" or had the "most weight" in clashes for dominance in any supervisory group can be charted clearly enough to show that formal and informal[5] authority do not always coincide and may in fact be far apart.

This chapter will cover only *one* set of struggles for dominance, that between managers of the production and maintenance branches of the line, and between the entire Milo unit and its Office over the same issue. The next three chapters will deal respectively with other struggles, those between staff and line groups, between union and management, and those involving the selection and advancement of executives. As we will see repeatedly, no division of conflicts into categories can avoid some overlap. For example, one finds members of a line faction cooperating with a staff group to defeat union demands. And simultaneously one might find line executives opposing efforts of the same staff to change some production method. Or again, circumstantial com-

pulsions may lead line chiefs to cooperate with union officers to exploit
a piece-rate system set up by the industrial engineers, while some members of the union confidentially agree with the engineers on a point
of incentive pay defeating the interests of other union members and
the aims of line executives. Easy to imagine, it is usually impossible
to spot the beginning and follow the course of a given display of
unofficial authority as it merges intermittently with the official.* And
for many reasons it may be unwise to try to enforce perfect departmental identity of members or to prevent confidential agreements across
formal barriers.

THE MILO MANAGERS

To follow these struggles in Milo we must first identify key managers
and rank them in terms of their observed daily working authority.
Then, as outlined above, we will follow the developing conflicts between
planned and actual ways of caring for maintenance costs inside Milo
and between Milo and the Office as a series of controls were set up to
prevent such conflicts. From our observations we can then sketch a
working theory of cliques and their role in getting the job done under
various conditions.

Official versus Unofficial Authority

A rough picture of the disparity between the formal and informal
authority of the major executives can be formed by comparing Figures 5
and 6. Excepting Forest, Figure 6 shows the officers of Figure 5
reranked according to their unofficial weight or influence. An individual's influence was judged less by the response of subordinates to his
officially spoken or written orders than by the relative deference of
associates, superiors, and subordinates to his known attitudes, wishes,
and informally expressed opinions, and the concern to respect, prefer,
or act on them.[6]

Fifteen reliable Milo participants evaluated the officers in Figure 6.
All judges were, or had been, close associates of the managers they were
rating. As only a staff member at Milo my part† in the judging was
confined largely to challenging the rankings. My criticisms were based
on my own experience and many conversations with executives and
their subordinates of all grades from the level of Taylor down.

In Figure 6 the central vertical, dropping from Hardy and Stevens
through Rees, Springer, and Blanke, ranks these officers in that order.

---

* Chapter 8 is a discussion of the interplay and interconnections of the two.
† See "Appendix on Method," chap. 11.

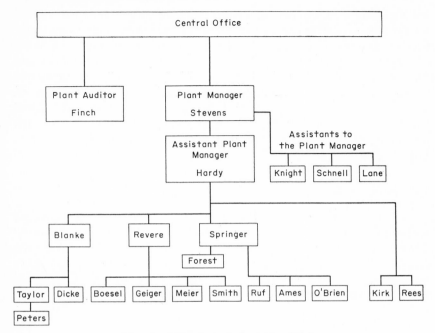

Fig. 5.   Milo formal chart simplified.

Rectangles on the same level and horizontal (Hardy-Stevens, Geiger-Revere, Kirk-Finch) indicate that the officers therein were considered to have equal influence.   At the same time each division is ranked according to the estimated power of its leader in plant affairs.   That is, Springer is above Blanke, and Revere below, as least influential of the division chiefs.   The department heads *inside* a given division are ranked in the same way but are not compared with those of other divisions.

As shown in Figure 5, Peters was not a department head.   But all the judges agreed that he should be put on the informal chart, and thirteen ranked him above Taylor.

There were minor disagreements on the placement of a few officers. For example, some of the judges who were line* officers objected to Rees' being regarded as more powerful than Springer.   But these same officers showed such fear† of Rees that if their behavior alone were taken as a measure of Rees' influence, he should have been placed

---

* This resentment was typical of line attitudes toward staff people.   See chapter 4.

† This was frequently expressed clearly as, "What he could do to you if you crossed him!"

above Hardy.   Two of the judges would have placed Peters below
Taylor.   These dissenters were general foremen who apparently disliked Peters because he had been brought over from a staff organization

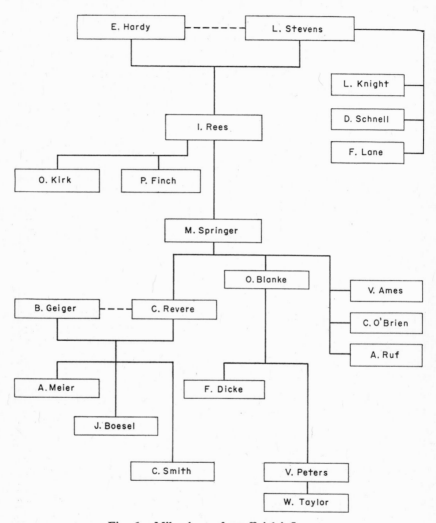

Fig. 6.   Milo chart of unofficial influence.

by his powerful sponsor, Blanke.   The informal chart does not of course
measurably show that the executives exercised more or less than their
given authority, but it does indicate that formal and actual authority
differed.   Scales and numbers were not used in the rankings because

the judges opposed a formal device and believed it was a misleading overrefinement.

/ To develop the ties between informal executive position and actions, note that assistant plant manager, Hardy, shares the same level as his chief, Stevens. This ranking was given for several reasons.

In executive meetings, Stevens clearly was less forceful than Hardy. Appearing nervous and worried, Stevens usually opened meetings with a few remarks and then silently gave way to Hardy who dominated thereafter. During the meeting most questions were directed to Hardy. While courteous, Hardy's statements usually were made without request for confirmation from Stevens. Hardy and Stevens and other high officers daily lunched together. There, too, Hardy dominated the conversations and was usually the target of questions. This was not just an indication that he carried the greater burden of *minor* duties often assigned to assistants in some firms, for he had a hand in most issues, including major ones. Other items useful in appraising Hardy and Stevens were their relative (*a*) voice in promotions, (*b*) leadership in challenging staff projects, (*c*) force in emergencies, (*d*) escape as a butt of jokes and name-calling, (*e*) knowledge of subordinates, (*f*) position in the firm's social and community activities.

For example, informants declared that Hardy's approval, not Stevens' was indispensable in the more important promotions. In the struggle over maintenance incentives (discussed later) the open opposition to Rees was made by Hardy, not Stevens. During breakdowns and emergency stops, officers in charge showed concern to "get things going before Hardy gets out here," or "before Hardy hears about it," without reference to Stevens. In too many significant cases staff officers saw Hardy, not Stevens, as the top executive to please or to convince of a point. Even production employees felt the difference. Seeing Hardy and Stevens approach together on a walk through the plant, they often remarked, "Here comes the dog and his master," with reference to Hardy as the master. /

Stevens was also called a "lone wolf" because he was "unsocial and distant," and "Simon Legree" as befitting a "slave driver." Especially active in civic life, the staff officials were outspoken against Stevens' "never participating in anything."

An assistant departmental superintendent pinpointed line feelings toward Stevens:

> [Stevens] tried to stop us from bringing newspapers into the plant. He barred the paper boy in the bus station from selling papers, but the [worker's union] broke that up in a week. It all started when he saw a couple of fellows reading papers out in the plant. He's a damned old grouch and

unreasonable as hell! He was taking a woman's club through the shops one day. He stepped on an oily spot on the floor and fell. Then he got up and called all the bosses of ＿＿＿＿ department and bawled hell out of them right there in front of the women. That's a hell of a way for a man in his position to act. He's not big enough for his job—he's always blowing up about things that [Hardy or Springer] would never say a damn thing about. A couple of years ago the street outside the plant was tied up with traffic. I was just going into the office when [Stevens] came tearing out wild-eyed to see what the trouble was. He looked like a damn fool.

On the other hand, Hardy's social activities and occupational experience—and possibly even his personal appearance—were material to his prestige in Milo. In community gatherings he was something of a social lion. Under forty, he looked and moved like an athlete, which contrasted strikingly with his white temples. Wives of his associates called him "very handsome" without offending their husbands. Hardy was a member of the Masonic Order, as were most of the Milo managers (Chapter 6) and community leaders.

The managers were impatient for the time when Stevens, a rejected non-Mason past sixty, would retire and be succeeded by Hardy. Hardy's tie with his subordinates was strong from his having been both a departmental and divisional superintendent at Milo, an experience Stevens lacked. This gave Hardy a personal knowledge of his associates that, with his other qualities, enabled him to outstrip Stevens as a power in the plant.

⌊Though officially head of Industrial Relations and presumably only a consultant on such matters, I. Rees at times inspired more concern than any of the other managers. This was partly attributable to his being sent out from the Office to "strengthen" the department. Aged thirty-six, with a degree in aeronautical engineering, he replaced "weak" F. Lane who was made assistant-to Stevens.⌉ The following incident points the error of the formal chart as a gauge of Rees' place in Milo affairs.

For some time the most widespread struggle in Milo had been between line factions favoring and opposing the use of maintenance incentives.* Otis Blanke, head of Division A, opposed the incentives and persuaded Hardy that dropping them would benefit Milo. At a meeting to deal with the problem Hardy stated his position and concluded, "We should stop using maintenance incentives. They cause us too much trouble and cost too much."

Then as only a staff head, and one without vested interest in this issue

---

* That is, the application of piece-rate pay systems to maintenance and repair work.

or the formal authority to warrant threats or decisive statements, Rees
arose and said: $c.2$

> I agree that maintenance incentives have caused a lot of trouble. But
> I don't think it's because they're not useful. It's because there are too
> many people not willing to toe the mark and give them a try. The [Office]
> put that system in here and by God we're going to make it work, not just
> tolerate it!

The surprise at these remarks broke the meeting up in embarrassment for everyone but Rees. His statement quickly spread to all of
supervision. Since Industrial Engineering had set up the incentives,
one of its supervisors asked the Maintenance Department to aid the pay
plan by having its foremen, in addition to the inspectors, count the
number of pieces done on various orders in their shops. The appeal
was made with the thought that report of nonexistent pieces might be
a factor in making the plan "too costly." Rees learned of the request
and described the idea as one that "would cause more trouble than it
would be worth." This remark was similarly flashed through the plant.
Early the following day all line executives who had been approached
by the staff supervisor telephoned apologies for their inability to aid him,
and they asked him to please consider their position in view of Rees'
stand. These and other less overt incidents led Milo executives to see
Rees as an unofficial spokesman for the Office. Because he had spent
three years there as staff representative of Industrial Relations, local
managers assumed he had been selected as "a bright young boy" and
"groomed" for the Milo post. His predecessor, Lane, was regarded as
"a grand old guy," but was removed to a "safe spot" for a few years
until his retirement because he was "not sharp enough to deal over and
under the table at the same time." Several of the executives explicitly
stated their belief that Rees had powerful sponsors in the Office and
that to provoke him would "just be suicide."

Although Hardy was overmatched by Rees on the issue of incentives,
he is placed above Rees in Figure 6 because he dominated more areas
of Milo life. Officially Hardy had authority over the line organization
and six of the staffs, including Rees'. But they were at swords' points
on any issue that Rees by loose interpretation could bring into the
province of his department—and maintenance incentives as a stimulus
to union-management friction was one of these. Hardy almost certainly
exceeded his assigned authority over all plant processes except those
which Rees interpreted as lying in his sphere. Here Hardy exercised
less than his formal authority.

M. Springer, Superintendent of Division C and formally on a par with
Blanke and Revere, is placed just below Rees in Figure 6. Springer

was thirty-six years old, held a degree in mechanical engineering, and had spent four years in the Office before coming to Milo as a processing superintendent in Division B. During the four years Springer was in this position, Hardy was head of Division B. They worked together as a clique in winning favors from a former plant chief. The understanding developed between them remained solid. Revere and Blanke recognized this. When seeking important favors from Hardy, they always first conferred with Springer, though all three had the same formal relation to Hardy.

Of the three superintendents in Springer's division, V. Ames was the most influential in plant affairs. This was partly due to his having the most important unit in the division. At the age of forty-five he was the youngest of the three, and had but one year of high school compared with O'Brien's four and Ruf's degree in engineering. However, Ames had great practical "knowhow" in terms of ability to get on with his men and the union while successfully meeting the typical pressures on department heads. This made him invaluable to Springer who had only recently become head of the division. Hardy, as well as Springer, was grateful to Ames for his support from below. Thus a place in a line of power enabled a department head to rank with division heads and at the same time to have an "in" above them.

Newly appointed to head Division A, O. Blanke, aged fifty, must be ranked above Revere. Blanke was hated by his subordinate department head, W. Taylor, aged fifty-five, who had counted himself as the logical successor of the retiring chief. Taylor and his close associates had "doped out" the line of succession without considering Blanke. In theory Blanke's surprise appointment should have damaged operations. But despite Taylor's resentment and covert attacks, Blanke had no serious trouble and actually strengthened himself. Earlier, as chief of a production unit, he had operated his department with remarkable economy. Evidence indicated that his friend, V. Peters, a staff specialist in the Auditing Department, "helped" him to control his costs. The records Blanke compiled, with his other qualities, convinced Hardy and Stevens that he was the "best man to head the division." Shortly after taking the new office he demoted a fifty-six-year-old general foreman in charge of the division's largest departmental subunit. He replaced the foreman with 29-year-old Peters and explained that the older foreman "handled costs poorly" whereas Peters* was an expert on such matters. This formally placed Peters below Taylor but in effect above him so

---

* Peters, and others, regarded his transfer from staff to line as a definite promotion. The meaning of such moves is discussed in the next chapter.

that Taylor could scarcely damage Blanke without exposing his hand. Blanke was further strengthened by his other superintendent, F. Dicke, reputed among cost analysts to have the most efficient department in Milo.

⌈Least influential of the division heads, fifty-nine-year-old C. Revere no longer aspired to dominate plant events. He was a widower with married children. This, and the rivalries he was caught in, made him less interested in greater income with the attendant responsibility.⌉ Chief of Division B for three years, he had reluctantly moved from department to division head. Though regarded as a person of "fixed habits" who "works automatically," his thirty-one years of experience in the division, and the lack of other worthy candidates, decided Hardy to give him the choice of accepting the higher post or retiring. His earlier role in the plant scheme will appear repeatedly.

⌈Officially a subordinate of Revere's and on the same formal level as Meier and Boesel, Geiger must be ranked above them and at least on a level with Revere. Aged forty-two, Geiger was born and technically trained in Germany. Part of his weight in Milo activities stemmed from his heading the major production unit.⌉ Undoubtedly he learned much from Blanke about the mastery of situations, when Blanke was head of the department and he assisted him. And informal bonds he developed in guarding Blanke from below helped him greatly when he moved to full superintendency. ⌈Heading departments that processed materials Geiger sent to them, Meier and Boesel worked closely with him. American born, they were of German descent and the three clearly were conscious of an ethnic tie that strengthened their cooperation. Probably as a side effect of the Second World War, they, with Blanke and Dicke were referred to by some as "Nazis." Enemies and gossips declared that all were under federal observation. This gossip had no basis in fact, but it revealed the ethnic, or national, consciousness usually at work in most organizations. And informally, the German ethnics did dominate Division B, while they had both official and informal command of Division A.⌉

The Elastic Role of Assistant-to

The position of "assistant-to" is often a temporary office. As noted earlier, its holder has no formal authority over subordinates of the executive. The office may be newly created, or reconstituted after having been vacant for a long period following the transfer, death, or retirement of the incumbent. The office has many uses.[7] Officially it serves to relieve the executive of routine work. He may, on the other hand, have a special task calling for the temporary appointment of a particular person. The office is used unofficially as a sinecure or position with uncertain duties but certain and flexible income. In this sense it may be set up as a reward for someone who has served long and well but has "got out of step" and is unlikely in the balance of his career to "make an adjustment," as in the case of Lane. Sometimes rather than have an able and ambitious person leave, the office is temporarily given to him in lieu of a higher rung until he can be better placed. In some cases the role is used only as a training and observation post, and in still others it becomes a berth for amiable misfits. In rare cases the post is held for a time by a seasoned older person who is really counselor to a young or new executive until he learns the ropes.

Although the office lacks official authority the incumbent may still have a certain power. For example, the assistant-to gains something from the status of the executive with whom he is associated. The fact that he is in a position to share some of the secrets of his superior, and to observe and report incidents, makes him a focus of attention and deference.

Obviously, past connections of the assistant-to in the firm are important in how he is seen. His former friends and enemies affect his current influence. Friends pass desirable information through him to his chief, while enemies conceal and conciliate. In either case he exercises an unspecified authority.

The known esteem, or disesteem, in which the executive holds an assistant-to obviously affects his influence. The chief's trust and regard show in assignments given him: whether he appears or not at important meetings; whether he merely reads a report or presides at the meeting; whether he is confined to his office, to the plant, or is given liaison assignments to the community and around the circuit of corporations.

Finally, his temperament and personal hunger for a larger hand in plant affairs are ingredients. When he chooses to voice an opinion out in the plant on some issue, his remarks, as in political matters, are interpreted as the views of his chief. Whether his view is acceptable or not at lower levels, the responses to it are calculated to avoid giving offense. His version of actions toward his chief can inspire new decisions and color pending ones. This factor finds fullest expression in the larger firms. There, size and impersonality join to blind foremen and others to official differences between the roles of *assistant* and *assistant-to,* which of course inflates the latter.

Among the assistants-to Stevens, Knight was closest to him and had the most unusual education of any member of management. He held two bachelor's degrees, a B.A. and a B.S. in chemical engineering from different schools. Aged sixty-two, he had been employed in various staff jobs for twenty-eight years and in his present one for eight years. Both aged sixty-four, Schnell and Lane were only recently appointed to the position.

[Knight is ranked above Schnell and Lane because of his wide knowledge of internal affairs and his influence with Stevens. Regular attendants to top level meetings reported that Knight's expressed opinions and suggestions were usually points of departure for Stevens. Others added that "anything worthwhile" done by Stevens was "really Knight's idea." At the least, Knight was a great source of strength to Stevens in his isolation. Geiger held that Knight was the only officer to whom Stevens "told everything."]

For over forty years Schnell had filled staff roles in the corporation. For the last decade he had been chief of Production Planning. During that period the department doubled its personnel. Increasingly, men with college degrees were brought in to be statisticians, accountants, cost analysts, and expediters. With only one year of high school and two of night school, Schnell often clashed with the new world of ideas and methods presented by his subordinates. Hence during his later years in the department his role became one of mock authority, with subordinates barely able to pay the official deference. But the period of expansion and his intimacy with operations of all departments enabled him logically to escape to a new post as liaison officer between Stevens and the various line heads. As described in the local press, his new job was an advancement; but at the same time it was a shelter from intolerable conflicts.

Though considered weakest of the assistants-to Stevens, Lane had served in all levels of the line but general foreman. He began with two months as a laborer and reached his job ceiling as *assistant plant manager* where he spent over two years. His duties as assistant-to varied, but he had power to appoint new members to the group privileged to eat in management's exclusive dining room, the significance of which is developed in the next chapter.

[Head of Production Planning, Kirk was regarded by many as having an ideal combination of training and experience. He also illustrates the drive and ambition of staff people—another topic for the next chapter. Holding a degree in general business from one of the greater universities, he had been employed for three years as cashier of a racing association, one year as educational director for a firm in another industry, nine months as an industrial engineer in another plant, three years as a public accountant, one year as an assistant line chief in another branch of the corporation, two years as assistant staff head in a second branch, one year as coordinator of inventory controls in a third branch, and finally three years as assistant-to Stevens before taking his present position at the age of thirty-six. Of the staff heads his opinions were most respected.

In addition to holding a master's degree in engineering and mathematics and serving for short periods in the role of engineer, industrial engineer, and cost analyst, Finch had the further experience of two years as assistant-to the plant manager of another branch of the corporation. Allegedly aided further by family connections, he became auditing chief at the age of thirty-one with the highest staff salary in Milo.

Line managers were much impressed by the fact that Kirk and Finch worked closely with Rees and that only these three of all the staff group sat by request with Hardy and Stevens at their table during lunch in the cafeteria.

We can classify the informally ranked executives in terms of why they exceeded, or did not fill, their offices. The existence of informal power positions creates a pressure on the formal framework to accelerate new positions and reassignments beyond the "normal" rate of promotion and retirement. Such officers as Hardy, Blanke, and Geiger move more rapidly than others from one formal framework to another. They are promoters and reorganizers in the sense that they do not see the firm as static. To them rules and procedures are not sacred guides but working tools to be revised, ignored, or dropped, as required in striking successive balances between company goals on the one side, and their personal ends *and* the claims of their supporters on the other. They command by example and by demonstrated competence to detect and control damaging situations and to reward those who aid them.

The power of Ames—and Hardy also—was dependent on such individual qualities as initiative in driving ahead, ability to please and to deliver great aid whether explicitly guided by a superior or not. This is something beyond just the ability to fully meet official directives with minimum creativity in new situations, which was apparently characteristic of Springer, Peters, Meier, Dicke, and Boesel.

Rees' power stemmed from his receiving, or assuming, the role of unofficial spokesman for the Office, and from his decisiveness, as will appear later. He, Hardy, Blanke, Geiger, Ames, Springer, Peters, Meier, Dicke, and Boesel were all in varying degrees adroit at moving in and out of clique activities, not as play in intrigue, but as a way of dealing with situations too urgent and dynamic for formal handling.

Stevens, Taylor, Revere, and Smith scarcely, or barely, filled their offices. They were unable to form cliques or to participate in clique behavior to win the informal strength eventually necessary for larger official action. Excepting some of the convenient departures by Revere earlier in his career, they were all rule devotees. They resisted change and were quick to fear any clique activity and to label it as "dirty."

The impression must not be given that Milo was more "ridden with politics" than other firms we will look at, or that personality, as a set of attitudes, is the only factor in struggles for authority. However, another aspect of personality, age difference, apparently influenced success in these struggles at Milo. It is almost a saw that older executives of an earlier tradition are less ready to take chances or accept new ways. Assuming that chance-taking and flexibility are a part of success and that both give personal influence, we find some support of this view in the informal chart. For example, if we divide the ranked line executives into the more and less influential, and average the ages of those in each group we find that those of greatest influence are decidedly younger than the others. Hardy, Dicke, Meier, Ruf, Geiger, Ames, Springer, Blanke, and Peters averaged 42.2 years as against the less commanding Revere, Stevens, Taylor, and Smith who averaged 55.5 years of age.

In terms of relative power to force a hearing or to "interfere" with the line, line members among the judges ranked the staff groups highest to lowest as Industrial Relations, Industrial Engineering, Production Planning, Auditing, Engineering, Chemistry, and Inspection. Before Rees became head of Industrial Relations, the staff would have ranked lower, largely because of Lane's indecisiveness. This does not mean that leadership alone gives force to a staff. Correctly or not, the head of Industrial Engineering was regarded as a "weak personality." But the work of his staff in methods and incentive plans thrust it into production planning, union-management relations, and such internal line problems as the touchy one between Operation and Maintenance.

OPERATION VERSUS MAINTENANCE

Cost Pressures

Operating costs are a concern top management vehemently shares with all levels of supervision. At Milo, cost meetings were the point at which top officers relieved their feelings on the need for greater economy. Middle and lower officers learned that an excellent cost record was directly related to their future. By graphs on bulletin boards, and semimonthly newsletters, departmental operating costs were publicized in much the same way as lost-time accidents and charity drives. The more efficient heads were lauded, the others shamed. This scheme of reward and penalty led to ingenious distortions of records to more nearly approach ideal cost figures. And divergent social rivalries hindered the hope that lower officers would compete with each other for rank on the efficiency scale.

For example, the maintenance department received an appropriation of $200,000 to cover installation of new equipment in one of the production units, but "lost" $130,000 of the allocation before it could be used for that purpose. According to a maintenance chief, eight operation heads applied pressure "for a divvy because Maintenance was always getting them into a jam." By the time work started on the project, only $70,000 remained. The eight chiefs then "tried to outdo each other" in the following months by redecorating their offices, installing luxurious plastic and tile floors or wall-to-wall carpeting, sumptuous furniture, and only electrically operated office machines. To a query as to how this could be done, the informant stated:

> Part of it was just taking money out of one pocket and putting it in another.
> Supposing a guy [department chief] wanted to paint his offices. Well, he wrote out an order for it and charged it against his cut of the $200,000. . . . He had an order number for it and he had a deal with Maintenance, so they had to do the job for him. He could go on charging things to that same number that had nothing to do with painting. He could go in the storehouse with that order number and get anything they had that he wanted as long as his honey [buying power that had been transferred to him] from Maintenance held out. I've seen a bench from the carpenter shop cost $400 [as a result of other work added to the order number for the bench]. If Auditing got to snooping around, what the hell could they find out? And if they did find anything, they'd know a damn sight better than to say anything about it. How could they prove that a bench didn't cost $400? [Hardy] might bawl hell out of somebody but he can't do anything about something that everybody does—especially when it's already done. All the work of installing the stuff was done by Maintenance. Buying the stuff was easy. All those guys [department heads] have got lines through Cost Accounting. That's a lot of bunk about Auditing being independent.*

---

* The nonindustrial reader should not regard these practices as peculiar to Milo. In the Fruhling Works, in Mobile Acres, a plant of 20,000 employees including 984 full members of management, much the same thing occurred on a larger scale. Fred Jessup, a division head, had sought for two years to get acceptance of his idea for changes in a refinement process, but was resisted by the Fruhling chief on the ground that Jessup's proposal was "phony." Taking a new tack, Jessup justified an increase of 20 new production and clerical personnel in his division and won appropriations to cover their payroll. Actually they were fictitious, but he created names and roles for them, and by his relations with the Auditing and Time departments he was able to use the funds for secret purchase of new equipment and experimentation in a vacant building. By support from associates (see "horizontal aggressive clique" below) the experiment was carried on for many months and established as successful. When the plant

The informant's inclusion of "everybody" was an exaggeration. Obviously those executives unsuccessful in such participation were under a burden of concern about costs and the need of comparing favorably with others. And as the covert nature of informal arrangements gave no assurance that one would be equally successful at all times, most of the executives did compete to please higherups and to win aid from them. These conditions bore directly on the struggles between Operation and Maintenance as production chiefs searched for loopholes in the tightening cost system.

R. Forest, assistant-to Springer, periodically called meetings of all operation heads. He went around the circle calling on each for an estimate of his working costs for the following month. The Standard Cost section of the Auditing Department recorded these estimates. All heads knew that Hardy and Stevens expected the estimates to be justified and consistently not exceeded.

To keep his record straight, each head was given a series of order numbers which constituted his "account." The Auditing Department prepared the wage and salary record of all employees in a given department. Consumption of utilities was recorded with similar precision. But upkeep of present equipment, purchase of new and replacement of old materiel, and the unforeseen costs attending expansion were all more difficult to control. Hence this area of upkeep was used by the department chief as one means of relieving cost pressures on himself. In using the escape he of course competed obscurely with other heads groping for similar devices. Hence at times calculating alliances were formed to share an expedient. As pressures for economy increased, many operation executives placed low short-run production costs above concern for equipment. That is, they favored continuous use of equipment with shutdowns only for breakdowns followed by minimum repair and quick resumption of production. Maintenance chiefs argued that long-run costs would be less, and equipment safer and more lasting,

---

manager shortly retired, the new technology was brought into the open, acclaimed, and labeled the "[Jessup] process."

Jessup declared that his "operations" were "really small stuff," that he had got the idea of "underground" action from the "shenanigans" of his retiring chief. According to Jessup, his late chief had several years earlier directed a major modernization of Fruhling. Only after the most careful planning, $30,000,000 had been appropriated for the program. But as the change advanced, the appropriation "came up short by $7,000,000 because of smart pencils and fattened payrolls." That is, a total of $37,000,000 was used, but nearly one-fifth of it was consumed to reduce social rivalries, to accommodate "empire-building," etc., and skilfully attributed to extraneous factors. Jessup incidentally illustrates the possible breach between given and exercised authority.

if thorough periodic overhauls were made.   Each sought to achieve
his goal without losing favor with Hardy.

For a decade the records of all repair work were prepared by the
maintenance shops in which the work was done.   This record included
time and materials for doing the work.   The shops sent a copy to the
Auditing Department which charged the cost to the given head.   Over
a period of several years friction developed between operation and maintenance groups.   Some heads of Operation complained about the backlog of over 1500 uncompleted orders in the various shops, while foremen
of Maintenance protested about being "pushed around" by operation
executives.

Hardy and the assistants-to Stevens investigated and found that some
heads had hundreds of unfinished orders while others had none.   The
condition was hushed to prevent invidious ascription of good or poor
leadership, when obviously there could be no poor leaders.

The backlog belonged almost entirely to the less aggressive and
less astute heads.   Once their orders and worn equipment were delivered
to the shops, they assumed that the work would be done as soon as
possible, and attended to more urgent matters.   Or if they did inquire
at the shops they put no pressure on maintenance foremen.   On the
other hand, the chiefs abreast of their repair work were there because
they checked constantly on the progress of their orders.   They expedited
the work by use of friendships, by bullying, and implied threats.   As
all the heads had the same formal rank, one could say that an inverse
relation existed between a given officer's personal influence and his
volume of uncompleted repairs.

For example, a dominant chief would appear in person and tell the
maintenance foreman that certain jobs were "hot" and were holding
up production.   Some operation chiefs threatened to block their flow of
informal favors to maintenance officers.   These favors included (1)
cooperation to "cover up" errors made by maintenance machinists, or
at least to share responsibility for them; (2) defense for the need of
new maintenance personnel; (3) support in meetings against changes
recommended by staff groups that maintenance forces opposed; (4)
consideration, and justification to top management, of materiel needed by
Maintenance for its success and survival in meeting the demands of
Operation.

Confronted by an aggressive executive demanding special service,
the foreman would look about his shop for machines with jobs that
could be removed with least danger of offending other executives concerned.   He would "pull" the partially repaired job of some less bel-
licose supervisor and replace it with that of the demanding head.

The use of fear to coerce favored service and its effect on foremen is illustrated by Revere's behavior at the time he was a department head. According to one of the foremen

> Charlie would come out here snorting that "By God I want this done and I want that done!" He'd throw his brass around here till he'd have everybody shaking in their boots. We all knew that if he got anything on us it would be just too damn bad—he was that kind of guy. If you tried to humor him and tell him you'd get around to it as soon as you could, he'd yell, "What d' you mean as soon as you can? Jesus Christ! I can see a dozen men settin' on their asses doing nothing! Get 'em to work!"
> His idea of a man not doing anything was all wrong. He'd see a lathe hand settin' on a box and say he was loafing. Well hell, you know as well as I do that a man can be taking a long cut that may take an hour before he makes another change. Why the hell should he stand up all that time? Yesterday the man might have had a job that made him ball the jack all day—and he might have one just like it tomorrow. So why not take it easy when he can? But that was Charley. Always riding you and always on the lookout to get something on you. I'll bet he ain't changed a damn bit, either.

Once the damage of maintenance tie-up to production was admitted by all, there was further dispute concerning the cause. Hinting at the play of personal relations, some executives declared that "politics" was the factor. Others held that maintenance mechanics were "laying down on the job" and that a piecework incentive plan would "clear the jam" and prevent such blocks in the future. This view appealed to the division chiefs and Stevens' group. They were reluctant to believe that supervisory behavior alone could have precipitated the problem. The new staff of industrial engineers agreed, for they would set up the pay plan and thereafter have a larger voice in all related matters. After many conferences, a faction of Milo and Office managers agreed on a twofold plan to harmonize different views. One part of the project was a control to prevent friction between the two line branches; the other was a wage scheme to speed up maintenance work.

The Control

The new system was called the Field Work Department (FWD). To tap all available knowledge, its personnel was drawn from a pool of experienced operation and maintenance men. In addition to having a broad knowledge of Milo technology and intimacy with blueprints, shop mathematics, and materials, each officer was a specialist in at least one of the areas such as pipe fitting, welding, machine operation, carpentry, boiler repair, motor repair, electrical maintenance, bricklaying, layout, statistics, and accounting. Several men were former supervisors.

Administrators of the FWD were at least second level managers from both Operation and Maintenance. The whole body, nearly one hundred personnel, was under a Superintendent of Maintenance who had earlier been in Operation. He was surrounded by a corps of consultants.

In theory, all members of the FWD would be working in a fresh atmosphere unhampered by the coerced cooperation or friendly ties of earlier jobs. Housed in a new, isolated building, the FWD was both the point of entry and termination for maintenance orders. And between these points the orders would flow in a circuit around the shops without the previous difficulties.

A scheme was introduced to lessen contacts between the personnel of Operation and Maintenance and to assure a fixed numerical and chronological sequence in processing the orders. The old system of "order numbers" and "accounts" was converted to give each department a specific annual series of numbers for use in writing maintenance orders. A department's series would run from say 5000 to 10,000. Any order in that range would identify the department and would take priority over any higher number from that department. The chronological sequence of an order from any department was determined on a time clock as it entered the FWD. Each order was then classified as an aid to rapid location of the job in process.

Frequently a job analyst visited the production site to get additional and confirmatory data on the newly registered order. Then the order was given to the proper specialists who determined the cost of materials and labor to do the job, and indicated the shops and routes among machines and operations that the job should follow. The FWD estimate of costs was then submitted to the executive who had issued the order. This enabled him to see how well he was remaining inside the budget he had submitted to Forest (above). He had a certain freedom to bargain for a smaller or larger estimate, but in the end he had to sign it, which gave him no justification for wide departures. Once he did, the order was placed in a pouch with blueprints and instructions and sent to the assigned shop. There again the order was clocked, recorded, filed; then completed as specified by the FWD.

As the job traveled about the shop, the time and course of each movement were recorded. On completion, a copy of the record was retained, another was sent to the Auditing Department, and one to the FWD where the "exact" cost of the job was analyzed and recorded for future reference. Throughout the job journey the FWD apparatus was expected to protect shop foremen from pressure by operation heads and to end recurring problems with the union over job placement.

The FWD in Practice

The new control was successful in permanently breaking the jam of maintenance orders. However, in a few months inconsistencies began to develop. The FWD discovered a mounting number of gaps between its estimates and actual costs as computed from the completed job records. Some differences were expected, but not multiples of the estimate or, as in some cases, jobs completed with no charge at all against them.

The social relations behind these unexpected results were complex, but due largely to the persisting cost pressures and the play of old enmities and friendships that the FWD had not considered and certainly had not erased. We can see this quickly by analyzing executive actions and regroupings. In group A were those chiefs who formerly dominated the shops and enjoyed priority on their orders: Geiger, Dicke, Boesel, Meier, Ames, and Revere before his promotion. In group B were those who paid for this advantage by having their repair work neglected: Smith, Taylor, O'Brien, Ruf, and others not on the chart.

Now, officers of group A covertly charged that work of the FWD was "slowing down production" because of the "red tape" and "no-good" estimates. They told jokes of the "soft jobs," "pencil pushing," "coffee-drinking," "loafing," and "sham work" of FWD personnel. Behind a mask of humor they asked FWD personnel if they were able to look the Paymaster's assistants in the face when receiving their checks. Finally, officers of group A became reluctant to sign estimates made by the FWD. Privately they indicated a fear that Hardy and Stevens would draw threatening inferences from comparing FWD estimates with (*a*) their actual costs and with (*b*) the advance estimate each of them submitted to Forest. Research showed a tie between their fear and the fact that their actual costs were markedly greater than FWD estimates.

In time the executives of group B also became averse to signing the estimates, but for a different reason: they were getting their jobs done for less, and sometimes so much less, than the estimates, that they, too, feared questions.

In terms of low maintenance costs and "smooth" operation, the two groups were reversing the positions they held before entry of the FWD. From a place of dominance, group A executives were in process of losing face with their division chiefs, while those of group B were moving from a condition of "poor management" to commendable efficiency in terms of cost figures. As group A was losing control over its repair costs, group B was gaining command, with some members reducing their costs by half. The major factor in this radical shift was action by new informal alignments *among* the executives and especially *between them and maintenance foremen.* The unplanned reorganization grew out of old friendships and enmities, and experiment to find loopholes in the FWD controls. It was reflected in the more startling gaps between estimated and actual costs.

These gaps—and jibes from maliciously perceptive cost analysts who had failed to "get in the brain department"—threw the FWD on the defensive. Several of its members visited the shops but learned little except that foremen were evasive and that some jobs were not on machines to which they had been routed. As members of the FWD, the investigators were seen, even by old acquaintances in the shops, as "dangerous" to the extent they "might make a slip" to key figures in the FWD.

Collaboration between group B executives and foremen to charge various amounts of group B work time to accounts of group A executives was the chief factor in the hiatus between estimates and final costs. The foremen were indispensable in this arrangement. They of course had to be willing participants—and were in most cases. Not only as individuals had they been bullied by many operation heads for years, but they had suffered the abasement peculiar to most foremen[8] over the past two or three decades, losses of authority to unions and expanding staff organizations. The cooperative maintenance foremen now derived a new sense of power from unexpected arrangements growing out of the FWD. They found themselves confronted by operation executives who could beg for favors but could not coerce them because of the buffer supplied by the FWD.

The physical details of charging time incorrectly were simple. The foreman had only to enter the pouch number (assigned by the FWD) of any uncompleted job in the shop on the time card of a mechanic. If a foreman remembered an enemy head, usually a member of group A, he could take revenge and simultaneously reward a friendly head by entering a job number of the enemy on the time cards of repairmen doing his friend's work. All "elapsed time" between clock punches was thereby charged to his enemy.

As competition developed to hold down costs and remain inside the agreed estimates, several of the smaller departments were cooperating with each other as well as with maintenance foremen to poach on accounts of the larger departments headed by executives of group A.

Other contradictory but interlocked social and technical practices helped clear a path for the developing evasion. All estimates, for example, assumed that maintenance equipment was in top working order. But this is rarely true in any shop and was not at Milo. Hence the FWD's allotted time was inadequate for some jobs. Also unavoidable change in mechanics, with different skill levels and motivations, frequently held a prior order to a given machine so long that the routing of other orders was thrown off schedule. This of course initiated departures. Again, some situations demanded that foremen substitute other job numbers, quite apart from agreements with friends in operation. For example, when a job was completed and all papers "closed out," it was established practice to regard it as "dead." However, a completed piece might be passed by Inspection and sent to its department only to be rejected there because it had been machined to fit *perfect* rather than the *worn* parts with which it engaged. Because the old order could not be reopened without embarrassment to the people who would have to make decisions and protect those responsible for the failure in communication, and because all time had to be charged to some account, someone's job number had to be used. Knowing the cost pressures on operation heads, and having power to assign a number, the foreman's sentiments toward executives who had been "reasonable" with him repeatedly influenced his choice of a number. Though relatively infrequent, this condition set a precedent for other deviations, whether demanded by work conditions or friendships.

A third long-standing job arrangement also afforded group B executives some escape from the FWD. The larger departments (group A chiefs) had more repetitive maintenance work than did the other departments. For use with only this class of repair service, they were given "standing order numbers." These numbers were always "open" in the shops. The new shuffle of strictures and freedoms made these numbers a useful but limited device that the foremen used to reward group B and to penalize group A chiefs.

At the height of the struggle among operation chiefs, Geiger learned by his own intrigues that the unnamed head, Whymper, in Springer's division was having much of his maintenance costs charged to Geiger's account. Geiger telephoned Whymper, gave enough details to show his knowledge of the poaching, and told him, "By God, you'd better pay up!" Expecting Geiger to go to Hardy, Whymper was terrified. He had shortly before received a $35,000 appropriation with which Maintenance was to enlarge a section of his department. Now he transferred the uncommitted portion — $3900—to Geiger's account. This was evidently more than he had poached, for according to staff informants Geiger used much of it for "fancy new storm windows, ten new fans, and a 9000 square foot paint job" in his own department.

Reactions of Top Management

Inevitably Stevens' office learned enough to respond by calling the heads with excessive costs to account. Some officers charged that "padding of books" by unnamed groups, was responsible for their costs.

All groups denied responsibility and professed ignorance of how the condition had developed.

Above suspicion at top levels, the FWD nevertheless elaborated the obvious fact that its data for actual costs came from the shops, and that its interest was to bring the two figures together, not separate them. The Auditing Department cleared itself by showing that its computations were based on only the workmen's time cards and the accompanying shop order numbers supported by the foremen's signature. The shop foremen declared that they always followed instructions to the letter and had not confused shop order numbers when assigning jobs. A similar defense was made by the shop clerical force which transcribed and dispatched the records. And some of group B heads even praised the FWD, maintaining that for the first time the more efficient executives were free to show their superiority. Hardy and Stevens were not convinced that they had the facts—or could get them inside the limitations governing everyone.

To uncover the maze of expanding innovations would have been a formidable task. Just the problem of gathering initial evidence, with the full cooperation of everyone, would require that hundreds of pouch numbers, continuing active for weeks on complex jobs, be compared with hundreds of time cards having five to twelve job entries daily, etc. Certainly the situation could not be brought out into the open for all to see without danger of exposing the involvement of close associates and dredging up old issues that would outweigh the current ones. Enough was suspected, however, to warrant their making changes. For some time several departments had had small maintenance forces of their own to care for trifling repairs. These groups were known collectively as *Departmental Maintenance,* as distinct from the larger system of shops dealing with the major work of all departments, called *Field Maintenance.* Several steps were now taken.

First, departmental maintenance crews were enlarged so that each department could do nearly all of its own repair work. At the same time the department head would have direct authority over his repairs and all personnel involved, including foremen. This was to prevent interdepartmental conflict. To expedite the change a large shop was closed and its tools distributed among the departments on the basis of individual needs. With union cooperation the personnel from this shop was similarly distributed among the various departments. Finally, the FWD was reduced to a "skeleton crew" of less than a dozen, and its forces were similarly absorbed around the plant.

Though no official charges of malfeasance were made from above, Operation and Maintenance covertly blamed each other for breakup of the FWD. Maintenance officers held that *their* wage plan had been effective in turning out repair work, and with less than half the men required before use of the incentives. Operation agreed, but declared that the financial cost was prohibitive. Under the money incentives some mechanics had so improved their skills after guaranteed pay rates had been set up on certain types of work that later they were able to perform at remarkable levels. Operation heads regarded these costs of repair as so great that they hoped to cut outlays by using certain machine parts until they were worn beyond repair and replacing them when possible with less expensive parts, thus eliminating the repair aspect of maintenance on these items.

The real issue—the wish to escape cost pressures and the resultant poaching of operation heads on each other's maintenance accounts— was not discussed, as both sides made a red herring of the incentive system. Operation forces convinced Hardy that their position was just. This led him to denounce maintenance incentives, and then to lose face in the unexpected clash with Rees mentioned earlier.

The FWD was theoretically sound as far as the knowledge on which it was based. But that knowledge was too limited. Created to reduce costs, speed repair work, and check "politics," it was undone by politics because such relations were not understood and were officially rejected as improper, which blocked understanding. At the same time the FWD actually increased cost pressures but did nothing to change the disparity in rewards which gave applause, prestige, and more income to Operation for "producing," and only toleration to Maintenance as a necessary evil. The failure was largely one of not adapting the control to what actually existed.

Departmental Maintenance

Friction between Operation and Maintenance reappeared *in* the department. Responsible to its head, maintenance foremen felt a special obligation to see that equipment was kept in top shape. Operation foremen, on the other hand, were unaccustomed to such interference.

A clash between two of my intimates, one from each camp in the same department, will illustrate typical attitudes. The operation foreman, S. Gilter, was disturbed by the actions of P. Higgins, his maintenance foreman. According to Gilter:

> It was bad enough when we had to put up with central maintenance. We at least felt free to run our production the way we wanted to. Now it's worse than ever. Higgins comes around and sticks his nose in to tell you your men aren't taking care of the equipment. He thinks they should work with one hand and hold an oil can in the other. He tried to tell me

last week when we had a breakdown, that it was my fault—that I hadn't
let the line stay down long enough the last time to let him do a good job!
What the hell does he expect? That line is supposed to be moving, not
standing idle. He comes nosin' around and tries to pass the buck.
Jesus Christ! I know my equipment. We never had any trouble in here
till they sent him over from the shop.

This statement followed an argument between the two men. The
following day when walking through the department, I met Higgins.

INTERVIEWER: Well, Pete, I understand you and Sam swapped punches
yesterday. Did he land any below the belt?
HIGGINS: You're damned right he did! That's the only way he knows
how to fight. He skimps on his maintenance costs to get a little extra
production. Hell, he could get a damn sight more production if he'd
keep his line lubricated. Go over and look at it, and look at his cranes—
the wheels and gears shine like the sun! In the long run he's going to
get less production and more costs. But you can't tell him a damn thing.
He knows it all. I came out a while last night to see that everything was
all right. And it's a damn good thing I did. I saved him a thousand
dollars in maintenance costs by spotting the leaky line and defective gauge
on his —— tank. He might have had a blow up with lost time cases.
And if he hadn't, he'd at least have damaged enough material so that the
re-processing would have cost over a thousand dollars and would have cut
hell out of his production. And that's not all. He's in the hole on his
costs now—I saved him from an ass-eating. But hell, he never has
a kind word for Maintenance, and least of all for me. It's always
"gimme, gimme," with nothing ever coming back.

Hardy soon learned of these disputes. He acted by *suggesting* that
in the future responsibility for maintenance costs would increasingly be
on maintenance foremen. This encouraged Operation to give less
thought to maintenance costs and to concentrate on production regardless of costs.

During the shift from field to departmental maintenance the Office
began developing its own plan to reduce internal line friction and control
costs simultaneously. Then as maintenance outlays expanded with
Operation's cryptically lowered accountability for such costs, the Office
began to prepare the way for its new plan.

THE OFFICE VERSUS MILO

Managers in the Office had learned that some of the local chiefs
wished to eliminate maintenance incentives, or at least to be free to buy
certain parts outside when and if repair costs for these items became
too great as a result of the incentives. As an unofficial agent, Rees
presumably gave the Office helpful details on factors and persons.

Hence the Office sought to fit its scheme to these attitudes, but at the same time to shift more control of Maintenance into its own hands. This approach changed the emphasis from concern about *who* in Milo would be responsible for maintenance costs, to developing a record of all replacement parts on hand so that each department head would have to *justify purchase of new parts.* This developing tactic of containment in response to covert evasions in Milo initiated new realignments. Struggle for dominance among groups of Milo managers shifted to one between Milo and Office managers as local chiefs saw their accustomed control of the plant being usurped by "chair-warmers" of the Office.

Dynamic steps were followed in developing and introducing the Office plan. It was shaped by exploratory interplays between groups of the Office and Milo. The Office pushed its logic with an eye to Milo morale, while Milo parried moves that threatened its authority and its social arrangements.

First, departmental maintenance was greatly reduced but, like the FWD, continued as a framework that could not be entirely dropped without encouraging potential rivalries and disrupting the newer productive practices. While details of the plan were being settled, repair work would be done wherever most expedient.

The plan itself can be discussed under (1) cost aspects and (2) personnel reorganization.

Cost Aspects

The major item to cut expenses was a "surplus parts program." This was aimed at compiling a record of all reserve equipment on hand in each department and developing a permanent system for keeping the record up-to-date. Next, the purchase of new parts was to be taken largely out of the hands of Milo chiefs,* though the plan was introduced so that they would seem to have a voice in the purchases.

To get the program going the Office requested a listing from Milo of the number of parts on hand that cost $500 or more, and of those parts currently needed or that would be needed by the end of a given period. The intent was to start with the more expensive parts and then systematically lower the figure as experience grew.

Personnel Reorganization

It was believed in the Office that a simple request for such information, to be reported in writing, was unlikely to accomplish its purpose. The realistic move, it was held, would be to create new specific duties

---

* See "Appendix on Method," chap. 11, for problems of learning what measures were underway in the Office.

and assign able men to enforce them. After collapse of the elaborate FWD, however, simplicity and directness were seen as basic to any reorganization, so only two new supervisory positions were set up in Milo.

Office representatives held conferences with a few Milo executives to work out details of the change. When the department chiefs learned of the developing plan, group A executives wished a voice in selection of the two new officers who would be liaison men between Milo and the Office. They were supported by their assistants as well as Blanke, Revere, and Springer. After conferences among themselves, these eleven executives worked as a clique to convince Hardy that the choice should be made *entirely* by Milo. Hardy was quite clear to his intimates that he regarded the pending control as interference with local authority, and he agreed with the executive clique that "we should pick some good men."

In the meantime the Office, ignorant of this attitude among local executives, was searching for a device to soften the shock of its plan. Failure of the FWD was seen by the Office as leaving Milo chiefs sensitive about the whole subject of cost control—and even indisposed to be cooperative. Hence the Office made a bland approach and voluntarily asked Stevens to suggest candidates from his own ranks.

The request precipitated meetings to choose candidates. Hardy met with the clique, some of the group B chiefs, and a few supervisors. These last two named no one but did stress the need for "able men." With Hardy still silent, the clique designated two persons who were generally regarded as *not able* men. Quickly it was seen that the clique of group A chiefs wanted only amenable candidates. When Hardy added his voice to theirs, the decision was made. The officers nominated were W. Taylor and F. Bingham. This was the Taylor who was out-maneuvered for the superintendency of Division A by the clique of Blanke, Dicke, and Peters. Both men were accepted by the Office. Opponents of the cause led by Hardy, including some of those who praised the FWD, ridiculed the appointments. They saw both candidates as "weak" and "impossible" in the roles given them. Taylor's failure to win the post of division head was considered proof of unfitness to "act on his own." They considered his private life as further proof. His wife had "disgraced" him and Milo by a noisy divorce in the local community. His heavy drinking and repeated defeats in clashes with the union were also evidence of his having "nothing on the ball" and of his "willingness to go along with any policy" of his superiors. Bingham, too, was regarded as a "soft touch." A low ranking staff supervisor, he was near retirement and pension and allegedly so fearful of losing these payments that he fell in with any demands by higherups. It was agreed that he lacked confidence and avoided responsibility. Without voice on this issue, many staff officers analyzed the choice of Taylor and Bingham as "manipulation by the top brass for their own ends."

In the assignment of duties, Taylor was to be responsible to no one in Milo but Hardy. And this was qualified accountability, for Taylor was expected to communicate *freely* and *directly* with the Office, a privilege that not over three of all the Milo managers possessed. Taylor's duties were to inspect and approve each "parts report" turned into his office and to verify its correctness by personal count of parts if necessary. He was the only officer in the plant with power to authorize the order of new parts.

Bingham was to assist Taylor, but he was responsible *only* to the Office for his duties. He was to initiate the reports periodically by requesting statements from each head of Operation. Thus he, not Taylor, made the face-to-face contacts. After obtaining the statements, Bingham turned them over to Taylor who approved them by signature and returned them to Bingham who mailed them to the Office. The Office then issued the superintendent in question a certificate of authorization which for a specified time enabled him to buy necessary parts from the outside without going through the Office, though each purchase, during any period, required Taylor's approval. By thus focussing on two individuals, neither of whom had authority over the other and both of whom had direct access to the Office to escape local pressures, the control was regarded as simple, direct, and manageable.

THE CONTROL IN PRACTICE

Initial Executive Reaction

Following introduction of the parts program, Bingham notified the heads that he was ready to receive statements. When two weeks passed with no response, he made further requests. A few officers gave excuses of being shorthanded, of having prior problems, emergency work, etc., but no records of parts.

The clique supported by Hardy had now compromised most of the executives, and they coerced the others to ignore and resist the control as long as possible while studying it "to find ways to make it work." Despite some oppositions in the past, Dicke, Meier, and Smith, with their assistants, favored compliance with the Office, but feared the outcome of not going along with the others. During meetings and in private arguments with members of the Hardy group, their vocal resistance was beaten down and they were finally frightened into silence. The arguments used against them showed the issue to be primarily one of *who* exercised authority in the plant—Milo executives or the Office. Hardy's remark was the keynote of the resisters: "The program is too inflexible and causes too much trouble." Blanke spelled out the dominant sentiments:

> The thing I've got against the whole damn setup is procedures. Every time you turn around you run into a rule that stymies you. Some chairwarmer in [the Office] cooks up a crack-pot notion of how things ought to be done. Maybe he was never in the plant but he don't let that bother him. He writes it up and sends it out. Then by God it's up to us to make it work. The way I feel about it is this: if the setup is so damned farfetched that you can't make it work, why bother with it at all? What the hell do they think we're out here for? We know our jobs. If they'd leave us alone we'd never have any trouble.

Statements of this kind and knowledge of Hardy's attitude indicated to the minority that their problems would multiply if they met Bingham's request at this time.

In the meantime, Bingham was increasingly disturbed by his failure but was helpless to do anything. He told confidants, "I need a psychiatrist. I'm so damned fidgety I don't know what to do with myself. I'd rather be out in the shop than sitting at this damn desk all day with nothing to do. I like to be doing something." After six weeks of growing distress over his inability to bridge the gap between expectations of the Office and the anonymous note from local executives *that he was to do nothing,* Bingham received a letter from the Office asking for a progress report. Devoted to the letter of official directives, and still having no statements, he notified the Office that the superintendents "refused to cooperate."

Response of the Office

On learning of Bingham's rebuff, the Office sent several investigators to Milo. Tightness of the informal bloc eluded their inquiry, but they prepared a statement praising Bingham's efforts and censuring the heads "for failure to cooperate" with him. Copies of the report were distributed at the Office and among local top managers.

Bingham's desperation and resulting action had not been foreseen by the executives. This open support by the Office meant that despite Bingham's docility, new devices were necessary to control him. Part of the assumed incentive of his new role was that he would enjoy the leisure of what was really a sinecure. But in his dilemma about what to do his leisure was spent in anxiety, and thus failed to be a reward.

Now supported by nearly all the heads, Hardy's group searched for indirect ways of winning him over. They sought to inflate his self-importance by installing him in a larger office with an immense desk, giving him a secretary, dictaphone, filing cabinets, etc. Need to control the character of his communications to the Office led the executives to reinforce these trappings of rank with a flattering personal appeal. Several of them, including Taylor, went to his new quarters and proposed that "we work this thing out together. After all, we don't want to do anything to stir up trouble." Apparently these inducements, with fear of reprisals, and the assurance that he would be protected by appearances, prevailed on Bingham. He agreed to go along.

Tactics of Escape

Though some of the superintendents continued to fear the Office, they cooperated to thwart an accurate tally of their extra parts. The motivation to prevent a count was complex. Probably satisfaction in outwitting authority was a minor factor. Certainly the managers felt an obscure urge to preserve their "right" to command the plant. However, judging from actions and spontaneous remarks, the major factor was their wish to keep a margin of funds beyond operating costs in the narrow sense. As we shall see in a later chapter, there are operating costs in the broad sense that include use of funds to meet the demands of daily personal relations—*the maintenance of a good fellowship structure as well as material equipment.* The financial costs of keeping social mechanisms in repair merge with those of the physical. If cataloged at Milo they would include such entries as (1) part or full time employment of relatives or friends of associates from both plant and community; (2) the executive's wish to have plush offices in his department; (3) possible emergencies in a period of change; and (4) use of plant services and materials (Chapter 7) to get more cooperation from subordinates and colleagues.

Before the executives showed resistance to the Office, Bingham's instructions were to make formal requests for a record of parts. To limit the evasion, the Office notified Taylor that his job would now include surprise inspections and count of parts in each department. He and Bingham were alarmed by this new directive for neither had the front or address to carry out the order as intended. After conferences with the executives, their solution was not to make unannounced counts, but to telephone various heads before a given inspection telling them the starting point, time, and route that would be followed. By varying these conditions on successive tours, Taylor and Bingham made each inspection *appear* to catch the chiefs off guard.

This use of official form as a mask was not new in the plant. Nominal surprise was a common device in Milo and between Milo and the Office in other actions also. For example, visits from members of the Office were planned but given a camouflage of spontaneity that served the needs of both groups. This spared Office managers the unpleasantness of seeing a condition of which they should be officially ignorant, and of feeling embarrassment in possessing knowledge that presupposed corrective action by them. The condition and the potential consequence of action would of course sully the friendly call and hence should be avoided. For their part, Milo officers reduced the time, cost, and interference with routine of setting up acceptable appearances by deciding in advance the specific path through the plant that the tour would follow. Then just on the fringes of the entire route, equipment was cleaned and possibly painted, walks and driveways were cleared and swept, and everything "put in order."

Inside Milo nominal surprise was also a preventive of conflict. For example, safety and health inspectors usually telephoned in advance of visits so that they would not see unsafe practices or conditions they would feel obliged to report. They thus escaped present embarrassment for themselves and avoided incurring hostility that might persist to a time when the good will of associates could be personally helpful in the ongoing and elusive structure of personal claims in which all the executives unavoidably moved. This fiction of surprise enabled the managers to preserve the official dignity so essential for any rules of the game, and to give the appearance of following formal procedures despite inevitable obstacles and frequent impossibility. They were experimenting to find workable means of dealing with problems too elusive to trap in formal procedure.

Notice that a count of parts was to begin provoked a flurry among the executives to hide certain parts and equipment, and thus save the faces of Taylor and Bingham. Motor and hand trucks, with laborers and skilled workers who could be spared, were assembled in a given department. Then the materials *not* to be counted were moved to: (1) little-known* and inaccessible spots; (2) basements and pits that were dirty and therefore unlikely to be examined; (3) departments that had already been inspected and that could be approached circuitously while the counters were en route between official storage areas; and (4) places where materials and supplies might be used as a camouflage for parts. Though complete inspections were required only four times a year, Bingham and Taylor had other duties so that with the size of Milo, inspections continued for longer periods than would be ex-

---

* Milo covered over a square mile and was broken into many units and subunits connected by numbered walkways and zoned driveways.

pected. Various evasive answers were given to questions raised by the work force involved. And in most cases the break in their routine was to them more of a lark than a question-provoking situation.

As the practice developed, cooperation among the chiefs to use each other's storage areas and available pits became well organized and smoothly functioning. Joint action of a kind rarely, if ever, shown in carrying on official activities enabled the relatively easy passage of laborers and truckers from one work area to another without serious complications for formal arrangements.

The inspections were meant to be both a control and a supplementary count. Once a month reports of parts were to be submitted to Bingham by each chief. The list of course should conform closely to Bingham's quarterly count. The reports now arrived regularly at his desk. Probably in no case were they accurate. But Taylor approved them, and Bingham dispatched them to the Office.

Thus a working adjustment was reached. The Office received its required flow of documents, which, though only roughly accurate, allowed planning within workable limits. Able to work behind a screen of assured formalities, Bingham and Taylor escaped nervous breakdown. Friction between Operation and Maintenance subsided to a low level. Finally, the Milo chiefs preserved their conception of local rights and at the same time raised morale. Conflict between principle and action in this area had not, of course, "ended," but it was contained and existed latently.

Maintenance and Operation in a Single Department

Another struggle, almost unclassifiably intricate, existed in Milo that well illustrates the problems of planning, as well as the dynamic complex of group actions in carrying out some plans. In O'Brien's department, Springer and Hardy encouraged competition among the three shifts to increase production. That is, the shifts were ranked in terms of their output. Posted graphs indicated their fluctuating standings. Although this was primarily a contest among shifts of total personnel, it also became derivatively a struggle between union and management, staff and line, upper and lower supervision, as well as between Operation and Maintenance.

On each shift there were four foremen and about sixty workmen. The foremen were quickly forced into various deviations from official procedure to protect themselves and win approval.

The commodity from this unit had a range of properties to meet specifications of different customers. Union and management had worked out a pay scale adapted to the degree of complexity and difficulty peculiar to each set of specifications. Because the pay rate varied, some orders for the product were regarded by workmen as "poor," some as "good." They of course knew the backlog of orders and the pay rate for various code numbers.

Workmen appreciated the pressures on foremen but were not sympathetic enough to respond as foremen wanted. They were willing, however, to bargain with foremen for some exchange that would be agreeable to both. The adjustment reached threw the department into conflict with Production Planning. That staff worked out rigid sequences for the processing of orders in all departments. The sequence was based on delivery deadlines reached with customers.

The deal between workers and foremen required that foremen rearrange the order sequence to allow higher-paying orders to be run first, regardless of the scheduling. Foremen reluctantly agreed to push back the lower-paying orders, knowing that a judgment day was inevitable. In the competition among shifts, maintenance of equipment became an issue. Having a run of good orders, a given shift sought maximum pay for itself and top production for its foremen. Focus on these goals caused equipment to be neglected, and to be pushed to the breaking point. Short-run demand to keep maintenance costs down also encouraged this indifference.

When breakdowns occurred during a run of good orders, say on shift A, the foremen and *production* crew worked frenziedly to make a scrimpy repair, which would barely last the turn. Frequently there was hope that the makeshift would fail on one of the intervening shifts so that the apparatus would be down for several hours to receive a thorough overhaul. (All delay time of course had to be accounted for.) This assured that the assembly would be in top shape 16 hours later when shift A returned. Satisfaction on shift A was heightened if the crew making a full repair ranked first in production for it would, happily, be checked somewhat. Shifts B and C behaved similarly under like conditions.

Repair of breakdowns by production workmen was officially forbidden because of possible accidents to the operators themselves, as well as the cumulative delays resulting from their unskilled repair work. Such work was officially the function of only maintenance forces. Wise to the danger of exhibiting idle personnel, maintenance chiefs who were ahead of demands objected to repairs by operators. As Maintenance usually bore the blame for all errors of repair, it had reason to prefer doing all the work. But at times it also wanted the work so it could charge more time and labor than was required and thereby gain resources for Maintenance. On its side, Operation usually was glad to have its crews do repair work, with the zest shown in O'Brien's department, for this reduced maintenance costs and increased production.

Another complication to the struggle among shifts was the fact that both production and maintenance workmen were unionized. In the endless jockeying for advantage among and between subgroups of union and management, union officers sometimes intervened to enforce official procedure, or to aid one group against another, or even to side with the managers when big issues were developing and larger gains would come later from soft approaches now. The managers involved behaved similarly. In the rare absence of ulterior issues or production pressures, Maintenance did the repair work.

When workmen coerced foremen to defer the poor orders until deadlines were reached, the storerooms complained. In some cases the customer had vehicles waiting for the product. Foremen then deferred starting the order until near the end of the shift so that not their men but those on the other shifts would complete the order and be penalized by low bonus pay. Production Planning was often brought into the issue by its own obligation and complaints from the storerooms. Angered at being "put on the spot by O'Brien," the staff head threatened him but was met by elaborate excuses. Though they did officially, neither Springer nor Hardy seriously condemned this evasion of planning, because *total* production was much higher with the competitive scheme than before, despite some friction with customers, and though expected routes were not followed, and the theory of motivation was misleading. And when they were processed, even the lower paying orders moved rapidly from the wish to get past them to better orders and to escape the emergency situation.

These internal struggles require a theory to cover their rise and movement. We have already viewed the organization as a set of official principles and routes for carrying them out. However, the picture of the FWD, the compromise between Milo and the Office, and the practices in O'Brien's department all show the organization as primarily a shifting balance between principle and action. We need now to see (1) how principles, or rules, must be modified as a result of contradictions that develop, and (2) how change is carried through by small groups, springing from the constraints of policy and bound by ties of interest and sentiment.

Planned changes, such as the FWD, were introduced into an existing system of conflict. That is, in the relations among various departments, ranks, official bodies, etc., there were already ongoing collisions between purpose and surroundings that interfered with direct approaches to goals. Purposes interlocked with cross-purposes. Among factors that variously influence these power struggles are: (1) the inability of higher officers to learn what is going on among subordinates; (2) the practices of executives who know but feign ignorance from fear that action will have uncontrollable repercussions; (3) the opportunity to gain personal or organizational advantages by side-stepping official procedures; (4) the use of change and confusion by some groups to establish footholds for future action; (5) the resort to expediency as a result of excessive formal demands; (6) the deliberate making and continued tolerance of ambiguous rules allowing any interpretation; (7) the claims of friendship, etc. These factors are slighted here because they vary, overlap, and may be symptoms as well as causes. Some of them are obvious throughout the book in specific contexts.

We cannot say how these unsystematic systems of opposition begin, but we can talk of influences that sustain them. We have just dealt with one factor, the drive by top officers to achieve economy of operation: one group with authority applying increasing demands on a subject group provoked contradictory behavior. Other factors are dealt with in succeeding chapters. Here we must dare to say in a sentence that the major factors in change are the firm's demand for efficiency, the impatience of personnel for promotion, the clash of extremists in theory and practice, the differences among organized interests, and the variations in ability among executives to deal with confusion. The initiation, blocking, and resolution of these contradictions are carried through in great part by cliques of various kinds.

CLIQUES AS FOUNTAINHEADS OF ACTION

Although the term "clique" *denotes* a small exclusive group of persons with a common interest, it too often *connotes* a group concerned with questionable activity. Without these moral overtones, the term can aptly apply to the initiating nucleus of many group activities in and out of industry. Certainly the negative feeling associated with the term is carried too far, for cliques and secrets are inseparable and essential for group life. We would question, for example, whether parents covertly checking on their children's activities in school and community are "conspirators"; whether the indirect attempts all of us make to learn more of our acquaintances than they voluntarily tell us is "immoral"; and whether the widespread "manipulations" by both leaders and followers in all areas of life in competitive societies to win ends is "villainy." Villainy may develop in all these cases, but not necessarily. Cliques may work for moral as well as immoral ends. Whether or not we are able to preach what we practice, the organization will fall apart without sustaining action by some clique. All organizations must have "privy councils" similar in some sense to the meaning of that phrase in feudal times. One may well ask, what organization is without secrets held by some members, usually the more responsible, from other members with the intent and eventual result of helping all *loyal* members? Too often uncertainty hallows and hides the developing defects of official doctrine for changing situations. Responsible members must nevertheless try to fit the department, or firm, to inescapable conditions. And in doing this they necessarily "socialize" and "discuss problems," which is easily seen by opponents as "clique" activity "undermining" the organization.

More of this later, but for now let us think of a clique as the informal association of two or more persons to realize some end. The end is usually a calculated one, but it may be multiple and differ for some members. Typical ends in an industrial plant are: to increase the status and reward of one or all members; to get more support in job activities; to find social satisfactions; to hide facts or conditions that would be frowned on by superiors; to escape unpleasant situations or annoyances; to get more privileges, especially those peculiar to higherups; and to share the limelight with superiors.

Many factors contribute to the rise of cliques. A few that are intrinsic or recur and that can be summarized quickly include: (1) division of labor, (2) variations in identification with the firm, (3) changes in the industrial community, and (4) compulsions of growth.

Division of Labor

Formal division of labor and assignment of responsibility encourages cliques, especially in a society stressing equal opportunity. Isolation of personnel in this way provokes a given group to magnify the importance of its function in the system and to ignore and minimize that of others. This leads to challenges and defenses. Work groups and their supervisors compare and rank contributions to the organization. This is particularly true of newer departments, and is of course not confined to industry. In the FWD, for example, there were numerous tiffs among material men, expediters, estimators, and job analysts, with each very status-conscious, defending his contribution as *the vital one*. The condition is probably commoner where education is higher and contribution is less tangible,[9] for the repetition and intensity of defenses seem greater in staff than line. In both, however, departmental boasting extends to accomplishments and competence of the department head.* In Milo's chemical department—and in at least two of the chemical firms in

---

* There is of course nothing "unnatural" about such behavior, but it is contrary to expectations. On the other hand, loyalty to the system rather than to the unifying leader, or department head, may handicap him severely. See M. E. Dimock, *The Executive in Action,* Harper and Brothers, New York, 1945, p. 249.

Mobile Acres—there were disputes between chemists on the one hand, and samplers and vat operators on the other, about whose function "is most important" and who "actually produces."* This job identity forces personnel into defensive action to get their share of credit and honors. Leaders call on subordinates for help to protect departmental interests and to expose the errors of others. Though seen as a distinct unit, the department is compared with others in performance of assignments, original contributions, etc., all of which encourages clique effort to conceal shortcomings and preserve appearances.

Clique action usually accompanies reorganization and the new divisions of labor that come with expansion. Departmental resistance to the new system is often apprehension that new procedures will limit old personal arrangements and "rights." Some supervisors are thrown into panicky opposition by talk of formalizing loose practices. They mouth platitudes about the threat to "democratic" relations, when they really fear the change and the unpleasant lag before they can build a new reservoir of unofficial advantages and in some measure again control the deference of subordinates. They argue that "formalizing things" will force them to "work for" instead of "working with" the company.

Differences in Feeling for the Firm[10]

Variations in the emotional ties of personnel with their firm are unavoidable. Differences in age, ability, expectations, and personal and community responsibilities lead to a *differential identification*. Given human agents in close association, with similar standards of what is desirable, and obviously they will clash over available rewards. Whatever the goals of the organization, there will be rivalry for higher posts, a voice in policy, and recognition from leaders. Without benefit of formal rules, and even forbidden, rivalries find expression in cliques.[11] Moreover, the individual's identification with the firm will vary with success or failure. The gap between his expectations and reality can never close, because our society almost demands that he never be satisfied. With this fluctuating identification a given employee is willing to engage in action at one time that he would not at another. We may say, overneatly, that his view of the firm changes with his success in advancing and protecting himself through participation in the inescapable aggressive and defensive cliques.

Other factors influence the degree of organizational attachment.† Some members are in a department by chance and are looking elsewhere. Some entered by choice but are disillusioned and remain to

---

* See chap. 4.
† Note the statements of various Milo officers in chap. 6.

please their families, or because they feel "too old to make a change," or "could not get the same money" elsewhere, or "have too much seniority." Some are indifferent or resigned and say, "All jobs are alike when you have to work for somebody else." Others are embittered and glad to see superiors embarrassed with problems. In other words, some officers are devoted career members, some are lukewarm toward the firm, while some hardly identify at all.

Changes in the Industrial Community

A changing market and technology, with plant expansion and turnover of personnel, promotes and requires cliques. New personnel and methods may make the organization more desirable for some but less so for others, so that one finds a range of commitments to the organization, as well as the department. This of course means that responsible officers cannot count equally on all members. Having to depend on some more than others their "interaction rate" is consequently much greater with some than with others. Hence despite formal equality, prescribed relations, and assumed objectivity, they draw closer emotionally to some and share community as well as job experiences with them. During work crises these persons turn to each other spontaneously. They share knowledge of developing events and judiciously withhold information from the untried, and especially from those who have "talked out of turn" or are likely to. Their ties are, of course, seen and variously interpreted. Some of the other members may be alienated and, intentionally or not, aggravate differences in the department. But in any case departmental affairs will be dominated by the necessarily small closed corps of officers who become the center of influence and attention, or a clique in our sense of the word.

Rapid turnover of personnel even in an otherwise relatively stable firm naturally weakens group unity. One finds "old-timers" drawing together into cliques because they "have been through things together" and "can count on each other." Irregular transfers of individuals in and out of departments, or the sometimes required systematic shifting of personnel around a circuit in the firm, gives a certain vagrant character to the movers and creates social instability and demand by some for closer relations. As a threat to existing informal arrangements these "floaters" are seen as strangers of a kind.

Under these several conditions demands for "loyalty" force departmental and subgroup identifications. But for some, or even many, this allows only tenuous concern with the organization as a whole, and limited or distorted awareness of departmental affairs. Alert and driving cliques then become the generators of action.

Compulsions of Growth

Organizations have an expansive force and they act to preserve themselves.[12] Milo's action toward its Office was a case in point, and we shall see in the next chapter that this also holds for departments. Often disparagingly termed "empire building," these strains of growth are typical and may be quite lawful, but they jar the organization and induce various clique actions. Two practices always present in organizations, decision making based on limited information and avoidance of decision when possible, increase with the firm's rate of expansion.

Repeatedly middle level executives must act on limited knowledge. Some pressures forbid delay: the placating of powerful associates or influential union officers; the creation of a suitable post for an able but impatient subordinate; the handling of covert internal practices long ignored but now suddenly big with threat to the firm. Here any action may seem like a gamble. These problems become more acute when carried to a superior who refuses to act, but directly or indirectly penalizes the subordinate officer for failure to act successfully on his own. As head of the department the latter turns to his subordinates for loyal support. At each level this is really a request (*a*) for closer ties to conceal current departmental actions and alternatives from outsiders; (*b*) for the keeping of secrets from emotionally marginal members who may be both ambitious and incompetent enough to exploit debatable points of policy; and (*c*) for obedience to understood orders. In effect it calls forth an action clique from the mixture of fit, half-fit and unfit subordinates.

Avoidance of decision may fall into several types, but two are noteworthy and stimulate clique action. In one of these, *sympathetic avoidance,* supervisory subordinates know that their chief is upset by decisions calling for ingenuity or marked departure from formal routine. Yet they see that official procedures are inadequate for meeting his demands. So to prevent the complications that might follow from forcing a decision on him, they develop clique action to protect him as well as to evade him. Their practices require that they keep key persons among interlocking departments informed of changes in unofficial methods, and that, at the proper time, they teach new members the distinctions between their practices and *official misleading instructions.**

---

* Quite apart from decision making, this coaching in the finesse of workable illegalities may be given in any organization. For example, embarrassing disturbances often result when new conductors come on the job and disrupt established practices between older conductors and daily commuting passengers on the interurban railway systems in metropolitan areas. Usually the commuter from

In the other escape from decision, *avoidance by misdirection,* the department chief or similar high officer wishes to elude a subordinate, or colleague in another department, who seeks to force a decision on him. To escape, the chief calls his closest associates to aid him by telling pursuers and telephone callers that he is where he is not—in some part of the plant or in the community "looking after company business." The chief's motivation frequently is fear of making changes in response to pressures from one quarter that will only bring pressures from another. Hence he engages in clique action to avoid action. Sometimes, too, he works on the theory that his pursuers will "cool off" and find a solution "if they are given a little time and *have* to." This was a common practice of Reynolds of the Attica Assembly Company (Chapter 5).

P. F. Drucker[13] praises skill in avoiding action and holds that in some cases any action would be equivalent to a "surgical operation." Also instructive are the comments from a roundtable of executives.[14] One executive says:

> Life in a large corporation is pretty much like politics. A fellow gets along pretty much on what kind of an organization he has been able to gather around him. . . . As far as I am concerned the lone wolf with no friends will get nowhere, either in business or politics.

TYPES OF CLIQUES

Though cliques arise from dynamic situations and engage in many actions, they can be classified roughly. Typing may be in terms of their recurrence, what they do, the situations they spring from, or their effects. Probably the simplest relevant scheme, however, is to label cliques chiefly on the basis of their relation to the formal chart and the services they give to members. Such a scheme is, of course, not exhaustive or exclusive.

---

the suburb to downtown on such trains carries a fifty- or sixty-ride monthly commutation book of tickets. Because the tickets are sold at reduced rates, the company declares tickets void that are presented separately from the book. That is, officially the conductor is to take the book from the passenger, tear out the ticket, and return the book. However, because trains at rush hours are usually full to standing room only, passengers, with the blessing of the conductor, speed up collection by tearing out the ticket and having it ready for him. Ignorant of this arrangement, the new conductor follows official precept and rejects tickets removed from the book. Passengers and conductor are of course outraged with each other. Fellow conductors in adjacent cars allow this to continue for some time, apparently as part of a hazing ordeal required of the newcomer, and to insure that he is sound before they acquaint him with their "illegal" but effective technique.

Approached in this way, cliques fall into three general groups: *vertical, horizontal,* and *random.* Vertical cliques can be broken down to vertical *symbiotic** and vertical *parasitic;* and horizontal to horizontal *aggressive* and horizontal *defensive* cliques. Vertical cliques usually occur in a single department. The tie is between the top officer and some of his subordinates. It is vertical in the sense that it is an up-and-down alliance between formal unequals. It could be represented as a rectangle with the altitude greater than the base, e.g., ☐. Horizontal cliques, on the other hand, cut across more than one department and embrace formal equals for the most part. The horizontal clique can be symbolized as a rectangle with a base greater than its altitude, e.g., ☐.

Vertical Symbiotic Clique

In this relation, the top officer is concerned to aid and protect his subordinates. He does this by concealing or minimizing their errors, occasional lapses, etc. He does what favors he can to meet their immediate needs and to solidify their future in the firm. He interprets their behavior favorably to critical members of the department and to his own superiors. He humanizes the painful impersonal situations and the demands he must make.

The subordinates fully advise him of real or rumored threats to his position. They tell him of current work situations, confer on ways of dealing with "troublemakers" outside the clique, and discuss interdepartmental maneuvers. When urgency demands action and the chief is unavailable or there is no time for consultation, lower members confer and make moves with the chief's welfare in mind, and in terms of

---

* The term *symbiotic* is adapted from the biological term *symbiosis* (*syn,* together, and *bios,* life) which refers to a mutually beneficial *internal* partnership between two different kinds of organisms. This is related to the term *commensalism* (*con,* together, and *mensa,* table) which is reserved by some students for *external* associations between two quite different kinds of animals, who live together in effect as messmates or fellow boarders. Examples of commensalism are the tie between the Dor beetle and its blind mite partner, the hermit crab (some) and sea-anemones, the Nile crocodile and one of the plovers, and the "tuatara" lizard and the petrel. Symbiotic relations include those between heather and its fungus partner, and termites and their flagellates. Our aim is not to force rigid parallels or to precisely follow biological usage. See R. W. Hegner, *College Zoology,* The Macmillan Company, New York, 1942, 5th edition, pp. 155, 702–703, and use of the term by sociologists: R. E. Park, "Symbiosis and Socialization: A Frame of Reference for the Study of Society," *American Journal of Sociology,* 45: 1–25, July, 1939; E. Gross, "Symbiosis and Consensus as Integrative Factors in Small Groups," *American Sociological Review,* 21: 174–179, April, 1956.

his known attitudes. Thus for all levels involved, there is a satisfying exchange of services. This is the most common and enduring clique in large structures. It is more than "team work" because only a nucleus of departmental personnel is involved. As it sweeps other members along they may follow gratefully, indifferently, or with some hostility. It is most effective when lower members are relatively indifferent about promotion or reasonably patient in waiting.

Vertical symbiotic cliques formed the real power centers in Milo, and they occurred at the divisional as well as the departmental level. Though not quite ideal because of Taylor's resentment, the Blanke-Dicke-Peters clique was an example extending into the divisional level, and the Hardy-Springer-Ames clique was another. However, several things make the clique less important at divisional levels. Personal ambitions and opportunities to move to other plants, for example, make the clique less stable there than at departmental levels. More subject to direct claims from the top, too, division heads usually want no official knowledge or part in taboo activities below them that they are sure department heads can contain. The latter understand that they are to serve as screening stations for conversion of unavoidable irregularities into reports befitting divisional dignity. Despite the weakness of a symbiotic vertical tie extending into the divisional level, these heads are caught in unofficial actions as we shall see (Chapter 5) was true at Milo.

Vertical Parasitic Clique

This is *the clique* of popular thought, the one that writers of supervisory manuals have in mind when they make such statements as, "No person may work under the direct or indirect supervision of an officer to whom he is related by blood or marriage."

This is a negative approach which assumes that collusive behavior is inevitable among persons with kinship ties who are in certain job relations. Apparently the implied dangers are thought to be confined to such persons and situations. This is not the case, and the approach explains nothing about how the clique works, or of its relation to other unmentioned cliques that may preserve it in some form. If this kind of clique is regarded as organizationally harmful, it deserves more study.

The term "parasitic" is used because the exchange of services between lower and higher clique members is unequal. The lower ranked person or persons receive more than they give and may greatly damage the higher officer. This clique need not be a family affair. It may be based on a friendship developed earlier in the plant or elsewhere, when the current higher and lower ranking officers were on the same job

level.   The subordinate person owes his position to one of his superiors.
He reports to this person what he regards as pertinent facts in his
work area.   His information may be of use to the superior, but often
its importance is exaggerated.   It is useful where it is accurate and the
higher officer has real need of it—but in such cases the clique relation
moves toward the symbiotic type.   The problem arises when the lower
member is thought to "carry tales" to the higher, whether he does or
not.   In this event his rejection by the group leads him to resentful
distortion and overstatement.

Since management theoretically places members on merit only, the
belief that special aid is given the lower member of the clique obviously inspires fear in associates that he has advantages they lack and will
win still more by informing on them.   Where this feeling is widespread,
the group resists the chief and misinterprets his best efforts.   He may exchange aid with the lower member, but group alertness to hide things
from the lower member cuts the volume of favors he can send up as
compared with that coming down to him.   Much of the harm of this
clique to the firm stems from its interference with operation of the symbiotic type.   Given the values of personnel, the fringe identification of
some members, and the incentives applied by higher management, *a
symbiotic clique is essential for a given department to compete on a par
with other departments* for favors from higherups and to set up workable
arrangements with other departments.

The uneven exchange holds when the clique includes members of
the work groups.   In at least two cases in Milo, workmen informed to
general foremen with whom they had been intimate before the foremen
entered management.   The foremen granted favors that eluded vigilance
of the union and were repaid with information and cooperation on rush
jobs.   But the exchange showed a more tangible balance in favor of
the workmen.

Formal regulations against the action we ascribe to this clique are
evaded in various ways to allow the soliciting member to receive special
aid and favors.   An arrangement used at Milo, similar to what is
described below as an aggressive horizontal clique, worked in effect
to establish the parasitic clique in at least six situations.   That is, two
or more higher officers on comparable levels agreed to aid each other's
relatives or friends on an exchange basis.   One officer made a place
in his department for the solicitee of the other, or promoted the person
ahead of others, or gave him more desirable work or more freedom from
regulations in exchange for like aid for *his* protégé from a colleague.
This cooperation, of course, promotes other understandings and joint
action across departments.

HORIZONTAL CLIQUES

Horizontal Defensive Clique

Cutting across departments and including officers, as we noted, of nearly the same rank, this clique is usually brought on by what its members regard as crises. Threatened reorganization, introduction of disliked methods or a control such as that of the FWD or the Office, efforts by lower and middle management to shift responsibility to each other for problems that have developed, or opposition among the same groups as reassignment of duties is made after a reorganization, are all conditions that bring on crises. This clique may also arise across departments when day and night supervision hold each other responsible as the source of illegal strikes, serious accidents, rejection of the product by a customer, etc.

Usually this clique is strong for only the limited time necessary to defeat or adjust to a threat. Since nothing is served by its persisting longer, it lapses to dormancy until another crisis, but when active it forces the symbiotic cliques into quiescence. However, it is inherently weak because of the vertical breaks likely to occur from action by resurgent symbiotic cliques. That is, as a horizontal structure the clique is made up of departmental segments, each restrained temporarily by the chief's preoccupation with interdepartmental action.

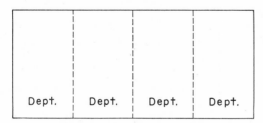

Fig. 7.   Horizontal clique.

Horizontal Aggressive Clique

This type is distinguished from the defensive clique chiefly by its goals and the direction of its action. Its members are the same, and they are likely to have some ties based on past cooperative victories in getting favors and outwitting others. Their action is a cross-departmental drive to effect changes rather than resist them, to redefine responsibility, or even directly shift it. As with defensive action, interdepartmental friction subsides as the clique becomes a mutual aid bloc. Its goals may be to get increased operating allowances; to bring on advantageous reorganization or to win favored consideration over other units of the corporation; to obtain an advantage in forthcoming union-management negotiations; to check the expansion of some staff group; or to advance some member to a higher post so he can help the clique. And of course any executive level, top management, division chiefs, department heads, spontaneously forms this clique when it sets out to correct extreme action by other cliques at lower levels.

When advancement of some member is successful his placement graphically distorts the clique toward the vertical form, but this does not of course necessarily destroy old horizontal ties. For in his new post, the promoted officer frequently finds that his present assistants do not measure up to his earlier ones.* He may then contrive to bring one of his former associates closer to him formally. Obviously the continuation of old ties and understandings hinders adjustment to a new circle. Where the promoted officer does work to draw advantages from earlier associations, he and its members behave remarkably like campaigning politicians. They introduce praise and blame into the stream of plant gossip where it will bring highest returns. If conditions allow, the upgraded officer criticizes the state of the product as it enters his department. He attributes defects to laxity under the responsibility of the person to be discredited. He cooperates with his favorite chiefs to decrease their costs at the expense of others. He talks and exchanges favors with intimates among the superiors of those he wishes to aid, as in the cases above where rules against nepotism were reinterpreted. To aid his own candidates he may omit the subtleties of faint praise and positively damn the chances of others by attacks on their personal untidiness, excessive drinking, extramarital activities; or their disgraceful family squabbles, unmanageable children, impossible personality, and the like. Or, if the condition is known to exist, he may stress the person's stomach ulcers as proof of his shortcomings.

Blanke, Geiger, Meier, and Boesel were an aggressive horizontal

---

* Frequently there is reluctance to break old emotional ties and to face the problems of developing new ones. His feeling is understandable if there are strong differences in attitude between his earlier and present associates on the issue of literal or loose interpretation of official doctrine. He may also be committed to aid one or more of his earlier associates. This last is related to a kind of spoils system and has been observed by numerous executives. See H. Frederick Willkie, *A Rebel Yells,* D. Van Nostrand Company, New York, 1946, pp. 186-88, and Eli Ginzberg, ed., *What Makes an Executive?* Columbia University Press, New York, 1955, p. 156, where it is noted that changes in top leadership often mean that the "new man promoted his own associates" to the detriment of other well-qualified individuals. Sometimes correction of this evil creates others.

clique. At one time they were all in the same division. As we noted, Blanke was then departmental chief with Geiger as his assistant. Meier and Boesel were assistant heads in other departments. When Blanke moved to head another division, Geiger succeeded him. Then with two other officers eligible in service and experience, Boesel became the next department head. Conversations with Geiger and others indicated that Blanke and Geiger greatly aided Boesel and that the three of them worked for Meier who came last to full superintendency. As superintendents, Meier, Boesel, and Geiger then cooperated closely to win favors from Revere. Through strong support from Boesel and Meier, Geiger had as much influence in the division as Revere. Although Blanke was in a different division and all faced new distractions, the old ties were revived on occasion to surmount official barriers.

The Random Clique

This clique is called *random* because its members usually cannot be classified in terms of formal rank, duties, or departmental origin, though they associate intimately enough to exchange confidences. Typically they have no consciously shared formal goal in the plant or point of company policy they are working to change, but the attraction is clearly friendship and social satisfaction. This can of course also exist in the other cliques, but friendship is not their end and may be hardly present. As compared with the more functional cliques this one is random in the sense that its members may come from any part of the personnel, managers and managed, and that they do not anticipate important consequences of their association.

As a rule, members of the random clique are not solidly in any of the more functional cliques. And usually they have never been in them, or if so, they are rejectees for indiscreet talk and failure in action. They are most often apathetic persons who are not sure why they are in the department. But being there they are given things to do, including the less desirable tasks, and they mechanically follow the routines. Consequently they resent, and do not fit into, the changing informal arrangements around them. They would like to escape the confusion to find simpler and more permanent recreational relations. As a result they get away from their jobs when possible to indulge in unguarded talk about people and events.

Their friends are like themselves. From the cafeteria to the showers they meet and gossip about their home departments and their dissatisfactions. Though only on the rim of events they do interact superficially with members of the other cliques. As would be expected, they learn few if any important secrets because of the barriers between themselves and these pivotal groups. And they may miss the meaning for larger issues of what they do learn. Nevertheless this relatively aimless association is important in plant affairs. As small unattached gossip groups moving freely around the firm, these cliques are both a point of leaks from the functional groups as well as a source of information for them. As such, the random clique intensifies informal activities in the plant.* The incomplete bits of information members exchange may mean little out of their larger context to an apathetic person, but much to an alert member of some functional clique. Discrete items supplied by a random clique on, for example, cost manipulation, or "gentlemen's agreements" at some level of union-management trading, may fit so well into the puzzle of an interested action clique that its members will clinch or change their pending action.

Instances from Milo show the circuitous routes of information leaks and the effects on others. The assistant chief chemist, Miller, received a confidential monthly salary "adjustment" of a hundred and twenty-five dollars. He wished to hide this from his subordinates, who were also pressing for salary increases to maintain the gap between themselves and the surging unionized stillmen and samplers. However, Miller did tell his wife, who belonged to a woman's club in the community. She told members of the club, one of whom was the wife of Sand, a line foreman from a third department. Sand was intimate in the plant with Wheeler, one of the samplers. Wheeler played golf with Sand and spent considerable time in Sand's office. Sand eventually passed the secret from his wife to Wheeler. Apparently seeing it as a joke on the chemists, Wheeler told them. Angered at Miller's "unfairness," some of the chemists wanted to face him with their knowledge and use it as a lever. Others overruled this, but "to get even" all cooperated with the samplers to conceal line errors and deviations from Miller, and to reduce the number of their own analyses.

In another case, superintendent Smith learned from his neighbor, Haller, a Milo employee whose loquacity was guarded against in his own department and encouraged elsewhere, that Boesel had arranged with his grievance committeeman to promote a workman contrary to the seniority record. Smith sought a similar deal with his own grievance man but was refused.† Smith's anger struck fear in Boesel and his

---

* The random clique is not, of course, the only source of leaks. Under stress, members of the functional cliques may tell things they would not normally, and for calculated purposes they may deliberately pass a secret to a known "two-way funnel." See chap. 8.

† It is common (chap. 5) for grievance officers and managers to pair off in cliques and to oppose like cliques as all pursue peaceful informal adjustments with small concern for their official roles under the contract.

union ally that Hardy and the president of the union local might be called in. They returned the promoted workman to his old position temporarily, though later both Boesel and Revere made deals with the union adverse to seniority principle. This incident made enemies of Smith and Boesel, and Boesel never learned the source of the leak.

CONTROL OF CLIQUES

Given the nature of personnel, and the official frameworks they create, even the cliques essential for intertwining official and informal actions occasionally get out of hand and must be curbed. These are the vertical symbiotic and the two horizontal forms. They normally function (*a*) to build working harmony from the differing skills and abilities, private feuds, and shifting identifications of employees in endless turnover; and (*b*) to adapt the personnel and changing technology to each other. But when this function fails, or other factors give one department a force in events unwarranted by its contributions, eventual action by a high level horizontal aggressive clique corrects the distortion.

Clique correctives are perforce applied expediently. Conflicting reports on the clique, questions of who the members are and their degree of involvement, and the indispensability of constructive clique skills, work to order the steps taken and to grade the rigor of correctives.

Restrictive action is typically initiated by (1) guarded attacks on the effects of the clique's expanding influence, and followed by a hint, from the presiding officer at a formal meeting, that not all sins are pardonable. If this is ineffective, and conditions permit it, (2) efforts are made to hold the structure as it is and to contain the clique. Greatly influenced by impersonal factors as well as the rank, quality, and extra-clique ties of members, this is a first step in some firms, a last resort in others. Failure to contain the clique may lead to (3) transfer or promotion of the clique leader, and, as in the case of Nevers in Chapter 7, he may receive surprising aid from the firm when he moves to another unit or another company. (4) If pretext and expediency interlock well, clique members may be dispersed about the firm. (5) Sometimes an offensive clique is nullified by neatly justified withdrawal and rotation of members about the firm. In other cases, (6) conditions and matching ingenuities may dictate direct or indirect change of structure or method in adjacent work areas to disrupt clique routines and thus weaken it. Instead of changes, circumstances may call for (7) informal punishments adapted to known sensibilities of key members. (8) Where the corrective clique agrees that certain members of the disruptive clique are expendable, demotions are made, with and without pretext, and members may abide by the change or quit the firm.

Since human ingenuity seems inexhaustible, and managerial structures and industrial technologies are so varied, these corrective steps obviously represent only some of the actions that are taken. Some of these points require further comment.

For example take the first point—complaints against an injurious clique in the hierarchy. Direct communication to top officers is taboo, as everybody knows, because intermediate levels may be involved. Formal "open door" policy may welcome detoured grievances, but subordinates fear leaks of their message and hidden reprisal from those they by-pass. The theory that each supervisor must know all that goes up through his level is sound but incomplete: it has not been news for at least two thousand years that the intermediate levels of various hierarchies wish to interpret and color reports on the way up to protect themselves and to please higherups.[15] Hence initial opposition to a hurtful clique usually resorts to anonymous communication by a letter typed on an outside machine and handled entirely by a non-employee. If the letter shows enough knowledge of irregular behavior, action of some kind is sure to be taken. Even though the behavior reported has been ordered or tacitly acquiesced to by the addressee, some changes must be made to preserve organizational decorum.

Containment is sometimes accomplished by setting up problem committees that include one or more clique members,[16] who share assignments, meet deadlines, prepare progress reports, and otherwise work with the group, which weakens the clique and promotes organizational consciousness.

Transfer or promotion of the clique's key member is sometimes possible and effective. New abilities are suddenly discovered in him that fit him for another post, usually staff, where it is hoped that neither the function nor new associates will channel his genuine abilities into aberrant action. The post may entail standard duties or be only a sinecure. As we saw with Blanke, who was not promoted to break up a clique, this may not entirely check old horizontal aggressive clique actions, but the new preoccupations are a powerful restraint. Sometimes intercompany relations allow cooperative transfers of gifted incorrigibles, as was done between Milo and Fruhling.

Where all members of a deviant clique are considered indispensable and above the humiliation of what cannot be concealed as obvious disciplinary action, all may be dispersed to different parts of the firm, or incorporated into some kind of rotating system to limit expression of excessive clique skills or to use them where they are needed. The potential tumult of dispersal may be more disruptive than the clique. But decisions usually favor the risk, for one finds the expanding firm expediently creating new posts for this purpose, and the more static company maintaining a reserve of active and dormant sinecures as a safety valve for this and other pressures.

Rotation as a remedy also has its pros and cons. It does hasten the breakup of undesirable cliques, hinders the formation of others and offers new promise to frustrated officers. But used injudiciously, it disturbs essential personal ties. The common pretext for its employment, "Everybody is more valuable to the organization because they know more about plant operations," is often suspected as a "trick" or resisted as "pushing people around," as any change is likely to be seen. In theory the rotated persons "get a fresh outlook." By the time they return, if they do, both they and the earlier situations have changed. Rotation is of course not always a mask, but is also used for broadening individual perspectives.

When personnel shuffles are inadequate or impossible, changes are made in methods and duties to balance pressures, reduce inequities, or to bring less troublesome realignments. Sometimes the problem area is seemingly ignored while the personnel and methods in an interlocking department are reorganized as needed to break routines of the troublesome clique and refocus its interests.

Where clique members are not regarded as indispensable, but their rank is such that a blunt release would raise questions about the original appointing officer's judgment, some one of the group may be singled out as a link to be broken, and as an example. Such a person habitually will not receive the information or aid he requires to function, or new "temporary" and logically sound but impossible assignments will be given to him. With calculated aid from others he will involve himself in trouble, grow weary of the job, become suspicious of clique members, and ask for a transfer or quit.

As implied earlier, almost never would an able executive be discharged for clique activity. Higher managers value these skills as necessary for cutting a way through or around chaotic situations. Public relations and the equalitarian ideology may require denial, but top managers are more disposed to pardon than punish occasional excesses of the social skill required for organizational coherence and action.

SUMMARY

In every administrative group, gaps appear between granted and exercised authority. Symptoms in a sense of disorganization, these divergences are inherent in a continuing process of reorganization, authorized or not.

As executive roles are changed by pressures inside and outside the firm, the role of "assistant-to" is utilized for formal as well as unofficial purposes. As an unofficial jack-of-all-roles, it gives the flexibility to executive positions and actions that formal theory and planning usually cannot. It serves as a reward, as an unofficial channel of information, as an informal arm of authority, as a safety valve for the pressures generated by a necessary surplus of able and ambitious developing executives, as a protective office for loyal but aging members rendered unfit by changes they cannot meet or from other failures, as a training post, etc.

The logically conceived plans of one executive level are variously altered by subordinate levels to fit their shifting social relations, as well as the emergencies of work. Inspired by fear of unofficial reprisals, the alterations are usually concealed and therefore not incorporated into future planning, so that the organization is always out-of-date in some sense. Therefore while planning must in general be logical, it must also be abbreviated, and even loose, in some areas to allow latitude for social contingencies. Achievement of organizational goals intertwines with individual and group ends near and remote from those of the firm. Much confusion among personnel stems from disagreement over the distance that can legitimately exist between the two. Persons able to deal with the confusion come to the fore as leaders, with or without the official title. They become the nucleus of cliques that work as interlocking action centers, and as bridges between official and unofficial purposes.

Springing from the diverse skills, attitudes, and turnover of personnel, cliques are both an outgrowth and instrument of planning and change. They fall into recognizable types shaped by, and related to, the official pattern of executive positions. Cliques are the indispensable promoters and stabilizers—as well as resisters—of change; they are essential both to cement the organization and to accelerate action. They preserve the formalities vital for moving to the goal, and they provoke but control the turmoil and adjustment that play about the emerging organization.

DOCUMENTARY NOTES

1. See the comments of E. P. Learned, D. N. Ulrich, and D. R. Booz, *Executive Action*, Division of Research, Graduate School of Business Administration, Harvard University, Boston, 1951, pp. 139–140.

2. For a study of such differences in two military units, see James D. Thompson, "Authority and Power in Identical Organizations," *American Journal of Sociology,* 62: 290–301, November, 1956.

3. One such anonymous person has said that the terms "conflict," "power struggle," "strife," "counter-tactics," and "struggle" are "loaded terms that carry certain inferences and innuendoes of undesirable motivation. These terms convey the notion of war." However, the consultant, R. C. Sampson, accepts in stride the frequent reference among his *clients* to "interdepartmental and intradepartmental warfares," and attributes these "struggles" to various things. See his *The Staff Role in Management,* Harper and Brothers, New York, 1955, pp. 79–80. Also Chris Argyris, *Executive Leadership,* Harper and Brothers, New York, 1953, p. 109, and especially Robert Bierstedt, "An Analysis of Social Power," *American Sociological Review,* 15: 730–736, December, 1950, and M. E. Dimock, *The Executive in Action,* Harper and Brothers, New York, 1945, pp. 53–68. Florence Nightingale actually praised such "scrimmages." See her *Notes on Hospitals,* Longmans, New York, 1863, p. 181.

4. See some implications in C. H. Page, "Bureaucracy's Other Face," *Social Forces,* 25: 88–94, October, 1946, and M. Dimock, *op. cit.,* p. 160.

5. Barnard distinguishes between influence and authority and insists that authority must always bear responsibility. In this sense there is only *formal* authority. See C. I. Barnard, *Functions of the Executive,* Harvard University Press, Cambridge, 1938, p. 174.

6. See the comments on authority and "power" in H. A. Simon, *Administrative Behavior,* The Macmillan Company, New York, 1948, pp. 129–130.

7. P. Stryker comments on American and British views of this office. See *A Guide to Modern Management Methods,* McGraw-Hill Book Co., New York, 1954, pp. 122–23; L. F. Urwick and E. Dale, "Profitably Using the General Staff Position in Business," *American Management Association, General Management Series, Number 165,* New York, 1953, especially pp. 10–25; T. L. Whisler, "The Assistant-To: The Man in Motley," *The Journal of Business of the University of Chicago,* 29: 274–279, October, 1956.

8. J. Carl Cabe, *Foremen's Unions,* University of Illinois, Bureau of Economic and Business Research Bulletin 65, Urbana, 1947.

9. See the remarks of Stein in chap. 6.

10. For general remarks on "identification," see Barnard, *op. cit.,* pp. 83–86; H. A. Simon, *op. cit.,* pp. 110–112, 204–214; C. L. Shartle, *Executive Performance and Leadership,* Prentice-Hall, Englewood Cliffs, N.J., 1956, pp. 156–161. And though expressed in different terms, see L. Reissman, "A Study of Role Conceptions in Bureaucracy," *Social Forces,* 27: 305–310, March, 1949.

11. C. I. Barnard notes the potential for covert action in democratic organizations. See his *Organization and Management,* Harvard University Press, Cambridge, 1948, pp. 39–47.

12. Dimock, *op. cit.,* pp. 53–68; Herbert Blumer, "Group Tensions and Interest Organizations" in Milton Derber, ed., *Proceedings of the Second Annual Meeting, Industrial Relations Research Association,* 1949, pp. 150–159.

13. Peter F. Drucker, *The Practice of Management,* Harper and Brothers, New York, 1954, p. 361.

14. Eli Ginzberg, ed., *What Makes an Executive?* Columbia University Press, New York, 1955, p. 148.

15. See the actions of Sejanus in Tacitus, *Historical Works,* E. P. Dutton & Co.

(Everyman's Library), New York, no date, especially Vol. 1, book iv, sections 1, 2, 3, 8, 39–59, book v, sections 6–9; and Frederick the Great's countermeasures in W. S. Dorn, "Prussian Bureaucracy in the 18th Century," *Political Science Quarterly*, 46: 403–423 (1931), 47: 75–94, 259–273 (1932); B. B. Gardner and D. G. Moore, *Human Relations in Industry*, R. D. Irwin, Homewood, Ill., 1955, 3rd edition, pp. 95–101.

16. C. L. Shartle, *Executive Performance and Leadership*, Prentice-Hall, Englewood Cliffs, N.J., 1956, p. 60.

CHAPTER 4

Relations Between Staff and Line

CONFUSION OF FUNCTION

The very phrase "staff-line" is a focus of dispute among students of management. Some frown on the term and deny that there is a "staff" function in industry.[1] Others say the phrase is too simple, that there are additional categories and functions.[2] Still others hold that the distinction between staff and line is vital.[3] Some theorists accept the distinction, but contend that the staff role should be sharpened and that staff personnel in any case should occupy a clearly subordinate position in management.[4] Against this view some students argue that staff personnel, as products of our competitive society, cannot be expected to function as "shrinking violets." [5]

Denying the staff role, Drucker believes that there are but two functions in management, "business-producing" and "supply," and no advisory function as such for no group advises another or acts for it. He even considers "staff" functions to be undesirable and, as currently used, to mean having authority without having responsibility. He admits that managers "need the help of functional specialists," but he sees these specialists as having a definite job to do, which does not include telling the manager how to do his job. These experts should belong to a given executive's unit, not a special staff. In another connection, however, he regards the Jesuit Order with its "systematic and codified" practices as "the most successful 'staff organization' in the world." [6]

Stryker quotes Urwick as ridiculing the idea that staff functions could be "purely advisory." Urwick views "line" managers as infuriated by the prospect of encroachment from the "advisers." [7]

Commenting on the Unilever Organization, H. J. van der Schroef agrees that a combination of knowledge and personality may carry some staff personnel "far beyond" their official authority.[8]

Ernest Dale is also dubious about the problem of overlapping authority. Through "authority of various kinds," he believes that staff personnel find many opportunities to influence line decisions.[9]

From his experiences as an executive in the War Shipping Administrations's Recruitment and Manning Organization, Dimock concluded that the chief difference between staff and line work is the "authoritative relationship." From his data he was often unable to distinguish staff from line work in terms of what people were actually doing in the organization.[10] Even in the more stable industrial firms, Sampson contends that the staff role has not been defined, that there is uncertainty about what staff work should include and how it should be carried out.[11]

A study focused on the "human aspects" of line and staff relations in twelve companies found only one in which both groups of personnel *appeared* to know "exactly what to expect of each other." [12]

Tead regards the staff-line distinction as real, but contends that staff technical knowledge becomes effective only when joined with "consultative skill" and "advisory persuasiveness."[13]

Although the research may not resolve these disputes, we will consider some of them, especially the question of authority, as we look at the day-to-day working of staff and line. As in the preceding chapter, we will see the difficulty of assigning authority quantitatively to any role, staff or line, and assuming, as some students do, that it will be exercised as though the role existed in a social vacuum. We will see the staff as a body sensitive about its contributions. We will see staff members who are not "shrinking violets." We will see staffs coerced to give and to withhold advice. We will indeed see some staff people exercising great unofficial authority, but also some engaged in morale-destroying genuflections because they lack authority but must justify their existence.

We have already sketched Milo's theory of staff-line cooperation (p. 16). Now we must describe and explain typical and recurring exceptions there and elsewhere, the unofficial roles and defenses that develop in staff groups, the line's unofficial uses of the staff branch, etc.

Typical of formal charts, Milo's map of positions does not indicate the excursions required of some staff roles: some staff people were "lent" to the line at different levels for varying periods. And some official staff communications to some line levels were almost experimentally broken off and rechanneled to other offices.

As mentioned in Chapter 2, staff officers lacked authority over line personnel. But such authority was delegated on special occasions. Naturally there was authority inside the staffs, as in the line, and staff officers corresponded to those in the line. Immediately above the lowest ranking staff people was the supervisor synonymous with the first-line foreman. Above the supervisor was the general supervisor, on a par with general foremen in the line. At the top was the staff head, equivalent to a departmental superintendent, and sometimes actually bearing the title of superintendent. Occasionally there were levels of assistant supervisors and assistant staff heads.

This logically satisfying picture of matching and interlocked experts and commanders rests on three assumptions: (1) that staff personnel will be reasonably content to function without formal authority over production; (2) that their contribution will be welcome, and (3) that it will be applied by the line if feasible. Cases supporting these assumptions are of course not problems. Our interest is in the recurring cases that required devious and inconstant adjustments between agents of the two groups to reach compromises. Following the course and conclusion of these oppositions is essential for understanding staff-line relations.

INFORMAL PRACTICES

The Staff as Monitor

An unofficial role of staff officers at Milo was to assist higher line executives in learning of irregularities at the production level.* Grateful to the upper line for their positions and wishing to stand in well because of their troubles with the line at lower levels, higher staff people fall easily into this function. In firms of Milo's size the strain of physical and official distance, with other factors, often snaps links in the chain of communication. Top management constantly desires more information on the behavior of lower officers, especially first-line foremen (many of whom at Milo were unionized for a time). Hence workable tips on shop level conditions are welcomed by departmental and divisional heads—provided that the message does not imply heavy counter claims. Given the usual "sweetening" of reports moving up the line, this circuitous reporting by staff people helps line executives in at least three ways. First, correct information can crystallize pending

---

* As discussed in chap. 7, organizations, democratic or undemocratic, frequently develop, and may require, internal espionage.

decisions. Second, if the staff officer's report deals with what he regards as someone's "poor shop practice," the line executive will know whether it is an "irregularity" he has already ordered, or one that he can tolerate. Finally, as a sympathetic and cooperative person he can count on this grapevine to help him solve his changing puzzles.

When known, this mode of communication of course disturbs lower foremen. E. Jones, a general foreman formerly in another unit of the firm, denounced "ratting":

> I missed a damn good job in the ————— plant because I wouldn't be a stool pigeon. [Jim Prentiss] was my division superintendent out there. He called me in one day and asked me how things were going in my department. I told him O.K. He said, "That's not what I hear. Come on and tell me about it. You've nothing to be afraid of. And I don't forget people who stand by me."
>
> I don't know, but I think [Prentiss] was trying to get something on my boss who was superintendent of the department. He was a damned swell guy and I wouldn't have told anything on him if it had cost me my job. So I said, "Mr. [Prentiss], I don't know what you're talking about. If there's anything going on in my department that's not on the up-and-up I don't know anything about it."
>
> He grinned at me and said, "Suit yourself. If you change your mind come in and see me. You won't lose anything by it."
>
> I went out and told my boss about it. He said I acted right. But in less than a month my boss told me that [Prentiss] wanted to move me out to [another department where working conditions were very undesirable] and that he couldn't do anything about it. He also said that he was transferring to another plant in three months. Well, I saw the hand-writing on the wall. I had a chance to take the job I'm on now so I quit the damn place. If I'd wanted to rat on my boss I think I could have had the job he left.

Line foremen sometimes react successfully to catch lower staff personnel in a scheme of commitments and thus limit what goes up. But the freer moving, more elusive higher staff people usually multiply news channels to receptive line chiefs. A specific instance shows the initial, and in this instance accidental, steps drawing higher line and staff together. The precipitating event was a practice that adulterated the product and made production more difficult. F. Haupt, in Industrial Engineering, learned from one of his roving subordinates that a certain shop was using substitute material for a customer's order to conceal shortages of the proper material that could not be explained. The condition was no formal concern of Haupt's, but he had had trouble with L. Kuester, general foreman of the shop, over adoption of Haupt's latest contribution, a new job routing system. Apparently his resentment led him to tell Tirpitz, a line chief from another division, about the substitution. Tirpitz had ordered that the makeshift material never again be used because of processing difficulties in his own department. According to Haupt, Tirpitz immediately called both Kuester and Kuester's chief, Taylor, "and bawled hell out of them. Tirpitz was so damn glad to learn what was going on that he invited me to have lunch with him." In Milo's executive dining room Tirpitz and Haupt sat at different tables, but this day they lunched together in Tirpitz' home, the better to cement the developing commitment to mutual aid. One of Haupt's intimates reported that he spent an hour in his office that afternoon "crowing about how Kuester had caught hell without knowing who had peeped." Later at parties, Haupt's wife boasted of the "new contact" her husband had made and what a "swell guy" Tirpitz was.

Conflicts Over Methods and Authority

As method refiners and technique formulators, the staffs are really specialists in change and reorganization. Sworn to stable technology, line people see changes as interfering with production. They particularly resist staff proposals from members who "give advice but couldn't do it themselves." Often seen as a threat itself, advice may also be rejected because of the manner in which it is given.

For example, R. Jefferson, assistant industrial engineer, devised a method for handling shop tools that would improve tool room operation and reduce costs by prolonging the life of tools. At least two line supervisors admitted privately that the plan had merit, but they rejected it. One of them, H. Claus, thought:

> . . . Jefferson's idea was pretty good. But his damned overbearing manner queered him with me. He came out here and tried to ram the scheme down our throats. He made me so damn mad I couldn't see. The thing about him and the whole white-collar bunch that burns me up is the way they expect you to jump when they come around. Jesus Christ! I been in this plant twenty-two years. I've worked in tool rooms, too. I've forgot more than most of these college punks'll ever know. I've worked with all kinds of schemes and all kinds of people. You see what I mean?—I've been around, and I don't need a punk like Jefferson telling me where to head in. I wouldn't take that kind of stuff from my own kid—and he's an engineer too. No, his [Jefferson's] scheme may have some good points, but not good enough to have an ass like him lording it over you. He acted like we *had* to use his scheme. Damn that noise! Him and the whole white-collar bunch—I don't mean any offense to you —can go to hell. We've got too damn many bosses already.

Jefferson's engineering associates disagreed on how he should have handled his plan. One believed he had been "too undiplomatic" and that:

He should have submitted his idea to the engineering department and let it be regarded by production as a contribution of the department rather than the work of any specific member. Jefferson wants to play for the galleries and he's afraid he won't get recognition. What the hell difference does it make whether production gives him the credit? His own boss is the one he should be worrying about. As long as my boss thinks I'm a good guy, to hell with other people. The way Jefferson went out on his own, he didn't sell his idea and he gave the department a black eye at the same time.*

A second associate believed the industrial engineering department "should have privately given full credit, then had a tool expert come in from the outside to sell it to the old guys [line]."

Jefferson himself contended that there was no reason to "hide" his contribution, that the line had always openly rewarded its members for private efforts. And he told his associates, "By God it's my idea and I want credit for it. There's not a damn one of you guys that wouldn't make the same squawk if you were in my place." [14]

To reduce conflict with the union, line supervisors frequently compromise on seemingly simple issues that shortly re-echo in a staff-line context. For instance, systems of bonus payment to production workers, once understood and agreed to by the many groups involved at Milo, usually could not be altered at one point without eventual plantwide reverberations. Yet repeatedly on the work floor Taylor submitted to pressures for misapplication of control factors set up by the engineers. The factor in question would correct for use of some abnormally difficult but necessary procedure by allowing compensation, usually increased pay, gauged to the condition. In staff eyes, Taylor's crime was to authorize use of the factors to cover normal working conditions. This nullified the engineers' work standards, for an unskilled operator could make "fat bonuses" without corresponding increases in production—a current, if not eternal, issue between workers and managers. Other aspects of this type of issue are discussed in the next chapter. Here we need note only how staff-line clashes developed around it.

After winning Taylor's signature to support a nonexistent condition,

---

* This admitted inability of the staff to keep its members in line contrasts with reported Japanese practices where individual contributions in management are considered as those of the chief or the department. Rewards for this submissiveness are advancement and the assurance of "life-long membership in the enterprise." See Solomon B. Levine, "Management and Industrial Relations in Postwar Japan," No. 42 in the reprint series of the Institute of Labor and Industrial Relations, University of Illinois, p. 66. We will note, too, the turnover of American staff personnel and the unconcern to remain for life with the firm when opportunity beckons elsewhere. Obviously different social structures are reflected here.

the involved workers typically had to "lay down" in order not to "kill" a good rate.*

Some supervisors were always uneasy about the workers' "slowing down" to the point of seeming idle. Aware of the condition, the engineers usually hesitated to intervene for fear they would bring both union and line management against them. So the general practice continued until H. Hampton, a foreman, received word from Taylor that an order, on which the factors were being used, must be completed at once. Hampton reported to Taylor that the operators refused to work faster for fear of "killing the rate."

Coming to the shop himself, Taylor saw at once his own responsibility for the state of things. Knowing that Blanke would not tolerate the slowdown, he reneged on his agreement and ordered the workers to step up production. At the same time he charged Industrial Engineering with setting up a rate that checked rather than increased production.

The foreman whom Taylor ordered to "sit on the job until it's done" kept the machines running at normal speed. Consequently the rate of production as measured by the standards exceeded 600 per cent, a performance four times greater than the outraged operators wanted. The engineers of course felt obliged to investigate a performance that had unexplainably moved from a normal to a phenomenal level with no change in job or methods. Enraged by Taylor's desertion, the operators explained their remarkable paper rate by exposing Taylor's part in the deception. He denied the charge and embarrassed everyone by further action in officially poor taste.

However the clash, with its implied fallacies in engineering "controls," reopened an old issue among the engineers: the meaning of a "day's work." To engineer Phillips, for example, the standards were not absolute and could not be relied on in all cases as a correct measure of a day's work. He held that one might arbitrarily call 125 per cent a day's work, but that "because of bugs in the rate" an operator "might have to kill himself to make it on one job, but could sleep on another job and still make it." As long as this was true, Phillips explained, "a man need not work at a killing pace but should still be doing something. As long as his machine is running, let him sit down if he feels like it. If he runs a 1000 per cent† performance, pay him off. That's what the

---

* To "kill a rate" meant to produce so much in terms of the rate that the resulting bonus, relative to production, would bring the engineers in to revise the rate downward.

† Actually both engineering and line officers would have regarded a performance of 1000 per cent as fantastic. For obvious reasons, at Milo, as in any profit organization, staff and service groups had to more than pay for themselves. Everyone knew that diversely aligned statisticians (themselves staff people) were seeking to prove and disprove that staff bodies "cost more than they are worth."

agreement is. If he feels you won't stand back of the agreement, he'll quit when he reaches a certain point."

Haupt and those who saw the standards as absolute disagreed violently. After recovering from his shock at Phillips' remarks, Haupt maintained that:

> If a man puts out a performance of 150 to 200 per cent a day, he's done a day's work even if he does it in an hour. The standards are correct. All of you know that they're based on hundreds of careful studies. It's up to the engineers to not make mistakes. Check and double-check your data and there won't be mistakes. A man simply can't produce 12 to 16 standard hours [150–200 per cent] without working like hell. If he does it in 2 to 4 hours he's entitled to do nothing the rest of the turn. I agree that we should stand back of the agreement and pay men for what they do, but I don't think a man has to work like hell for eight hours to do a day's work. As long as a man can put out 10 to 20 standard hours for every eight actual hours he puts in he's a damn good man. If you guys don't believe that, then you don't believe in your own standards and your whole line of thought is phony!

Though never settled, this debate reveals the typical self-conception of staff groups and their sensitivity when challenged by the line.[15]

Milo's major production unit was the focus in a third case of dispute between staff and line over methods and authority. Originally costing millions, the unit was rebuilt and modernized recently at a cost greater than that of the original installation. The Office was displeased with the resulting production and said so. Geiger comments on these pressures with a grasp of organization rare among the department chiefs. Though he does not always mention them by name, his attack is really against local or Office planning, sales, and engineering staffs.

> We're always catching hell about our maintenance costs being so damn much higher than those of the [Colloid] plant. Well, let me tell you something about the facts. The [Colloid] plant is nothing but a production unit. All they do is make [what my unit makes]. They don't have any processing units. All their work is done on big orders—they make the same damn thing for days. This means that they're not having to stop or slow down or make changes in their setup. Now we don't have anything like that. Most of the time the hodge-podge of orders we have will take only from thirty minutes to two hours—after we get set up—to run out one order. Well, setups and changes take time and cost money. Local Production Planning does the best they can, but [the Central Office] decides just what we'll run and there's not a damn thing we can do about it. In spite of all this, yesterday we came within less than one per cent of the [Colloid] plant's record for the same period. . . . The [Colloid] plant is the pet of the corporation. It's new and it was set up just to be a pace setter. In that plant every damned motor and part is standardized. They're all the same from end to end. If anything goes wrong, they've

got the parts and the skill to do a quick job—men changing the same kind of parts all the time get till they can do the job with their eyes shut. It's not that way here. On my unit I've got [production machinery from a great variety of equipment manufacturers] in the way of motors and parts. When they come in we've got to rework them and make changes so we can use them. Well, by God, that takes time and money. . . . Local sales force—and the guys you know as well as I do—are always working on a reciprocity basis. . . . That's why we can't have standard parts here in the plant. . . . They buy equipment from people who will buy our products for somebody else. There's a lot of subletting that goes on. We sell to people who don't use our products but who get a hand in the profits from combines who do use the products or who get in on the subletting done by people that we order directly from. They're always making deals of that kind. They don't give a damn how much we're inconvenienced and they don't think about the costs until they get the maintenance bill. Then hell really pops.

Another point where we're on the spot in being compared with the [Colloid] plant is that that plant was planned and laid out from scratch. We're always tearing down, rebuilding, and changing to meet technological advance, competition, and changes in the market. We've really got a bastard plant, all because the original planners couldn't see far enough ahead. Then we're a damn sight bigger than the [Colloid] plant. There's a hell of a lot more here to coordinate and keep going. And regardless of how carefully planned a plant of this size is, you can't rule out politics. There's just as much politics here in the plant as there is in Washington.

Larry Donovan, one of Geiger's general foremen, laid their problems at the doors of the Industrial and Mechanical Engineering departments. He and Geiger, with associated foremen, won Revere to this view. According to Donovan:

The whole damned engineering bunch from [the Central Office] on down ought to be cleaned out! They're responsible for the [millions] that was spent reconditioning this unit—and a lot of their work was nothing but waste. They sent parts that we tried and rejected ten years ago as being unfit for our use. The shifters, guides, and sluices just wasn't designed right. Hank [his assistant] and me have wrote out nearly five hundred orders for parts that hadn't even been thought of up the line for the new unit. That's how damn poor things are run by the engineers.

[Revere and Meier] spent most of their time out here last week. [Revere] asked me, "Larry, what the hell's wrong? Why isn't it running right?" I told him it was because the parts wasn't right—poor designing. [Revere] said, "What the hell should we do?" I told him, "I've caught hell several times for not scrapping the old [shifters and heat exchangers] because they was taking up room. I've still got them. I think they should be put back in." Revere told me, "Well, by God put them back in!" Just then Reardon [Geiger's assistant] stuck his nose in and yapped, "Yeah, but the Engineering Department has a hand in that." Revere yelled, "God damn the engineers! Put them back in."

Well, we shut her down and put them back in. We'd had the new unit running four months and still hadn't broke the old record. Two turns later we broke the old record and we'll be breaking everything the [Colloid] plant has done. We'd have broke it a long time ago if they'd put that bunch of chair-warmers to work instead of having them set around and dream up cockeyed designs.

Plant Protection and Evasion of Staff Rules

At both Milo and Fruhling the staffs of Industrial Relations greatly influenced the job routine and rules governing plant police. We will see later how plant materials and services, protection of which is a major duty of the police, fill a social function with and without the aid of the wardens. However, spontaneous submission to claims of the work force leads these armed guardians naturally to undo various staff regulations. As everyone in industry knows, on the "graveyard" shift there is cat napping, and even periods of genuine sleep among the personnel, both supervisory and nonsupervisory. This is usually done by prearrangement for certain people to "spell" or to awaken others and to warn them if discovery is likely. However, there are accidental slips, as well as feigned ones, that lead to discovery by the roving protectors, who are required to report all such cases. But even in the best protected firms there are impersonal cases of failure to report deep predawn sleeping because the discovery is so near quitting time that preparation of the report is omitted as a nuisance. Oftener, however, the omission stems from the policeman's friendly relations with the sleeper or his department head. In a widely known case at Fruhling, a plant guard maintained a farm and delivered food products to many executives and general foremen, on whom he allegedly reported nothing.

Safety Rules

As noted in Chapter 2, safety rules* were incubated in the staff of Industrial Relations. Stevens and Hardy gave the staff such strong support in its safety program that lower management tried to conceal many accidents. The staff used bulletin-boards to advertise the rank of all departments in terms of safety performance. The admonitions of manuals prepared in the Central Office made clear that a relation existed between the safety record of a department and the future of its supervisors.

Hence to protect themselves and escape detection, lower supervision and workmen cooperated to resist the staff control by keeping many accidents off the record. For example, a workman caught his foot in a

---

* The rule against sleeping in the plant is usually interpreted as being a safety rule to make its evasion the more abhorrent. This despite the proud pointing to statistics showing that one is safer in the plant than at home.

conveyor and broke several toes. P. Hancock, the foreman, took his car and drove the man to a private physician in the community rather than to one of Milo's three hospitals. The workman was treated regularly and was driven to and from his home daily by either his foreman or general foreman. During the day he sat or lay on a pile of waste in a secluded part of the tool room reading pulp magazines. His time card was punched in and out for him, so that he received his regular hourly pay throughout the period of disability. His company (group) insurance was of course not touched, for claims would have exposed the case at once. The medical bill was paid by the foreman and general foreman. Union officers cooperated* in the deception, though some foresaw complications in case the workman "had lost his foot."

In another case a department chief succeeded in having a plant physician give aid but keep the treatment of a mashed toe off the record. The individual was similarly paid but sat in a chair directing his replacement.

All such cases were interpreted by the Industrial Relations Staff as a rejection of its preventive device of wearing "safety shoes" with steel reinforced toe boxes. The staff used many lures to win use of the shoes in "hazardous work areas." Always selling the shoes at cost, the staff met each objection to them with a new tack. Spurned as "too heavy," the shoes were reduced in weight. Criticized as "too hot," they were lowered to the height of oxfords. When the shoes were ridiculed as "clumsy," the staff asked the manufacturer to finish them as dress shoes in various styles and colors. This increased their adoption among many older men who did use them for all purposes.

Chemistry and Engineering worked with Industrial Relations to frame safety rules covering the use of gases and liquids. But when executive pressures were great for completion of certain work line foremen demanded that safety limitations be ignored, or they cooperated with workers in breaking the rules. Both were of course accountable in case of accident.

Rules required that only bonafide electricians change blown fuses on overhead traveling cranes, but most foremen allowed or asked cranemen to change the fuse to avoid the delay of waiting for an electrician to arrive.

Staff rules also forbade the use of crane *limit* switches except in

---

* This case was of course union-management cooperation at one level. The complications of unofficial cross-organizational claims and conflicts evade precise containment. Where possible, illustrative incidents are categorized according to how they are precipitated. But this, too, can be disputed.

emergencies. These switches were electric stops located above all crane hoists. Their function was to prevent the hoist from rising to the point of striking the drum and snapping the cable, which would of course endanger life and property.

Some line chiefs seriously tried to enforce the rule. The problems involved and the attitudes toward the staff, as well as line superiors, were most feelingly expressed by M. Dillard, an assistant superintendent.

Cranemen let the hoist travel until it hits the limit switch to save themselves the trouble of pulling a lever. This wears the limit switch out and keeps it from working in an emergency. And every day some of them [limit switches] crack up and quit working. But you don't find it out till you've got another breakage bill or an accident. The first time the switch fails to work is too damn late to prevent some kind of an accident. Handling equipment like that breeds carelessness and disrespect for rules. Yet when you give some foreman hell for allowing this to go on he'll have the brass to stand up and tell you the limit switches must be used daily to be sure they're in working order! A foreman with attitudes like that will look around for rules to break. Honest to Christ, I could put my finger on a dozen foremen that ought to be canned! One of my foremen got so bad I called a meeting of the cranemen and had him tell them while I was there not to use limit switches except in an emergency.

Making up breakages cuts like hell into our appropriations—it keeps us from getting essential things. Yes, and that don't include the hell you catch upstairs trying to explain your breakages. This stuff is all tied up together—you make one little slip and you're in a hell of a jam on a dozen points.

The whole safety setup would drive you nuts if you worried about it. There's a rule that says every time there's an accident it must be written up. Then there's a rule that says the accident write-up must be passed around and read and signed by all the workers. Once they've signed, they're on their own if they have that kind of an accident. One of the things that beats hell out of you is the way you have to break the rules. For instance there's a rule forbidding men to work around defective equipment. Yet the heat to produce is on so damned heavy that Maintenance has to send men in to do repair work with parts moving all around them. Half the time we want something repaired we don't dare shut the unit down. The rules say no repairs can be made on moving machinery, but production comes first. Just let somebody get hurt and you'll get the ass-eating of your life. Production comes first but safety is supposed to. You hear it dinned into your head till you're sick of it. Then you have to forget it but take your medicine when an accident happens. You follow the rules when you can—maybe that's half the time, not a hell of a lot more.

When a serious accident could not be hidden, the reporting of it usually distorted the facts to protect the person who would be held responsible. Part of the rationale behind distortion of reports is the theory that all possible accidents have been experienced or foreseen and therefore catalogued. This means that future accidents are blocked off by rules and can occur only if rules are broken. The theory is so true in most cases that the responsible person describing an accident must ignore the many rules that were broken to single out one, that may or may not have been breached, to protect himself and those nearest him, as well as the injured person. To the more sensitive officer, describing an accident and specifying the rules broken is not a simple thing but a *social* problem with *ethical* overtones.

Such cases would usually occur in the line, but an instance involving line and staff shows the force of social factors in subverting logic both in the occurrence and reporting of the accident.

R. Neilson, an incentive applier from Industrial Engineering, left his work area and went to a machine shop to request a favor of his friend, the foreman, Fitzhugh. Neilson asked for a buffer with which to polish an object he had earlier made in the shop—another common but illegal practice. Fitzhugh nodded assent and pointed to the tool room. Neilson obtained the buffer and carried it to an open bench. Soon after securing his piece in the vise and applying the whirling buffer with pressure, he slipped on an oily spot and fell against the buffing wheel which cut his left forearm to the bone. He was hurried to the hospital where the diagnosis automatically made him a "lost-time case." Since the accident occurred in Fitzhugh's shop, he was obliged to report it. His description stated:

> Incentive-applier from outside shop requested buffer but was refused. He then got buffer from tool room in absence of attendant [the attendant gave Neilson the buffer]. Accident caused by breaking shop rule 7 which forbids all use of tools except by shop employees qualified and authorized to use them.

Neilson was "disciplined" by an additional two weeks lay-off without pay after convalescence. He offered no objection to the penalty and felt no resentment toward Fitzhugh, "because it was all my fault anyhow. I wouldn't have got Fitz in trouble if I'd lost my arm."

Industrial Relations at Milo was slow to uncover and counter disregard of its rules. It did not require the signatures of witnesses to the accident and to the accuracy of the responsible officer's description. Fruhling and Attica staffs did require witnesses, but repeatedly line officers either coerced associates into signing or gave tacit favors for signatures and thus still eluded the restriction to some extent.

Among "minor" safety commandments breached more than obeyed, are those forbidding the individual (1) to use a ladder not fastened at the top to its supporting object; (2) to walk under a ladder; (3) to ascend a ladder or stairway without having one free hand; (4) to work in certain areas without a dust mask; (5) to do certain work without goggles; (6) to handle certain chemicals without rubber goggles and rubber gloves; (7) to fail to report unsafe conditions; (8) to engage in "horseplay"; (9) to fail to go immediately to the hospital with minor lacerations, etc. The attitude here is not active opposition to the staff so much as apathy and boredom. But of course the staff suffers as though it is met with organized resistance.

The condition stems from several things. Often there is physical inconvenience in following a rule. Many workmen are supported by foremen in thinking the rules too general and petty. Finally, personal advantages are frequently gained by breaking or misinterpreting regulations. The last two points need further comment.

Meeting the command to hold safety meetings, workers and foremen hash and rehash safety methods until the process becomes a mummery. Foremen read the latest list of accidents, including those from departments with hazards they never encounter. The foremen point to the "causes" of the accidents and ask for comments and suggestions. In some situations workers are accused of being unobserving and unimaginative if they have no suggestions to offer. If they do, their comments are frequently interpreted as personal attack on the foreman in charge of the pinpointed area. Or the suggestion itself may be ridiculed. Workers listen with respectful boredom. Where morale is high and they know the real feelings of their foreman, they assist in the pretense by feeding in hypothetical constructs of accidents that could occur in different areas of the plant under certain conditions. Even in departments where safety meetings are held daily because of the real dangers, there is a limit to the number of possible accidents that the most imaginative can conjure up. Occurrence of simple and preventable accidents shows the empty character of the meetings.

To some persons the most rewarding safety rules to break are those requiring the ill or injured person to go to the hospital at once and as often as requested by the doctor. But going to the hospital after work often means waiting for 15 to 45 minutes as one of the crowd. Going before work may mean loss of a day's pay, and the travel time and cost to and from home if the physician discovers the patient is running a temperature and sends him back home.* Hence many workers establish relations that enable them to leave early and have someone else punch out their time card and thus "beat the crowd"—when too many do not do it.

---

* Less bureaucratic physicians sometimes advise the worker to sip a glass of cold milk just before leaving home to make the temperature acceptable when examined.

But here, too, staff aims are often circumvented. Some employees arrange to go early to the hospital but go on home instead. In some extreme cases at Milo, when employees were to receive diathermy treatment for wrenched backs, they went only two or three times and quit, but continued to leave the job early for weeks with the understanding that they were going to the hospital. Staff discovery of course leads to friction with responsible line people. A common excuse offered by foremen and workers is that return trips to the hospital are usually superfluous: physicians and nurses "dress scratches until the scars disappear just to build up a record for themselves" (that is, allegedly to justify the function and existence of hospital personnel).

Production Rules

We need not repeat the case of discord between the line and Production Planning cited in Chapter 3. But that staff's commitment to maintain a logical tie between production and customer's orders was incidentally blocked by internal line problems. And, as we saw, even when aware of the problem, higher line gave the staff little real support in its effort to be logical because, however done and in whatever order, *total* salable production was the dominant line interest.

Feigned acceptance followed by expedient rejection of staff offerings raised internal staff problems that aggravated friction with the line. To reduce friction and solve problems they thought too dangerous to take to superiors, middle and lower staff personnel in some cases covertly collaborated with similar line levels. The obstacle to wise decisions by upper staff and line is clear.

Rifts in the Chemical Staff, for example, led its samplers to exchange favors with the lower line that kept leaders of both branches in the dark about working conditions. In one line department, the solution in a series of vats was supposed to have a specific strength and temperature and a fixed rate of inflow and outflow in order to give desired qualities to the product. However, because of production pressures, unreported defects in earlier processing of the material, and occasionally large gaps between laboratory and plant practice, the expected conditions were not maintained. The solution was about triple the ideal strength, the temperature around ten degrees above normal, and the rate of flow double that expected. Yet the chemists sampled the solution at regular periods daily and by "graphite analysis" showed that all points met the laboratory ideal. This was done from expedience, as well as from sympathy toward hard-pressed foremen and from resentment toward superiors. While the chemists worked to hold conditions inside the tolerance essential to avoid damaging the product, they were handicapped and failed at times. They then helped to hide or reclaim damaged items. In return line foremen notified the chemists, rather than their superior, of anything "going wrong" that would reflect on them, and cooperated to reduce the number of analyses the chemists would have to make. This is lower level staff-line harmony based on the staff's expedient collaboration to evade its own minor rules in order to win cooperation on major rules and to carry on. We will return to this, but here let us see how this kind of harmony makes for staff-line disharmony higher up. When the graphite analyses going into the chief chemist's office are acted on, mysterious troubles develop in the processing departments. Top line requests the staff to do something about it. The head chemist and assistant get their own samples and analyze them. Finding errors, they too are likely to submit ideal figures. This was done at both Milo and Fruhling. Whether the line chiefs involved denounce the whole staff as not worth its keep or say nothing, the social problems will overshadow the technical issues for a time.

Lower staff-line disharmony sometimes arises from logically irrelevant and disguised issues that set off erroneously based recriminations between the two branches at high levels. At Fruhling, for example, professional consciousness among routine chemists and their enforced close contact with "uneducated" line samplers led to great bitterness and eventual ending of face-to-face relations between the two. Laboratories were built at a distance and samples and reports exchanged through pneumatic tubes. The rise of conflict in this case deserves special attention. Although the chemists usually had college training in chemistry, their work required more manual than analytical skill. Nevertheless they regarded themselves as very superior to the line samplers who had much less formal schooling. However, the samplers received only slightly less pay than the chemists and taunted them about their pretensions. Finally the samplers' union obtained a pay increase for them that boosted their incomes beyond those of the chemists. In time, jibes and insults were exchanged. On night shifts the chemists had no staff supervisors present to protect them. Alert for a chance to punish the chemists, the samplers brought in more samples than necessary or than could be analyzed correctly. To be sure the chemists were properly degraded, the samplers, aided by their foremen, arranged to load rush orders at night when laboratory samplers were unavailable. The product had to be sampled at once. Line samplers could not do it because they were not trained in that kind of sampling. The chemists therefore suffered the final outrage of having to do the work of subordinates, and, when line personnel could arrange, do it in freezing temperatures. The volume of work, and the distractions of the conflict, forced the chemists to make graphite analyses. Errors and impure products resulted. Line samplers escaped all responsibility by pointing to the chemists' signed analyses. The economic costs of returning and refining the product from storage areas, and from loading and shipping points, as well as the turnover of staff personnel were, of course, the surface issues at top levels. There the problem was attributed to cussedness among the chemists.

FACTORS IN STAFF-LINE CONFLICT: SOCIAL BACKGROUND DIFFERENCES

Attempts to explain these frictions must consider the total conflict in a plant. Staff-line problems are separable only to a degree from collisions among the line departments as each tries to increase its operating funds and reduce its costs. Various managers inspire fear through the organization by pushing to win promotion, expand influence, etc. Then, tensions between union and management may aid or interfere with either of these movements. This complex of unconsidered variables, clashes of interest, and unplanned disruptions makes any analysis of staff-line relations incomplete and artificial to a degree.

If we keep this general conflict system in mind and pretend that we have frozen two additional disturbing factors, we can get a better picture of events. The two other factors are (1) the differences in what staff and line officers bring to the job and (2) the differences in what they can do when they get there.

The chief points of difference making for personality clashes can be discussed under the topics of education, age, professional consciousness, and social distinctions.

Education

Milo's group of 36 staff heads, assistants, and staff specialists had an average of 15.2 years of schooling as compared with the 13.8 years for the 36 line superintendents who, however, had more schooling than their line subordinates. This difference was statistically significant at better than the one per cent level. The 270 nonsupervisory staff personnel, with an average of 13.1 years, had more schooling than all line groups but the superintendents.

These educational gaps clearly affect interpersonal relations. Staff people, as did the Fruhling chemists, show a smugness about their training that irks line supervisors, who react by referring to staff personnel as "college punks," "slide rules," "crackpots," "pretty boys," and "chair-warmers." College-trained executives whose theory has been harshly revamped by experience, criticize "college boys" as "trained too much to follow fixed steps—they don't know how to use short-cuts." Top executives elsewhere have questioned the ability of those with nothing but "technical competence" to deal with the "more intangible . . . facets of business."[16] And some line chiefs encourage resistance by generalizing that "engineers make a lot of mistakes," "set phony standards and try to cover themselves by finding fault with production methods," etc. Line attitudes toward staff personnel, especially industrial engineers, came out most pungently in various line definitions of engineers at Milo. One of the best of these was Geiger's phrasing: "An engineer is a guy who comes around and picks your brain on the fine points of your job, then goes to your boss and gets his approval to come back in two weeks and *tell you how to do your job.*"

Surprisingly, the staff man's verbal facility often blocks communication with the line. Quicker in argument, he holds in contempt line personnel who grope for words or mispronounce and misuse them. Too concerned about their future to openly ridicule the line in meetings, staff members imply that line people do not know what they want or even what they are talking about. And the advisory officer's ingenious phrases suggest that "lack of education" is no shortcoming of his own. On the other hand, his theory and proneness to treat abstractions as real become a blind spot* when he is confronted with the practical arguments of line figures who can match words with him. Communication is also blocked by seasoned line officers who, one time only, see gaps between an adviser's theory and practice and thereafter suspect any of his offerings as "all theory."

---

* Too great preoccupation with theory stimulates rifts even between levels inside a staff. For example, on sultry days a Milo chief engineer once too often insisted on supervising the placement of oscillating fans on the floor of an office in which his subordinates were writing up their field work. His aim was to achieve maximum circulation of air in all parts of the room. The lower engineers, however, resented the implication of his knowing more engineering theory than they. And they especially wanted to resist any theory that prevented them from placing the fans in a pattern related to their informal ranking of themselves—so that some received "more air" than others. Their gestures forced the superior to withdraw apologetically. For comment on the "blind-spotting" effects of specialization, see A. N. Whitehead, *Science and the Modern World,* Macmillan, New York, 1925, chap. 13; K. Burke, *Permanence and Change,* New Republic, New York, 1936, pp. 11–18, 54–70; F. J. Roethlisberger, *Management and Morale,* Harvard University Press, Cambridge, 1941, pp. 137–174; R. K. Merton, "The Machine, The Worker, and The Engineer," *Science,* 105: 78–81, January 24, 1947; H. J. Laski, "The Limitations of the Expert," *Harper's Magazine,* 162: 102–106, December, 1930.

Staff groups are more enterprising and impatient for quick reward than line forces. Here, too, education is a factor. Usually selected because of their outstanding academic records, staff newcomers believe their contributions are indispensable, and they expect quick advancement. The case of R. Jefferson, the assistant industrial engineer, cited above, was typical.

In time the educational differences between staff and line personnel are likely to be much reduced.

Age

The same 36 staff officers had a mean age of 42.9 years. This figure would have been well under 40 except for the inclusion of several indecisive executives in their fifties who were dropped into a staff to spare them the greater stress of making decisions in the line. Nevertheless, the age of 42.9 was still significantly less than the average of 48.7 years for all line superintendents. The difference was about the same through the other two levels of line supervision, with whom the staffs had their greatest trouble. For example, the 61 general foremen averaged 50.0 years and the 93 first-line foremen 48.5 years. But the greatest age spread between these two functionally different branches was between the line and the 270 ambitious, salaried, nonsupervisory staff people who averaged only 31.0 years and, as mentioned above, had almost the same amount of schooling as the superintendents. They were also the explosive pool of future leaders: always studying both staff and line managers to note their health, ages, and retirement dates; obsequious, and prayerful for whatever event would create openings.

These age distinctions[17] were more than just figures. Like the educational gap, they interfered with understanding and cooperative effort. Claus' rebuff of Jefferson was in part an older officer's dislike of being advised by a younger person. Staff personnel were made conscious of this line attitude. When the two faced each other in meetings, staff suggestions were often ridiculed by line officers. This disillusioned the less experienced staff men. Lamenting his staff's many failures to "sell ideas" to the line, Fred Haupt, an assistant staff head, told me:

> We're always in hot water with these old guys in the line. You can't tell them a damn thing. They're bullheaded as hell! Most of the time we offer a suggestion it's either laughed at or not considered at all. The same idea in the mouth of some old codger in the line'd get a round of applause. They treat us like kids.

One of the staff specialists assigned to Taylor's department devised what he regarded as a survival technique for close living with a line chief. His remarks are also a staff stereotype of line executives, comparable to Geiger's picture of the engineer given above.

I never tell him anything point-blank. It doesn't pay to. I *hint* at something or give him a bare idea of what I have in mind. I may even joke about it as something too silly to consider—anyhow I don't bring it up again. Then he'll come around in a week or so and tell me the same damn thing in different words and ask me how I like it. I tell him I think it's a good idea. Then he says, "Let's go ahead with it." We both pretend it's his idea* but we both know it's not. On the other hand, sometimes I think he fools himself into thinking it's his. When you've got to live with a guy like that, what else can you do?

Individual drive for recognition, type of staff-line incident, and internal complications for the staff are all illustrated by the activities of Haupt. Then aged thirty-seven, he was the son of a consulting engineer. Three of his models for living were maternal uncles who retired early from industry (outside Mobile Acres) and law practice. They were each "worth from $200,000 to $400,000." Second in rank in his department, Haupt was eager for the top position, but depressed by the "damned healthiness" of his chief, also under 40. Of a plantwide wage system, that part administered by Haupt became a farce when lower staff personnel—who applied the system—"weakened"† under the pressure of workmen to increase their bonus. All efforts to correct the situation failed. Haupt volunteered to show his associates and line chiefs "how the situation should be handled." To withdraw the pay plan without union trouble, he bargained privately with the griever to adjust past job records so that the guaranteed "average pay" after recall of the plan would be satisfactorily high. This agreement meant that regardless of what the production level of workmen had been for the periods concerned, their pay would be equivalent to time-and-one-half, given only for overtime and holidays.

Higher engineers in the division refused to support Haupt "because it would mean professional suicide." His subordinates sat and sulked. They felt that their pay plan had been perverted, and their efforts as engineers wasted.‡ They agreed among themselves that Haupt "sold us out." Fearful of opposing him verbally, they attacked him in other

---

* The thought of making the other fellow think it is his idea is of course the common "buttering up" practiced by subordinates in all organizations. But doing this is most painful for experts.

† These personnel were so few in number that they were easily isolated and coerced to "be more reasonable," or, as with the chemists in another staff, to make out "graphite" reports. Even when deceptions were suspected and partially established they were not likely to be thoroughly uncovered because of inherent complications.

‡ One study suggests that engineers have a greater fear of failure than line executives. See Harriet B. Moore and Sidney J. Levy, "Artful Contrivers: A Study of Engineers," *Personnel*, 28: 148–153, 1951.

ways. When he walked through their office at 8:10 A.M. they were too busy to look up or answer his greeting. When he was busy in his office —behind a closed door—they called him by telephone. When he answered, they listened for a moment without response to his repeated "hello's," then hung up. During a national political campaign they put a ticket of the Democratic presidential candidate on the rear of his car. Because Haupt was a Republican, as all the managers at that level were or pretended to be, and did not know how long the emblem had been there, he feared his superiors had seen it. He complained that "whoever did that ought to consider the spot it puts a guy in. What would Hardy think if he saw that damned badge on my car?"

Haupt's action stood, but the engineers thought it "hurt the department," and line chiefs saw it as "the wrong way out," and as "costing too much."

Staff people of this type are understandably more dynamic and driving than most older line officers. They are less well established in life in terms of material accumulations, occupational rank, and job security. At the same time they have greater expectations, more energy, and more life ahead in which to make new starts elsewhere. At Milo, this drive was reflected in the staff group's having gained their current positions in less time than had members of the line. Though their rank was roughly comparable to that of line heads, assistants, and general foremen, the 36 staff officers (including the former line executives) had spent only a median of 10 years attaining their positions as compared with 11 years for first-line foremen, 17 years for general foremen and 19 years for line chiefs.

Differences in Professional Consciousness[18]

As a factor in personality clashes, professional sensitivity was noteworthy in other firms as well as at Milo. Professional sentiments were shared by all the engineers, and to a lesser degree by all staff members with specialized training, even in some cases where the specialty was not being used, as with a salary rate expert who had a B.S. degree in geology. We saw how this feeling among even routine chemists snapped the staff-line tie and brought humiliation to the technicians. With still greater education and scientific commitment, the research chemist is indeed a professional. Where staffs of such experts exist in industry, feuds with the line are likely to multiply. Moreover, because of differences of function this occurs even when the executive himself is an expert. Also in Mobile Acres, the Marathon Research Company was a firm of 260 employees, most of whom were staff. The director was a former staff man with a Ph.D. degree. As a small firm with limited resources,

Marathon's clash of economic and social factors was different from that in the larger plants, but the outcome for staff-line relations was similar.

Nearly all the researchers had received some graduate training and some had higher degrees. But the director's narrow outlook and responsibility as coordinator apparently limited his understanding of the research group. To cut down clerical expenses he reduced his office crew and then required the researchers to do their own paper work. Each of them spent three or more hours each night and about five hours on Saturday and Sunday in tabulating research and preparing reports. Almost without exception they saw themselves as becoming "glorified clerks." Then to increase its resources, Marathon arranged to get restricted research funds from a nearby university. The school expected certain of its graduate students to do research in the firm and to be "guided" by the staff people there. Despite preoccupation with their own problems, personal relations developed between the researchers and students so that shortly the chemists were unofficially aiding the students. Learning of this, the director took the next step of asking the researchers to "help the students graduate on time." The researchers, however, did not want the official responsibility of being "nursemaids." Hence they retarded graduations as often as they aided them, and they complained that if they "had wanted to be schoolteachers," they would "have taken up teaching."

The final insult to professional pride and commitment came when the director's ideological biases blocked some of the Ph.D.'s from what they regarded as essential sources of data. Two of them read German and Russian research journals. They asked the director to make the journals available and pointed to specific findings they regarded as in advance of ours. The director said Marathon could not afford the extra costs, and that "America leads the world in research. Those Krauts and Commies can't tell us anything!" One of the specialists, who has since left Marathon, told me with cynicism that the influence of formal education is overrated: "For here's a case of a man's ambitions and job making him forget his professional obligations."

In one of the Fruhling laboratories employing only analytical and research chemists, line pressures defeated professional expectations of the newer chemists and thus aggravated staff-line conflicts and stirred professional jealousies among the chemists themselves. For example, younger chemists in this laboratory often wanted to publish their research findings in the professional journals. Regulations required submission of such papers to the Office thirty days in advance of giving them to the journal editor. The Office justified its screening on the ground of concern for public relations and the need to guard its competitive position.

One of the chemists submitted such a paper for clearance. After some cuts, the Fruhling Office approved publication. The paper was accepted and the chemist patented the major ideas he had developed.

However, line chiefs of his division had been unofficially opposed to both the publication and the patenting. The division head had told the chief chemist that certain processual changes inherent in research facts of the paper were not desirable at the time. The chief chemist and his assistant submitted to this pressure. As the research chemist thought, they even agreed warmly with the line executive because they were professionally jealous of their subordinate and did not "want their own insignificance exposed around the corporation."

The chief chemist had long followed the line policy of keeping his junior chemists on hourly pay "until they proved themselves." The policy also enabled Fruhling to claim any profits from the beginner's research, for the chemist, not the company, received the profits from findings he patented when on salary. In this instance, the chemist patented his idea, thinking that he was going on salary. But he remained on hourly pay, and his freedom to do research was sharply limited for disrespecting the unofficial request that he not publish or patent his research. He responded by resigning.

Social Differences

A differential focus on dress, poise, ease in meeting visitors, fluency in conversation, speech consciousness, personal grooming, recreational interests, and concern to avoid giving offense all served to raise a barrier between line and staff groups, especially from the middle line down.

Staff members were particularly concerned about their dress, a daily shave and a weekly haircut. The staffs ostracized the rare member who did not measure up. One competent and cooperative individual who shaved only every other day, rarely got a haircut, suspended the knot of his tie far below his unbuttoned collar, and wore the required white shirt beyond the one day limit was shunned and heckled till he quit his job.

Below the level of superintendent in the line there was relative indifference to such matters, often from necessity as well as disinclination. General and first-level foremen were usually in such intimate contact with production that dust, grime, grease smears, and emergencies prevented meticulous dress. The surface distinction of "dirty" and "clean" jobs with the implied status differences inflated the self-esteem of staff people. This galled the two levels of line foremen, most of whom had no objective grounds for feeling inferior in terms of pay, authority, and contribution. Nevertheless many foremen saw conspiracy against themselves in the visible similarities of staff people and higher line managers.

Staff sophistication in making personal approaches, in speaking, and in writing reports gave its members an advantage in the struggle for favors from top management. The lower line was quick to interpret actions of higher managers as showing sentimental ties with the staffs. A typical practice shows the contrary attitudes of top and lower line toward the social qualities of staff people.

When official visitors came to Milo, Hardy usually picked an urbane staff assistant to show them about the plant. Or he would select several such persons to be attendants on the route. As the visitors and guides came down through a given bay, line supervisors typically looked up and declared among themselves that the visitors would know less on leaving than on entering because (with reference to staff guides), "you can't cover up your ignorance with a fast line of patter!"

The aversions of some general foremen to staff personnel were so great at Milo that, though expected to attend, they remained away from the cafeterias reserved for management in order to avoid staff people. One of Geiger's foremen expressed more graphically the many similar outbursts made by other line officers.

> There's a lot of good discussion in the cafeteria. I'd like to get in on more of it but I don't like to go there—sometimes I have to go. Most of the white collar people [staff officers] that eat there are stuck up. I've been introduced three time to Svendsen [engineer], yet when I meet him he pretends to not even know me. When he meets me on the street he always manages to be looking someplace else. God damn such people as that! They don't go into the cafeteria to eat and relax while they talk over their problems. They go in there to look around and see how somebody is dressed or to talk over the hot party they had last night. Well, that kind of damn stuff don't go with me. I haven't any time to put on airs and make out I'm something that I'm not.

Thus educational, professional, social, and age differences (1) discourage easy informal ties between staffs and many middle and lower line supervisors, (2) prevent staff people from getting close to situations, and (3) dispose both groups to draw unflattering stereotypes of each other.

STAFF AND LINE CAREER PROSPECTS

The social and functional differences of staff and line personnel are reflected in their diverse expectations and job destinies. We can see the meaning of this for staff-line cooperation by following the staff beginner through his early experiences in the restless and expanding staff groups.

Position of Staff Personnel

Entering industry for the first time, the logical but unsophisticated* young staff officer is usually shocked to find himself caught in the cross fire of staff-line skirmishes that must never come to open battle. He expected to engage in specific and clear-cut relations with everybody. He assumed his training would lead him to a precise, methodical round of duties. Now he finds that his freedom to apply himself is checked by shifting arrangements. To get his bearing he must first uncover and explore an intangible world of private understandings. Frequently he finds that the academic specialty† he counted on is not related to his duties. Instead of cut-and-dried social relations and job duties labeled with their rewards, he finds that the important thing is to learn who the informally powerful line officers are, and what ideas they welcome that will not offend his staff superiors.

Frustration and Turnover

Often the staff beginner's reaction to these conditions is to look elsewhere for a job. If not, then he adjusts toward protecting himself and finding a tolerable post from which he can plan his future. When he follows this second course he is likely to be more concerned with social relations to aid his advancement than with creative effort for the firm. His frustration in finding the avenues blocked to full expression and quick recognition is reflected in the high turnover of staff personnel. These data are fully available only on Milo. Table 1 shows the turnover‡ there of both line and staff for four successive recent years.

---

* Of course, not all staff people are engineers, but see the remarks of a retired research engineer on the worldly naiveté of some engineers: John Mills, *The Engineer in Society*, D. Van Nostrand Co., New York, 1946.

† Only fifty per cent of Milo's higher staff people were in their college groove. And in the division (7800 total employees) of Fruhling on which data are available, 59 per cent of upper staff worked outside their specialty.

‡ Turnover was determined by dividing the average number of employees (line or staff) into the accessions or separations, whichever was smaller. Percentages do not include salaried supervisors of either staff or line, but cover all other employees of each group.

TABLE 1.   STAFF-LINE RATES OF TURNOVER, 19___ TO 19___

| Year | Per Cent Turnover | |
	Line	Staff
19___	24.2	78.9
19___	28.3	88.0
19___	31.7	88.0
19___	31.5	81.5

In addition to the restraints inherent in a firm's general conflicts, the formal structure itself frustrates the ambitious staff person. That is, the levels of authority are usually fewer in the staff than in the line branch. At Milo, as the chart shows, staff levels were numbered only three or four as against up to seven in the line. At Fruhling there were more staffs, but they were rarely over three levels whereas line ranks ran to ten. This allowed fewer possible positions of distinction and authority for staff personnel to move through, and stimulated empire-building among the staffs. Supercharged with youth and aspiration, but blocked by low ceilings, the staffs expanded laterally.

Expansion

Staff growth pains were shown by the demand for more personnel and the numerical increase* of staff as compared with line personnel. The increases were justified to "carry on research," "control new processes," and "keep records and reports up-to-date." With staff growth came boasts about "the number of men under me." As needs for personnel were understood, several conditions inside the staffs did not square with these requests.

One of these was staff concern with its "privileges." Members wished to be free of the regulations they ingeniously devised and applied to line personnel: they arrived late on the job, maintained a radio in the office, left the plant—sometimes for long periods—during working hours, and quit early. Grouped in large offices, the staffs participated in another condition not shared by line groups, prolonged and recurrent social activities on the job. These embraced talk of sports, politics, parties, and sophisticated buying; the operation of raffles; petty gambling, especially the double charm of settling issues by coin matching; the

---

* See C. Northcote Parkinson, *Parkinson's Law*, Houghton Mifflin Co., Boston, 1957, chap. 4. Though factual-satirical, and riding on humor and ingenious interpretations, this little book insightfully touches on a variety of administrative organizations. And if approached in the proper spirit, chaps. 4, 5, 6, 7, and 10 have a certain relevance for our chap. 6.

solving of mental puzzles, etc. Most discussions necessarily moved on a superficial level, for attempts at wit so interlarded the talk that wise-cracking was often an end in itself, as two or three members of every staff competed to entertain the group.

Finally staff forces were vehemently defensive about their functional importance for production. They engaged in theoretical jousts that sporadically lasted for hours as they challenged each other's contributions and ideas or attacked line groups and other staffs. Where they regarded time spent in this way as a privilege of their status, line people saw it as a threat to themselves and the organization's resources.

Dimock[19] has described similar expansive behavior in governmental staffs. He sees executives enlarging staffs because they feel "more secure . . . surrounded by brain-trusters." And seeing them as "his" people also makes the executive "feel more important." Finally the very growth of staffs emphasizes to outsiders the volume of research and planning that goes on and thus gives the "enterprise a reputation for being aggressive and forward-looking." Baker and Davis[20] develop the idea of staff expansion in terms of a "law of functional growth," but they ignore social functions as an aid and hindrance to their law.

The results of pressure from within the staffs to expand can be shown by comparing Milo's total staff and line groups* at a recent time and again three years later. The times selected were arbitrary because of the availability of data, but were not atypical in terms of technological expansion or fluctuations in production. Total plant personnel actually declined by over 400 (about 0.5 per cent) during the period.

TABLE 2. MILO STAFF AND LINE GROWTH

	Initial Period	Three Years Later	Per Cent Increase
Staff	400	517	29.3
Line	317	387	22.1

As Table 2 shows, with 400 members at the initial period, the staffs were already 20.8 per cent larger than the line. Three years later the staff forces, with 517 members, were 33.6 per cent larger than the line with its 387 members. The 29.3 per cent increase in staff people

---

* Staff personnel included staff heads, assistants, staff supervisors, engineers, industrial engineers, chemists, accountants, statisticians, planners, schedulers, routers, dispatchers, analysts, estimators, providers, secretaries, and all kinds of clerks, etc.

Line membership was confined to all administrative officers and their immediate clerical force of secretaries and expediters. Production workers were not included.

as compared with the 22.1 per cent growth of the line in three years was statistically (C.R. 2.43) almost too great to be accidental.

Transfers from Staff to Line

Although officers in both staff and line were impatient for older high status figures to move off the scene, frustration was higher in the staffs. The engineer, Jefferson, for example, merely echoed what we have heard others say. The top figures in his department, Carlson and Enders, ". . . are damned healthy. I'm stuck right here. If I could get a spot in the line, I'd have something to look forward to."

However, casual remarks at both Milo and Fruhling pointed to greater inducements than the line's many-runged ladder: there was also more income, authority, and prestige[21] there at any level. Although the actual number of people moving from staff to line was small, it was great compared to the reverse movement. During the last seven years ten staff officers entered Milo's line at levels of general foreman to assistant-to Stevens. During the same period only one person moved from line to staff and this was a created office for an executive who failed under the strain of matching his official and unofficial decisions.

One top executive observed a similar trend in his company over a period of thirty years. The firm hired "engineers, chemists, and technologists of all kinds" and put them beside line executives. In time the specialists took over the responsible line jobs. This displacement evidently had shortcomings for this executive declares that the managers coming up "through the ranks became educated in human problems, but the technicians" did not.[22]

In the same vein another executive cautions that in moving people from staff to line you may lose a "good contributor and get a bad manager, usually with a nervous breakdown." *

In the 1940's the executive Willkie recommended more general education for specialists and rotation about the firm to broaden them.[23] More recently this is becoming a policy in some of the larger firms.[24]

V. Vance, top administrator of one of the Fruhling divisions, explains why some line groups admit many specialists.

> In our selection of potential executives we've stressed college boys—all engineers—for the last five or six years. We call them "training engineers." We want them to have actual experience on the job, and we want them to try out their research ideas. Maybe they won't do much at first but look on, ask questions, and offer suggestions.

---

* Eli Ginzberg, ed., *What Makes an Executive?* Columbia University Press, New York, 1955, p. 118. Milo administrators implicitly recognized this in dumping subdued line executives into the relatively safe staff posts.

Coming right from college, the boys can never have any first-hand experience with workers, so it's easy for them to get management's viewpoint. You can see that a man coming up from the shops will have a worker's viewpoint. He may not be able to shake it off, but go around the rest of his life *appearing* to have management's view of things.

Hiring college boys pays off in other ways, too. At least one out of three of these fellows will have real ability and knowledge that he can apply. In spite of what first-line foremen say about the college boy's not having "know-how," he can learn, and he'll usually have a hell of a lot of sound theory and good ideas. They help us in this way: In the past when we increased the capacity of a production unit, we had to enlarge all our processing units to accommodate the new volume of production. That's not always true anymore. These young engineers often show us how to use our same processing equipment in new ways. They make minor, inexpensive changes that let us take care of our greater production without installing new equipment all over the plant. That means a hell of a lot of savings. In addition to paying for their salaries many times over, these young engineers are grateful for their jobs and have nothing but management's interest in mind.

POWER OF THE LINE

Vance's remarks have implications often overlooked by new staff personnel. One is that the line *is* the firm. It is established and brings in the staff groups. It demands that staffs prove themselves, and it decides issues between staffs and itself. But for staff careers the most oppressive power of the line* is that to appoint and promote all members of management. And of course staff promotions are greatly influenced by information coming from middle and lower line. Hence every staff member knows that if he aspires to higher office the weightiest part of his record must be a reputation for "understanding" line problems and getting along with line people.

In meeting the expectation that he contribute practical ideas, the staff man comes to view himself as an expert of top management. As such, he must appear infallible once he has committed himself on some point. He strains to develop and deliver new techniques. But he frequently becomes so impatient for applause that he tries to force acceptance of his ideas, and thus gives already suspicious line chiefs the impression that he is reaching for more authority.

Against this, the production chief holds his authority as something

---

* The case of Rees in the preceding chapter was of course a glaring exception to the rule of staff subserviency to line. An instance in the Attica plant is detailed in the next chapter. Some pertinent discussion based on a survey appears in Charles A. Myers and John G. Turnbull, "Line and Staff in Industrial Relations," *Harvard Business Review,* 34: 113–124, July–August, 1956.

sacred. He resents the implication that after many years of success in the line he now needs the guidance of an inexperienced newcomer. When this sore spot is touched, staff-line cooperation cools. The thwarted expert attributes his failure to "ignorance" and "bull-headedness" among "the operation boys."

Even before presenting an idea to the line, staff agents must face the obstacle that many first-line foremen view them as tools brought in primarily for control of the lower line. Foremen are likely to regard most staff projects as manipulative devices. They cooperate with production workers and general foremen to defeat insistent and uncompromising staff people. As we saw, foremen may cooperate with lower staff personnel in trouble with superiors. But this is also an attack on staff chiefs. The staff function inherently threatens some part of the line because any contribution is likely to mean change in the line.

Staff innovations are opposed for several reasons. In view of their longer experience, intimate knowledge of the work and higher pay, line chiefs feel an obligation to make the contributions themselves, and they fear being "shown up." They know that changes in methods may bring personnel changes, break up informal arrangements, reduce their authority or enlarge that of rivals (including staff people), and bring reorganization with possible change of superiors. To some line chiefs, change based on staff ideas will be disastrous for they represent instability, impracticality, and unpredictability. They are "snoopervisors" who may uncover workable but forbidden practices and label them "inefficient" and "unscientific" in terms of their holy procedures.

Hence middle and lower line will often oppose staff-initiated change openly until top line shows firm support. Then verbal conformity will screen lower level resistance and malpractices to bring a return of the earlier arrangement. Knowing this, staff officers may withhold real improvements when they believe attempts to introduce them will be defeated or that forcing resistance into the open will hurt their future.

Though they may not sketch the engineer as neatly as Geiger did, many first-line foremen have similar attitudes toward all staff people who rove the plant in search of meat for their recommendations to top line. In Fruhling's division of 3500, the foremen conspired to withhold ideas and information from methods engineers:

> . . . because they always gobble up everything you tell them and then take credit for it. Sometimes things get so bad that we have to help them out to make it easier for ourselves—even if they do get credit. But most of the time we don't put out anything—we ask them. And believe me, if you want a cockeyed answer, that's the way to get it!

STAFF COUNTER TACTICS

Actual or probable line rejection of their ideas provokes staff groups to (1) strengthen their ties with top line; (2) adhere to the staff role, but "lean over backward" to avoid trouble down the line that could reverberate to the top; and to (3) compromise with the line below top levels.

The Top Line as a Staff Haven

At Milo the staffs regularly sought means to bring them intimacy with Hardy, Stevens, and the division chiefs. The most widely used device was to get membership in management's "Cafeteria Association," which was closed to officers below general foremen in the line and general supervisors in the staffs. Movement to one of these offices did not automatically make the incumbent a member of the Association or qualify him to eat in the cafeteria. Membership came by invitation not application, though informal probes were made to learn what chances one might have of being invited.

Eating in the cafeteria gave staff officers the opportunity to (1) make personal contacts at high levels that would aid survival out in the plant; (2) introduce ideas and send up trial balloons in the easy noncommittal situation and to study initial responses; (3) receive hints of interpretations the top executives were making of reports on staff activities sent up the line; (4) drop hints of line resistance to policy and practices that have been officially accepted; and to (5) apply advance pressures against known, suspected, or possible cores of rising opposition to staff ideas not yet fully developed but already leaking to the line.

Thus for the Milo staffs at least, the dining hall was also a rejuvenation clinic and a camp for maneuvers. Here, of course, the ideal camaraderie prevailed. Formal commitments and the educational and social ties of staff and top line generated a sympathetic atmosphere. Anxious staff heads and assistants were reassured even if no specific issues were talked out. Warm acceptance by the status-givers enlivened the staff and cheered them back to the working arena. The social and professional importance to staff officers of admission to this sanctuary came out in the comments both of those in and those aspiring to enter the Association.

F. Rivers, a production planning supervisor, commented:

> Eating in the cafeteria means that you're really *in*. When you're one out of the top one hundred [only one hundred could be seated at one time

and rarely more than this number attended] in a plant of this size you're doing all right. Being in really means a lot. Before I was in I've had occasion to call on Jim Bimble [line head] for something. Right away he'd have someone take care of it for me. He thought I was just a clerk. Now when I call on him he looks after it personally and falls all over himself helping me.

R. Merritt, a cost supervisor, outside the cliques in his department, fantasied in this way:

There seems to be a committee that passes on you. [F. Lane, assistant-to Stevens, made the decision on who would be invited.] I've had my application in for three years, but no soap. Harry [his superior] had his in for over three years before he made it. You have to have something, because if a man who's in moves up to another position the man who replaces him doesn't get in because of the position—and he might not get in at all. I think I'm about due.

Avoidance of Trouble

Since harmony and cooperation down the line are interpreted as absence of trouble, staff groups also specialize in good appearances. This is essential for subordinates as well as heads. Though the staff head may be content to remain where he is, he must still guard and strengthen his position. As he defends his personnel and fights to enlarge operating and research allowances, he perforce builds friendly ties in the line to counteract the concern there about staff growth and influence. Hence ability to give favorable impressions of oneself and department becomes a survival item in the catalog of staff skills. The importance of pleasing[25] may outweigh contributions. Inside the staff future rewards and penalties are also colored by impressions made concrete in a day-to-day record of merits and demerits locked in the individual personnel file. Events support these generalizations.

The cases already mentioned of the Fruhling chemist, and of engineer Haupt's treatment by his subordinates illustrate the penalty of forgetting to please. Haupt learned his lesson well. When the tensions of a situation weakened his self-control he quickly apologized.

In a clash with Kuester and Taylor, for example, he was much concerned to placate them. His staff had developed corrective factors to be used discreetly on certain jobs in the shops, and had agreed to Kuester's right to say when the factors were to be used, as in the case above involving Taylor and Hampton. Haupt's agents in the shop notified him that under pressure from the union, as with Hampton, Kuester was mis-applying the factors. Since Haupt was formally responsible for "fair and impartial application" of the factors, he chose this time to challenge "loose application" resulting in "bad precedents." During the altercation in the shop, Kuester, referring to periods antedating the factors, asked, "Why do we have trouble now when we didn't use to?"

Haupt became very angry and shouted, "You know damn well why we have trouble! And by God I don't want to hear about it again. You come up with that same old stall every time!" Haupt resented the implication that his group was responsible for Kuester's problems, and he insinuated that Kuester's trouble was really his well-known tactical weakness, like Taylor's, in dealing with the union.

Haupt's assistant, A. Riley, was silently present during this exchange. Just as they neared the shop exit, Haupt told Riley to go on to their offices, that he was going back for a moment. The next day Haupt explained to Riley that he had gone back to apologize to Kuester and to Taylor, another silent witness. Haupt then added, "I think maybe you'd ought to go and see them, too, and make your peace. We want to get along you know. They'll feel a lot better if you apologize."

This fear of unseen reprisal from irate line executives was acutely evident when the staff man considered himself a likely candidate for a higher post. T. Wohler, a Milo second level supervisor, was a case in point. Responsible for three supervisors and eighteen non-supervisory employees, his department had developed the unconcern about punctuality that staff groups accept as their perquisite. The official starting time was 8:00 A.M., but the practice was to arrive up to 8:25. The lunch period, from 12:00 to 12:30, was observed from about 11:45 to 1:15 with story telling, games, news reading, and radio listening. Midmorning and afternoon coffee breaks were extended by coin tossing to determine who would go to the restaurant for coffee and rolls. Then the ten minutes observed in the shops became a leisurely half-hour in the staffs.

This behavior was visible through a glass partition separating the staff rooms from a suite of offices held by C. Kother, a processing head, and his associates. Hardy, Blanke, Geiger and other prominent executives visited Kother. Hardy sometimes came to Wohler's office and drank coffee with the staff force, so all these line figures personally knew Wohler's administrative style. Yet when Wohler learned of a possible opening above him in his staff he called his force for a meeting and addressed them as follows:

Boys, I think we've been getting too lax here lately. I've let it go on for sometime without saying anything. It's time we started checking up on ourselves. There may be changes around here. Some of you may be in line for promotion. If you are, you want everything to be in your favor. Well, one of the best things anybody can do for himself is to make a good impression. I know you boys don't mean anything by it, but do you realize that when you have coffee and rolls out there in the room it looks as though you're having breakfast? At lunch time you sit around and tell jokes and read the paper half an hour after you should be back at your work. You know, that doesn't look good to Kother's bunch over there. They think we lead the life of Riley. And another thing, Mr. Hardy pops in and out of here a lot. What do you suppose he thinks when he's been around the plant and seen everybody else working like hell, then sees some of you boys sprawled out as if you owned the place? I know you boys are all damned good workers, but what will he think? When he catches you doing nothing he's likely to think you loaf most of the time. I make a motion that we stop having rolls and coffee at nine o'clock. What do you say? Let's take a vote—show hands. How many are in favor of having breakfast at home instead of on the job? I see, well—it's up to you. But the least you can do is to be inconspicuous when you eat your rolls. And if you're going to have coffee on tap, don't be surprised if you see me carrying a cup in to Kother once in awhile. You can see the position we're in. We've had several run-ins with Kother. I can tell you he's not going to sit in there and watch us make a play-house in here without talking his head off. You know what that means. He knows all of you. If you don't want to help yourselves, at least think of the organization. I'm not bawling you out. I'm just telling you for your own good. It's up to you to make the choice.

Driving in late two mornings during this period, Wohler advised the supervisor who rode with him that, contrary to their habit, they should enter the opposite side of the building to avoid being seen by Kother, who had no formal authority over them. Wohler's mental state is suggested by his confiding to the supervisor that he had slept little these two nights because he was "curious about who's going to get the vacant position."

Staff Compromises with the Line

Since the staffs are only partly successful in winning favors from the top and concealing their friction with other parts of the line, members are often reduced to compromise. We have already seen cases at lower levels. These adjustments are usually of three kinds. The first and most common, and probably least crippling to the staff, is toleration of minor rule-breaking by the line in exchange for aid from the line in crises. Second, and potentially more damaging to the staff, is *delay* in applying changes already accepted by top management. Third, and most illegal but not as dangerous for the staff as it sounds, is transfer to line accounts of staff research funds in order to get more, or continued, cooperation. This last may never be expressed in such terms, but is understood.

Toleration of rule-breaking, and even cooperation with the line to sidestep some regulations, is essential at times to prevent the line from revealing staff errors to the top. Failure by the staff to "cooperate" with the line is countered by the line's "standing pat" on its own rules at a time when the staff wants evasion. Experience shows both groups that tomorrow can be a day of distress for the side standing on a regulation. For instance, a Milo staff assistant was caught in a three-way contradiction: an indefensible error by one of his subordinates stopped a production line; the line chief was running a strange and special order against a deadline; the staff personnel who were necessarily used on the experiment were inexperienced and irritating to line workmen. The line executive could have exposed the staff error to soften Revere's criticism. But he took the blame, controlled his workmen, and concealed the staff blunder. Yet before and after this incident he had (1) used short-cuts forbidden by staff-line policy, (2) refused to allow inspection of the product at the required time, and had (3) charged the staff unjustly with blame for defects in the material. Repeatedly his behavior compelled the staffs concerned to falsify reports. These sometimes dealt with expensive operations that called for reworking of the product and manipulation of funds, time, and personnel.

Sometimes demanding line heads persuade a staff to delay the release of new methods, processes, etc., that have been, or are ready to be, officially accepted. In return they may tacitly offer the consolation of more aid in making the project work when it is brought out, as well as a word of credit and appreciation to higherups.

In a case at Milo, a staff head ingeniously stalled delivery of his project for nearly three months and hid its completion from the impatient top level, which of course included Hardy, an expert himself in stalling movements. Under threat of an illegal strike, the line executive involved agreed with the griever of his area to not introduce the change during a stipulated period. Already beyond his margin of safety in a circle of tightening commitments, he could not avoid the concession. With its current number of personnel, the union stood to lose certain pay bonuses if the new system were applied at once. Knowing that if he opposed the aggressive and resourceful committeeman he would only raise greater problems elsewhere in addition to the threatened walkout, he exploited the weak staff. He and the union officer agreed that during the period of delay they could work out transfers of workmen by seniority and without pay losses for most people concerned.

On his side the staff head was in no position to refuse the demand. However, meeting the exaction called for maneuvers not imparted by his formal training. First, his subordinates, who had developed the plan, were impatient to see it in action. They were not deceived by his excuses for the delay and they planned by some means to bring the issue into the open at the next staff-line meeting.   He met this threat by requesting them to prepare an inventory of materials and to make a long postponed revision of older methods.   Then, fearing these assignments might not occupy them for the required time, he divided them into groups for intensive research on setting up a merit-rating plan for the department.   This final task, as he knew, was extremely controversial in the staff because of individual aspirations and rivalries.   Thus he tied the group down with busywork and gave excuses for the absence of his supervisors from meetings.   Although this blocked formal communication that the plan was ready, it was fear of his acuteness and reprisals that prevented unofficial revelation.

The personnel manager or teacher is correct who surmises that there was fall of morale in the staff and that none of the assignments was completed.   But to weigh this staff-line settlement organizationally, or morally, calls for appraisal of the possible effects of the threatened strike.

The third survival tactic of the staffs is to surrender some of their funds, granted by top management, to middle and lower line.   These heads typically ridicule staff research as "money wasted on blunders." Some heads contend that their departments "can accomplish more with less money."   But staff people attribute their failures to line "sabotage" and refusal to "cooperate."   Line officers counter by citing specific costs of "crackpot experiments."   At both Milo and Fruhling, executives talked of "the $160,000 oversight" made by a Fruhling engineer.

In any case, the evidence supported by intimates in both groups at Milo indicated that pressures below top line did lead to something more than sporadic "kicking back" of funds previously assigned to staffs. The transfer was accomplished by personal relations and the legerdemain of skilled auditors and accountants, who were also career minded staff people concerned to "do what is right."   These kickbacks were of course not embezzlements, but were similar to those we earlier saw Milo Operation coerce from Maintenance groups.   These transfers were literal purchases of line tolerance and cooperation.   And on these compliances some aspirants successfully staked a claim to consideration for line membership.   In view of the repeated failures of logic to accomplish what was needed in the maze of shifting ties fashioned by natural aptitude, departmental overidentification, etc., the critic might have difficulty showing that this was not at times a wise use of staff funds in the tortuous career of the total organization.

If such practices were universally extreme, the staffs obviously could not survive.   On the other hand, the remedies sometimes offered by presumably qualified people have a specious ring.   The thinking of a former Fruhling chief is an example.   Lured to Milo to serve as a combination local counselor and liaison man between Milo and the Office, he favored eliminating all staff personnel "except a few chemists, accountants, and . . . engineers." He would replace them with "highly-select front-line foremen who are really the backbone of management." He would train these foremen in all the behavioral sciences and reward them with very high pay. This has some merits but gives no thought to the reactions of the superiors* of such extraordinary foremen, or of the multiple functions this builds into low-ranking people, or of the conditions existing at the work level. Like the abortive FWD, this would apply a new control to poorly understood situations. This may be intellectually satisfying but is hardly control. Sampson contends that there are too many controls.[26] There are indeed too many irrelevant controls, but possibly not enough based on intimate knowledge of people and conditions and kept up-to-date. Developing such controls is of course the great task of all organization.

SUMMARY AND CONCLUSIONS

Intermeshing staff and line is the impossible problem of wedding change and habit. This natural conflict increases to the extent we are able to perfectly fit men to different functions, for then no one remains to reduce the clash of functions that never interlock automatically or perfectly. We of course expect the executive to do this, but we admit the problem by filling our libraries with how-to books for him. Fortunately no one fits his job as well as he should in theory, or we might all be the automatons some novelists and intellectuals say we are becoming.

However inadequate, some form of the staff-line arrangement is necessary—and has been as far back as Darius' installation of an independent informer-secretary in each satrapy of the Persian Empire, or Plato's later role of adviser and pedagogue to kings. It is sounder than the other theories of industrial organization. Like them though, it overlooks the complex conditioning of human beings and their varying abilities to escape conditioning, especially when forced to deal with contradictions inside formal limitations. There are, as we have seen, men in both staff and line groups who can perform both functions, and seek to, regardless of their official tie.

But entering industry as college trained specialists oftener than line people, the staff force brings unlike views of the firm and unlike poten-

---

* Lack of space forbids detail, but repeated attempts in these plants to increase the rewards of bottom ranking people, in both staff and line, without comparable adjustments up the hierarchy to maintain status distinctions was, as a Fruhling lawyer put it, "always explosive as hell!"

tials for action. Once in the plant their further differences in age, professional feeling, recreational tastes and social outlook interfere to a degree with cooperation. Irritatingly theoretical staff ideas, use of funds, impatience, and focus on prestige symbols are all suspect to hardheaded line executives. Hence for the typical young staff member, reality is far short of expectation.

With its authority, necessarily practical bent, and long tradition of control over production and careers, the line demands that staffs justify their existence *inside the limitation of not endangering the organization.* This restriction explicitly refers to economic stability, but implicitly includes informal social arrangements and ways of doing things.

The career chances of staff personnel are inferior in terms of possible income, prestige, and authority. They may quit in frustration, or remain to expand staff numbers and functions by their pressures for place and reward, or to move over to the line with its greater prizes. They jockey to insulate themselves from uncertainty while they work to build understandings with the top line.

Despite these hitches to cooperation, line authority is at least unofficially shared by staffs who are authorized to devise, refine, and impose numerous regulations on production workers and lower supervision. This authority is evaded to a degree by the workers who are often aided by their foremen. And line managers below top levels variously resist staff growth and influence as a threat to themselves.

However, in the ongoing conflict, the staffs do statistically justify their contributions, and find informal means to please the line, clear a way for acceptance of their offerings, and soften the effects of their changes.

The way may be painful, but apparently all creative effort arises from some measure of tension and conflict. There is no reason to suppose that production—a dual process requiring the few to follow careers as they both feelingly and perfunctorily find ways to serve the many— is an exception. It would be more nearly so if staff people did not share the personal success values of line people, but this is a big *if,* since both are products of our society, which sees all divisions of labor as career paths first and moral obligations second.

DOCUMENTARY NOTES

1. Peter F. Drucker, *The Practice of Management,* Harper and Brothers, New York, 1954, p. 241.

2. Lyndall Urwick, *Some Notes on the Theory of Organization,* American Management Association, New York, 1952, pp. 67–75. See also Albert Lepawsky, *Administration,* A. A. Knopf, New York, 1949, chap. 10.

3. Ordway Tead, *The Art of Administration,* McGraw-Hill Book Co., New York, 1951, p. 105.

4. Robert C. Sampson, *The Staff Role in Management,* Harper and Brothers, New York, 1955.

5. Edward C. Schleh, *Successful Executive Action,* Prentice-Hall, Englewood Cliffs, N.J., 1955, p. 122.

6. Drucker, *op. cit.,* p. 146.

7. Perrin Stryker, *A Guide to Modern Management Methods,* McGraw-Hill Book Co., New York, 1954, p. 116.

8. Chapter 4, "Conditions for an Equilibrium," in H. J. Kruisinga, ed., *The Balance Between Centralization and Decentralization in Managerial Control,* H. E. Stenfert Kroese, N. V., Leiden, 1954, especially p. 53.

9. Kruisinga, *op. cit.,* p. 36.

10. Marshall Dimock, *The Executive in Action,* Harper and Brothers, New York, 1945, p. 112.

11. Sampson, *op. cit.,* pp. 26–27.

12. See E. P. Learned, D. N. Ulrich, and D. R. Booz, *Executive Action,* Harvard University Graduate School of Business Administration, Boston, 1951, p. 155.

13. Tead, *op. cit.,* p. 104.

14. Sampson (*op. cit.,* p. 27) allows no place for such "self-seeking" in staff work. As noted above, Schleh would, as would W. H. Whyte, Jr., whose demand for more "individual dynamics" reaches a crescendo in his *The Organization Man,* Simon and Schuster, New York, 1956.

15. In addition to internal staff frictions there are of course clashes between staffs. For a study in part of staff-line relations as well as frictions between industrial and development engineers, see Harriet O. Ronken and Paul R. Lawrence, *Administering Changes,* Harvard University Division of Research, Graduate School of Business Administration, Boston, 1952.

16. Eli Ginzberg, ed., *What Makes an Executive?* Columbia University Press, New York, 1955, p. 164.

17. See E. A. Ross, *Principles of Sociology,* D. Appleton-Century Co., New York, 1938, pp. 238–248, for comment on the consequences of age differences.

18. See John W. Riegel, *Administration of Salaries and Intangible Rewards for Engineers and Scientists,* Bureau of Industrial Relations, University of Michigan, Ann Arbor, 1958, Part 2, pp. 1–81.

19. Dimock, *op. cit.,* pp. 96–97. Elliot Jaques in *Measurement of Responsibility,* Tavistock Publications Limited, London, 1956, pp. 104–106, also considers ages of personnel as a factor in expansion.

20. A. W. Baker and R. C. Davis, *Ratios of Staff to Line Employees and Stages of Differentiation of Staff Functions,* Ohio State University, Columbus, 1954, p. 57.

21. See also Learned, Ulrich, and Booz, *op. cit.,* p. 188.

22. Ginzberg, *op. cit.,* pp. 43–44.

23. H. Frederick Willkie, *A Rebel Yells,* D. Van Nostrand Co., New York, 1946, pp. 268–286.

24. Editors of *Fortune, The Executive Life,* Doubleday and Co., Garden City, New York, 1956, p. 213.

25. Learned, Ulrich, and Booz, *op. cit.,* p. 61.

26. Sampson, *op. cit.,* p. 30.

CHAPTER **5**

Local Meanings of
High Level Labor Agreements

THE LABOR CONTRACT

This chapter deals with union-management relations under national labor contracts. In most cases, these agreements will be used as a foil or background for illumination of case materials. Though representing local plants the national, or industrywide, work contract is drawn up at high levels and cannot consider all the complaints from labor and management in the firms represented. The contract may respect certain local practices, but in disputes over which shall prevail, local customs go by the board, and this outcome is usually promised in the contract. Furthermore the contract is likely to be ambiguous* both by chance and intent. Representatives of union and management, sitting around the table, seek to give each clause a meaning favorable to their respective camps. At the same time, each camp tries to block or limit advantages the other attempts to embody in a given clause. In the completed document each camp sees advantages for itself in most clauses, though what this is in specific articles for one camp would usually not be clear to

---

* Ambiguity, of course, has the advantage of allowing varied interpretations, which fits in well with the expediential nature of labor-management relations at high levels. See Herbert Blumer, "Social Structure and Power Conflict," in A. Kornhauser, R. Dubin, and A. M. Ross, eds., *Industrial Conflict*, McGraw-Hill Book Co., New York, 1954, pp. 232–239.

the other. Some articles may of course be stalemates that frustrate both groups. In any case the final document is likely to be broad and in effect ambiguous, however specifically its clauses may be itemized and qualified. Hence when the document is delivered to the local plant, it inspires more contempt than awe.

In the case of the Milo, Fruhling, and Attica firms at least, the central office managers had some awareness of the contractual ambiguities for they sent along for each supervisor a manual of interpretations for use with the contract. Presidents of the Milo and Fruhling locals had similar but somewhat less detailed manuals, and the Milo president said such manuals were necessary "because every statement's got a half dozen meanings"[1]—this despite the fact that the top managements and the national unions periodically sent questionnaires to their respective local officers inviting suggestions for improvement of the agreement.

Behavior in local plants under the agreement can be discussed topically as (1) resistance to the contract, (2) individual initiative among workers, (3) managerial expediency, and (4) economic and production pressures.

RESISTANCE TO THE CONTRACT

Each of the local managements and unions alike saw the agreement as restrictive and damaging because of the attempt to fit it to a hypothetical national scale.* And all the local groups resented the authority of parent organizations. Consequently, the understanding was in general to ignore the contract when both parties were willing. One of the Milo line executives declared:

> Hardy and Stevens have both said they don't give a damn what kind of arrangements are made with the union just as long as things run smooth and it's kept out of writing. Hardy . . . told us that we can ignore the contract but keep it out of writing. If anything blows up and it's in writing we'll be reversed at once—and whoever puts it in writing will get more than a reverse!

Milo's grievance committeemen† confirmed this statement and one of them specifically said:

> Top union and management are always bothering the local plant. We can work out our own arrangements if they'll leave us alone. Hardy

---

* Geiger's attack on the Milo Central Office, and Milo's resistance to the Office in the rift over maintenance costs are typical expressions of management feeling about outplant interference with local autonomy.

† In all the three plants union grievance officers were elected by the rank-and-file for specific terms. The total of such officers in the plant constituted the "grievance committee." Each officer, commonly called a "griever," was responsible for grievances in a specific area of his plant.

and Stevens told us they don't care what arrangements we make but if
we get in trouble the contract will have to be followed to the letter. . . .
Taylor told me the same thing—and said he wouldn't know anything
about me having someone else punch me in and out [forbidden by plant
rules] so I could attend meetings and look after business.

In the words of another Milo committeeman:

> The top people lay down too many hard and fast rules to follow. But
> we get around the contract by doing a lot of things we can work out and
> keep off the record.

In the smaller Attica plant a tradition of *personal,* rather than contractual, relations was so strong that grievance committeemen wanted
no part of the contract except in rare critical cases.   There was no
evidence that Attica managers were more "autocratic" than those of the
other plants, but new grievance men in most cases visited the chief of
Industrial Relations to get evaluations on the "important" parts of the
contract.   From past experience and hearsay they knew that few parts
of the contract had constant meanings during its life.   The game
was too changeable and the rules too out-of-date because even the
newest contract, shaped by high level expediency, could not consider
the myriad differences among firms.

The situation at Fruhling was similar.   But as the largest unit in its
corporation, Fruhling problems were best represented in the contract so
that presumably it had most reason to adhere to the articles.   Also
favorable to contract procedure was the anomalous condition that the
president of the local (brother-in-law of a Fruhling executive) insisted
on following the letter of the contract and demanded that neither union
nor management be allowed to depart from it.   But as neither side
wanted to be bound by rigid procedure, they jointly forced the president
to resign.

The practices in these firms were apparently not confined to Mobile
Acres, for the assistant head of a Fruhling division who had earlier
served in an Eastern unit reported similar behavior there.   Oddly
enough, in his own division at Fruhling a racial problem forced close
attention to the contract.   Grievances there quickly reached a "paper
stage," and:

> Once a grievance gets on paper there's no way of avoiding discussion
> of it.   [This, of course, was also essentially true at Milo and Attica.]
> There's no horse-trading at all in our division because the majority of the
> workers are Negroes and the griever is a Negro.   You won't find many
> Whites forcing grievances because they don't want a Black going to bat
> for them or feeling that he had got something for them.   But they have
> shenanigans down on the other end.   I hear about them.   [That is, this

informant knew of settlements outside the contract in other parts of Fruhling.]

These practices were clearly a winking at the contract. However, because settlement of differences outside the contract was not subject to guidebooks or official rules, the course of action was thrown open to the ingenuity of participants in finding means of simulating conformity to the contract while adjusting behavior to the pressures that could not be escaped. The result was use of precedents, experiments with new devices, and the drafting of discreet members. This occurred inside and, as we shall see, cut across both camps. Some workers never filed grievances, but influenced others to do so. Supervision also had its "strategists" who never came into the open. But some individuals were prominent in both front and background activities. The movement and intensity of these necessarily covert negotiations were qualified by individual insight and influence, degree of personal involvement, weight of issues, and the urgency for action.

The problem then is to show how union-management relations were carried on under a contract honored more in the breach than in the observance, and to explain why, with little guidance but the taboo against exposure of practices embarrassing to the dignity of high officers, behavior still followed a pattern.

ENTERPRISE AMONG WORKERS

Over ninety per cent of the production employees in each of these firms were members of their respective unions. They responded to strikes called by the national union. They showed much solidarity in holding their production near levels established by themselves when working under piece rates. This conformity doubtless sprang more from emotional identification with the union than from anything else. Part of it though was inspired by a wish to escape friction and to maintain easy relations with fellow workers in the daily elbow-rubbing of shop life. This was visible conformity strongly, but not entirely, supported by inner convictions, as shown by other behavior in the shop.

Personal Interest

Despite appearances, during the predominantly peaceful periods, numerous workers actively sought private advantages. They saw the union less as a persisting body and more as a part-time emergency association that could be called out as needed. Some regarded their needs as so private that the union could not openly aid them.

It is common knowledge that Americans have no bureaucratic tradition and dislike formal procedure.[2]   But they do have a tradition of getting things done and of advancing themselves privately.   Speaking or "politicking" for oneself was typical in Attica and unexpectedly common in the other two more formalized firms.   The focus for private bargaining included pay increases, desirable days off during the work week, preferred weeks of the year for vacation, a better work position, escape from restrictions applied to others, and so on.   The drive for personal advantage could be directed to the shop steward, or to him and a griever, or to one or both of these with some member of management. The point to be stressed is that not just the lukewarm, but also the militant members of the union, those who criticized others for "not sticking together," practiced this behavior.   To labor the point, though unions were a legally established powerful force in these plants, and were made up of persons who clung together in crises, still the sincerest of these members as persons with private interests might on occasion behave in a manner contrary to group expectations.   And though concerned not to flaunt their departures, if discovered they were not severely condemned by the majority, except during election campaigns when peccadilloes were blown up to deadly sins.

The impulse to use one's own wings at times was apparent even in conversations not related to specific incidents.   For example, the urge to "make a dicker" needs no comment in the remarks of B. Phelps, a forty-six-year-old worker devoted to the union for over twenty years.

> There used to be satisfactory handling of grievances before the check-off was put in. The union put that damn thing in without a vote—only the local heads voted.   Before the check-off, the griever used to come around to collect dues.   In that way a man had some contact with the griever.   When he come to collect . . . you could tell him your beef. And by God if he didn't promise to do something about it you could refuse to pay up. . . . You could make a dicker and be sure of getting something for your money.   Now you're damn lucky if you can find your griever.   And if you do bring up something to him, as like as not he'll walk off and tell you there's nothing he can do about it.

A shop steward in his fifties, T. Kincaid had suffered much in his work career.   In the following remarks he cites his experiences in another firm to convince a staff employee that even he, a member of management, had no security against the machinations of his superiors.

> You know what they done over there [an earlier job]?   They kept all the records of every man—how much he'd put out—sheets to show how his work'd run all the time he worked there. . . . They had a chart for every man.   They'd have his high point.   When he'd begin to fall off from that, they figgered he'd had hell beat out of him and was done.   Then they'd put another dub on the machine.   You don't know what that is!

We'd work so damn hard for ten hours that all we could do was go home and eat supper and go to bed. When you work like that you just ain't got any life left in you.

This company's gonna do the same damn thing. You guys [incentive-appliers] don't know how you're playin' into their hands. All the company needs to keep this system goin' after they get . . . records . . . is two or three men. They need a man in the office to keep the files goin' and to dig out the right sheets for the man out here in the shop who gives him the dope. Just press the button and out'll come the sheet. There's a lot of these [incentive-appliers] think they're gonna get someplace in the world. Hell! The company don't care a damn bit more for them than it does for anything else that don't pay. They're cuttin' their own throats just like the damn fools [members of the union] who won't stick together.

Despite this clear statement of hostility to management and of the need for solidarity among production workers, Kincaid a few months later participated in a private arrangement with management and his griever that allowed him to move from "B" to "A" rating as a machinist without demonstrating the skill required of others to make the change. This is not to condemn an act, but to illustrate the common lack of concern for organizational principle and theory by both union and management when important advantages were seen as possible by one or both parties, or a repayment of favors was demanded by unwritten protocol.

Except that he was an active campaigner for the re-elections of Beemer, his griever and close friend, the factors in Kincaid's advancement were not clear. However, to get it he needed to demonstrate mastery in the use of one more cutting tool in the shop. Rules for the test required that the candidate himself, unaided in any way, set up the machine and operate it competently for one hour. Except for the appearance of meeting the rules, Beemer and the department chief agreed to sidestep formal procedure. When Kincaid stepped up to the machine, the job was already set up. The cutting heads were adjusted, the tools had been ground to the proper dimensions and inserted to the right depth, and set at the correct angle. The feeds, speeds, and timing were arranged so that the job could have run unattended for well over the required hour. Kincaid went through the motions of checking gauges, tightening fasteners, etc., then pressed the starting button and stood before the machine for one hour. At the end of that time he was signaled to press the stopping button, which ended the test and gave him the promotion.

Behavior of Grievance Committeemen

For the most part grievers were eager to rise in the union and fought for re-election. Maneuvering for personal advantage by individual workers fitted in with their goals. Those who were re-elected were politically astute,[3] though some workers on occasion might refer to them as "slick tongued" and "two faced." At each election some candidates for the grievance office were bitter toward management. They attacked current grievers as liars and "stooges" for the company. But over a period of seven years at Milo, with a committee of nine grievers, only two fiery individuals won office, and both served but one term and were not re-elected. Grievers who were re-elected were skilled in dealing with both their constituents and the managers, and they held as a principle that political subtlety was necessary for success in office. Conscious of his craft in negotiation after winning Kincaid's promotion, Beemer grinningly told me, as a naive and sheltered staff person, "I could even make *you* an A-machinist!" Ken Brady was another esteemed griever. Explaining his third re-election, he said:

> Industrial relations is all based on good relations. You've got to be friends to some extent. You can't have industrial relations without giving and taking on both sides. You'll always win more cases by getting along with supervision than by being tough. You've got to swap for swap and make trades. I always make a boss or soop [Supt.] think what I want him to do is his idea. If they think it's their idea they're a damn sight easier to get along with. Some of the boys are sore at me and go around telling lies on me—but I'm still in.
>
> Lots of times a griever gets caught between two of the men he's representing. And whatever he does, one of them's going to be sore. And when you're handling a case you've got to always remember that you'll want to run again. You may have a program started that'll be shot if you're not re-elected. If somebody else is elected, he'll have to establish new relations again. A griever has the problem of holding the union together and keeping peace in it while he tries to please both the union and management. Some of the big shots don't like me—they want to win all the time. But I figure that some of the best friends I have are the big shots here in the plant. Sometimes I have to talk like hell to explain some of the deals I make with them—and sometimes I keep what I'm doing to myself if I see a chance to get something good later on. The thing some grievers never get through their heads is that a lot of the bosses are on the spot theirselves. If you go a little easy on them when they're on the pan, by God you make friends—they'll stand by you sometime when you're back of the eight ball. Sometimes when I have a rotten grievance [one interfering with present arrangements], I'll take the case up to the soop and let him know I won't push it hard.*

In terms of getting re-elected, the more successful grievers followed a pattern. By fast talk and action, they became heads of the shop

---

* Some students regard such grievers as "management-minded." This is one "explanation," but it becomes awkward to say that the managers who are involved are "union-minded."

cliques in their areas of the plant. Each shop clique was, of course, made up of its informal leaders. These leaders were political whips in the sense that they defended the griever's behavior, kept him informed of pertinent developments, and fought for his re-election. In return he rewarded them with favors growing out of his bartering with individual managers. These favors were usually of a kind too rare to be granted promiscuously, hence members of the rank and file were recipients only infrequently or as they made outstanding contributions to the cause.

There were also cliques of grievers and executives. Working inside the demand for obeisance to the contract, their arrangements were at times necessarily secret. This made strong bonds between one griever and one or more department chiefs. The more "illegal" their pact, the closer they were drawn to each other, and the greater their fear of exposure. Sometimes leaks led to conflict between grievers, and at times there was the paradox of friction between a griever and "his" superintendents on the one hand, and another griever and his allied executives on the other hand. The friction of course arose from (1) envy of those in an alliance who successfully avoided the contract, (2) demands by rank-and-file members or first-line foremen for similar benefits and free-lance dealing, and (3) horror among those few in both camps who made an end of mastering procedures and clauses and now saw themselves and their labor undone by "politics."

Grievers having poor relations with management fished for the secret of those who got on well. The same was true of foremen. Inevitably leaks occurred, denials were made, and new fronts were set up. Here, as with the alliances we saw earlier among managers, fear of consequences and knowledge that the enemies of today might have to be the friends of tomorrow usually prevented open breaks. However, the strength of personal ties that sometimes developed between griever and executive came out in casual remarks. According to the griever, Brady, "A griever does best when he gets a gentleman's agreement. I'd rather have Ames' [see formal chart] word than writing from anybody else." During a conversation I had with Ames on a union election that was coming up, he remarked, laughing, "It won't bother me. Brady has it in the bag, and I hope he keeps it for life!"

In some cases these personal ties seemed immortal. At the Attica plant several executives and departments collaborated with the union to keep a griever from leaving the company. Failing in this, they and staff groups cooperated further to make possible his return with full seniority. The executives explained, "He's a good guy! We never had a griever around here that had the brains and horse sense that guy has!" A member of the rank-and-file merely said, "He's a real politician. He could do anything that had to be done." The griever evidently also had business ability, for he acquired a night club and was giving full time to its operation. At the time of research, he had been held on the Attica payroll for two and a half years. However, he was required to return for a half-day's "work" every six months to justify in some sense his remaining on the payroll.

Though Beemer at Milo usually flouted official procedure in his union role, he was esteemed by the rank-and-file. His relations with O'Brien led him to the latter's home for dinner on Christmas Day. And his understandings with management in general allowed him privileges that a minority of his constituents objected to. For instance, during one period of over a month Beemer was presumably doing his official job in the shop while also looking after his union duties and assisting Red Cross and Community Chest drives in the plant. Yet with the approval of management and most of the rank-and-file he did none of these things. He appeared in the plant only to punch his card in the morning and evening. And part of the time he did not appear at all, but had friends punch him in and out. During the interval he spent much of his time in the union hall attending to minor things. His actual work was to elude the demands of a minority in the plant that wanted him to process grievances, which he and the managers involved had agreed to not consider in their current balance of claims on each other. Beemer's enemies among the workers tried to bring the case before higherups in the union but his friends were in the majority and blocked the action. One of his supporters commented:

> What the hell! [laughing] He was just resting up—having a little fun. Some of the guys are jealous and want his job. We couldn't get a better man to represent us. He's got us more than any griever we ever had. He's the best damn griever in [Milo]. He can prove black is white and make 'em like it. He knows how to get along. If we had a sorehead in there, he'd never get us anything.

Sometimes the influence of grievers grows beyond purely union-management affairs. For example, at Milo, Taylor felt obliged to ask his griever, L. Spencer, to recommend some member of the work group to fill a foreman's position that was opening. At another time Spencer learned that the tie between Taylor and him was being used by two general foremen who were "out to get Taylor's job." He of course warned Taylor of the threat. In these tradings it was inevitable that isolated members of the rank-and-file would occasionally be sacrificed for the group. We shall see that the same principle holds in management, where higher executives are prone to regard first-line foremen as expendable for the winning of larger issues and the control of conflict. This of course has occurred in many kinds of organizations throughout history, but it is currently fashionable in some circles to deny it as existing in modern organizations. One of the Fruhling grievers stated the truism as he saw it:

A man can have a good legitimate grievance, but the union may pass him and his grievance up to keep on good terms with the company. The union'll do it every time when there are big grievances coming up and backed by most of the boys.

Sacrifice of foremen can damage management and aid the union. In an atypical but instructive case at Attica, a foreman insisted on dealing with the union as though he and it existed in a vacuum. He was in trouble with the union, his fellow foremen, and superiors. Demoted to the work level on the charge of inability to carry out orders, he took revenge on his superiors by following their orders to the letter, especially when he knew trouble would result. In mock respect for official directives he stifled his own initiative and did nothing without supplementary instructions. At the same time he distinguished himself as an indispensable workman so that he was almost above discipline. The rank-and-file elected him to the grievance committee. With full knowledge of techniques and personalities on both sides he became such a figure in the union that he forced management to reckon with him on all grievances, whether he or another officer presented the case.

In all these firms when the grievance process was allowed to follow official steps, management's action was based on the predominantly personal relations surrounding the process. In order, management was concerned to know what worker and griever were involved, how the worker stood with his griever, what cliques each were in, and how the grievance was related to other grievances in terms of possible precedents, although officially each grievance was unique.

MANAGERIAL EXPEDIENCY

Reversal of First-line Foremen

As is generally true elsewhere,[4] first-line foremen in these plants had little authority over workmen as compared with what they had exercised in earlier periods. In a span of around two decades, this level of supervision had gradually lost the power to hire, fire, and influence the pay of their employees. Entrance of the unions had been largely responsible. With other functions, hiring and firing had passed to the Industrial Relations Departments. Control of wages above the minimum levels established in the contracts was now chiefly in the hands of the Industrial Engineering Departments. Though gradual, this loss of authority was so painful that many foremen were quick to make decisions contrary to union demands. Then frequently they were reversed by higher executives as a matter of expediency. In time the foremen adjusted in one of two directions. They refused to make decisions on grievances that came to them and instead passed the grievances up the line for others to handle. Or they initiated activity with grievers that checked formal grievances. Actual behavior of foremen in the grievance process was less sharp than this classification indicates.[5] Probably all of them, and certainly the older ones, had ambivalent feelings.

Refusal by some foremen to deal with grievances tended to do away with the first step in the grievance procedure.* A foreman for thirty years, J. Randall criticized his chief and revealed the typical feelings of lower supervision on reversals.

> O'Brien [Supt.] is an easy guy to get along with, but he'll sell you out in a pinch. Just to give you an idea. I had a man that made a habit of coming on the job late. He'd do it week after week. Well, I got damn tired of it. We'd want a full crew so we'd know just where everybody'd fit in. I'd decide we had everybody out that was coming out. Then I'd send the floaters† around where they was needed. We'd just get the turn started when here that dead-ass would come dragging in. I jacked him up about it again and again. Finally he come out late one turn and I sent him home. He filed a grievance, and O'Brien sent him back to work. I went over to O'Brien's office to find out why he had overruled me. He handed me a line of salve about "having to do it." Said it "was a small item after all" and that he "might want a big favor from the union sometime in the future." He said, "We have to trade back and forth. Sometimes we give in, sometimes they give in. That's why we never have any big trouble." Then he said he might have to reverse some of my decisions again sometime, but if he did, not to get sore about it, because he wouldn't mean no offense by it. Well, damn that noise! If O'Brien wants to make me look like a fool every time I make a decision, why by God he can make all the decisions. You know, two can play that game. I can give the boys [workers] every damn thing he can give them. Then when

---

* According to the contracts, attempts to settle grievances should begin at the work level with (1) the foreman. Failing there, the grievance should move to (2) the department head, next to (3) the plant chief, and then to consideration by (4) a representative from the national union and one from management. Still failing of settlement, the grievance would go to (5) arbitration. All the contracts allowed grievances of certain kinds to be introduced in the second, or even third, step. References here to grievances by-passing the first step means grievances *supposed to enter the first step.*

† Floaters were workers without fixed positions who filled vacancies made by the absence of regular employees.

they come up with a big one that I know damn well he can't give 'em, I'll tell 'em to take it to him—that I don't want anything to do with it.

Thirteen of the Milo first-line foremen reported similar experiences and cited those of others. Some of them mentioned specific cases of being reversed, while others merely said they would have nothing to do with signed grievances. Staff officers in both Milo and Fruhling often assumed that grievance inquiries were directed to no line officer below general foremen. In the tabulation of Milo grievances given later in the chapter, most of those listed as first-step grievances began with general foremen.

At Fruhling some department chiefs attempted to force settlement of grievances in the first step to avoid their own involvement in the second step. Data are inadequate to follow the full effects of this pressure on the first level, but at least in some cases, the number of paper grievances was reduced by the responses of first-line foremen. They worked out tacit exchanges with stewards and committeemen to check the filing of grievances. In effect they passed on the pressures of department chiefs to the work group itself. There, of course, an exaction was required for pulling punches. As their part of the exchange, the foremen involved drove to the homes of grievers (and some members of the rank-and-file), picked up defective appliance motors and parts, delivered them to the shops for repair* at company cost, and returned them in person. As we shall see in Chapter 7, these and similar practices were organizational safety valves and morale cement quite as much or more than they were "theft."

Unofficial settlements between first-line foremen and the union covered all matters that both were sure of keeping inside the ban against explosive noncontractual settlements. Risk of detection was small, for the minority of workers who opposed certain settlements were discreetly silent and averse to filing grievances frowned on by the grapevine. Bitterness over a gentleman's agreement was usually limited to an expended minority of workers, foremen, or lower staff personnel, while the majority of workers who gained an advantage promised the losers "a better deal next time." These agreements between foremen and union officers were not collusive. Initially there might be such intent, but the always suspicious rank-and-file were not dupes. When a

---

* All such repair jobs are referred to as "government jobs." The origin of the phrase need not be discussed here and is obvious to some readers. At Fruhling, as at Milo, all such work was charged to someone's account. The transport of parts was facilitated by the foreman's privilege of driving into the plant and parking adjacent to his work area. Workmen, of course, parked on company lots outside the plant walls.

minority did not push a grievance it was because they were opposed by the majority and the griever. They feared reprisals that in some form could be applied on most jobs by the foreman or the griever. For example, the majority would support the withholding of high bonus jobs from "troublemakers," or approve their receiving jobs that were unpleasant in terms of being dirty, monotonous, difficult, etc. These penalties could be disguised as impersonal observance of duty. Two cases at Milo will illustrate unofficial bargaining between grievers and foremen that in some sense hurt a small group while favoring a majority of those concerned.

In the first case, foreman Kustis had an agreement with Beemer that allowed Kustis to give his low-skilled brother, a machinist, certain high-paying jobs whenever they entered the shop. Normally such jobs were distributed equitably. In this case, however, about eighteen men failed to get their full share of the "gravy" jobs. Beemer's part of the pact was that Kustis, with his authority as foreman, should be liberal in O.K.'ing the use of certain "bonus-fattening" factors when questioned by incentive-appliers as to whether "good shop practice" warranted application of these factors. Against the eighteen men who confidentially considered themselves "robbed" by Kustis' support of his brother, ninety-five men stood to gain under increased use of the factors. Where Kincaid's reclassification was individual bargaining, this was collective bargaining that led to what a majority of workers in the subunit regarded as a substantial wage increase, legally guaranteed or not.

While the eighteen men were irate and made covert threats at times, they did occasionally get "good" jobs which they would not have if they had filed grievances on this issue. And even if they had filed grievances, Kustis and Beemer would have denied the charges. Both had an elaborate but specious body of statistics to show challenging higherups that the brother was a very high producer on jobs that the complaining minority was not, and they were prepared to use these data, in case of exposure, as an argument for giving the brother "a little extra reward." Furthermore, as all the disgruntled minority knew, revolt on this issue would have thrown Beemer into a listless reverse in the processing of many of their future grievances. The high bonus on the "gravy" jobs was less the result of errors in the pay system than a misapplication of the system that started as an error and became customary. The error arose because of aggressive action by Kustis' brother toward a new and poorly trained incentive-applier. By the time the engineers learned of the error it had become a practice. Then they feared that attempts to correct the error would spur the union to charge unfairness in management and to expose the staff to higher line criticism—another example of the logically inextricable entanglements in which staff-line-union-management entities involved themselves. Poorly trained incentive-appliers were a product of urgency. The highest turnover in the plant was among this group of staff people, largely because members could not endure the conflicting demands on them, and requests for these employees did not allow time for adequate training.

In the second case at Milo, conflict between two members of management embroiled a griever, as well as the rank-and-file, because of his informal ties with the participants. Mike McGovern, a general foreman, was searching for a pretext to have the system of fixed turns, which his foremen worked, changed to one of rotating shifts. He wished to get his favorite foreman, Phil Bailey, who worked the evening turn of 3 P.M. to 11 P.M., on day turn, 7 A.M. to 3 P.M., with him for at least one week out of three, and to be rid of Jim Keeley, now on steady days, for at least two of every three weeks. But despite the friction with McGovern, Keeley wished to continue on day turn. Since both Bailey and Kissel, the "graveyard" foreman, favored rotating, only Keeley held up the change. McGovern's pretext was that rotation would acquaint foremen with the problems of other turns and thus "make them more valuable to the company." Keeley said this argument was "phony." Having long worked on nights and only recently coming to the day turn, he argued that the "work on days" was "more important" and that, "besides, I have a good crew on day turn and I don't want to leave them."

Bailey and Kissel enthusiastically followed McGovern's proposal that they agitate workmen on their turns to demand rotating shifts from the department chief, "or even higher." McGovern then suggested to Spencer, the griever, that the change would be good for all. Spencer agreed, but said nothing of his own preference for day turn. He and Keeley had dovetailed their barters so that his card was punched and proper excuses were made for him when he was off the job attending to miscellaneous affairs. Keeley now asked Spencer to meet the agitation of Kissel and Bailey and convince the night workers that rotating shifts were undesirable. Spencer could only use the hollow argument that all straight night workers console themselves with: it is better to work a fixed turn than rotating shifts because eating and sleeping at all hours damages the health.

The night workers laughed at Spencer. Several of those on the 3 to 11 o'clock turn declared they were having trouble with their wives because they were "always tied up when other people are out having a good time." Apparently as a result of their inclination and the agitation by their foremen, one of the night workers filed a grievance demanding rotating shifts. Also a petition, circulated on nights, showed a great majority of workers favoring rotation.

Working to recapture his popularity with night workers, Spencer, with Keeley, made several night visits to the shops to meet the activities of Kissel and Bailey. In the meantime Spencer carried the grievance in his pocket and evaded the complaining employee. By the time the latter caught up with him, Spencer had lined up enough votes on nights so that with those of the day group, he had a solid majority against rotation. He then tore up the grievance and explained to the employee that the month before union elections was a poor time to "play into the hands of management." The issue was not reopened. McGovern did not press Spencer because he was indebted to him for obtaining a vacation schedule that had been difficult to get production employees to accept. McGovern and the night foremen were aware that they had been out-maneuvered, and Keeley remained on days.

As we noted earlier, Milo higher chiefs actually encouraged under-standings between workmen and supervision that reduced and contained conflicts at the work level, but the top stratum was concerned when union-management relations got out of hand to the extent of alienating first-line foremen. Hardy sought ways of keeping foremen in the fold. Conferences among department chiefs, general foremen, and foremen to pinpoint incipient grievances was one device used. An outline of the sore area was turned over to Rees for study. Sometimes he conferred with the people involved and sometimes not, but in any case he made a decision that was given in person or handed down to the first-line foreman. The theory was that, knowing he was supported from the top and would not be reversed, the foreman could speak out forthrightly, which would save his face and avoid embarrassing his superiors. However, among other things, (1) the foreman's not having made the decision, as well as his suspicion that no decision would be ironclad, and (2) his inability to escape the web of commitments binding him to the rank-and-file, stewards, and grievers, defeated Rees and Hardy.

Fruhling was more successful in placating its foremen. At least every six weeks, the plant manager and his associated chiefs invited several dozen foremen, from a different series of departments each time, for a conference. This became a notable event for it was preceded by what the foremen variously called, "a royal feast," "a swell feed," or "a dinner with all the trimmings." This was served in top management's plush club.

The "conference" itself was apparently of little importance. For by the time the foremen spent upwards of two hours leisurely consuming several courses of food, with extra servings delivered by attractively uniformed girls (including the daughters of chiefs), and followed by choice wines and expensive cigars, they lacked both the alertness and heart to raise many issues.   Interviews indicated that even the bitter and cynical foremen were softened by the experience and refused to believe that these events were entirely calculated.   And possibly they were not.

The Foreman's Blind Alley and Frustration

Statistics on the foreman's inability to climb the formal ladder is a topic for the next chapter.   Here we will touch on his resentment over his inability to climb, without abandoning values dear to him, and its expression in his dealings with the union and his superiors.

At both Milo and Fruhling, but apparently less so at Attica, first-level foremen often yielded to pressures from the union with something of a feeling of revenge on higher managers.

Some Milo foremen were members of a foreman's union.   According to informants, they had earlier been 90 per cent organized.   The union was nullified during a strike by the workers when many of the foremen remained in the plant.   Each was paid in excess of his regular salary by more than $1200 during the several weeks of the strike.   But despite defection of the majority and lack of legal support by the Taft-Hartley Act,[6] some of the foremen continued in the union after the strike.

Hardy and the division heads showed enough concern about the foreman's union that some of the foremen felt a new freedom.   They considered that though the strike and its aftermath did not increase their chances of rising, they could still relieve union pressures by informal exchanges, and by the tacit threat of such activity check pressures from higher managers.

Some higher managers were aware of these tactics.   Reflecting Blanke's feelings as well as his own, and his reputation for economical operation, Dicke questioned the validity of trying to buy the loyalty of foremen:

> Some of these foremen have got the idea we couldn't do without them. It was dead wrong for the company to throw that money away on them and coddle them the way they did [during the strike].   Hell, anymore most of the front-line foremen are workers at heart.   They'll play monkey-shines on management every time they get a chance, and thumb their noses at you to rub it in.   That money made them feel good for a few days but it won't last.

In one of the Milo shops I overheard a quarrel between a foreman and general foreman with the lower officer making threats similar to those the foreman Randall made in his criticism of O'Brien.   The general foreman resented his subordinate's failure to get two workmen to put in overtime. He was suggesting that the foreman tell the men they "had better work over if they know what's good for them." In answering his chief the foreman implicitly threatened to use forbidden favors as inducements to the workers:

> By God I asked them to work over! They don't want to. *You* go tell them they've *got* to do it. I've got myself in too damn much trouble already trying to *make* these guys do something. I get along with them all right. But it takes more than just talk to get special favors out of 'em. I can do that too, if you want it done. I can give 'em what it takes.* They don't send up grievances on me!

Compromises at Departmental and Divisional Levels

Distant from clashes in the shops, some higher chiefs see the union as another control over lower supervision. For example, E. Meiner, a recently retired Milo divisional chief, declared:

> As a group, top management feels that it's benefited by dealing with the union. It's a lot easier to deal with a group than with each of the individuals in it. But one of the best deals for top management is the fact that the union keeps front-line foremen and general foremen—yes and department heads, too—on their toes. They all have to strain a little to do the right thing all the time and keep grievances down. They know damn well that top management doesn't like third-step grievances. And they know the only way to keep them down is not to pull any shenanigans on the union. Top management is bound to gauge the quality of its supervision by how smoothly they can keep things running.

Meiner correctly saw middle supervision's wish to present a proper front in dealing with the union. However, he was either misinformed or wished to mislead me in giving the impression that they need only follow rules to avoid grievances. He also implied that division chiefs were above "having to strain a little" to get along with the union. The data contradict this and show that this group also solves problems by unofficial trading.

Kincaid's reclassification from "B" to "A" machinist was a case in point. The agreement between Beemer and O'Brien was outside the contract and opposed to plant policy. The repercussions forced repeti-

---

* Hundreds of miles outside the region of Mobile Acres, an executive in a firm doing contract work for various governmental bodies, assures me that my researches have much less relevance for firms like his own, where "penny-pinching" is not important in relations with the union. He notes that his firm never has strikes or fear of them. The company voluntarily gives wage increases or submits without conflict to union demands, "because it's all charged to costs." As part of the "cost plus" procedures his estimating staffs are instructed to triple their closely figured estimates before adding the agreed margin of profit.

tions and variants of the "illegal" incident, which required deviation from other plant rules. Shortly after the original incident Beemer was pressed by two other workers for a similar favor. He sought to get O'Brien to allow the same arrangement as with Kincaid. After weighing the complications, O'Brien refused. Then Beemer and his informal shop leaders decided to claim that danger of accidents existed in the requirement that a man prove his skill on a new machine or in a new position without communication with others.

Beemer argued that those workers near a candidate being tested should be allowed to step forward and caution him, if and when they saw him about to endanger himself or others because of his inexperience in the new position.

Since O'Brien was still troubled, Beemer added the qualification that only the more experienced workers (!) should step forward to warn the novice, and *only when genuine danger existed.* O'Brien agreed, knowing that operating instructions would be given to candidates under the guise of advice on safe procedure. The two workers sponsored by Beemer thus passed the tests.

O'Brien had no intention of giving such a favor without some return. For months he had sought and failed to get acceptance of a "frozen" schedule among several groups of workers in his department. This would allow him to fix the working days of his personnel weeks in advance. Departure from such a schedule would be allowed only in case of death in the family, etc. Since much of Milo operated 168 hours a week, management desired tables of this kind to (1) reduce squabbles by showing that everyone was treated equitably with respect to holidays and Sundays off, and (2) guarantee a daily work crew. O'Brien now requested Beemer to agree to such a schedule. After considerable review of the balance of favors interlarded with joking about what constitutes friendship, the schedule was accepted with the usual concession demanded by the union, "that there be some flexibility in getting days off to take care of exceptional cases."

Similar exchanges apparently occurred at Fruhling's departmental levels. Though no such specific data were available, Charley Bozar, a Fruhling griever, generalized in these words:

> One of the deals we make with the bosses is when layoffs are coming. They'll want to keep certain men and we will too. What we do sometimes is to agree to them keeping a man whether he has seniority or not—you can always make excuses to cover up. Then we'll get to keep a man we want, even if he's somebody management don't like too well.

The impulse is to theorize that such exchanges are a function of the large plant, but there are exceptions. In the smaller Attica firm, the president of the union local in effect requested that management cooperate with him in presenting a common front to the rank-and-file. An Attica engineer, for example, introduced a piece-rate system in one of the departments. The existing labor agreement did not require union approval of the system. The union was glad of this, for it planned to utilize the expected conflict to buy other favors. Hence when the pay plan was unexpectedly well-liked by workmen, the president of the local requested management to announce that the plan was introduced as a result of negotiations between management and him. It seemed "unfair," he said, "for management to take full credit for it" in view of his having "raised no objection to putting in the plan."

This type of struggle and compromise, utilizing but overriding formal restraints, also reached into the divisional level. At Milo the griever Brady had had trouble with Dicke in trying to apply Beemer's technique of getting workers private pay increases by change of job title without change of duties. Notorious as the most cost conscious of Milo Executives, Dicke remained unassailable. When Brady presented three men for reclassification in Dicke's department, Dicke gave them the usual standard tests under close observation. They failed, and Brady complained that the tests were "too damned tough." When Dicke was unmoved by argument or hints of "how other people take care of their problems," Brady carried the case to Blanke. Blanke himself had two union employees in the division whom he wished to promote because of their uncommon ability. But he knew that the men lacked seniority and that the union would object if he attempted to promote them. So when Brady came to him seeking help for the three men he was sponsoring, Blanke presented the case of his two protégés. Brady agreed to the promotions if "his" three men were given a test they could pass, and if he could witness the testing of the other two. The exchange was concluded in that way. In this case, as in others, Brady escaped trouble with his constituents for allowing promotion of two workmen over those with greater seniority. He was exultant over the case and remarked, "I don't win five per cent of the cases that go over Dicke's head."

Fruhling had numerous cases of unofficial settlements reaching into the divisional level. I shall cite two, one a racial problem and one concerning expendable professional employees.

In the first case a Negro had attained the departmental seniority to operate delicate and complicated refining equipment in one of the divisions. He had the basic knowledge of processes, and some manual practice with similar but less intricate apparatus, but he lacked experience with the more complex machinery. All the employees at this skill level were Whites. They professed to like the Negro as a person but did not want him to take the job and set a precedent. They requested the union to consider this. But the union held that to bar the Negro would be undemocratic and its officers asked him to file a grievance. He did. The griever processed it and won at the departmental level against resistance by the foremen. On Friday of that week the division chief and department head called the Negro in to tell him that the job was his and that he should appear on Monday morning to take it over. They also stressed that he would be "entirely" on his own and would "assume all responsibility for the job." They meant that he would not receive the usual preliminary guidance given to others taking these jobs. The processes in this department were dangerous in that both the product and chemicals used in its refinement were either corrosive, lethal to inhale, or highly inflammable and explosive. Management expressed fear that hostility of the Whites toward the Negro might lead to distractions that would endanger all employees, as well as destroy equipment and halt production for an indefinite period. Before management's meeting with the Negro, conferences with the union, which was also concerned to check its internal friction, had established that the griever would not process a second grievance that the Negro might file. The Negro, however, withdrew his request, and notified the managers on Monday morning that he no longer wanted the job, but would remain in his old position. He had not been overtly intimidated, but withdrew because he either learned or guessed what was going on.

In the same Fruhling division a group of chemists, all on rotating shifts, complained of suffering from irritating vapors in the air on third turn, 4 to 12 P.M. On this shift only a "recovery plant" operated to reclaim some of the expensive materials consumed in preparing the product for its final processing. In the recovery operation pungent gases were evolved and spread to adjacent areas. Other employees could retreat for most of the time to less affected work areas and suffer only minor discomfort. But the laboratory was in the direct path of the vapors as they were pushed by prevailing breezes. Regular deliveries of samples to the laboratory confined the chemists there. The vapors induced coughing and respiratory irritations that required the following week to disappear. Hence the chemists usually felt the effects of the vapors for two out of every three weeks. Their complaints to the chief chemist, who was not around the plant at night, were treated as fanciful, allegedly because of his own fear of confronting line chiefs with the condition. Anonymous letters from the chemists to the division head brought only curses on the chemical department and a reprimand for its chief.

So the chemists, a vocal but trifling minority, asked the workers' union to do something for them. Interested in winning white collar workers, the union promised to act, and began by giving the chemists union buttons to wear. Learning that the chemists had signed union cards, management objected that as "confidential employees" and "part of the management group," they could not belong to a union. The union ignored this and asked the local Board of Health to send a committee to investigate the condition.

In the meantime management quickly appropriated $35,000 to nullify the vapors by changes in the recovery plant. The exact "negotiations" between union and management over this group are unavailable. The chemists were, of course, not members of any legal bargaining unit. Both union and management knew that the objectionable condition was confined to third turn. However, this was apparently not mentioned to the Health Committee, for it was invited in, and they accompanied it, to make the investigation on the day turn when the vapor producing part of the recovery process was not running. The committee found nothing. Union spokesmen apologized to the Inspector and to management for having been "taken in by grieving crackpots," and promised to ignore such complaints in the future. My informants at Fruhling would only say that the $35,000 was "used for more important things." The union did not accept the chemists as members. Months later, a small "bath" was installed in the recovery plant to "wash" the vapors before they passed into the air. Since the vapors were partially soluble in the liquid, the basis for complaints was reduced.

We have described cases at Milo in which the favor bartering of union and management skirted the intent of job reclassification by standard tests. These departures were not typical of job reclassification. In most cases the intent and content of the tests were followed much more closely. But here, too, the logical channels were sometimes inadequate to relieve pressures by official means—pressures generated by individual and group rivalries for available rewards, the side effects of clashing interests, and the obligation of working toward official ends regardless of confusion. For example, the actual job reclassification could follow the steps of the contract and yet be used irregularly by both union and management to solve other problems and to strengthen the union while evading the intent of a national statute.

At Milo, a worker seeking reclassification used a standard form and petitioned his divisional superintendent for a "job assignment." The division chief then notified the worker's foreman to give him the test. This procedure was especially satisfying to the union, because it went to a high level and in theory prevented foremen or other intervening officers from denying the test. Brady and Blanke conformed to this intent, but they introduced an ingenious variant enabling them to sidestep the contract and to give Brady a new control over luke-warm members of the work group.

When Blanke received applications from the shops in Brady's jurisdiction, he telephoned Brady to see whether the man had signed the check-off before he approved the application. If the man had not, Blanke held the petition until Brady called back to say it should be approved. If the impatient applicant tried to learn what was holding up the approval, he was avoided or given excuses. Finally, in disgust he would turn to Brady. Brady then feigned inability to do anything for him because he was "not a member in good standing." When the man signed, Brady called Blanke who authorized the job test and returned the form to the man's foreman. Thus the worker in Brady's area who had not approved dues deduction from his check could not get a reclassification test.

Provisions in the Labor Management Relations Act (Taft-Hartley) of 1947 made such coercion illegal. But whatever legal and moral judgments are made of this arrangement, Brady was serving his fourth successive term. According to Brady, the control was not known to top union officials. These latter had officially notified the local that unwilling workers were not to be coerced to grant deductions. As in other situations, however, formal commands were variously adapted to social and personal demands. Though possibly less original and effective than Brady's device, pressures were used by other joint cliques elsewhere in Milo and in Fruhling for the same end. The motivations of management in connection with the check-off are discussed below.

Brady's stratagem was in principle the reverse of Bob Phelps' criticism that the check-off destroyed the individual worker's bargaining power. Here Brady was demanding that the worker "pay up" before receiving the favor he was requesting.

We saw how petitions for "job assignments" at Milo by-passed the entire department by going directly to the division chief. Sound in theory, this tactic did not completely block interference by resentful first-line foremen. Each with a different purpose in mind, the griever, Spencer, and the superintendent, Smith, formed an ambiguous alliance to check intrusions by foremen in the process of job testing in Smith's department.

Once a job test was granted, the practice had been for foremen to set the date on which the test would be given. The worker's pay increase dated from the day he passed the test. However, instead of giving the test at once, after the right to it had been granted, some of the foremen delayed for days and even weeks. Pressure of production, tie-up of machines, etc., were excuses given. In the meantime, some foremen seized the situation to unofficially revive their lost authority. For example, in the interim they gave the worker some "stiff jobs," such as cutting concave or convex surfaces, to show him he "wasn't a top man," even in his present classification. This was a last chance to win deference and put the man through his paces.

Spencer and Smith agreed that the worker granted the right to take the test must be given it at once. And if he passed, his new pay rate was retroactive to the date his assignment was approved by the division chief. This practice was later approved by Revere, and locally requested to be written into the next contract.

Wanting this settlement for different reasons, Spencer and Smith revealed the sinuous meanings attached to shop experiences. Spencer held that the agreement allowed full expression of individual skill (craftsmanship) without overthrowing the principle of seniority. However Smith, who thought the union's emphasis on seniority blocked recognition of differences in ability, saw their arrangement as happily putting seniority in a minor role. He believed that if a worker could get a job assignment with retroactive pay from the day the assignment was approved, he could receive top rate in a short time regardless of his lack of seniority and would, even though he remained in a general job category, be receiving promotions on the basis of ability.

Executive career ambitions were important in some of these cases. Fear of the wrath of Hardy and Stevens drove many of the Milo executives to extreme measures to settle grievances below the third step. Those with this concern who were less adroit than others in clique activities sometimes found themselves in professionally shocking alignments.

One such case involved Beemer and the executive, Taylor. They had agreed that an operator on a complex finishing job was entitled to "allowance factors" that would raise the pay of the job from 10 to 16 bonus hours. Taylor's signature at the staff level of incentive-appliers made the change official. In less than a week he signed another request of Beemer's that increased a job from 39 to 48 hours.

This maneuver to avoid union-management friction precipitated staff-line conflict. Frightened at the implied criticism of their studies, the engineers restudied the two jobs and declared that unperformed and unnecessary operations were being paid for. They reduced the time to the original figure. Beemer notified Taylor of the cut in time. Taylor went to the engineering office for a conference with Haupt. When Haupt declared that the jobs had been carefully rechecked and that he could do nothing about findings of the engineers, Taylor demanded, "What the hell is it to you what the jobs pay? It's not out of your pocket. All you guys act as though you're paying for it. Forget about it!" There were further studies and conflict. Taylor won a slight increase. But the victory hurt his future. His attempts to have "smooth relations" with the union trapped him into the unforgivable sin of *openly bargaining for the union with a group of his colleagues.* This was not forgotten when he was under consideration for the divisional post that Blanke won.

Company and Community Compromises

Though no older than the Milo and Fruhling companies and, like them, subject to a distant central office, Attica labored under a small town tradition that gave its union-management relations a different character from that in neighboring companies. The plant was originally set up by several hundred men imported from another area. Mostly in their twenties, they lived adjacent to the plant in houses put up by Attica. They formed Community and Athletic Clubs. At the time of research hundreds of the men had lived and worked together for nearly twenty years. Tradition was reflected by stress on face-to-face dealing with superiors and the use of first names; promotion was from within, especially from lower line positions to newly developing staff posts. Long employment and low turnover of supervisors reinforced the original orientation, as did Attica's type of industry and relatively simple administrative pattern. Attica was not completely successful in resisting attempts by its central office to rationalize processes and refine roles. A few high officers from distant places were sent in. They forced changes, but were covertly resisted. Their efforts to win acceptance of systematic personnel forms, reports, filing systems, etc., largely failed. Hence the data from these sources are fragmentary. However, available data show the lack of refinement in job duties, the multiplication of roles in one person, and the persistence of outworn methods. The complex of Attica's union-management relations and staff-line conflicts were as real on paper as those at Milo and Fruhling, but to the participants they were secondary and attributed to different things, when considered at all. Most behavior was personal and functioned with little reference to abstract systems or expectations.

Anomalous in the sense of differing from practices of the nearby giants, Attica is important in showing how both internal and community factors combined to push an imposed contract into the background.*

---

* Students of the controversy over the relative weight of internal or community factors in company problems will find pointed comments and references in Abraham J. Siegel, "The Economic Environment in Human Relations Research," *Research in Industrial Human Relations,* Publication 17 of the Industrial Relations Research Association, Harper and Brothers, New York, 1957, pp. 86–99.

Attica's grievance committee consisted of two Whites and a Negro. Although they processed the usual kinds of grievances, the records were so abbreviated and distorted that they were unreliable for determining the number and seriousness of grievances.   However, in the preoccupations of Attica's Industrial Relations Department, and the axis of reverberations between there and the community, most issues were concerned in some way with job discrimination and racial problems, though these did not always erupt into formal grievances.

Attica's technology required little skilled labor, and its pay scale was near the bottom for the Mobile Acres region. Consequently over half the work force was unskilled, and a large but varying percentage of it was Negro.   Usually, however, the percentage of Negroes was less than at Fruhling, and only slightly higher than at Milo.   Attica's unskilled work was shunned by many skilled Whites who worked elsewhere for more money when possible.   Turnover ranged between twenty and thirty per cent with minimum seasonal fluctuations.   Thus unskilled local Negroes and Southern Whites, unable to meet the higher standards of most of the major firms, gravitated to Attica.   This tended to increase the Negro and Southern White population of the plant.   Yet some skilled Whites were willing to take laboring jobs temporarily rather than be laid off when layoffs were to be made. This involved seniority problems, but some Whites, both Northern and Southern, favored layoff of Negroes first, regardless of seniority. They applied pressures to keep Negroes from getting enough seniority to displace Whites in case of layoffs.   The union was usually able to defend the contract's seniority principle.   The dormant race problem, which flared openly at times, led management to adopt an unofficial policy of holding Attica's percentage of Negro population to the same level as that of Magnesia, and to give preference to Northern over Southern Whites with no industrial experience.

This policy was constantly threatened by (1) the local labor market, (2) political ties of the Chief of Industrial Relations, and by (3) Attica's need at times of an increased number of workers of a specific skill.

Expanding job opportunities elsewhere in Mobile Acres led a stream of Whites away from Attica.   Those remaining were upgraded, and replaced to some extent by Negroes.   E. Reynolds was Attica's head of Industrial Relations and also in charge of all employment.   Then in his sixties, he was one of the pioneers.   He had been a line foreman for years before taking over the staff post, which was a *promotion* in Attica.   Reynolds also held a public political office in the community. This was known and approved in the Central Office as "good for public relations."   Attica supervision envied Reynolds his extra income and his status in the community. They attributed numerous internal problems of Attica to his allegedly spending more time in the community than in his office. Reynolds' political role involved him in the race problem. His party battled with the Democrats for the large Negro vote. Part of the return for vote-getting demanded by Negro community leaders was that he employ as many as possible of their job-seeking friends and relatives. These occasionally included large 14- to 15-year-old boys, who were sent with the understanding that their employment record would show them to be of legal age. Attica's expanding Negro population stretched Reynolds' ingenuity to the limit to preserve himself in the contradiction.

Several times a year, Attica advertised for personnel to fill a certain skilled and well-paid job category. Magnesia's interested Negro population knew of these periodic openings, created by Whites leaving for slightly higher pay elsewhere, and prepared their members by free training in the local night schools. With their higher job status and income, Negroes in these jobs became targets for the malice of some Whites and recipients of open abuse by the Southern Whites. As all were lined up to receive their checks on paydays, some of these Negroes responded to insults of the Southern Whites by flaunting their larger checks. When all of the Whites were stirred to near violence by this, management, with a limited police force, sought ways out of the problem. It suggested that the Payroll Department pay Negroes on other days, or at different windows. The department objected that this would "make too much work." The union objected that it would be discrimination. So the plant manager unofficially ordered Reynolds to hold the percentage of Negroes in this choice class of jobs to that of the community, and also to cut down as much as possible on the hiring of Southern Whites, because, "We can't fight the Civil War all over." Reynolds answered that he could not reduce the number of Southern Whites unless he found "somebody else to do the work." The manager retorted that the responsibility was Reynolds'—"Do what you have to do!"

Applicants for this skilled job were hired only after passing an actual work test given by the foreman of the department. Reynolds' compromise was to hire, subject to testing, Negroes who applied, and to instruct the tester to "flunk them, regardless of how good they are." Shortly the Negro griever was approached by some of the rejectees. Both the griever, as an officer in a Negro welfare organization, and the Attica union filed protests but were unable to prove that the tester discriminated. Top management was concerned that there be no disturbance about this in the community. Reynolds called on the

Negro community leaders to control the welfare organization and to aid him with his problem, which they apparently did.

Reynolds then shaped Attica's old-fashioned employment methods into a device to balance the claims of plant and community on him. He did this by processing Negroes and Whites differently, by developing a code system on his employment cards to deceive the union, and by exploiting the work habits of both Whites and Negroes to defeat the paper control systems of the various staffs. True to his earlier experiences, and contrary to our pat generalizations and the usual departmental distinctions, Reynolds became a line wolf in staff clothing.

In the hall just outside his office at 8 A.M., he usually found two or three Whites and fifteen or more Negroes seeking employment. He thought it politic to give the appearance to these Negroes, and therefore to the Negro community, of hiring many more of them than he actually did. He first hired the Whites, had them take their physical examination, and sent them to work at once, even though they might be two hours late on the job. Then he called out the name of one or more Negroes he had hired the previous day and told to report that day. At this moment he would also hire one or two of the other Negroes, thus usually seeming to have employed twice as many Negroes as he had. After taking their physical examinations, the Negroes entering for the first time would be sent home to report for work the next day, or later. When they did appear they were called in before the changing group of job hunters and seen only as two more Negroes hired, not as the same Negroes entering twice.

A variant of this procedure was to give the Negroes requesting employment an application form, ask them to go home, "study it carefully," fill it out, and return it the next day. The second day the Negro would take his physical. The third day he would go to work. In this way he would probably be seen three times, but never as the same Negro. If he were recognized as the same Negro, Reynolds believed that at least he would be seen as "getting a lot of special attention from management."

To put a convincing face on the situation, Reynolds had to know in advance whether the prospective employees he called from the crowded waiting room were Negro or White. He determined this at first by having his secretaries put a red check in the upper right corner of job applications (and later personnel forms) to signify Negroes. In grievance meetings this mark was detected by the grievers for what it was. Reynolds was condemned. He next used a small red dot. This was seen in time and denounced. Finally he had his secretaries put a small blue dot in an agreed letter "o" of the form. This escaped detection.

The work habits of many of the Negroes and particularly of the Southern Whites, were irregular. Reynolds learned they could often be "counted on" to lay off three or more successive days every month without reporting off in advance. And this occurred frequently following the two-week pay periods. Studying this pattern, Reynolds decided to have all persons dropped from the payroll who were off a minimum of three successive days without notice. He found he was catching more Southern Whites and Negroes than Northern Whites. So to reduce the percentages of Negroes and get rid of troublesome Southern Whites he reported both as "quits." But he suffered conflict in "getting rid" of Southern Whites because this increased his percentage of Negroes. Hence he temporized and met as best he could the new formal demand for a monthly report on percentage of Negroes. One device was to submit the report at a time that would allow the maximum number of Negroes to be classified as "quits." This report in and read, he then reported "vacationing" troublesome Whites as quits. In the interim, he rehired many of both because he needed them and regarded them as "good workers when they work" and because some foremen demanded certain workers. During this month he of course met other claims* while remaining alert to exploit voluntary and pseudo-quits to aid his percentages. When the rehires were Negroes, he also profited by putting them through his employment ritual. But at the same time he aided some Negroes by protecting their seniority. Thus he discriminated among the Negroes. Those he favored were usually the ones sponsored by Negro community leaders, or individuals demanded by shop foremen. However, all these he rehired he pointed to as Negroes *hired* when meeting community political claims on himself. At times the union was ignorant of how Reynolds utilized absenteeism. At times it blocked him, but at times it collaborated with him. An assessment would show him to have gained more for his purposes than he lost.

---

* During the summer, pressures were heavy from Negro political supporters to hire Negro college boys. Hence, on one summer day when five Negroes quit, Reynolds slapped his thigh and said, "Fine! Now tomorrow I can hire five Negroes." This community involvement is highlighted when we remember that at times shop foremen were yelling for men when men were at the gate seeking employment but were blocked by the percentage protocol which Reynolds—and others— opposed. In at least one case, a foreman told Reynolds, "I need men. I don't give a damn if they're black, white, or green!"

The speciousness of Attica's paper logic is thus seemingly exposed by, and attributable to, a staff head's (1) dominance of much of the line, (2) bullying of other staffs, (3) permitting community ties to order employment policy. However the personal, rather than impersonal, structuring of union-management relations was not established by Reynolds. He did color events, but largely because a basis for the events already existed. Probably the most revolting fusion of personalities, in terms of what was planned and hoped for by Attica's central office and the union's national office, occurred in one of Attica's strikes. This was against top management and was called to "protect" a supervisor who was liked very much by his men. Reynolds had nothing to do with the incident. The strike was led by one of the grievers and included 92 men from two departments. Their general foreman had failed to get an assistant superintendency, in a shake-up, that they thought he should have had. The strike lasted only four days and failed of its purpose, but its meaning seems clear.

Formal Grievances as a Measure of Compromise

As the Milo griever, Brady, noted above, the wish to avoid written commitments led to "gentlemen's agreements." Oral understandings apparently multiplied as a griever continued in office, for the total number of paper grievances, as well as the number at each step, declined with time in office. It would seem that decrease in filed complaints became (1) a rough measure of developing pledges between grievers and managers, and (2) an indication, as a griever remained in office, that the rank-and-file approved the results of his actions in their behalf. The casual comments of rank-and-file already reported suggest this, but the records of re-elected grievers are stronger evidence.

Milo, Fruhling, and Attica had a total of 46 grievance committeemen. Of these, 17 had served more than one term, but workable data could be had on only nine. The annual total grievances for each of these nine declined with each successive year in office. The same was true, almost without exception, for each of the first three steps in which the grievances had been settled. For example, the total first step grievances during the first year in office for each of the nine ranged from 149 to 194; total second step grievances from 65 to 91; total third step from 15 to 31. By the fourth year in office the same steps varied from 30 to 98, 10 to 44, and 2 to 9.

More detailed personal knowledge of the Milo grievers Spencer, Brady, and Beemer warrant a closer look at their grievance records. They, and a fourth man who could not be persuaded to give data, were the only ones who had served continuously on the Milo committee for at least four years. Tables 3, 4 and 5 show their recorded grievances through four successive years. The first two years of Spencer's record were unobtainable. Total grievances for a given step and year were divided by twelve to get the average number of grievances a month. With few exceptions each year shows a decline in number of grievances in each step. The exceptions are for Spencer, the second step in his fourth year, and the first step in his sixth year; for Brady, the third step in his fourth year; for Beemer, the third step in his third year.

Decline in grievances filed does not necessarily mean decline in tensions. It could mean this, but more likely means growing facility in compromise. Bred in conflict, union-management cliques make covert containment an ideal. When they fail, they follow the law. Sometimes, too, one or both parties may send up the written protest for reasons other than conflict.

Managerial Behavior toward the Union as an Organization

In actions toward the union in their firms, many of the managers departed from the popular picture that the interests and attitudes of industrial administrators are always solidly opposed to those of production employees.* On the contrary, numerous department heads, gen-

TABLE 3. ANNUAL GRIEVANCES OF COMMITTEEMAN SPENCER

Year	Step	Total	Grievances per Month
Third	First	117	9.7
	Second	41	3.4
	Third	12	1.0
Fourth	First	105	8.8
	Second	42	3.5
	Third	6	0.5
Fifth	First	71	5.9
	Second	33	2.8
	Third	3	0.3
Sixth	First	73	6.1
	Second	23	1.9
	Third	1	0.08

---

* It should be obvious, that in the firms we have dealt with, the managers themselves were also employees in the sense of receiving specific pay from an employer who in theory could drop them from the force as easily (actually more easily than unionized employees) as any other employee.

TABLE 4.   ANNUAL GRIEVANCES OF COMMITTEEMAN BRADY

Year	Step	Total	Grievances Per Month
First	First	157	13.1
	Second	74	6.2
	Third	20	1.7
Second	First	129	10.8
	Second	58	4.8
	Third	8	0.7
Third	First	101	8.4
	Second	24	2.0
	Third	7	0.6
Fourth	First	44	3.7
	Second	11	0.9
	Third	7	0.6

TABLE 5.   ANNUAL GRIEVANCES OF COMMITTEEMAN BEEMER

Year	Step	Total	Grievances per Month
First	First	182	15.2
	Second	68	5.7
	Third	17	1.4
Second	First	133	11.1
	Second	67	5.6
	Third	14	1.2
Third	First	96	8.0
	Second	41	3.4
	Third	16	1.3
Fourth	First	30	2.5
	Second	14	1.2
	Third	4	0.3

eral foremen, and staff people showed feelings of good will and gratitude toward the union.   These feelings went beyond the expedient union-management cliques to include executives who at one time were regarded as unrelenting foes of the union.   This is not to deny that the managers were calculating, or to say that they were fond of unions.   But certainly those above the level of first-line foremen did not hold a clear-cut unchanging enmity toward the union.   Unions and managements were more than two perpetually and unalterably hostile camps forced to live together. The data show that management's mixed feelings were based on (1) personal ties with members of the union, (2) indebtedness for favors and cooperation, and (3) direct economic advantages arising from union activity. Examples will show these points existing separately in some cases and combined in others.

Milo's chief chemist, J. Larsen, had been bitter toward the union from its entry until the Second World War. During that period Milo's Office began giving the managers confidential salary increases each time the union received a general wage increase. After an "equity" adjustment in his salary followed by a series of general increases that enabled him and other officers to maintain, or increase, the pay gap between themselves and production workers, Larsen gave thanks in this way:

> After all these years of just existing [$300 to $475 per month] now for the first time [$1150 per month] my wife and I are able to get our noses up for a breath of air. And by God we owe it all to the union! If the union hadn't come in we'd have stayed in the same damn old rut. In the last few years I've put four kids through high school and three of them through college. They're all on their own now, but they'd never have had a chance if my income hadn't shot up! I still believe in the law of supply and demand, but by God I know which side my bread's buttered on, too.

The economic factor showed also in frequent and open management pressure, at both Milo and Fruhling, to get workers to sign the check-off. We have noted the liaison between Brady and Blanke in part for this purpose. Taylor, O'Brien, and Smith were other Milo executives who directly urged workers to authorize dues deductions for their "own good." And according to some of his workers, the Milo general foreman, Hampton, threatened them, as they felt, in saying, "If you don't sign the check-off, you'll be laid off."

Some of the chiefs in the Fruhling division of 3500 made similar approaches with the explanation that "You cause too much trouble by not signing." Their motivation could have been desire for harmony in the work group, but they, too, showed indebtedness, more muted than Larsen's, for the impetus to their salaries given by the unions. One of them jokingly told me with reference to copies of the well-known satirical parody, "The Free Rider's Psalm," being circulated by the union, that "I don't have to pay dues either."*

---

* These conditions and feelings in management are evidently not peculiar to Mobile Acres. I have recently come across large and small unionized firms, all in unlike industries, in a region reputedly more "reactionary" than the areas of our study, in which at least lower management expressed similar reasons for "liking" unions.

Leaks of these supervisory proddings to sign the check-off reached the president of Milo's local during a recent political campaign. The union interpretation was that this was "a trick" to mislead the rank-and-file into "thinking that management is for them a hundred per cent just to get them to vote for the Republican presidential candidate." But these promptings were made by some of the managers from the time of the Taft-Hartley Act and continued after the political campaign.

During the campaign other management action revealed both their economic interest and their lack of consistent enmity toward the union. The union raffled off several automatic washing machines and radio-phonograph-television sets that listed on the market for three hundred to eighteen hundred dollars. Everyone knew that the proceeds were going to be used for political purposes, since the union announced its support of local and national candidates of the Democratic party. At Milo the president of the local, the grievance committee, and shop stewards went about freely, entering all offices, selling one membership ticket in the union's political agency with three raffle tickets for one dollar. Each purchaser signed a ticket and was given a receipt. Among many others, Stevens, Hardy, Blanke, Ames, Dicke, Rees, Lane, Schnell, Haupt, Revere, Smith, and Geiger bought chances. In a negligible number of cases, middle and lower supervision showed concern that the signatures required of them might "turn up in some anti-Communist, spy-investigating committee." Meiner commented above on the union's direct economic and disciplinary benefits to the company. Cooperation in maintaining order, and service as a communication link between management and the rank-and-file were additional aids that aroused friendly sentiments among the managers. Noncollusive cooperation in controlling its members was seen as a real virtue of the union. According to Taylor, who was so often in need of help:

> The union helps a lot in maintaining discipline among the men. Before the union came in, any attempt by management to explain its position on anything just made the men more suspicious. Now we make our position clear to the union heads and the men accept it. This enables us to get by without penalizing individual workers which always stirred up a hell of a lot more trouble.

Possibly the most objective indication of management's lack of antipathy toward the union was the fact that some persons were often "illegally" permitted to be members of both union and management. At least twenty-seven hourly-paid foremen at Milo were dues-paying members of the union. Policy was inconsistent on the point of whether this condition was legal or not. In practice it was good if convenient to both, or if favored by one and tolerated by the other as part of the economy of favors. Both camps preferred this condition, for all my efforts to get definitive statements were monotonously countered with, "It all depends." Privately, individuals in both camps saw merits in the ambiguity. Although some of the foremen involved suffered status dilemmas, others apparently felt they were able to play off one against the other.

One union official made this "off the record" comment:

> We don't try to hold our men back to keep them from entering supervision. We've got a number of men in supervision who are in the union and pay their dues regularly. We're glad to see them get up. It helps us as long as they remember who helps them out and keeps things running smooth for them. We help them by seeing that their seniority runs unbroken. If they go on salary and become officially part of management, they can still pay their dues and keep their seniority. Officially they're full members of management when they're on salary and just can't be in the union. We don't feel that way about it. In case they get bumped, we'll stand back of them. When cases like this come up, we argue that we only lent the man to the company and that they never ceased being part of the union.* So far we've got away with it. It's a good policy for us to follow. You know, the company could dislike a man and get him on salary so they could can [fire] him. But they can't do that the way we work it.

Management views were similarly tied to specific gains. For example, Hampton's remark about his foreman, Kim White, whom he knew to be in the union:

> Kim can get a hell of a lot more out of the men than I can. And the thing about it that tickles me is that he's up to all their tricks. He'll fight like hell for them, but if they don't put out he cusses hell out of 'em and they have to take it! If I just looked at one of 'em the way he does, I'd get a grievance, but they don't dare sign a grievance against him.

In addition to utilizing the judgment of grievers in selecting foremen, management called on union officers of all kinds to replace vacationing foremen through the summer. And at Milo, the president of the local substituted the year around for foremen off ill, as well as those on vacation.

Like that of the union toward management, managerial behavior toward the union was guided more by expediency than by ties to its own camp. Solidarity was prevented at least by (1) inescapable events

---

* In another union and industry, the rank-and-file have an effective control over their members who enter management. The new-fledged supervisor does not pay dues and no one contends that his union membership was never broken. But in case he should return to the work level, the rank-and-file who worked under him vote on whether he shall retain his seniority.

that forced compromises; (2) friendships and personal concerns over-riding all containment; and (3) attempts to avoid the complications of an agreement never covering all local issues and never up-to-date.

ECONOMIC AND PRODUCTION PRESSURES

Production Pressures on Foremen

Top management's demands for greater output encouraged informal settlements between the union and foremen. We saw the foreman caught between his chiefs and the union, and heard his threats to do something about it. As with the Milo supervisors who found holes in the FWD, many foremen sought ways to escape mounting production pressures. But steady growth of bureaucratic controls at Milo and Fruhling, combined with the foreman's limited contacts and negligible influence with higher staff and line executives, allowed only the most extraordinarily ingenious personnel to maintain convincing production reports when production was short. But such inventive persons were typically moved up in a hurry to levels befitting their astuteness.

Usually the foreman was reduced to covertly stimulating and re-warding the more responsive and helpful workmen. He remembered those who "put out" and rewarded them discreetly with better paying and/or more desirable jobs, and with overtime in his own as well as in other departments in which he knew such time was available. The foreman's latitude for giving these rewards was narrowed by watchful fellow workers and alert shop stewards weighing the expediency of intervention. So usually those rewarded were people with leanings toward the "rate-buster" type—the thick-skinned employee who, with his other features, is little concerned about the hostility of his work group and ignores their wish to hold production at some agreed level.[7]

A Milo foreman had two workers of this type whom he counted on to do unpleasant emergency work that others resisted. When he could, he openly rewarded them with easier higher-paying work, even though costs might be greater to the company than if done on available auto-matic equipment. With aid from grievers, he successfully countered complaints by reminding complainers why he was giving the reward. Foremen also used negative rewards, such as giving the relatively less undesirable jobs to the higher producers. Some foremen were able at times to rearrange a work group so that many or most of the higher producers could be in an area free of the high temperatures, unpleasant odors, vapors, and drafts that occurred intermittently in certain proc-esses, and plagued others.

This use of rewards complemented supervisory penalties as discussed earlier in the section dealing with reversal of foremen. In giving rewards, however, relations between foremen and workers were usually direct and confidential without mediation by steward or griever. Here, too, exchanges were made easy by the typical willingness of workmen to bargain privately and to accept and understand the reward. There were cases, however, in which grievers collaborated by (1) denying to suspicious workmen that the condition existed, and (2) refusing to recognize this as an issue warranting a grievance.

Cost of the Fourth Step to the Union

The fourth step in the grievance procedure was between representatives of the national union and of the company, and was argued in the "area office." This office was far enough from Magnesia that most union locals regarded the cost of travel and maintenance as too great a strain on their economic resources. Hence union officials tried to limit grievances in this step to those they felt sure of winning. Depending on the number of men involved and the trips required, each grievance carried to the fourth step cost the union two hundred to six hundred dollars. This disposed the union to pull punches at the third step to keep the grievance from going higher. Union officials frankly admitted that bluffing was their major tactic at this level. Some committeemen feared to let grievances reach the third step lest management throw it into the fourth step out of vexation at not having it settled sooner. Thus economic limitations made the unions concerned to settle disputes as advantageously as possible below the third, and certainly below the fourth, step. This interest, of course, spurred unofficial settlements as near the shop as possible.

The fear that top management would spitefully throw grievances into the fourth step was not fully justified. For as Meiner of Milo indicated above, local top management had its own brake on fourth step grievances, fear that central offices might interpret them as a mark of poor management in the local plants. Supervisory anxiety at lower levels was reinforced by local management's soft-spoken approval of any controllable informal settlements and implied warnings against eruptions involving the top.

SUMMARY AND CONCLUSIONS

Official commitments demand that top leaders of union and management, like opposed generals, bear themselves with formal hostility, though rank-and-file on both sides may fraternize.

Remote from the units represented, negotiations lead to ambiguously phrased documents that cannot fully reflect local concerns and practices. Yet as a symbol of authority and identification, as well as a truce, for both camps the negotiated contract demands ostensible conformity down through the work level. This expectation is but one of several conditions that contribute to a complex of unofficial interpretations and practices at the plant level. Intrusion of side issues such as friendships, disputes inside both camps over professional rights and functions, and changed roles often involves followers down through the work level and leads key persons to see contract provisions more as irrelevant abstractions and obstacles than as aids to cooperation.

Preoccupation with these as well as orthodox but bafflingly complex issues forces members of both camps to drop official identifications and makes their relations a blur of conflict, cooperation, and compromise initiated and guided by cross-cliques.

Intricate and pervasive systems of conflict at local levels prevent separation of purely union-management issues for discussion. The ideal subject matter is promiscuously intershuffled with staff-line conflict, interdepartmental struggles for resources, and confusion over the changing line between official and unofficial procedures. Endless compromises result as one conflict area intrudes into another, but all distract from continuous isolation of any one set of issues.

Leaders are limited by these systems of conflict, but unwittingly contribute to them as members of both management and union groups use expedients to win personal goals, check enemies, aid friends and supporters, and to protect themselves both when they are involved and when they wish not to be. Union rank-and-file intuitively recognize this condition and elect leaders with relevant survival skills, who also assist in perpetuating the system.

Finally, adherence to the contract is weakened by (a) economic restrictions on the union, (b) production pressures on middle and lower management, and (c) top expectations that differences be settled below certain levels of argumentation.

DOCUMENTARY NOTES

1. Some unions have well-known manuals. See *How to Win for the Union.* 7th edition, UAW–CIO Handbook for Stewards and Committeemen, 1945.

2. See a sociological analysis by Alvin W. Gouldner, "Red Tape as a Social Problem," in R. K. Merton, et al., eds., *Reader in Bureaucracy,* The Free Press, Glencoe, Illinois, 1952, pp. 410–418.

3. Some readers referred to my earlier report ("Unofficial Union-Management Relations," *American Sociological Review,* October, 1950) on plant life under high-level contracts as an "exposé." That was not the intent of the report. Later research suggests that such behavior is typical. For a detailed account, see Leonard R. Sayles and George Strauss, *The Local Union,* Harper and Brothers, New York, 1953; Jack Barbash, *The Practice of Unionism,* Harper and Brothers, New York, 1956, especially chap. 15. Also see Barbash, "Ideology and the Unions," *American Economic Review,* 33: 868–876 (December, 1943); and *Labor Unions in Action,* Harper and Brothers, New York, 1948, pp. 176–181.

4. There is a broad literature dealing with the foreman's decline in status and his present condition. See J. Carl Cabe, *Foremen's Unions,* Bureau of Economic and Business Research, Bulletin 65, University of Illinois, Urbana, 1947; F. J. Roethlisberger, "The Foreman: Master and Victim of Double Talk," *Harvard Business Review,* Spring, 1945; Donald E. Wray, "Marginal Men of Industry: The Foremen," *American Journal of Sociology,* January, 1949, pp. 298–301; D. Miller and W. H. Form, *Industrial Sociology,* Harper and Brothers, New York, 1951, pp. 207–217; M. Dalton, "The Role of Supervision," in A. Kornhauser, R. Dubin, and A. M. Ross, *op. cit.,* pp. 176–185; Reinhard Bendix, *Work and Authority in Industry,* John Wiley and Sons, New York, 1956, p. 215.

5. For a concise discussion of the grievance process, see Van D. Kennedy, "Grievance Negotiation," Kornhauser, Dubin, and Ross, *op. cit.,* pp. 280–291.

6. Section 2 (3).

7. See M. Dalton, "The Industrial 'Rate-Buster': A Characterization," *Applied Anthropology,* Winter, 1948, pp. 5–18.

CHAPTER **6**

The Managerial Career Ladder

CAREER STUDIES

Like other aspects of executive behavior, the subject of careers in management is discussed with voluminous disagreement. Students of various backgrounds and interests have (1) made questionnaire surveys of high-level executives; (2) explored biographical dictionaries as far back as the 1870's in search of data to reveal career patterns; (3) recorded the anonymous remarks of executives called to research conferences for group discussion of their world and its activities, with psychologists and psychiatrists present to put questions and to assess exchanges made around the circle; (4) built on other studies and brought them up-to-date in the search for backgrounds as career-shaping forces.[1] These reports variously suggest that industrial leaders are more likely to spring from some social groups than others; that opportunity for certain types of individuals to achieve success in business and industry is greater or less at one time than another; that individual success in some respects means probable losses in others; that formal or informal selection of executives is more effective; that one kind of executive training is superior to another; that selection and promotion should be from within or from without; that leaders should or should not be "bureaucratic-minded," etc.

Most of the studies have focussed on the origins and traits of individuals as related to their social and occupational rank at the time of study. The correlation among these variables is often made a conclusion. This slights the functioning of executives in their various positions, their struggles for success, their gains and losses from moving in and out of cliques and other informal groups, their explanations and feelings about success, and the attendant complications of their progression through formal offices. Treated as the controlled digestion of information fitted to specific job categories, their formal education is over-stressed, while the meaning of what is often simultaneously acquired—an unwitting but pertinent education in social skills—is not recognized. The search for quantitative bulwarks often leads students to treat their admittedly indispensable factual data as terminal answers, rather than as starting points for questions.

THE FOCUS ON MILO

It is easy to attack and hard to conclude, but in this chapter the stress will be on some of the "related factors" and "attendant complications." This will limit the report to Milo and comments on the findings of others, for Fruhling files were closed and those at Attica were undeveloped and inadequate for study of training,* and steps in careers. Our aim is to look at factors affecting the success of Milo officers in winning high place. Who was recruited and advanced? What were the bases on which people were chosen for preferment?

---

* "Misleading" would be a more correct term. As the Attica Central Office extended its rational controls, it requested copies of the personnel records of department heads and other high officers. These records were to go in the Office payroll files so that the local managers could be paid directly from the Office. Reynolds and the others of the pioneer group believed that "it would not look good" for their favored group to have a background of, say, ten years as a laborer, eighth grade schooling, and a commonplace title throughout the period. So with the understanding and cooperation of the plant chief, they "doctored" the personnel records of the fifty-eight men who would be known in the Office chiefly by these documents. This was, of course, meeting rationalization with rationalization. Those who had a labor record were given a respectable clerical title for that period. All members were reported as having at least a high school education, and one or two years of college was preferable and commonly reported, though many of them apparently had no high school training at all. Some of the drab current titles, such as "department foreman," were changed to "Master Mechanic," "Director of," "Administrative Head," "Plant Accountant," "Works Paymaster." The extent to which these records had been altered could not be determined.

These practices were of course not confined to Attica, nor are they unique to business and industry. For some comment on background enlargements by individual job-hunting executives, see Perrin Stryker, et al., *A Guide to Modern Management Methods*, McGraw-Hill Book Co., New York, 1954, p. 259.

What did "ability" mean, and how weighty was it in success as over against seniority, etc.? How did people go about climbing in the ranks?

Though method is covered in the appendix, the problem of answering questions of this kind requires comment here. As a participant observer, with all the implied evils of self-deception, I of course asked questions on the basis of what I thought I already knew. But logical procedure demanded the corrective of checking my warped vision against other sources of information before returning for systematic soundings of several dozen intimates among the managers. The official sources of information also serve as a background for presenting the other data. In order, therefore, the research steps were to (1) formally interview several high officers with whom I was not intimate, (2) explore official statements in various supervisory manuals and handbooks, (3) get unofficial statements from intimates by systematically posing the same questions to all, and finally to (4) check these accumulated data against those found in plant files which a group of intimates were working to open for my study.

Formal Interviews

The answers of one high line and one high staff officer to a question indicate the typical official statements that were made on qualities essential for success. The comments of these men, both Roman Catholics, on the topics of religion and secret societies were not provoked by me. Although ages and years of service, etc., will be presented later for all the managers, some of these items are usually given with each person's comments for whatever additional relevance such information may have for more specialized students. The question asked was, "What are the things that enable men to rise here in the plant?"

L. Bierner, an inactive divisional superintendent suffering from heart trouble, aged fifty-seven, and employed by Milo for thirty-eight years, answered:

> Integrity, loyalty, and honesty! Nobody can keep an honest man down! If you deliver the goods, you'll be pushed. If you help your superiors they'll help you—they'd be fools not to! I've heard a lot of stuff in the plant about Catholics and Masons and how you have to be one or the other. There's nothing to that! It's just in men's heads and has no basis in fact! If you're loyal, your boss doesn't give a damn what your religion is—he'll probably be glad you've got some and that's all. Men come in and raise hell because somebody got to be a foreman and they didn't. They bring up all this stuff about being a Mason or a Catholic or something else. There's nothing to it! The men who say this sort of thing are merely trying to find excuses for their failing—because they don't have anything on the ball. All you've got to do is to show people you're

a right guy. All you've got to do is get on the ball and hit it, and nobody will raise any questions as to what your religion is or what you belong to. Any unbiassed objective person can see this. The guy who's always making charges of this kind has nobody to blame but himself—he won't take the necessary steps to improve himself. When men complain about not being foremen, I tell them the truth. I tell them so they can improve themselves or go somewhere else, but I never want to ruin or discourage them. I've often turned men down who later improved themselves and were given foremen jobs. There's no substitute for honesty and fair-dealing among men in industry.

You talk about people getting up in industry. Do you know that seventy-five per cent of supervisors don't want to advance if it means more work and responsibility? They want money but not what goes with it!

The staff officer, T. Cowper, was forty and had been with Milo nine years. His formula was simple.

I think there are three important things necessary to success in industry: First, ability. There's nothing that can replace ability. Second, freshness and flexibility of viewpoint. A manager must be able to meet changing situations. If he can't do this he won't be a successful supervisor or manager. Finally, a man must have willingness to work. It takes no end of hard work to be a manager. You've probably heard talk here in the plant about the company requiring you to be a Mason or a K. of C. to be a member of management. That's a lot of bunk. Nobody ever told me that I have to belong to anything. Sometimes management names certain people to be members of the Chamber of Commerce. But that's not forcing them into anything. Membership in that is not a social affair but a business relationship. It's part of the job. It's just helping to look after the company's interests. There's a lot of people in management who are Masons, and who belong to the Country Club, but they aren't required by management to join. We had a man who was chairman of the Ration Board and quite a number of the boys were on draft boards during the War, but nobody required them to be. People in management can belong to anything they wish. I'd say the organization is fairly democratic. It was once said that the Masons were prominent. Now the Masons don't show their rings and buttons as they used to.

Where Bierner stresses character attributes and implies the need of an unspecified kind of ability, Cowper is saying that dynamic plant conditions demand originality, flexibility, and hard work. They both say in effect that the essential qualities are obscured by the excuses and lamentations of those lacking the qualities.

Supervisory Manuals and Handbooks

These were little more instructive than Bierner and Cowper. They spoke of "ability," "honesty," "cooperation," and "industry" as qualities important for advancement. "Merit-rating" plans were referred to as a means for appraising fitness, but no sample plans or enumeration of important characteristics were cited in these booklets. Nor were leads given concerning the steps for the managers to follow in getting a rating, etc. The term "ability" was not defined anywhere in the manuals or interviews. Still it was obvious that, though unarticulated, many of the managers could agree on what they meant by the term. They used the term to mean capacity (1) to maintain high production, but low operating costs and a low rate of grievances (without illegal strikes) and of accidents; (2) to make "good contributions" toward the solution of critical issues, (3) to preserve "good relations" in the department and between departments, and (4) to subordinate personal to organizational aims. Some of these tacitly acknowledged factors could have been measured roughly, but no record of such indexes in relation to a promotional scheme existed. Some of the staff groups did, however, make periodic though conflicting appraisals of their members with possible promotions in mind.

Unofficial Statements

Most intimates, from the work level, to near the divisional level, strongly denied that promotions were subject to any formal system, or that such a plan would be followed if it did exist. The following ten partial statements are selected as representing those who in theory would be most eager for promotion—skilled workers, first-line foremen, and staff personnel. Their responses are to the same question asked of Bierner and Cowper.

J. Bennett, a skilled worker of forty-seven with thirty-one years in the plant, gave this explanation:

> Promotion comes about by being a Mason. Twenty-five years ago Henry Blair brought in the Masons when he was made division boss. Now ability or nothing counts so much as being a Mason. Look at Hall and Diller—[his foreman and general foreman] they're both Masons, but Rolland [another foreman of Diller's] ain't, and he's got a college education. And that's why he don't have Diller's job. Rolland knows more about mechanics than anybody in the shop. You need to get wise. Look around. Hell, all the bosses are Masons. You can get by with murder if you're a Mason. Take Diller. He'll "yes" a man to shut him up, but if it goes higher, he'll "yes" whoever's above him. Hell, you don't have to be a Mason just to get a promotion, you have to be a Mason to keep your job.

The first-line foreman, Hall, to whom Bennett referred, was content to remain where he was in the ranks. At fifty-three, Hall had eight years of schooling and had been with the company thirteen years. He had been a machinist four years before being promoted. His answer:

> By hard work. I got where I am by hard work. I always done what I was told and was willing to do more. I never asked for any favors, but was willing to help others.

With the corporation for twenty-two years, Sam Perry had been a first-line foreman for nine years. He was forty-five and had attended school eight years. His comment:

> Well, I think a lot of things help a man get ahead. I think a lot of the old-timers around here got in by having friends. Some of them got up by ability. But it beats hell out of me how some of them got their jobs and how they keep them. I got my own job by helping people and doing things I wasn't expected to do. When Taylor was assistant superintendent over here I always helped him out every time I saw a chance. He asked me one time how I'd like to come up and see them install officers in the Masons. I knew damn well that was an invitation and that I couldn't lose. I went up and applied to get in. When he got to be soop, [superintendent] he asked me to take a foreman's job. Well, here I am. I wouldn't want to get any higher though—you catch too much hell. I always dread vacations. I have to take Hampton's [general foreman] place for a week every year. The least little thing you do you'll find you've stuck somebody's neck out. When I used to just work in here I couldn't hardly wait for vacations,* but now I hate 'em.

H. Trimble, a sixty-three-year-old first-line foreman with eight years of schooling and thirty-seven years' service with the corporation, answered:

> Mostly their own ambition. If they do their work well and anything else that comes along, they'll do all right. A man has to do more than what's expected. First you'll be trusted with a few small jobs to see how you handle them. If you do well—you're on the way up.
>
> I used to be ambitious when I was a young fellow, but I never knowed how to keep my damn big mouth shut. I'd just as soon tell my bosses to go to hell as to look at them. If I'd used my head I could have been someplace. Two different times, after I got to be a foreman, my bosses got big jobs in some of the other plants and wrote to me asking me to come and be a superintendent for them. I had five kids in school and owned my home and just didn't want to tear up and move to a strange place. Besides, back in 1929 when I got the first offer, I was making pretty good money then—about $360 a month. I thought I had the world by the tail with a down-hill haul. When the depression come I lost all my savings and wished I'd taken the job. It pays to have friends but it's my own fault it didn't pay me.

---

* See chap. 8 for the significance of Perry's remarks.

J. Evans, aged fifty-three, was an outspoken foreman who had been
with Milo for thirty years. A high school graduate, he boasted that
he had "read more" than his college trained children. He laughed at
my question:

I'm surprised that anybody who's been around here as long as you have
would ask that question. You know as well as I do that getting in and
running around with certain crowds is the way to get up. Nearly all the
big boys are in the Yacht Club, and damn near all of 'em are Masons.
You can't get a good job without being a Mason [Evans was a Mason].
Hell, these guys all play poker together. Their wives run around together, and they all have their families out to the Yacht Club hob-nobbing
together. That's no mystery. Everybody knows it. It's the friendships
and connections you make running around in these crowds that makes
or breaks you in the plant.

Look at Rupert [the assistant superintendent]. He's the misfit suckass in his department. By his toadying in the Yacht Club—making
boats, repairing them, making models, giving parties, and so on, he's been
able to keep in their good graces. That's why he can fall down on job
after job they've given him. He gets by with murder.

Rutherford [predecessor of Stevens] got up by family connections. His
father owned a plant in the East. It finally became a part of our corporation. Rutherford was manager of a plant six years after getting out of
college. Now by God that's not working your way up from the bottom.
You're a college man, too, but by God you couldn't do that—you've got
nobody pushing you. Take Geiger. I don't want to take any credit away
from him. He's a damn good man. There's no doubt of it. But he was
a good friend of Berelson [predecessor of Rutherford] who used to be the
big shot. Berelson was thick with Rutherford. Geiger was Berelson's
private chauffeur and took over the same job for Rutherford when Berelson retired and moved South. That's how Geiger got up.

There's no promotion system whatever. Seniority, knowledge, or ability
don't count. You've got to be a suckass and a joiner. You've got to
polish the old apple and have a lot of "personality." I was once asked to
join the Masons, and it was hinted that there'd be a good job in it for
me. I told them it was against my religion. They said, "Why Jim!
You're not a Catholic. What do you mean, it's against your religion?"
"I mean that if I can't have a job on my own ability I don't want it!"
Well, I cut my legs off by talking like that. I didn't realize it at the time,
but when I was passed up three times in favor of somebody else, I caught
on, but I raised hell anyway. They told me I "wasn't a good salesman,"
that I wasn't "known—nobody knows you!" Since then there's been two
more promoted past me. There's fifty men right here in the plant who
could tell you a story just like mine. That's why over a dozen of us
ignored the invitation to the big dinner and a medal for twenty-five years'
service. Some of them went, but half of them didn't.

Bridges [president of the corporation] sent out a letter a couple of years
ago to every member of supervision. In this he requested that any foreman or supervisor having a grievance should carry it up step by step

through his superiors until he received satisfaction. If he's turned down at one level go to the next, and so on, even if it comes to Bridges himself. That's a lot of bull! There's not a man in the plant that would do it. They're all afraid to go above whoever made the decision on it. They know damn well how they can be made to suffer without being able to prove that everything's not on the up-and-up. They'll all accept whatever decision is made about their beef and do nothing about it.

A night supervisor, aged sixty, J. Cunningham had two years of college and had been with the firm seventeen years. His views were similar to those of Evans:

> Well, by God, it's not by ability! I can tell you that! It's who you know that counts, not what you know. Take Dick Pugh. He knows nothing about accounting but he has a man under him who's a trained accountant. Hell, that's not right. Anybody can see it's not. The accountant gets a little over $400 a month while Dick pulls down better than $600. Do you see any justice in that? Look here [showing a list of supervisors], there's one, two, three, four—nine men who are drawing the pay of foremen and carrying the title. Yet none of 'em have over five men under them. One man could easy boss the whole damn bunch. Why do you think they get away with it? Because they're Masons? Not by a long shot! That's part of it, but there's other reasons. Fisher's uncle is one of the directors. He thinks we don't know that, but that's how he gets by. Jones is a son-in-law of the assistant superintendent. Brown is always flunkeying out at the Yacht Club. And the soop [Cunningham's superintendent] gets a hell of a kick out of dancing with Davis' good-looking wife. If she's going to dress well and keep on looking good, Bill's got to make his $515 a month and feel like staying up nights—and a lot of these nights he spends home with the kids. His kids are damn nice. Two little girls. But Bill wants a boy, and Liz [the wife] says there'll be no more kids.
>
> Look at my own job! On nights I'm responsible for the same thing that it takes Blaine, Taylor, Hampton, Vick, and Streeter to do on days. They average about $850 a month while I get only $575. Figure it out— five hundred seventy-five bucks compared with forty-two hundred and fifty. [Total monthly salaries of Blaine, Taylor, Hampton, Vick, and Streeter.] Now you tell me. How do you think men get up in industry? [All salaries mentioned have been increased considerably since the interviews.]

L. Wilkins, forty-eight, assistant staff head with twenty-two years' service, answered by comment on his own lack of success in the organization.

> I've quit raising hell, but I don't let it get me down. I go ahead and do a good job because I know there are a lot of innocent people dependent on my doing a good job. They [his superiors] know I've got three kids and that I'm not as young as I used to be and that I probably couldn't get as much money starting anywhere else. I don't think [the Office] would

tolerate the things going on here in the plant if they knew about them.
There's some people around here that think they're little tin gods and
they want to draw a group around them that'll treat 'em that way. And
if you treat them that way you won't have any honesty or principles left.
That's the part I can't take and that I've never been able to swallow.
I've got to live with myself, and I regard my own self-respect more than
I do dollars, when I've got enough to live on. Most of these fellows are
boot-lickers with a set of principles made of rubber. If you study the
matter closely you'll find that to succeed here in the plant you've got to
be unfair—favor some and mistreat others. That's why Phillips [his
former superior] left. He couldn't be unfair with people—it just wasn't
in him. If you get ahead around here it won't be on ability but on
agreeing with everything you're told whether you think it's fair or not—
and keeping your thoughts to yourself. When election time comes around
and you think the Democrats have a good man, keep it to yourself and
pretend you're a Republican. Now I never do that. Sometimes I vote
one way, sometimes another way—and I never hide who I think is a
good man. [Wilkins was recently demoted to a low rank in a different
staff and put on hourly pay. His associates say "the reason was, he talked
too much."]

A college graduate, aged thirty-nine, E. Stein was a staff officer who
had spent much time in the Central Office. His response was:

The company naturally talks of having a promotion system. But this
thing of "ability" is damned hard to pin down. It's easier to get at when
you've got something concrete to work on. For example, when you're
down on the lower levels in industry—say a machinist or a time-study
man—you can always be checked on your worth to the company. Your
superiors can see that you're doing something. If you were suddenly
asked at the end of a month or a year just what you'd contributed to the
company's cause you could point to some statistics. It's not that way
when you get up higher. The higher you get, the more your advancement depends on impressions that your superiors have of you. And these
impressions are based on almost no real evidence. If a high staff officer
or a division superintendent were asked what he'd done for the company
during the last year he'd have a hell of a time pulling up anything concrete. When you're in a position like that you know all the time that
other people want your job and are trying to get it—and you know that
impressions are constantly being formed of you. I know it goes on. I
see my supervisors here. I find that people up in the front office have
impressions of them. They're typed. And the whole damn thing is
usually wrong and always unfair. Vaughn or McNair will see my supervisors for maybe twenty minutes once or twice a month and will form
impressions of their merit on such evidence as that. Hell, you can't
judge a man's capabilities from no more knowledge of him than that!*

* Based on wide experience in both large and small firms, T. K. Quinn supports Stein's observations. See *Giant Business: Threat to Democracy,* Exposition
Press, New York, 1953, p. 139. Stein's observations on "ability" have been
echoed elsewhere and from much higher vantage points than his. See Eli Ginz-

Yet these guys insist on getting first-hand impressions. They know damn well they don't have any foolproof means of rating men so they're conceited enough to think they can look at a man and size him up—find out how he stacks up alongside others and how much he's worth to the company. And their impressions just boil down to whether they like a man or don't like him. When you walk into a room with them you can see that they're intent on getting every impression of you that they can. You've got to always be on guard about your dress, speech, manners, and general conduct. All that has nothing to do with brains or ability. Look at Edison, or Lincoln, or Henry Ford—they were too busy doing things to be fussy about how they looked. Yet even if I'm an hour late of a morning, I'll shave. Some people will skip their shave if they were up late the night before. But it doesn't pay. I first noticed this when I was in [the Office.] There, the higher you went the more you got involved in politics. Everybody was uneasy and trying to beat everybody else in making a favorable impression. [Stein was recently promoted to the top post in his staff.]

C. Gregg, a low-ranking staff supervisor, aged twenty-eight, had been with Milo for four years. He responded with rambling attacks on the "front," the "sham" and the "insincerity" of Milo managers as a group. He noted that ten years earlier, Milo had

. . . decided to do away with the hard-nosed boys of the old school. They want men that can pat you on the back and hand you a smooth line without meaning it. They want guys who can put on a front. Men here in the plant get their jobs by connections, not by ability.*

In most cases the heads get a good man under them and let him make the decisions. They bear down on the assistants because the assistants are afraid of their jobs and have to carry the major part of the responsi-

---

berg, ed., *What Makes an Executive?* Columbia University Press, New York, 1953, pp. 67–68, 71, 73–74 and 79, in which various top level executives (1) deny the existence in their firms of any "list of qualifications . . . for promotions," and admit that they promote on the basis of their liking the person and his success on the previous job; (2) confess they do not know what leadership qualities they are looking for and doubt the validity of much of the writing on leadership; (3) reject all formal promotion schemes and instead judge the merit of a man for promotion by "how loud an outfit screams when you want to take a man away," a device recommended by the late sociologist, Louis Wirth, for discovering the operations and effectiveness of an institution. The existence of an abstract, transferrable ability is scouted by some. See C. Wright Mills, *The Power Elite,* Oxford University Press, New York, 1956, pp. 140–141.

Stein's concern for "some statistics" supports W. H. Whyte, Jr.'s (*The Organization Man,* Simon and Schuster, New York, 1956, p. 167) observation on the search for "some index of achievement that no one can dispute."

* Production workers, elsewhere, have observed that after meeting all formal qualifications, "pull" and "connections" were still needed to become a foreman or advance from that position. See Eli Chinoy, *Automobile Workers and the American Dream,* Doubleday and Company, Garden City, N.Y., 1955, pp. 52–60.

bility for their decisions, as well as the few the head himself may make. Take [a reorganized and newly tooled department]. Word comes down that being more modern they shouldn't have to use as many men as before. That's a damn lie—it nearly always takes as many workers as before, but skip that. The point is that everybody gets the shivers. They're all afraid of their jobs, and rumor increases the fear. And ability plays only a small part in their getting or holding their jobs.

Among line personnel, only Hall, Perry, and Trimble suggest that "work" and "ability" are factors in advancement. Evans admits that Geiger has ability but does not see this as the major factor in his success. Evans, Cunningham, and Wilkins clearly think ability is lost in the shuffle of personal relations and the requirement that candidates know the right people.

As staff men, both Stein and Gregg suspect ability is a minor item. But Stein more perceptively does not deny that ability is sought and considered so much as he laments the absence of techniques for uncovering it, and the association of inappropriate earmarks with it.

These contradictory statements mean little without the more objective evidence that comes from study of ages, job experience, years of service and time spent in each level, amount and kind of education, etc.

OCCUPATIONAL DATA

If a firm selects and advances its supervisors on the basis of skills and experience that fit them for more important and difficult work, we can assume that some detectable relation exists between job rank and the factors we have just mentioned. Certainly we could expect some fairly clear age limits for people entering at the bottom and at each successive level if there were to be regular advances. For responsible administration of others we might also expect a minimum term of service as a measure of fitness before appointment to higher levels, not that age and experience guarantee wisdom. Then too, in a firm with great specialization and division of labor, such as Milo, we would expect a close tie between job and type of training. Let us see how the Milo data fit into some of these categories; for example, age at time of appointment, years of service at appointment, and education in terms of amount and subject matter. This last, as the assumed open-sesame to all rewards, deserves close attention.

Age at Time of Appointment

Table 6 includes current ages and all but one of the above items for the three line groups and the staff. The "superintendents" include all

TABLE 6. OCCUPATIONAL DATA ON MILO MANAGERS

Managerial Group	Data Categories	Mean	Median	Range
First-line foremen	Age at appointment	36	37	16–58
	Years service at appointment	12	11	0–38
	Years education	11	11	6–20
	Current age	48.5	48	31–65
General foremen	Age at appointment	44.4	44.5	26–62
	Years service at appointment	16.2	17	1–31
	Years education	11.8	12	8–16
	Current age	50	50	35–65
Superin- tendents	Age at appointment	41.4	41.5	25–58
	Years service at appointment	19.8	19	3–35
	Years education	13.8	14	9–19
	Current age	48.7	49	35–65
Staff group	Age at appointment	36.6	33	24–54
	Years service at appointment	13	10	3–35
	Years education	15.2	16	9–19
	Current age	42.9	41	29–61

levels and categories—full, assistant, and assistant-to. The staff includes the classes discussed in Chapter 4. The first entry for each management group shows the age at appointment to that group expressed as the average, the median, and the range for all. The age range of 42 years for foremen, 33 for superintendents, and 30 for staff people shows only—excepting the one adolescent first-line foreman—that entrants must be adults, young or old.

Years of Service at Appointment

Here, too, we see that some members of all levels were with the corporation as little as three years before achieving their present rank. In the two lower line levels some members entered as supervisors without previous experience in that role, at Milo or elsewhere. The narrowest range of service was 30 years for the general foremen. With their average of 16 years, this suggests no clear service prerequisite for entry. Six general foremen had less than 5 years' service, whereas 11 had 25 or more years as they came to the job.

The relation between years of service and entry for the staffs and superintendents defies classification. Sixteen superintendents starting as production workers required 8 to 30 years (M. 19.3, Md. 20.5) to make the grade. Six of the 16 by-passed the level of general foreman. The other 10 were caught as general foremen for 1 to 8 years. Nine superintendents came from staff organizations where they had been employed 3 to 35 years (Md. 14).* Six superintendents entered Milo as first-line foremen and spent 3 to 12 years there before taking superintendencies. The remaining 5 superintendents took the office after 14 to 33 years (Md. 21) in the line as clerks or secretaries.

The absence of regularity is clear. Seventeen superintendents served in some line supervisory role, but never as general foremen. Only 16 of the 36 superintendents started as workers and became first-line foremen, and 6 of these got double promotions in skipping the rank of general foreman. Five members became superintendents with no previous administrative experience. However, we must note for its later relevance that, apart from systematic promotion, these five, with their average of 21.8 years of handling confidential records and observing events, undoubtedly had immense knowledge of internal affairs, both economic and political, and used it.

In terms of their job histories, education, and ages, the staff force fell into two clusters. One group of 23 with an average of 16.5 years of schooling entered Milo as staff employees and rose to current positions in from 3 to 11 years (Md. 7), at which time they averaged 31 years of age. The other group of 13 entered the line organization with 12.8 years of formal training. In various clerical and minor supervisory roles they remained there for 17 to 35 years (Md. 22), where apparently they were tolerated as near failures for various reasons. They were gradually moved over to less rigorous staff positions at 39 to 53 years (M. 48) of age.

Looking at the median years of service at time of appointment for the 190 line officers we may fancy we see a pattern of promotion: personnel became first-line foremen after 11 years, general foremen after 17, and superintendents after 19 years. But this is misleading. First, the obviously disproportionate numbers would bar most foremen from rising to the top. Ignoring this limitation, the foreman's case was still hopeless, for fewer superintendents were being drawn from the bottom and the rate of progression for foremen was falling sharply. We saw above that over half of the superintendents did not start at the bottom, and that six of those who did skipped a step. Study of current ages (Table 6) shows that foremen were moving up more slowly. For

---

* Dispersion of the data was so great in some cases that the mean values, having coefficients of variation in excess of 50 per cent, were deficient as measures of central tendency. See T. C. McCormick, *Elementary Social Statistics,* McGraw-Hill Book Co., New York, 1941, p. 130.

example current foremen had already held their positions 12.5 years,* which was 5.2 years longer than current general foremen had served as first-line foremen. Also the foreman's remaining years before retirement were little more than those of his superiors: he was only 1.5 years younger than the general foremen and only 0.2 years younger than the superintendents. If the first-line foremen had immediately become general foremen and held that office for only the time that the general foremen had served (M. 5.6 years), and had then become superintendents, they would have been 54.1 years old and would have been employed 30.1 years, as compared with the superintendents who served 19.8 years to reach that office, but after being there 7.3 years† were still less than three months older than the foremen.

Despite the weakness of this kind of statistical discussion, it is clear that movement through the hierarchy varied greatly and that age and years of experience were not important for appointment and promotion at Milo.

Education

Years of schooling expressed as an *average* for each group was related to rank in management. Education included time of attendance in grade school, high school, college, trade schools, night schools, and years of study by correspondence. As seen in the table, each ascending level in the line had more education than the one below it.‡ These differences were not due to exaggerations of time spent in night school or correspondence study. For even when averages of only the grade, high-school, and college totals were considered, the difference persisted: first-line foremen, 10.5 years; general foremen, 11.2 years; superintendents, 13.1 years. And though only trifling, differences in the same direction persisted when night, trade, and correspondence schooling were totaled and averaged separately for each level: first-line foremen, 0.5 years; general foremen, 0.6 years; superintendents, 0.7 years. The tie between education (grade, high school, and college only) and rank was also found when the 36 superintendents were broken down into their formal levels: departmental chiefs, 12.5 years; divisional chiefs, 13.7 years; plant head and assistants, 15.3 years.

This bond between rank and schooling suggests several things. First, that those with the greatest amount of relevant subject matter and

---

* Current mean age minus mean age at appointment.

† See preceding note.

‡ Differences between educational means of the line strata, as well as between the latter and the staff group, were statistically significant at better than the one per cent level in all but one case, which barely missed that level.

formal skill logically earned higher rank. However, this was not true at Milo. Only a minority of the managers were in positions associated with their college training. Lumping the 226 managers together, the formal duties of at least 62 per cent of them did not relate to their specialized education. Considered by rank, the percentages whose duties did not match their training were: first-line foremen, 61 per cent; general foremen, 81 per cent; superintendents, 61 per cent; staff, 50 per cent.

As examples of training among first-line foremen not directly applied, one man had two years of schooling in traffic; another, three years in physical education; a third, two years in advertising; a fourth, two years in journalism.

Among general foremen, one had three years in chemistry; another, two years in pre-medicine; a third, trained in engineering, was in charge of a warehouse.

Among the superintendents, one trained in medicine; a second in law, and so on.

In the staffs, an M.A. in engineering was an auditor of nonengineering matters. Another, with the same degree and subject, was a cost accountant. The head of industrial relations had a degree in chemical engineering; his assistant, aeronautical engineering. These gaps were also common at Fruhling, and are probably widespread* for reasons discussed below. Thus the subject matter of education was not a magic key to success.

A second theory might be that amount of education was important as a test for elevation. Certainly this is often used as a rough screening device. Some executives see it as a measure of ambition, reliability, persistence, and character.† Volume of education was not ignored

---

* The Wharton School of Finance reports a low relation between the training and later work of some of its alumni. Cited by W. H. Whyte, Jr., *The Organization Man,* Simon and Schuster, New York, 1956, p. 88. See also W. Lloyd Warner and J. C. Abegglen, *Occupational Mobility in American Business and Industry,* University of Minnesota Press, Minneapolis, Minn., 1955, p. 29, who note that only one-third of the business leaders in their sample had commercial training in college.

Comparing the vocations and inventions of inventors, David Cort points to a frequent gap between formal training and the products of creative output. See "World's Most Valuable Men," *The Nation,* December 8, 1956, pp. 497–500.

† Ginzberg, *op. cit.,* pp. 50–51. Strong criticisms of currently fashionable criteria for recognition of executives are offered by the English writer, Aubrey Silberston, in *Education and Training for Industrial Management,* Management Publications Limited, The Millbrook Press, Ltd., London, 1955. He holds (pp. 15–16) that "systematic selection methods, however carefully devised, are

at Milo, because some reference was almost invariably made to education when promotion was discussed. But specific merits of education were not stressed, and the fact that some men rose to high levels without college training[2] while others with it remained near the bottom speaks for itself.

Another common explanation points to family origin as the source of both education and aid to success, so that the father's occupation and background become the clue. Students disagree on this[3] and the incomplete data on Milo managers gives little support to the view. Data on father's occupation were available for only 31 of the 72 superintendents and staff officers, and these show little that could be regarded as a definite pattern of impetus accounting for placement of the sons. For example, the fathers were: 4 small farmers, 2 grocers, 9 skilled workers, 2 school-teachers, 1 telegrapher, 1 police officer, 1 barber, 2 sales clerks, 1 insurance agent, 4 industrial foremen, 1 consulting engineer, 1 realtor, 1 streetcar motorman, and 1 locomotive engineer. The sons had a median education of 14 years, and 18 were on jobs not related to their training.

The most workable theory in the present case is that increased years of schooling at the college level are directly, but complexly, related to managerial skill in carrying on the endless round of unavoidable compromises. This is to say that the total experience of going to college may be more important for the executive than the technical courses he takes. In the last decade or so, executives themselves, with various educators and students,[4] have questioned the adequacy of some subject matters and have proposed curricular changes, but they have given little if any attention to the career consequences of the student's campus life, drives, and competition as an *experience*. It is much too simple to say that candidates are selected because of their education. Doubtless they are to a degree, depending on how status-givers interpret education. But in view of the controversies over subject matter and the evidence that years of schooling relate to rank, there is merit in thinking that educated candidates select certain ranks. Education in this sense means the student's total growth during his tenure on

no substitute for long acquaintance with a person." He doubts (p. 6) the "universal validity" of any of our pet traits and categories, such as "high standards of integrity and loyalty, courage, imagination, initiative, acceptability to others, intelligence, pertinacity, and optimism in the face of adversity." He quotes an "experienced manager" who suggests that "the quality which matters most of all is resilience under adversity." In other terms this quality is examined below in chap. 9. He admits that (p. 12) "some technical understanding is required in nearly all managerial jobs," but ranks personal qualities as probably more important in most cases.

campus; the formal doses, yes, *and* the inseparable unintended acquisitions.

Before we can talk of the transfer of college experiences to executive tasks, we must compare the unofficial executive and student roles. Chapters 8 and 9 deal with the administrative situation and the interplay between it and the executive, but here in a paragraph we must note salient features of the executive's environment. He deals with ambiguity. Though he has defined goals and understood ways of reaching them, he functions only as he fashions new routes that are always out-of-date. Yesterday's guide often fails him in today's contradictions. His indispensable ability is not to act out cut-and-dried precepts, but to carry on where there are no precepts. If he is to escape "ulcer gulch," survive as a leader, and protect himself without permanently alienating associates, he must precipitate but channelize crisis, and aptly compromise to preserve the uncompromisable.

The student's career on campus is trivial as compared with future rewards and responsibilities, but given certain common conditions, his experiences are an unwitting preparation for the executive role. Years of "education" have many implications for the type of student (*a*) who attends school with more vocational than intellectual purpose; (*b*) who wishes to participate widely on campus and yet craves good marks; and (*c*) who for these and other reasons is forced to budget his time. Such a student may have both vocational aims and intellectual fire, but the first is essential and seems typically dominant. He may have received a financial and psychological boost from his family, or his campus cronies may have awakened his career consciousness. Knowledge of employers' expectations may give him the "A-fever" if campus honors do not. Long before he completes high school, the student has learned that in our society he must participate or be a "grind" in danger of becoming "introverted" or "maladjusted" or even "antisocial." Social activities take time but may pay unexpected returns. These activities would of course include the efforts to enter and climb in fraternities, most recreation, and dating.

Taking a part in campus politics gives the student an experience he may not get outside of college, at his age, short of entering professional politics. He tries his hand at helping select and elect officers, and may himself serve. His part in the intra- and inter-organizational struggles is educational. He learns to move in and out of cliques and organizations with minimum friction. He mixes with the mentally elect and competes with those who also have pangs of status- and career-hunger. Success as a campus "wheel" is instructive and good for his record.

If with all these activities, and the helpful obstacle of part-time work, he is still able to make good marks, he has learned how to function inside limitations. Probably he has become adept at analyzing his professors and utilizing his social contacts whether he is consciously calculating or not.* If his limited time demands more short cuts to maintain his grade points, he studies his professors to (a) isolate their pet theories; (b) outguess them in preparing for examinations; and (c) to please them. Although apple-polishing may not always pay off as expected, the exercise in grappling with the unknown still enlarges his executive potential. He compares notes and impressions with other students. This requires cooperative exchanges and sharpens skill in cracking cliques that have a corner on past examinations. Some of his circle of friends may be part-time library personnel and help him to monopolize hard-to-get books, and/or to keep them out overtime, as well as escape fines or have them reduced.†

However, competition for grades and contacts, the deadlines for delivery of term papers and reports, and the occasional baffling professor, may defeat all these maneuvers. This is good, too, for developing possible administrative talent. For in addition to the skill of easy cooperation with others, the student now has to gamble on his own and determine the unascertainable. He becomes sensitive to intangibles, and learns to live with the elusive and ambiguous. This unofficial training teaches him to get in his own claims and gracefully escape those of others that he must. He learns to appear sophisticated and to adjust quickly to endless new situations and personalities.

Despite what we have said against subject matter, some of the student's courses may contribute to his developing social skills. The first two years of college are usually designed to "broaden" and "give perspective." His travel through time and space on the wings of biology, history, anthropology, politics, sociology, philosophy, psychology, may bring him home with a new view of family and neighborhood precepts. He may lose some dogmas about what is worthwhile, what is good and bad, and about the virtue of fixed ways of doing things. Even if he doesn't change deeply, some desperate situation may provoke him to activate his inert knowledge of successful means used by dead heroes. At least he may avoid the error of thinking that "politics" and "rat races" are peculiar to our time or to a particular kind of organi-

---

* Those who cringe at the activities of this alert student were obviously never campus "wheels" and will not be executives.

† Some of my successful intimates (in terms of their high marks in college and quick rise in industry) at Milo and Fruhling and acquaintances in other firms have boasted of these practices. Also see Ginzberg, op. cit., p. 175, on executive performance in relation to overcoming obstacles in getting a degree.

zation. Thus subject matter of this kind may combine with the unofficial education acquired under various stresses to produce a type of person with hidden executive possibilities.* Such students receive much more "vocational education" than they bargain for or pay for.

This is not to say that all college graduates are executives in the rough. Obviously not all fit the type we have posed, which was based on rather narrow but close study of such people as Hardy, Springer, and Rees at Milo and others at Fruhling. For instance, a kindergarten teacher might fit our type, though there is a question about the force of her status aspirations, and never show the qualities we attribute to the successful executive because her role is very different from that of executives—however much she might protest to the contrary!

Whether experience in college gives the urges or merely stirs latent qualities born elsewhere, or whether earlier conditioning and college are necessary, at Milo the drive for personal† success as the major end of life was the goal of the college-bred oftener than the noncollege.

Evans, as we saw, was widely read and verbal but was not "college-processed," and was most critical of the behavior he saw as essential for success. Also noncollege, Trimble admitted the "error" of his earlier views. Perry, with eight years of schooling, frowns on what is needed for success. Gregg, a high school graduate, is of the same view, and Wilkins, with two years of high school, thinks the formula is to "be a bootlicker with a set of principles made of rubber."

On the other hand, Cowper, with a degree, emphasized the value of "flexibility" in success. In another connection he remarked, "I'm always willing to deviate in clearing up problems. By that I mean to ignore principle for the moment in order to follow it in the long run."

---

* Some top managers argue in favor of recruiting campus "big shots" as potential executives, while others say such persons are "spoiled" and can function happily only as "adulation" is heaped on them. This second group would focus on candidates who make high marks without concern for their popularity. But a third group, supported by some evidence at Milo, reports most satisfaction from hiring those students who were both big men on the campus and high scholastically. See Ginzberg, *op. cit.*, pp. 45–47. For executive impressions of formal knowledge versus judgment as factors in success, see The Editors of *Fortune, The Executive Life,* Doubleday, Garden City, N.Y., 1956, pp. 213–214, 216–217.

† D. Starch, "An Analysis of the Careers of 150 Executives," *Psychological Bulletin,* 39:435 (1942); A. W. Kornhauser, in *Industrial Conflict,* First Yearbook of the Society for the Psychological Study of Social Issues, The Cordon Company, 1939, XI, pp. 210–211; Warner and Abegglen, *op. cit.,* p. 132, show that, in their sample of around 8000 executives, college graduates required 20 years to reach their positions, as compared with an average of 31 years for those with little or no formal schooling.

Haupt, a college graduate, usually successful in compromising on unessentials to preserve the sinew of policy, made a maxim in Milo by his repeated defense, "I always try to make two and two equal four. Sometimes I wind up with three-point-nine or four-point one, but that's close enough."

Cunningham was an exception. With two years of college, he denounced the behavior associated with success.

The few cases of noncollege men who practiced and approved the compromises essential for success were atypical. Successful practices are of course contagious and can be variously imitated by some, but many of this group were barred by moral feelings from adopting the more rewarding conduct. Implicitly preaching the morality of fixity, they demanded simple and unvarying practices in their daily relations —as did the foreman, Randall, in Chapter 5. Their potential for accommodation, or ability to adjust to change, was low. Rank seems to relate directly with this potential. That is, success as an executive requires aptness in fitting means to ends inside the limitation of preserving the organization, which includes its indispensable personnel. The intruding moral issues are part of our problem of explaining how the managers rose in the structure, but we too must compromise and ignore them for the present.[5]

Thus age, work background and service, and formal education as training adapted to positions, all showed such variations at Milo that none of them could regularly be formal tests for recruitment and promotion.[6] Scattered cases indicated the same was true for Fruhling's 940 managers.

Case materials are a threat to the researcher. His loving care to turn his matchless insights on every crumb of his findings easily trips him into platitudes. With this threat as a monitor, I should like to comment quickly on typical unofficial events attending (1) the choice of candidates for open positions, (2) demotions, (3) sinecures and competence for office, and (4) salary variations.

CAREERS IN PROCESS

Vacant Position and Promotion

Inconsistencies about the official route upward naturally provoked fears, speculation, and search for unofficial routes. Vacation of an office by the advancement, death, or transfer of its occupant was followed by a period of silence and suspense as to who the successor would be. Except in case of sudden death, there had usually been some planning for the vacancy, but this was often vague even to those who counted themselves as likely candidates.

At Milo a small group of superiors, which included Hardy, conferred and prolonged the suspense by delays of one to three weeks in naming a successor. Importance of the office was naturally a factor. Sometimes it was allowed to die, but no notice would be given of this intent. Assuming the office would continue, the field was left open for speculation on the criteria* that would be used.

The behavior of both those with and without hope of being chosen showed conviction that personal factors would decide, and that the choice would have personal consequences for subordinates. During this period, subordinates who professed to have excellent grapevines would slight their duties to impress others with their knowledge of what candidates were most in favor. Wagers were made with odds given and taken on two or more possible candidates. At the same time there was debate as to who *should* have the office with expressed fear and hope as to the consequences. While supporters of a candidate pointed to his favorable qualities such as age, experience, education, personality, influence, and family conduct, others noted cases where these factors meant nothing. Some of those fearing a certain appointment, assured the group they would transfer or quit "rather than work under him."

Unexpected appointments or promotions brought excited analyses of the selection. In some cases personal competence as a factor was never mentioned, though theorizing about the matter might recur for months.

The assumption that all members of a firm perpetually crave to move upward, and that only the aggressive can rise, has noteworthy exceptions. The case above of Perry could have been multiplied several times, even up to the divisional level. The mere wish not to go higher in the ranks, as in Perry's case, did not prevent the person from rising. Though some individuals successfully declined invitations to take higher office, others were coerced into entering management, or into taking higher supervisory posts.

The case of Evans illustrates successful rejection of higher rewards and the variations of upward drive in one individual. Despite the fact that he denounced the conduct associated with success, and that he

---

* On occasion some of the high managers implied a certain essential behavior in aspirants. Brady, the Milo griever, told me that at the time of Taylor's failure to get an expected post, he (Brady) asked Blanke why. Blanke replied: "Nobody knows him. It wasn't because he lacked ability but because he didn't use the plant politics the way he should have." As we have seen, this was *an ability* Taylor lacked.

"raised hell" with his superiors when he "was passed up three times in favor of somebody else," he recently declined the assistant superintendency when it was offered to him. His explanation to me:

> Goddamn the job! When I was younger and needed the money, I couldn't have it. Now that my kids are all grown and nearly through college the old lady [his wife] and me can get by without it. It would have been damn good ten years ago to have a little extra cash. But I'm fifty-three now and I don't have the expense I used to have. There's a lot more hell goes with the job than used to. I don't mean to be catching hell the last twelve years I'm here. Some guys'd sell their souls to be a superintendent, but not me.

Some workmen of great skill and technical grasp were encouraged by Milo managers to enter the ranks, and in some cases were forced to.

L. Jackson was one of these. As a practicing Fundamentalist from a farm community he possessed certain presumed virtues for ascendancy. His habitual hard work, reliability, and often stated belief that "man was meant to earn his bread by the sweat of his brow," were not lost on H. Warren, general foreman of that area. Warren was convinced that "Jackson is a man you can trust when your back's turned." He asked him to accept a foremanship. Jackson declined. Warren offered uncommon privileges, including the right to select individual members for his work crew. Jackson still refused and explained that he was "not qualified to be a boss." Accustomed to bitter rivalries for foremanships, Warren was delighted and redoubled his efforts. Just before taking his vacation, Jackson again declined. Returning on Monday two weeks later, Jackson was approached by a work crew who asked for assignments. He responded with "Why ask me?" They quoted Warren as having ordered them the preceding Friday to report Monday to their new boss, Jackson, and they referred him to the bulletin board for proof. Jackson tore the notice from the board and went to Warren's office where he also found Warren's chief, O'Brien. They both apologized for their action, and explained that they were "on the spot. Please help us. There's not another man we value as much as you. We've got to get the work out and nobody else but you can do it." Jackson accepted, but rejected the position in less than three months. Division chief Springer had complained to Warren over some production detail in his province. When Warren conferred with his foremen and found that one of Jackson's men was responsible for the difficulty, he spoke sharply to Jackson. Jackson quit his job and went home. Warren and O'Brien drove over to see him that night and explained that they meant nothing "by bawling you out. That's part of the job.

We have to do that to make things look right upstairs. You know there was nothing personal meant. Won't you reconsider?" Jackson refused to return except to his old job as workman.

When Warren was later made top manager of one of the corporation's smaller units he again turned to Jackson, and this time asked him to come and head a department. Jackson declined. His case shows that Milo directors were concerned to reward some kinds of ability.

The division chief, Revere, took that office under protest. Starting at the bottom at age twenty-two, he climbed to department head in twenty-two years. After ten years there he was asked to take his present position. He declined and gave bad health and diminished family responsibilities as reasons. However, his reluctance was based less on these considerations than on status and income factors. After having been department head for four years, Revere had seen Hardy take over this very division at the age of twenty-nine. Informants said Revere wanted the job at that time and was bitter over Hardy's getting it. And Hardy's moving into his present post six years later did not soften Revere's feelings. As division head Hardy had received $17,500 as compared to the $12,500 received by Revere when he took over the office. Although this was an increase for Revere of $3700 over his salary of $8800 as department head, it was still $5000 less than a rival had received. The gain of $3700 did not cover the injury to Revere's feelings and had to be supplemented by the command that he take the vacated position or retire.

The cases of Jackson and Revere point up both the complexities of career motivation and the play of personal relations in planned organizations.

Demotion

Little attention has been given to the fall of individuals in organizations.* Possibly as a status tragedy, the whole subject has been shunned, except for superficial post-mortems on "reasons for failure," which usually skirt the errors of status-givers, the validity of criteria used in selection, and the social factors in organizational defense tactics.

Demotion from failure is typically disguised to protect not only the individual ego and the organization's investment in him, but also his original sponsors. If the demotee has high status, a post is created for

---

* Demotion for failure is part of "social testing." See Pitirim Sorokin, *Social Mobility,* Harper and Brothers, New York, 1927, pp. 182–211. Where Sorokin's concern is the institutional testing of individuals for fitness to remain or be rejected, ours is how failure of the individual in a given position leads not to rejection but to his retention and reclassification in the organization.

him, or he is made an "assistant-to" (Chapter 3), where "his skills will be most helpful to the company," or he is fitted into a staff (Chapter 4) "to round out his experience," etc. He retains his previous salary.

B. Schwann was Rees' second assistant (not shown on chart). We saw in Chapter 5 how Rees sought to hand down unofficially official decisions to strengthen first-line foremen. When Rees was visiting the Central Office or busy with other things, much of this work fell to Schwann. At other times Schwann was expected to "troubleshoot" and aid in nipping developing grievances by keeping Rees informed on shop affairs. At all times he was expected to have on tap a supply of effective suggestions. Because he was always available, hard-pressed executives called on him more and more for informal suggestions which were treated as decisions by line chiefs—at their wit's end, or eager to involve the staff in trouble. Son of a school teacher, Schwann had little background for making potentially hazardous decisions. He took a degree in education, and in his own words, "led a soft life in college." He then taught in a small high school for several years, became "disgusted" with the work and pay, and took a job as timekeeper in industry. From there he entered Milo by personal connections. He moved to second assistant in five years and was transferred two years later to a newly created clerical office with routine functions in the same staff, "where we can make better use of his psychology." But according to superintendent Meier:

> Schwann was eased out because he couldn't do the job. He'd complain of his stomach hurting him. Right in the middle of a meeting with a dozen people sitting around a table, he'd jump up in pain and run out into the hall to get a drink of water and come back with tears running down his cheeks. He knew of the relation between nervous strain and stomach ulcers so he'd pretend he had indigestion. Hell, we all knew he had ulcers. His nervous system just couldn't stand up under that sort of strain.
>
> You'd go up to his office for an answer on some squabble you were in with the union. He'd listen and tighten up all over. Then he'd squirm and twist and strum his fingers on the table. Finally he'd give you an answer and say, "How's that? Is that about right? What do you think?" Well, hell! That's no answer! You go in to see him because you don't know what to do, and then a guy shows you *he* doesn't know what to do! You want a quick, decisive answer and no beating around the bush—something sharp and final, the way Rees hands it out. You're usually holding up things waiting for that answer.
>
> Well, you know what happened. Schwann had to give up. He was too soft. He didn't have the nervous system to take it.

Lane's move (Chapter 3) from Industrial Relations to assistant-to Stevens was similar in origin and action to Schwann's case.

Sinecures and Competence for Office

Thinking of sinecures as flexible offices with pay but few if any fixed duties, we can see that the office of "assistant-to" was frequently a sine-cure. In addition to the functions of "assistant-to" that were summarized in Chapter 3, sinecures were used to accelerate and bolster careers. They could be created at nearly any level, be dropped arbitrarily, or they could be semipermanent and be succeeded to. But not all posts of "assistant-to" were sinecures, nor were sinecures confined to this office. Whether to reward those who were failing but had served well, or as a substitute for unavailable higher posts, to protect an overrated person from claims beyond his revealed strength—as in the case of Schwann, as an inducement (Bingham, Chapter 3), to cover errors in judgment of appointing officers, or when given in rare instances just as a favor, in all cases sinecures could have the dignity and façade of any office. For example, the formal organization chart shows that superintendent Ruf had a first-line foreman reporting directly to him. Informants said this foreman had no "real" responsibilities, but was only a "stooge." The same statement was made of the similarly-placed foreman in the charted department between Geiger and Meier. The chart also shows at least a dozen general foremen* without first-line foremen. Some of these offices were clearly more than sinecures, though several of them had few routine duties, and all the occupants received the pay of general foremen for no more than the duties, without the pressures, of first-line foremen. Confidential complaints by some foremen and "authentic" general foremen indicated that several of the offices were given as direct rewards for various reasons.† And during reorganizations some had been preserved for morale purposes or to hold highly competent general foremen who might have quit if demoted. Like that of "assistant-to," use of these offices had followed expediency and social demands more than economic logic. However, it is likely that the long-run gains of Milo were greater than if rigid formal theory had been followed.

Never referred to as such, sinecures were common enough to be talked about a great deal at Milo. Informants estimated that the number of "good" sinecures, including those in the staffs, varied from fifteen to twenty-five, while those of less value might fluctuate to forty-five or more. The failures who held sinecures were spoken of as persons who had "fouled out" or who "couldn't cut the buck." Others were "just on

---

* As bearers of the title, all but three of the most questionable cases of these general foremen were included with the sixty-one on whom occupational data were presented.

† See the discussion of unofficial rewards in chap. 7.

the payroll" for unexplained reasons, or were "fair-haired boys," or possessed "flashy personalities," or had "a lot of get-up and go."

Attitudes toward sinecures were by no means always unfavorable. Much like our senators and their attitudes toward lobbying, few officers, including those at top levels, could be sure that changing conditions or ill-health would not at some time find them glad to be protected or rewarded by a similar post. However, there was resentment in some cases because the real nature and operation of sinecures could not be publicized. Hence some persons mistakenly regarded them as permanent positions and grew embittered after hungering for one specifically only to see it remain vacant for months, or even die. The unofficial existence of sinecures was obviously contrary to organizational theory as well as the ideal in American business and industry that measurable contributions and reward should clearly match in all cases.

Variations of Income

Salary variations inside specific limits were officially thought to be natural if not inevitable because of tacitly recognized differences in seniority, experience, etc. However, as with other features of planned action, various conditions[7] intrude to produce unplanned results. Set up in part to protect morale, the limits for a given salary range are overstepped to (*a*) encourage the nearly indispensable person to whom material reward is uppermost; (*b*) correct negative errors in appraisal and protect the appointing officer by allowing the granted status to stand, but with reduced salary; (*c*) lift the spirit of certain persons during presumably temporary reorganization by lowering their rank without salary change, as with demotion of assistant superintendents to general foremen; (*d*) induce an officer to submit to being "loaned" to another department where his title will continue unchanged to conceal the salary increase and prevent disturbances.

We can get at these variations by comparing an official statement with the beliefs, actions, and analyses of those involved, and with some of the actual salaries.

Cowper (mentioned earlier in this chapter) was very close to the administration of Milo's salary and wage rates. He spiritedly defended the ideal of a one-to-one relation between individual ability and pay. In his words:

> Incomes are confidential. They're an outgrowth of an agreement between a man and his superiors. Each man is correctly merit-rated according to his ability. I'll admit there have been cases where some superintendents have wanted to promote a friend without inquiring whether there was somebody else in another department better qualified

for the job.* But that stuff doesn't go around here. In a small loosely-knit plant [sic] people can get away with that. But in a large well-knit plant like ours [sic], you won't find that kind of thing. I think you'll find that's usually true of most big corporations. You wouldn't find it here anyhow, because Stevens doesn't stand for monkey business.

Our salaries are set up on a sliding scale. A man coming on a job is paid according to where he falls on that scale. There's no question of his being correctly placed on the scale, but *where* he's placed is nobody's concern but his own.

Contrary to Cowper's statement, there was widespread belief that amount of income was influenced as much by "connections" as by ability. The general eagerness to discover even approximate salaries revealed these suspicions. A piece of mail delivered to the wrong office was opened by an officer. When he discovered that it contained code numbers and related data that with other available information and long calculations would reveal the annual salaries of officers in another department to within fifty dollars, he called an assistant and began the computations. Foremen, general foremen, and finally the assistant superintendent stopped all work to await the results. The withdrawal of nine men from regular duties for over two hours reflected the disbelief that incomes measured only ability.

Superintendent Taylor professed a lack of interest in the income of others but revealed a knowledge of techniques for finding out:

Many people in management get a kick out of feeling that they know something other people don't—that they're on the inside. And sometimes they just pretend to know. There's a lot of ways used for finding out about other people's income. People are always alert around tax-paying time. If they can hear just a word out of a man about his taxes, it'll mean a lot. People here in the plant do a lot of figuring on their taxes right in their offices. If you come in suddenly on a man and he gets a phone call just then, you can always let your eyes wander around his desk [laughing]. If you know how many kids a man has and how much taxes he paid, you can come close enough to feel good. People are always straining for a glimpse of somebody's pay stub—that's all it takes—you know right where to look, and one quick look does it. If you know the charging rate† in small departments you can come awful

---

* Silberston, *op. cit.,* p. 14, reports this as common in England: "It seems inevitable in most firms that certain appointments should be made without consulting the appropriate official. This is particularly likely to happen when a suitable person is available within the department where the vacancy occurs." Neither he nor Cowper analyze the system of claims in the department that requires such action.

† The "charging rate" was the total salaries of technical and administrative employees of a given department divided by the total hours of the year which that department operated, and expressed in dollars.

close to figuring what the big wheels get. If you hear a man drop a word about how much company insurance he has, you can come within a hundred dollars or so of his yearly income. If you can learn what the general foreman gets, you can come close to the departmental superintendent. Or if you know a departmental superintendent's salary, you can hit close to the general foreman and the divisional superintendent. There's no doubt that you can learn a great deal about incomes if you compare points with others and give a lot of time to cultivating it.

Taylor also implies that there was always a fixed relation among the salaries of different levels throughout the firm. The evidence shows that, despite the official scales, the managers did not invariably stand in a fixed salary relation to each other. Excluded from the functional cliques, Taylor here again was apparently unaware of practices known to others.

Income data are deficient. At one point in the research at Milo, exact incomes were obtained for ninety-six officers. But while inflation progressed with the research, the timing, rapport, and hazards of my personal contacts lacked this regularity. And as the sources of my information closed, some salaries were increasing more sharply than others. For example, some of the divisional officers received as much as three $600 increases in one year, with two of the increases coming in the last three months of 1956. Some officers at other levels received only one increase for the year. Hence annual salaries for first-line foremen through department heads are $1200 to $2800 more than given, whereas divisional heads are $3000 to $8000 more. Estimates of varying reliability roughly double the salaries for the plant manager and assistant but "substantially increase" the distance between them. Since the increases were not to correct imbalances except in a small minority of cases, the original figures still serve our purpose.

The scale of first-line foremen ranged from $475 to $600 per month. Yet at least eight salaried foremen were below the minimum with salaries of $425 a month. Years of service were no key to where foremen were placed on the scale, for one foreman of seven years' service received $550 for the same job that a foreman of ten years' service received $475.

The scale for general foremen ranged from $575 to $675. Here at least one man was below at $550, and another was beyond the upper limit with $750.

The incomes of departmental and divisional heads were given as annual salaries. The actual departmental salaries, with no mention of a scale, ranged from $8500 to $14,500. Smith received $8500; Dicke, $9500; Taylor, $10,600; and Geiger, $14,500. The divisional heads ranged from $14,500 to $16,000 with Springer and Revere receiving $14,500 each,* and Blanke $16,000. P. Finch received the highest staff salary in Milo, $15,000. Hardy received $20,500; and Stevens, $21,000, as against a salary of $27,000 paid to Rutherford, his predecessor, several years earlier.

Since need and informal compacts could force salaries below and above "fixed" ranges, they could obviously make changes inside the official ranges even more readily. An officer in the Auditing Department told me:

> In the last three or four years certain jobs have jumped up to around $750 a month. A new man comes in and gets much less, maybe only $500. Yet inside of six months he'll be getting $750. There's a lot of politics in here somewhere. It looks to me like some of the flashy personalities† get themselves liked and get around the rules. Some guy that's not liked, or steps on somebody's toes, is held to the rules, or maybe he don't even get the advantages of the rules. It looks to me like Smith [the line superintendent] is one of these. He's a damn good man but he don't click.

Stein sought to justify income variations as largely the result of impersonal necessity:

> Many appointments are made on the basis of expediency. Sometimes when things are all snarled up, management has to put in a much bigger man than will be needed later on. Since he's going to have to do something really tough he's going to be paid well. When he gets things going, he'll be taken off the job and the next man will get less for less, which is only natural. Then again once in a while you'll come across a man who's tops in pleasing. He makes the right impressions and pleases everybody concerned. Since everything high up is based more on impressions than on anything concrete, his real abilities may easily be overestimated and

---

* Revere had received increases totaling $2000 since taking the office, possibly in part to ease his feelings about discrepancies noted earlier.

† These are the "highly visible" people observed elsewhere—those, *e.g.*, in Evans' remarks (above) who were "known" (as against his not being known) and who in Stein's remarks (below) are "tops in pleasing." See Blanke's remarks in footnote on page 168. Also see P. F. Drucker, *The Practice of Management*, Harper and Brothers, New York, 1954, p. 155. Phrase-makers have only recently named the practice "high visibility," but the behavior has long been advocated for personal success. For example, a master of many roles in the Italian Renaissance privately counseled, "If you . . . are the follower of some great lord, and would be employed by him in his affairs, endeavour to keep yourself always in his sight. For every hour things will occur to be done which he will commit to him whom he sees, or who is at hand, and not to you if he has to seek or send for you. And whosoever misses an opening, however small, will often lose the introduction or approach to matters of greater moment." Francesco Guicciardini, *Ricordi,* trans. by N. H. Thomson, S. F. Vanni, New York, 1949, p. 85.

he'll get promoted to a job that his abilities don't justify. Before long this will show up. Well, you'll have to move him, but he stays right on at the same pay. If you were paying him what you thought he was worth, and now you had to move him to some little piddling job, why his pay'll sure as hell be out of line with other jobs of that kind.

Stein begs the question. Seeking to show that salary variations for a given position flowed naturally from the play of impersonal forces, his reference to people who are "tops in pleasing" suggests that personal action to protect failures also contributed to salary differentials. At another time Stein declared that "one big reason" why salaries could vary on the same level at any time, was that younger men were coming in and "finding things all set up for them." Hence they "could not be expected to get as much as the men who had worked long and hard to get things organized." Unless one assumes some unrevealed differences in abilities or initial problems to be overcome, this explanation hardly covers the case of Springer's receiving $12,500 on taking office at the age of thirty-five, whereas Hardy, taking an office on the same level, several years earlier when inflation was less, received a salary of $17,500 at the age of twenty-nine. The same holds for the salary of $27,500 that Rutherford commanded at the age of twenty-nine as compared with $21,000 given Stevens several years later at the age of sixty-one and after thirty-five years of service with the corporation.

Thus the character of demotions, the use of sinecures and the office of assistant-to, the events attending promotions, the unofficial variations in salary and the multiple contradictions prompting them all complement the conclusions drawn about the data on personnel histories. These findings are of course not breath-taking but are a prerequisite to examining the recurrent charges that a set of unofficial standards was used for regulating careers.

Many profess to know that ability is only one factor in success, but scorn attempts to explore other influences as time wasted on the "obvious." Yet it is equally obvious that when speaking for the record, these same persons deny concern for any individual quality but "ability." Barnard[8] is a sophisticated exception. And another top executive ironically observes: "I really don't know how we find the natural leaders. I suppose mostly by smell. However I would not want to deny that there is an element of patronage and pull there [utility field] as everywhere else."[9] Stryker[10] sees executive criteria as "strictly nebulous," and "based 20 per cent on the record and 80 per cent on the personality." These figures are admirably neat. However even in organizations requiring a high degree of formal education and originality for entrance, as in academic and other institutions, personality can outweigh scholastic fitness in the eyes of both recommenders and selectors of candidates. Aspirants in some cases have stood in the top one per cent of their classes but have been damned as in only the top fifteen per cent because of attitudes and interests dissonant to "sponsors." Unacceptable attitudes can, of course, also lead "recommenders" to overrate the person in helping him move elsewhere.

UNOFFICIAL REQUIREMENTS FOR SUCCESS

In the excerpts from interviews we saw spontaneous references by Bierner, Cowper, Bennett, Perry, Evans, and Cunningham to the Masonic Fraternity, with contradictory implications about membership as a factor in success. Their statements were cautious beside dozens of assertions from other people, non-Masonic Protestants and Catholics alike, that membership was essential. But other unofficial factors were also mentioned. In all we need to look at four alleged career aids: (*a*) membership in the Masons, which, as we shall see, had the negative aspect of *not* being a Roman Catholic; (*b*) having a predominantly Anglo-Saxon or Germanic ancestral, or ethnic, background; (*c*) membership in a local Yacht Club; and (*d*) being a Republican in politics.[11]

Masonic Membership

Endless direct and allusive remarks about Masonry, and the fantasies among workmen about its importance, led me to question representative intimates about these charges.

C. Bicknell, an assistant superintendent who was a Thirty-second Degree Mason, held that:

> Being a Mason doesn't help you get a better job, but it does make for better relations. The fact of being brothers in the lodge and being of service to each other is never mentioned, however. You always know that you can get service and help from each other because of that, but it has no direct bearing on you getting a better job. The Masonic Order demands that each man stand on his own feet. Being a Mason may help a man, but only in a general way. The Masons in a sense are a religious organization. If you know the Bible, you've got the principles of Freemasonry. We've nothing against the Catholics being Masons, but the Church don't like us.

Superintendent Ames, a Mason, avoided discussion of Masonry in connection with Milo but implied a great deal:

> If you and I go into a strange town, and we're both broke and have no friends there, I'll have friends at once and you won't. That's what it means to be a Mason—you'll have friends among strangers and your

friends who are Masons will do more for you than they would for people who're not Masons. Let me give you an example. I was down in St. Louis at the airport and wanted to get a plane for Chicago. I was in a long line. By the time I got up to fourth place, the three people ahead of me were all turned away—they wanted tickets to Chicago, too. I was about ready to leave when I noticed a ring on the finger of the ticket agent. I was smoking a cigar, so I casually put my elbow on the window and held my hand up where my ring could be seen. When the agent asked me what he could do for me, I told him I'd like two seats on a plane to Chicago. He looked me over and said, "Wait a minute, I think I can fix you up!" He stepped over and made a phone call and came back and said, "Yes, it's okay." What do you think of that?

C. Waring, a general foreman and a Mason, was noncommittal, but smiled and said, "I guess you know there's plenty of Masons around here. Well, that's not all. There's going to be a damn sight more of them!"

A staff supervisor who was not a Mason declared:

I think the Masons are a good organization, but not the bunch they've got around here. There's too many social climbers and ambitious people getting in. They're ruining the Masons. They don't want in to do the organization any good; they want it to help them get a better job. There's so many of the big wheels in the Masons now that they just about run the plant.

Younger Catholics regarded the Masons with rancor. But a fifty-four-year-old staff specialist of that group was more temperate:

I think the Masons are getting too strong in the plant, but a fellow has to be fair. You probably never heard of it since it was before your time, but we've had two managers here in the last twenty-five years that were Catholics. And one of them put in quite a few Catholics when it was convenient. Maybe not the way the Masons do now, but it was done. The big shots in [the Central Office] know that things work that way. I think they sort of alternate Catholics and Masons to keep the thing balanced up.

There was no evidence to refute or support this statement.

Another general foreman, J. Clancy, aged sixty-one, had received hints that his application for membership in the order would be welcomed, but he hesitated to apply:

I think the Masons are a fine organization. I've wanted to get in for years, but I'm afraid to. More than three-fourths of my men [workmen] are Masons. If I was a Mason they'd be on my tail all the time for special favors. That would worry the life out of me. Some bosses don't mind things like that—some of them might even want it like that. But I want to treat all my men just the same. I don't want to play favorites.

Blanke gave an indirect testimonial of Masonic strength among the managers. He advised the griever, Brady, who had applied and was acceptable to the Fraternity, "Don't join while you're a griever. You'll find too many of your boys (rank-and-file) yelling that you've sold out to management."

Catholics were acceptable to the Fraternity, but they considered themselves ineligible, they said, because of the Church's opposition to certain oaths required of Masons. Yet their conviction of the importance of being a Mason led several of them to drop out of the Church and join the Order. O'Brien was one of these. Appointed by an earlier Catholic plant head, O'Brien sat in one of the front pews with that manager during his tenure. But when this sponsor died and was succeeded by a Mason, and O'Brien saw various retiring Catholics replaced by Masons, he dropped out of the Church and joined the Fraternity. Most of the Milo Catholics were embittered toward him, but two Catholic general foremen and five first-line foremen followed him in a few months. Fraternity members admitted this. Several aspiring Catholics of Polish, Italian, and Lithuanian descent who made the change also changed their names. Younger Catholics were naturally uneasy about their future. They asserted that where the Catholics were only five per cent, or less, of management, they should be a majority as they were in Magnesia, where the current and preceding Mayors as well as the district national congressmen were all Catholics.*

Intimates were quizzed to establish who was Catholic and Mason and who was neither. The count and percentages of officers in these groups among the 226 managers are shown in Table 7.

TABLE 7.   Masons and Catholics in Management

Managerial Group	Masons No.	%	Catholics No.	%	Neither No.	%	Total Officers
Staff	19	52.8	5	13.9	12	33.3	36
Superintendents	28	77.8	3	8.3	5	13.9	36
General foremen	39	64.0	12	19.7	10	16.4	61
First-line foremen	70	75.0	10	10.9	13	14.1	93
Total	156	69.0	30	13.3	40	17.7	226

* Their statements concerning the community and its public officials were correct. Senior priests in Magnesia observed that the number of Roman Catholic managers at Milo had been "declining for years," and they estimated Magnesia's Catholic population at 59 to 85 per cent of the total.

We see that the Masons, 69 per cent,* were considerably less than the 95 per cent alleged by the Catholics. But if we drop the Catholics from our calculation, because as a group they considered themselves ineligible, we see that nearly 80 per cent of the eligible managers were Masons. This is a highly significant difference and suggests, with the other data, that Masonic membership was usually an unofficial requirement for getting up—and for remaining there.

Assuming that Masonic membership, with the superintendents 78 per cent strong, was an unofficial test for success, we might expect the next highest concentration to be among the general, rather than first-level, foremen. Status uncertainty among the latter was probably a factor. In their confusion over whether they were in the fold of management or worker, they saw Masonic rings and buttons as symbols of being solidly in management. Also, 25 per cent of those foremen, more than any other level, were members of minority groups as foreign born or first generation Americans. Many had changed their heavily consonanted Central-European surnames to Anglo-Saxon names similar to those of top management. These first-line foremen also contributed most of those who dropped Catholicism to show another item of similarity to the status-givers, and to make a tacit plea for the opportunity to conform still further by becoming Masons.

The age, educational, and job differences we discussed in staff-line friction probably held the staff group to low Masonic membership. Most of the seventeen nonmembers aspired to be Masons, but feared that blackball by one of the lodges, any of which might contain line enemies, would jeopardize future entry at a more favorable time. Hence they waited. Also most of the staff Masons were older (only five under forty), former line men untrained in staff duties. Their ineptness, lack of contributions, and use of the staff as a refuge with known line sponsors protecting them, all generated internal frictions disposing these older officers not to vote the younger "pure-bred" staff people into the Fraternity. Cowper, as a staff non-Mason, was the highest placed Catholic in Milo. He was secure because of his contributions and personal charm, because he showed loyalty in crises,[12] and because he had been around long enough to destroy doubts and to win the esteem of all groups. In the staffs he was a sustaining nucleus for the non-Masons.

The informal power chart also shows the importance of Masonic membership: of the twenty-one officers, only Stevens and Knight were not Masons.

---

* The difference between the 69 per cent who were Masons and the 31 per cent combined Catholics and "neutrals," would, by Chi-square, occur by chance about 7.5 times in 100.

Ancestry, or Ethnic Composition

In Mobile Acres, as elsewhere,[13] there were feelings of varying intensity about differences in national origin. Talk of this was of course more open and crude on lower levels than on the higher,[14] but some feeling was common on all levels. Those in the groups least acceptable to the majority naturally missed nothing of the animus against them. Especially, low-level minority staff employees made the common lament of minority groups, "You've got to be twice as smart to get half as far." Obstructors were identified by the repeated charge that "there are too many Johnny Bulls and Kraut-eaters around here." At the work level one might find brunette Scottish, Welsh, Irish, Scandinavian, and German extractees referring to those (sometimes blond) of Italian, Polish, Slovak, and Lithuanian descent as "dagoes," "hunkies," and "wops." Thus both majority and minority members identified each other more, or as much, by personal knowledge sharpened by rivalry than by physical traits.

We have already referred to name changing. Workers and first-line foremen of Slavic origin were especially sensitive about their polysyllabic names and the related problem of spelling and pronunciation that brought ridicule on them. Several minority families developed permanent rifts over name changing by the children.

Resentment over failure to rise sometimes led minority persons openly to charge discrimination. Paul Sarto, a first-line foreman of Italian descent, despaired of becoming a general foreman and resented the fact that two German-born associates had reached that level. His resentment exploded during one of the weekly cost meetings held in his department after regular quitting time. Some thirty minutes into these meetings, he typically arose, announced he was going home, and left. On one occasion his chief, Ames, objected. Sarto answered:

> I've told you what I had to say and I've listened to you guys beat around the bush for half an hour after quitting time. I've got nothing to stick around here for. I'm not going any higher. I've got the wrong complexion to get any place. I'm going to stay right where I am regardless of how much I do. I don't want any hard feelings about it, but facts are facts. See you tomorrow.

The meaning of other cases was similar.

The alleged exclusive selection by ethnic stock was checked by studying the national origins, surnames, and birthplaces of the managers. This was done in part by personal knowledge, by checking with intimates to uncover name changes and get the family name, by use of personnel records, by free interviewing with doubtful persons, etc. The total

TABLE 8. THE ETHNIC CHARACTER OF MANAGEMENT

Ethnicity	Staff		Supts.		Gen. Fore.		Foremen		Total % in Sample
	No.	%	No.	%	No.	%	No.	%	
Anglo-Saxon	18	50	26	72.2	41	67.2	47	50.5	58.4
German	12	33.4	10	27.8	16	26.3	22	23.6	26.5
Scandinavian	5	13.9					10	10.8	6.6
Italian	1	2.7			2	3.3	3	3.2	2.6
Polish							4	4.3	1.8
French					1	1.6	3	3.2	1.8
Croat-Serb					1	1.6	2	2.2	1.3
Spanish							1	1.1	0.5
Negro							1	1.1	0.5
Total	36	100.0	36	100.0	61	100.0	93	100.0	100.0

members of each ethnic group and their percentages in each class of managers are shown in Table 8.

We see that Sarto was both wrong and right—2 Italians did make the grade of general foreman, but 16 German ethnics did also. The important thing for the minorities though, is that the Anglo-Saxons constituted at least half of each group of managers, that the German ethnics were next in number, and the two together made up all the superintendents. And the Anglo-German combination increased directly from bottom to top. In percentage the Anglo-Saxons were lower and the Germans higher in the staffs than elsewhere. Together they made up 83 per cent of that body, their lowest combined proportions in any group but the first-line foremen.

Differences* in the various levels leave little doubt that one's ethnic make-up was a factor in his success. But the differences take on still greater meaning when, as the Milo Catholics did, we look at Magnesia's ethnic pattern. Using a new city directory and making surnames† the gauge of national origin, a random sample showed the Anglo-Saxons to make up only 26 per cent, and the Germans 12 per cent, of Magnesia's

---

* Differences in percentages of Anglo-Saxons between first- and second-level foremen and between superintendents and first-line foremen were significant at the 5 per cent level. But between general foremen and superintendents the difference could have been due to chance nearly three times in ten.

† This device of course overlooked the extent to which names may have been changed and the fact that migration weakens the criterion. Since nearly all of Magnesia's Negro population had Anglo-Saxon names, all such names from the area in which Negroes resided were counted with the non-Anglo-Saxon and non-Germanic ethnics.

population.   And though only a minority of Milo's dominant ethnics were foreign born, the census data showed that this reservoir in Magnesia was also limited: those born in Germany and the British Isles together constituting less than 15 per cent of the city's population.   Thus ethnics composing probably less than 38 per cent of the community filled 85 per cent of Milo's advisory and directive forces.*

Membership in a Yacht Club

Discussions of outings, week-ends, the "blowouts" of past seasons, party planning at the Yacht Club, and plant gossip about the meaning of social activities there—all indicated that the Club was indeed a place where careers might be influenced.   In the next chapter we shall see the social significance of the Club as a community organization drawing on the materials and services of Milo and Fruhling for maintenance. Here we need to view the Club (a) as the less successful supervisors saw it, and (b) as it related to the managerial group in terms of the alleged bearing of membership in it on rank in Milo.   Milo managers

---

* Ethnic stratification has long been documented by students.   See, among many others, P. Sorokin, op. cit., pp. 11–128, 280–312; W. L. Warner and L. Srole, The Social Systems of American Ethnic Groups, Yale University Press, New Haven, 1947; R. M. MacIver and C. H. Page, Society: An Introductory Analysis, Rinehart and Co., New York, 1949, pp. 349–416; J. O. Hertzler, Society in Action, The Dryden Press, New York, 1954, pp. 232–234.   Selection by ethnic affinity, other things equal, is not of course confined to industry or to the present. My colleagues have pointed out to me cases in the academic world.   Barnard (Functions of the Executive, p. 224) notes the need, in order that men may function together, of using many social characteristics and personal traits as tests of fitness in selection.   Specific situations may stress some and exclude others. But these criteria, including "race, nationality, faith, politics, sectional ante-cedents," etc., represent "in [the] best sense the political aspects of personal relationships in formal organizations."   He believes these informal tests to be "most highly developed in political, labor, church, and university organizations," because "the intangible types of personal services are relatively more important in them than in . . . industrial organizations."

History is replete with cases of ethnic selection, even where there is zeal for reform as in the Emperor Diocletian's administrative reorganization in the third and fourth centuries.   With ability scattered through dozens of provinces, he, an Illyrian peasant, chose Maximian, of similar origin, for his co-Augustus.   For their subordinate Caesars they selected Constantius, of Illyrian origin; and Galerius, born in adjoining Thrace but tested in the service of Aurelian and Probus, two earlier Illyrian peasant emperors.   Whether or not Diocletian chose these associates explicitly because of the ethnic tie, there seems little doubt that their common backgrounds were assumed in some sense to give a common out-look, as well as the promise of deference to his judgment on doubtful questions. See the Cambridge Ancient History, Cambridge University Press, 1939, Vol. 12, pp. 200, 325–330.

had no exclusive control of the Club. The managers of Fruhling, Attica, and other firms, and high civic figures of Magnesia shared its social activities. The Club in effect was (*a*) an outpost of Milo social life (managers and aspirants), (*b*) a center for the city's unofficial interindustrial communication, and (*c*) a major bond between all the industries and the community.

Evans and Cunningham referred above to the Club, but others attacked it as the center for self-advancement for those who lacked "ability." The implication was that in the softening atmosphere of beach picnics, group swimming and water games, dancing in the pavilion with each other's wives and daughters; and in the small intimate gatherings for cruising and fishing, many ideal situations arose for making personal contacts and demands that extended to the plant.[15] These claims allegedly would be applied directly by climbers and reinforced by community figures intimate with both the aspirants and various high managers. The community career brokers included two former mayors, the leading bank president and several of his officials, lawyers, physicians, and various business leaders.

Activity in the Club was statistically less of a test for entry in management than was ethnic background and Masonic membership. Club activity aided the candidate who had other things in his favor. Hence we find that Milo members of the Club were less neatly ordered by rank than they were with respect to national origin and membership in the secret society.

One hundred fourteen Milo employees were members. This included 14 superintendents of whom Geiger was one and president of the Club, 24 general foremen, 29 first-line foremen, and 47 staff personnel. The latter group contained 14 officers in the sample, and 33 lower supervisory and nonsupervisory personnel outside the sample. With what we have seen of staff ambition and insecurity, the total of 47 suggests that staff people saw life in the Club as solid preparation for the future, but their greater preference for parties and clubbing (Chapter 4) must also be considered as a factor in their membership. Observation in the Club, and many casual but revealing remarks showed that freely given efforts to increase and maintain the Club's physical plant were not forgotten by higher officers pondering the future of this candidate as against that one.

Political Affiliation

As we noted in Chapter 4, all the managers were Republican in politics, or feigned to be as an essential for their success. Three conditions showed this. (1) With newspapers at hand representing the usual range of political views, the managers almost to a man carried a famous "isolationist" paper into the plant. (2) Discussions among managers favorable to Democratic ideologies were covert and occurred chiefly among first-line foremen. (3) All managers who at some time had served in public office did so as Republicans.

The fear of seeming not to meet this expectation was illustrated by Haupt's reaction (Chapter 4) to his subordinates who put the badge of a Democratic presidential candidate on his car. However his fear was no greater than that any of the middle and lower level managers would have felt in his situation. Wilkins' case (mentioned earlier) was well known. He found himself demoted "for talking too much," and part of the talk was open attacks on Republican ideology and supporters.

However, there were Democrats among the managers, including at least twenty-nine of the first-line foremen. Cunningham was exceptional in being a Democrat in middle management. When questioned as to how this squared with the typical feelings about the need of being a Republican, he replied:

> I *am* supposed to be a Republican. Don't get the idea I pop off to other people on politics the way I do to you. I'm just trying to help you with what you're doing. And don't think that they [top management] don't know you before you get to be a general supervisor! You've got to be a damn good actor or you don't get that far!

Bearing the stamp of an authentic Republican was in some cases an open-sesame to placement at high levels. Superintendent J. Lambert (not on chart) had held a political office for the Republican Party in Magnesia, and he had been state auditor for several years on the same ticket. On losing the auditorship to a Democrat he entered Milo, without industrial experience, as "chief"[16] of a department. The title was changed to superintendent two years later, though informants say he started with the salary of superintendent. Lambert's political experience and party loyalty filled his conversation. Many of his employees, known by their friends to be Democrats, felt coerced to echo his political sentiments to escape suspicion of holding contrary views. Their friends ridiculed them for having "no guts."

Milo also employed the county auditor following his defeat after five successive terms on the Republican ticket. He too lacked industrial experience and specific training for his Milo post, but was made assistant staff supervisor at once and general supervisor six years later. Without supporting evidence, informants made much of the probable ties between the earlier political roles of these officers and tax assessments on Milo properties, with the implication that Milo was indebted to them. Since these were the only cases of this kind, it is not known whether persons of similar experience but other political leanings would have been chosen in this way or not.

Assuming that Republican dogma reflected the convictions of Republican managers, one can see how a theory of private enterprise would operate in career activities to resist or evade formal step-by-step procedures for advancement.

DISCUSSION AND CONCLUSIONS

Use of unofficial tests of fitness for entry and rise through the levels should not imply that appointing officers are interested only, or even primarily, in the aspirants meeting these tacit standards. The problem is more complex. The replacement of Lane by Rees, the choice of Blanke over Taylor, the movement of Schwann, the manipulation of Jackson, the use of sinecures, etc., all indicate concern with ability in the sense of getting the job done with minimum disturbance for the organization. Talent to carry on in this vaguely pragmatic way was understood to be a requirement in all selections. Certainly no superior at Milo or elsewhere would want a subordinate in a responsible position who could not passably meet both stated and tacit expectations. This basic competence was understood, despite occasional errors in the judging and selecting of candidates.

Why, then, the use of informal standards of fitness? Milo chiefs were like Reynolds of Attica, Jessup of Fruhling, and several executives cited by Ginzberg in having little interest or belief in the merit of formal selection. Even where there is interest, the means usually proposed do not measure what is essential.[17] Dimock's[18] contention that the executive must be a "tactitian and a philosopher," a "statesman," and a "responsible manipulator," is relevant for our data, but these concepts have not been formalized into schemes for appraisal of executives. These labels refer to varieties of leadership the meaning of which often varies with the speaker.[19]

Barnard's[20] discussion of leadership continues to be one of the most penetrating. He is concerned with the executive's problem in making personnel changes. Any change is likely to bring demand for more change when individuals and groups are competing for advantage and reward on the assumption that all are equally able and deserving. Dealing with the democratic situation, in which subordinates have the right to talk back and to do something about their dissatisfactions, requires political skills in addition to formal competence. However open discussion of differences in this respect is taboo because of potential discord, loss of confidence among members, etc.

Nevertheless higher officers must consider the capacity of competing candidates to utilize and aid necessary cliques, control dangerous ones, etc. Too often the search for men who combine formal competence with this unspecified skill throws a top officer into despair. He is likely to put a premium on "loyalty" in terms of the candidate's seeing the job as he does. Wittingly or not, he begins to look for attitudes like his own as assuring a basis for understanding and cooperation. But he knows the difficulty of getting at the disposition and probable behavior of untried and artful people, however overwhelming their credentials. Hence at varying levels of conscious purpose, the appointing chief gropes for more valid marks of loyalty. This does not of course mean that he does not value subordinates who on occasion differ with him.

With considerable scientific support, his search moves on the assumption that those with qualities and interests like his own will think as he does. Hence in his quandary he finds it good that the prospective candidate is also Irish, went to such-and-such a school, came from a "good" family (socioeconomically like his own),[21] and has civic activities and recreational tastes similar to his own. These likenesses would naturally not be advanced as proofs of fitness in general discussion, but tacitly or unconsciously they predispose judges to see the prospect as one with a "good job outlook" and readiness to act jointly on critical issues.* Moved by these pleasing characteristics, the desperate personnel assessor may easily overlook other qualities. He receives every encouragement from the ambitious and "highly visible" subordinate who is probing for ways to please, and for marks he can copy to show the chief how much they have in common.† This aggressive self-advertisement

---

* See Bicknell's remarks above on Masonry.

† Stein frankly stated that he became a member of Hardy's church because he "thought it would help." He pointed to others who variously followed the practice. Currying of favor by simulated likenesses is immemorial. In his *Letters* to his son (especially the letters of May 11, June 26, November 11 and 16, 1752—in Dobrée ed.) Chesterfield confidentially recommended it, and he successfully practiced it. Machiavelli openly advocated it (*Discourses,* Bk. 2, D. 2), but was much less successful in practicing it than his contemporary Guicciardini, the historian, who publicly denounced it but privately advised it (H. Butterfield, *The Statecraft of Machiavelli,* Macmillan, New York, 1956, p. 115). Hazlitt attacked it (*e.g.,* the essay, "On Patronage and Puffing"), and suffered from his refusal to practice it. Writing on industrial organization, as an active executive, Willkie (*A Rebel Yells,* D. Van Nostrand Co., New York, 1946, p. 191) declares that "all men tend to ape those above them in the hope of becoming socially and professionally acceptable." Also see the systematic comments of Samuel Haig Jameson, "Principles of Social Interaction," *American Sociological Review,* 10: 6–10, February, 1945.

and social mimicry may quite naturally be interpreted as a sign of the desired political skill. Certainly it indicates strong desire and a will to succeed which can push the inert excellence of other candidates out of the picture. But such behavior is not a guarantee of executive finesse, and may well indeed conceal the lack of it as well as other necessary qualities. It is thus quite possible for the highly visible appointee to be attitudinally out of step with his sponsors, and yet misleadingly appear to have been lifted by favoritism based on his successful mimicry. He may of course fit both the formal and informal tests and still fail if the official criteria are not based on what is needed in the executive role.

Willkie,[22] however, fears that all such aping is likely to get out of control. The "powerful executive" surrounds himself with "a corps of hardened yes-men . . . who pick up ideas from their superior, amplify them, and parrot them impressively. . . ." In industry an "unconscious conspiracy" develops "a strong, secret, and tacit organization which maintains itself by accepting only those with similar ideas, or those friends, relatives, and class-conscious equals who can be counted on to support the hierarchy."[23]

Without being an apologist, one must note that this condition is the ultimate consequence of selection purely on the basis of social traits; it is not true of all industry,* nor confined to industry, nor inevitable. As a "rebel," Willkie is of course overstating what has always been present in varying degrees in most organizations in the more complex societies. It is pedantic even to mention that this can be documented voluminously by various students. Obviously an industrial firm is fossilizing when selective criteria—as any set of attitudes and characteristics—become ends in themselves. However when concern with social traits is limited to avoidance of what would be blatantly negative items to most members, the threat to the organization is much less than the other extreme of focus on purely formal qualifications. A fetish of formal tests can lead to their use as a blind to prevent charges of favoritism.[24] Employed with this intent, status-givers may still (a) select with attention to formal and social skills as without the test, and at the same time (b) adroitly inject various personal, cultural, and ethnic preferences to maintain a "balance of power" among two or more factions. Here, as elsewhere, men can decide what they want and then wilfully reason their way to a conclusion.

Those concerned to avoid this might first limit the pool of candidates to the technically fit,[25] so that the final focus can identify those most

---

* Since about three-eighths of the Milo managers had relevant formal training, and most of them had years of industrial experience, this was not true there despite the weight of informal factors.

able to deal with internal tensions and the more subtle phases of group actions.

This dual focus promises (a) more judgment and less moral anguish in those who must communicate things forbidden to the dignity of formal channels,[26] and gives (b) some assurance of the approximate homogeneity basic to ready cooperation.[27]

Despite mountains of print on the subject, there are still no generally accepted indexes of competence in office. We cannot say how much of what develops after a decision is the result of the decision maker's insights, and how much arises from unassessed factors in the ongoing complex. Some executives[28] see the situation as so ambiguous that "most people don't live long enough to get blame or credit" for their decisions, and that one's decisions may never be proved wrong.[29] Drucker[30] expects a steady increase in the time-span for testing a decision, and even stronger, Urwick[31] feels that an indefinite future is required to tell the effects of a decision.

Our showing the minor role of formal as compared with informal factors does not mean that no effective managers* made the grade at Milo, or that if they did, it was by chance. Certainly not. For if we see the able executive as one who inspires confidence, who finds a way where apparently none existed and adapts rules without destroying their intent, who balances official and unofficial claims with minimum damage to himself and the organization, then Hardy, Ames, Dicke, Boesel, Meier, Geiger, Blanke, Springer, and others were competent leaders who met the informal tests as well as the few explicit formal requirements. On the other hand, Stevens, Taylor, Smith, Revere, Ruf, and O'Brien were lesser leaders—by this standard—who met the ethnic and Masonic test (excepting Stevens), but did not meet the subtler requirements of sharing off-the-job activities that interlocked with those of the community. Certainly they did not meet the expectation that they effectively move in and out of clique activities as necessary, and compromise readily on smaller things to preserve greater ones. To push the theory, their high visibility and smiling haste to meet the more obvious informal requirements led to overevaluation of their fitness, relative to the other group.

Since higher officers eventually move, die, or retire, obviously no specific social earmarks can be fixed, however much a given set may

---

* In terms of profits and dividends paid, Milo was definitely successful and presumably well-managed. However, one former "insider" in another industry declares that if capital and market are large enough, a firm may be a "huge financial success" and hide the fact that it is poorly managed. See T. K. Quinn, "Sovereign State of G.M.," *The Nation*, May 26, 1956, pp. 447–448.

be the focus of imitation today. Given the internal struggles that play around every important replacement, there is each time some unavoidable departure from the current balance of formal and informal factors. As at Milo, gradual changes over thirty years converted the item of a Catholic majority to a minority and a Masonic minority to a majority.

In terms of democratic theory, any set of informal requirements may become discriminatory. And when they are made ends in themselves, they certainly become undemocratic. But when controlled, they are likely to form a basis for cooperative effort. Men need not like each other to cooperate, and people with similar characteristics may dislike each other. But mutual liking—which is more probable when key characteristics and viewpoints are similar—assures a cooperative tie that formal selection and guidance, with all its merits, cannot guarantee.

Movement up any organizational ladder is subject to many influences outside individual and official control. Among these are (*a*) the effects of rivalries for personal success; (*b*) the limited number of positions; (*c*) the loose and shifting nature of our society, which weakens existing formal means of ascent and biases personnel against new ones; (*d*) the unavoidable influence of personal feelings in any interacting group; and (*e*) the clash of individual and organizational interests, which minimizes the official ways of getting up and encourages the unofficial.

DOCUMENTARY NOTES

1. See for example, such reports as "The Nine Hundred," *Fortune,* 42 (5) 132–135, November, 1952; William Miller, ed., *Men in Business: Essays in the History of Entrepreneurship,* Harvard University Press, Cambridge, 1952; F. W. Taussig and C. S. Joslyn, *American Business Leaders: A Study in Social Origins and Social Stratification,* Macmillan, New York, 1932; Suzanne I. Keller, "Social Origins and Career Lines of Three Generations of American Business Leaders," Columbia University Ph.D. Thesis, New York, 1954; C. Wright Mills, "The American Business Elite: A Collective Portrait," *The Tasks of Economic History,* Supplement V to *The Journal of Economic History,* December, 1945; Eli Ginzberg, ed., *What Makes an Executive?,* Columbia University Press, New York, 1955; Mabel Newcomer, *The Big Business Executive,* Columbia University Press, New York, 1955; W. Lloyd Warner and J. C. Abegglen, *Occupational Mobility in American Business and Industry,* University of Minnesota Press, Minneapolis, Minn., 1955, and the same data prepared for the nonprofessional reader, *Big Business Leaders in America,* Harper and Brothers, New York, 1955.

2. See also "The Nine Hundred," *loc. cit.;* Delbert C. Miller, "The Seattle Business Leader," *Pacific Northwest Business,* College of Business Administration, University of Washington, 15: 5–12, 1956; Gordon F. Lewis and C. Arnold

Anderson, "Social Origins and Social Mobility of Businessmen in an American City," reprinted from *Transactions of the Third World Congress of Sociology,* 3: 253–266, 1956.

3. Delbert C. Miller and William H. Form, *Industrial Sociology,* Harper and Brothers, New York, 1951, pp. 717–774; C. Wright Mills, *The Power Elite,* Oxford University Press, New York, 1945, chap. 6, p. 386.

4. Wallace B. Donham, *Education for Responsible Living,* Harvard University Press, Cambridge, 1944; Chester Barnard, "Education for Executives," *The Journal of Business of the University of Chicago,* 18: 175–182, 1945; H. Frederick Willkie, *A Rebel Yells,* D. Van Nostrand Co., New York, chaps. 12, 14–24, 1946; W. H. Whyte, Jr., *The Organization Man,* Simon and Schuster, Inc., New York, 1956, p. 79.

5. See T. V. Smith, "In Accentuation of the Negative," *The Scientific Monthly,* 63: 463–469, December, 1946, and his scintillating little book, *The Ethics of Compromise,* Starr King Press, Boston, 1956. Also pertinent here is chap. 12 in Ralph Barton Perry, *Realms of Value,* Harvard University Press, Cambridge, 1954.

6. P. F. Drucker, *The Practice of Management,* Harper and Brothers, New York, 1954, pp. 154–155, admits this condition is widespread in industry. C. Wright Mills, *The Power Elite,* Oxford University Press, New York, 1956, pp. 133–134, 386, contends that corporate careers in America are not "bureaucratic" in the sense of regular upward movement by virtue of specific fitness and examination at each step. Studies touching this topic in government agencies include Peter Blau, *The Dynamics of Bureaucracy,* University of Chicago Press, 1954; R. G. Francis and R. C. Stone, *Service and Procedure in Bureaucracy,* University of Minnesota Press, Minneapolis, 1956.

7. Robert K. Merton, "The Unanticipated Consequences of Purposive Social Action," *American Sociological Review,* 1: 894–904, December, 1936.

8. C. I. Barnard, *Functions of the Executive,* Harvard University Press, Cambridge, 1945, p. 224.

9. Ginzberg, *op. cit.,* p. 62.

10. Perrin Stryker et al., *A Guide to Modern Management Methods,* McGraw-Hill Book Co., New York, 1954, pp. 259–261.

11. See the comments of Donald E. Super, *The Psychology of Careers,* Harper and Brothers, New York, 1957, p. 134, on the use of informal criteria in research designs.

12. Everett C. Hughes, "Queries Concerning Industry and Society Growing Out of Study of Ethnic Relations in Industry," *American Sociological Review,* 14: 218–220, 1949.

13. Orvis Collins, "Ethnic Behavior in Industry: Sponsorship and Rejection in a New England Factory," *American Journal of Sociology,* 51: 293–298, 1946; Everett C. Hughes and Helen M. Hughes, *Where Peoples Meet,* The Free Press, Glencoe, Ill., 1952.

14. See comment on the effects of "spurious tolerance" and "human-relations mindedness" in the organizations of today. Charles H. Coates and Roland J. Pellegrin, "Executives and Supervisors: Informal Factors in Differential Bureaucratic Promotion," *Administrative Science Quarterly,* 2, No. 2, September, 1957, pp. 212 ff.

15. For discussion of the weight of informal situations in decision-making, see Floyd Hunter, *Community Power Structure,* University of North Carolina Press,

Chapel Hill, 1953, and "The Decision-Makers," *The Nation,* August 21, 1954, pp. 148–150.

16. *Chief* was his title. The term was rare at Milo, though I have used it loosely throughout the book as synonymous with *department head* and *superintendent.*

17. Aubrey Silberston, *Education and Training for Industrial Management,* Management Publications, Ltd. The Millbrook Press, Ltd., London, 1955, p. 6 ff.; Ginzberg, *op. cit.,* pp. 164–165.

18. M. E. Dimock, *The Executive in Action,* Harper and Brothers, New York, 1945, pp. 4–5, 8, 65–66.

19. See the introduction in Alvin Gouldner, ed., *Studies in Leadership,* Harper and Brothers, New York, 1950; P. Selznick, "An Approach to a Theory of Bureaucracy," *American Sociological Review,* 8: 51–54, February, 1943; R. Tannenbaum, V. Kallejian, I. R. Weschler, "Training Managers for Leadership," *Personnel,* 30 (no. 4), 2–8, January, 1954; L. Urwick, *The Pattern for Management,* University of Minnesota Press, Minneapolis, 1956, pp. 56–73; Dimock, *op. cit.,* pp. 195–205.

20. C. I. Barnard, *Organization and Management,* Harvard University Press, Cambridge, 1948, pp. 24–47.

21. See the provocative, humorous, and over-neat book of W. H. Whyte, Jr., *Is Anybody Listening?,* Simon and Schuster, New York, 1952. And on the influence of family at the start of industrial careers in a southern metropolitan area, see Coates and Pellegrin, *op. cit.,* pp. 200–215.

22. Willkie, *op. cit.,* p. 186.

23. *Ibid.,* p. 188.

24. Ginzberg, *op. cit.,* pp. 74–75.

25. Drucker, *op. cit.,* pp. 154–155.

26. Barnard, *Functions of the Executive,* Harvard University Press, Cambridge, 1938, p. 225.

27. *Ibid.,* pp. 147, 224; E. Dale in Kruisinga, *op. cit.,* p. 33; Stryker, *op. cit.,* p. 259.

28. Ginzberg, *op. cit.,* p. 126.

29. *Ibid.,* pp. 128–129.

30. Drucker, *op. cit.,* p. 15.

31. Urwick, *op. cit.,* p. 31.

CHAPTER 7

The Interlocking of Official
and Unofficial Reward

PROBLEMS OF LANGUAGE AND DEFINITION

In chapters 3 through 6 we repeatedly saw cases of unofficial favor-bartering and of one-sided rewarding. Like the ongoing action, and buried in it, these rewards are fitful and expedient. They accompany the informal phases of many settlements to smooth the way for action, to bind cliques, to cement larger groups, and to heal ruptures. We saw in the preceding chapter how official compensation in the form of salaries admits of irregular variation in the firm's effort to reward uncommon merit.* Nevertheless the obstacle of formal controls, and limits to the proportion of organizational resources that can go into salaries, often forces unofficial use of company materials and services as supplementary rewards for variable contributions from people on the same level, and from the same person at different times.

Use of materials and services for personal ends, individual or group, is, of course, officially forbidden, for in both plant theory and popular

---

* Drucker recognizes the internal pressures for more elastic rewards in noting that "the salary system should never be so rigid as to exclude special rewards for 'performance over and above the call of duty.'" See *The Practice of Management,* Harper and Brothers, New York, 1954, p. 152.

usage this is *theft*. But our concern to pinpoint the informal phases of administration where possible requires scrutiny of this generally known but taboo subject.

Such practices are as delicate to discuss as they are to apply. For as long as rivalries can generate "reasons" there will be double talk around the concept of "reward," especially in organizations that stress "fair-dealing," "job evaluation," "merit-rated salaries," etc. The dynamics of individual and group action do not require that one agree fully with those who say that no word[1] ever has the same meaning twice, but they do demand that one recognize the difficulties of assigning absolute meanings to terms describing the kinds of situations we are dealing with.[2] What in some sense is theft, may, in the context of preserving the group and solving present problems, lose much or all of its odious overtones. We only need note the gradations of terms referring to theft to suspect this. As theft requires more ingenuity, becomes larger in amount, and is committed by more distinguished persons (whose power is often related to their importance in the operation of society), its character is correspondingly softened by such velvety terms as *misappropriation, embezzlement,* and *peculation,* which often require special libraries to define. To spare the living[3] and some of the recent dead, and to ignore differences in time and place, we can point to Cellini—and remember Pope Paul III's judgment of him that "men like Benvenuto, unique in their profession, are not bound by the laws"—Aretino, Casanova, and even Voltaire. These men were all scoundrels of a kind who, nevertheless, were esteemed for their commendable contributions to society.

Always there are genuine transitional nuances, with debatable margins, between covert internal theft and tacit inducement or reward. Immemorially the esteemed personality who also performs unique services can move closer to "theft" than others without censure.

MANAGERIAL MOTIVATION

To talk of rewarding is to talk of motivation, and students declare, and show by their disagreement, that little is known of managerial motivation.[4] Distinguished executives and specialized students admit that the whole subject of reward is so dynamic that attempts either rigidly to define motivation,[5] or specifically to reward managers[6] are both likely to go amiss.

Our data have shown that what is a reward for one man is not for another[7] (Bingham, in Chapter 3); that the rank a manager craves at one time, he rejects at another (Evans, Revere); that the same inducements cannot be given to all on a given level because of differences in ability and demand for reward (Hardy); uses of the office of assistant-to, etc.;[8] that the organization's contact with the community may demand greater reward for some managers than for others; that "power struggles" are forbidden but do occur and must be disguised;[9] and that more than financial reward is necessary.[10] We know that some managers are more venturesome and more inclined to "play the game" than others are.[11] This may mean unexpected errors, losses, and gains for the organization. In any case such managers must have greater resources and rewards than rigid planning will allow.[12] We saw in Chapter 3 that Milo managers were concerned to maintain social as well as productive mechanisms, and that, in addition to the use of materials and services for this purpose, they juggled accounts to (a) allow full and part-time employment of the friends and relatives of plant and community associates, to (b) justify plush offices stemming from their rivalries, and to (c) keep a margin, or kind of "slush fund," in the naval sense, for emergencies—social and mechanical.

Although these practices may vary among cultures and inside a given culture,[13] and with the size, age and financial state of a firm,[14] as well as by industry,[15] they nevertheless occur widely and point to further problems for the manager who deals with other firms or other plants of his own corporation; we have but to recall Geiger's problems from having his unit compared with that of the Colloid plant.

As a result of these gaps between the inherent limitations of formal reward and the obscure complex of activities that must be rewarded, an organization's services and materials, designed for its official functioning, are repeatedly drawn on to fill the breach. Used injudiciously, this may lead to plunder.

THEFT: REAL AND QUESTIONABLE

Before we present cases, let us admit the probably universal existence of internal theft, individual and organized, that is more damaging than helpful to the firm and that would strain the term to be called reward for specific contributions. Various informants report almost incredible cases of empire-building with minimum functions or contributions for many members; of favors and perquisites granted to some for no obvious important service in return; organized pilfering rights—including regular paid frolics for some of the company's members as "representatives" or "spokesmen" at some "event"; and the purely personal use of plant resources under the guise of "community relations," and sometimes not honored with a pretext. This is reported as common in some of the large firms doing contracted work for various governmental bodies where, as we saw in Chapter 5, the pressure for economy is less.

There is, of course, widespread individual theft in which tools, clerical supplies, home fixtures, etc., are taken for personal use without the knowledge of superiors or concern for one's group or the organization, and which could not be justified in case of detection. Similar internal theft by subgroups and cliques, with lifting-license tied so closely to rank that stealing beyond one's station is punished by death, can occur even in sacred organizations.[16] Civic bodies of antiquity were similarly tapped by members.[17]

Theft may also be enforced in the group and occur systematically over a long period. For example, in a small cabinet factory in the Mobile Acres region, the employees of one department, on piece-rate pay, regularly turned in more pieces than they actually completed, and coerced newcomers to do the same to protect old hands.

Between theft and informal reward is the gray-green practice of expense-accounting, which is also related to rank. "Theft" is softened to "abuse of privilege," but the feeling of some companies is clear in their demands for explanations. Others, however, including those sensitive to the tax factor, see large accounts as "part of the man's compensation," or as necessary to "attract and hold top men," or as a practice comparable to the "employee medical program."[18]

One organization reflects this attitude in its contract with a well-known top executive. After defining his duties and authority, the company says that:

> During the continuance of the employment of [the executive] hereunder he shall be paid a weekly salary of Twenty-five Hundred ($2500) Dollars, and in addition a weekly general expense allowance of Five Hundred ($500) Dollars which shall not include travelling expenses or other items generally related thereto, which shall also be paid by the Company. There shall be no abatement or diminution of the compensation or expense allowance of [the executive] during such time, if any, as he may fail to perform the services required to be performed by him hereunder solely because of illness or physical incapacity even though such illness or incapacity may prevent the performance by him of any duties whatsoever for a period up to six consecutive months. . . . [If the executive shall be required to change headquarters around the Company operating areas he shall receive] such suitable office accommodations and such clerical and other assistance as shall, from time to time, be reasonably required by him, and of such type, character and extent as shall be consistent with the position of Chief Executive Officer of the Company. . . . [He] shall receive fair and reasonable vacations with pay, commensurate with the position and duties undertaken by him hereunder.[19]

Coercion in expense-accounting can function as in the cabinet factory cited above. An informant from an optical company reports that lower-ranking, and obviously less imaginative, employees who rarely used expense accounts were not permitted by higher-ranking members to list their costs exactly. Rather they were forced to inflate the report, sometimes very much, so as not to "show-up the fat accounts" of the habitual users. Internal coercion to protect one's own masquerade might at times be justified, but apparently was not in this case.

Though parallel cases only at times, feather-bedding by labor, and the various professional and managerial practices embracing pay-backs, split-fees and rebates,[20] also lie in this twilight area.

UNOFFICIAL INCENTIVES

In crossing the middle ground between understood theft of materials and their controlled use as inducements and rewards, one must always fight the sheep-or-goat concept of truth. Responsible persons who succeed in this apparently broaden the system of rewards and are able to stimulate those not lured by standard appeals, or who also require other[21] incentives for greater effort.

Individual

Because of the tacit stress on flexibility and supplementation of the more common inducements, unofficial reward is naturally directed more toward specific contributions and situations than toward rank as such. But obviously if such reward is not confidential, or if it is known and not justified in the minds of others, it is likely to follow formal rank and become systematic theft of the kind we noted above.

Although informal reward ideally is given for effort and contribution beyond what is expected of a specific rank, it is also granted for many other purposes, often unexpected and formally taboo yet important for maintaining the organization and winning its ends. For example, it may be given (1) in lieu of a promotion or salary increase that could not be effected; (2) as a bonus for doing necessary but unpleasant or low-prestige things; (3) as an opiate to forget defeats in policy battles or status tiffs; (4) as a price for conciliating an irate colleague or making, in effect, a treaty with another department; (5) as a perquisite to key persons in clerical or staff groups to prevent slowdowns, and to bolster alertness against errors during critical periods; (6) as a frank supplement to a low but maximum salary; (7) for understanding and aid in the operation, and the defense, of the unofficial incentive system; (8) for great personal sacrifices. There are, of course, more subtle supports which may not be articulated but are intuitively recognized and rewarded where possible. These include: ability to maintain morale in the group or department; skill in picking and holding good subordinates; habitual tacit understanding of what superiors and colleagues expect but would not in some cases want to phrase, even unofficially; and expertness in saving the face of superiors and maintaining the dignity of the organization under adverse conditions. This last may be aptness in masking and supporting the fictions essential for regulation of error, and in perpetuating symbols considered necessary by the dominant group.[22]

These performances are not exhaustive and may overlap in the same person. There is no fixed tie either, of course, between services rendered and the kind of material reward or privilege granted. Though we are confining our discussion to positive rewards, there are also negative ones, such as exemptions from rules binding on others, which, as we noted in Chapter 5, was but one in the first-line foreman's repertory of inducements for production workers.

Though his general contributions were great, the Milo foreman, Kustis (Chapter 5), illustrates the privileges given for personal sacrifice. Kustis dropped his Catholicism, from choice but with suffering, to become a Mason and thus demonstrate his fealty and fitness. His freedom to "feed gravy jobs" to his brother was outlined in Chapter 5. But with the knowledge of his superiors, he built a machine shop in his home, largely from Milo materials. He equipped his drill press, shaper, and lathe with cutters and drills from Milo. He supplemented these with bench equipment, such as taps, reamers, dies, bolts and screws. Finally, piece by piece and day by day he removed a retired grinder from his shop. Normally such tools were sent to another department or unit of the corporation.

Ted Berger, officially foreman of Milo's carpenter shop, was *sub rosa* a custodian and defender of the supplementary reward system. Loyal beyond question, he was allowed great freedom from formal duties and expected, at least through the level of department heads, to function as a clearinghouse for the system. His own reward was both social and material, but his handling of the system unintentionally produced a social glue that bound together people from various levels and departments. Not required to operate machines, Berger spent a minimum of six hours daily making such things as baby beds, storm windows, garage windows, doll buggies, rocking horses, tables, meat boards, and rolling pins. These objects were custom built for various managers. European-born,* Berger was a craftsman and eager to display his skills. However,

---

* In a study of production workers on piece rate in a plant of Mobile Acres, I earlier indicated some of the differences in feeling for craftsmanship between European-apprenticed and American-born workers. See "Worker Response and Social Background," *Journal of Political Economy,* 55: 323–332, August, 1947.

his American-born associates with their folklore of "one good turn deserves another," often gave him a "fee" for his work. Since everyone knew his thirst, these gifts* were usually wines, ranging from homemade "Dago Red" to choice imported varieties. But he also accepted dressed fowl, preferably duck and turkey. In some cases he made nothing, but used his influence to aid with a problem. In other cases he found a place in his department for the summer employment of someone's son, and again usually he received some unspoken favor. The transfer effect of these exchanges needs no elaboration.

Jim Speier, one of Peters' (formal chart) foremen, gave Peters great support in the latter's conflicts with Taylor. An understanding foreman and bulwark of the unofficial directorate, he made great use of both the structural and carpenter shops with Blanke's approval. He had a wood and steel archway for his rose garden prefabricated in the plant, and removed it piecemeal. Incentive-appliers estimated that exclusive of materials† the time spent on this object would have made its cost at least $400, in terms of the hourly charging rate. Also in Berger's shop, Speier had fourteen storm windows made, and a set of wooden lawn sprinklers cut in the form of dancing girls and brightly painted. For use on his farm, Speier had a stainless steel churn made that cost over a hundred and fifty dollars by the charging rate. In the same shop Speier had several cold-pack lifting pans made, also of stainless steel. According to self-styled experts on such matters, the design and workmanship of these pans was superior to anything obtainable on the market. Incentive-appliers declared that the welding, brazing, grinding, and polishing costs made the pans "worth their weight in gold."

Pete Merza, a general foreman in Springer's division, was given enough freedom in the use of building materials that his reward was seen by some—ignorant of his unofficial contributions—as approaching theft. Like Kustis, he had withdrawn from the Church to become a

---

* A colleague suggests that this "looks like bribery." It is hardly that. Rather these gifts were gestures of good will, and in some cases substitutes for favors due that could not be exchanged in the course of carrying out regular duties. One can argue that people were being persuaded to violate their official duties. With no more casuistry one can also argue that "bribes" of this kind contribute to the carrying out of official duties, and that, inside varying and debatable limits, they are a legitimate cost for the maintenance of solidarity. This is not to deny that bribery occurs in industry, as elsewhere (Flynn, *Graft in Business*, The Vanguard Press, New York, 1931, pp. 55–76), or that bestowal of gifts cannot be bribery. See "Should Companies Give?" *Newsweek*, December 24, 1956, pp. 59–60.

† No estimate was made of the cost of materials, since many of these came from the scrap pile and would have been discarded anyway.

Mason, but this was more a gesture than a personal sacrifice for him. An inimitably warm and helpful person acceptable to all factions, he was really rewarded as Milo's peacemaker in the clashes between Operation and Maintenance. Informants stated that he "carried out several hundred dollars worth" of bricks and cement and used Milo bricklayers on company time to build much, or most, of his house.

In another Milo case, reorganization dropped two general foremen to the first-line level. At that time, salary decreases followed automatically. Since the two men did not wish to continue at Milo as first-line foremen, they were put in charge of warehouses as positions there opened. They understood that discreet use of nails, paint, brushes, plumbing and electric fixtures, safety shoes, etc., was acceptable as long as inventories balanced.

Unofficial rewards are of course given for uncovering *pure* theft and misuse of materials. But this calls for internal espionage, which is a harrowing and impossible role for some people. This informal role of theft intelligencer is essential in many organizations. House detectives, various guards, and company police are the conventional guardians in business and industry. But this official role advertises itself. Everyone knows who to watch, and many resent the implications of being watched. Those who play the formal role of guard and investigator are not only likely to be compromised in various ways (see below), but they cannot function at the expected level of efficiency. For as they begin to accomplish official purposes they become the focus of informal attack and are made aware that they can be put in a bad light, as Bingham was (Chapter 3) from the outset. The theft intelligencer compensates for this defect. Simultaneously filling a formal role,* he must be one who has the tact and address to conceal his role of developing intimacies to discover misuse of materials.

At Milo, such investigations were usually carried on by selected persons in both staff and line. However as rule-makers and refiners who had to justify their existence, staff groups were especially eager to avoid blots on their professional escutcheons. Meeting this inherent perspective of the staff role limited the means of unofficially rewarding staff people. Materials and services would usually be inconsistent as a reward. Hence the staff agent who successfully carried out "intelligence" assignments was usually given his next promotion six months early, which admirably fitted *his* needs, and job logic.

---

* In diplomacy, the old role of papal *legatus a latere* was similar in the sense that a formal role, usually that of cardinal, embraced a confidential unofficial function.

Some inducements were both rewards and rights, but for different people. For example, what was at first a reward to some younger officer grew with his rank and seniority into a right which he in turn doled out judiciously as a reward to demanding subordinates.* Services and materials from the company garage, and long distance telephone calls were among the items spread along this axis of reward-rights. Line officers in good standing above the level of general foreman, and certain anointed staff figures including Rees at Milo and Reynolds at Attica, frequently, if not regularly, filled their gas tanks from company stock and received car servicing including washing and waxing. Rank was exercised, with the understanding for all that interference with garage personnel and use of materials culminating in defective operation or tie-up of company trucks and tractors, or accidents of any kind attributable to such interference, would threaten or even cut off reward-rights. As the balance of rewards and rights became too heavy with rights, inevitable crackdowns cut the rights and led higher executives to call on skilled machinists from the shops, instead of garage personnel, to give tune-ups, minor repairs, etc. Machinists in a sense shared these rewards and rights by (*a*) escape from repetitive work; (*b*) association with superiors whom they never met socially and seldom officially; (*c*) the privilege of taking Lincolns and Cadillacs out of the plant for "trial-spins" after tune-ups, and driving home "on company time" to take their wives shopping and "be seen." All time of machinists in such activity was of course charged to their regular jobs.

The axis of reward-right has another common phase: some executives ambiguously feel a "right" to use materials and services whether granted or not, and if questioned would defend their practice as a due reward. These are the managers who put in much overtime (emergencies, meetings, etc.) without extra compensation, and who resent the time-and-a-half overtime pay of hourly-paid workers, and who assist in compiling and circulating lists of these workers whose annual incomes exceed, say, six thousand dollars. Frequently these are also the officers who angrily agree that the organization owns them and in turn, quite within the range of normal madness, protest a counter ownership of its resources. These

---

* Naturally, friendship was sometimes a consideration in meeting pressure from below. But where demands were made without significant contribution—and in the tone of "a right to share"—the "reward" given was sometimes a disguised penalty. At Attica one such aggressive person demanded a "share" of the house paint he knew others had received. He was given all the usual bulk-purchased and unmixed ingredients—except the drying fluid. Elated, he mixed and applied the paint. When it did not dry, the accumulations of dust and insects ruined his work. He became a laughing-stock without recourse.

managers would say, sociologically, that unofficial demands call for unofficial rewards. Where people have been "oversold" by higher management's attempt to win their identification, they may of course expect greater reward than they receive and resort to supplementation.

Use of materials to supplement low salary is apparently rather common in some of the smaller firms that are less formalized and less able to pay incomes comparable to those of larger companies. In the Argo Transit Company, a firm of two hundred employees, several of the office force were variously rewarded to keep them from moving elsewhere. One individual who had reached the top pay bracket, was given an extra day off each week with pay. Another person, considered as an indispensable secretary, was each week given any half-day off she desired with pay. Since she sewed much for her family and was the only secretary in that office, she did most of her handwork there in connection with sewing. She also did all her letter writing on the job and used company materials and stamps. Use of stamps at Christmas time amounted to a bonus. As she was expected to conceal her unofficial pay and to guard the box from other employees, she evidently also received a certain psychic reward. As a practice this is of course not new. Saintly Charles Lamb, known to have hated his job at the East India Company, used his employer's time and materials and franked letters to his friends, whom he requested to write collect to him. This was probably understood and acceptable, and was not a positive reward as in the case above.

An X-ray technician—of unknown quality—in a general hospital reported that his salary was so low he was "expected to steal hams and canned food" from the hospital supplies to supplement it. Though not in the same hospital, this may be related to the Midwestern hospital thefts nationally reported in October, 1953. There many additional items were taken, but the thefts may have started as an internal reward system and then have grown to a pilfering right extending to outside persons. The typical internal use of materials is suggested by the defense of one of the hospital attendants who allegedly said she had "never seen a hospital where they didn't take things," and the hospital administrator's apparent knowledge of the thefts and reluctance to intervene.

Evidently leaks of information at the technician's hospital transformed the plan of salary supplementation into a problem of theft. For one person rewarded by the informal plan was also unofficially paid for his suggestion for keeping the system in bounds. Despite its obvious complications, his proposal that nurses leave the hospital by the rear exit was accepted. As they passed through this door their clothing and bundles were inspected. But professional indignation and the rights of rank ended the inspection when one nurse objected that she had worked there "twenty years only to be reduced to sharing the scrub woman's entrance!"

Unofficial Incentives for the Group

Berger's remarks above indicated the private use of work groups by some Milo managers. As one of those referred to, Hardy's worth to the firm was unquestioned. Presumably Stevens knew of his more overt use of materials and services, which included the necessary labor and supplies for building a fireplace in his home under construction. Through Milo offices he also ordered a plate glass for his picture window and removed the glass from Milo on Sunday. He may have paid part of the cost of the glass since one reward-right in many firms is to allow elect members to buy through the company at wholesale prices, and less.

A recently retired Milo executive, who was a bird lover, had an eleven unit aviary built in Milo shops and installed on his large rear lawn. Each spring he sent carpenters from the plant—and continues to receive this service possibly as a phase of his pension—to remove, recondition, renovate, and re-install the bird houses. This person, who started the emphasis on Masonry as an unannounced requirement, frequently used the same carpenters for redecorating his home. Lack of comparable maintenance skills apparently checked this practice at Attica, but it occurred at Fruhling though documentary support is inadequate for that plant. As with the use of materials alone, this double employment of facilities and stores obviously may become abused "rights" that blur the line between theft and reward. However, managers in both firms raised defenses that fluctuated between double talk and sound argument. My bantering of intimates raised certain questions. For example, when unavoidable emergencies, errors in planning, and market changes made work shortages, was it better to let "idle" men be seen by those who were busy, to reduce the work force, or to take the idle men out of the plant to do something else, something that was usually a lark for them? Management argued that unrest is promoted by "task inequities," and that men with nothing to do are pleased with a break in the monotony. Inquiries to Beemer, Brady, Spencer, and various maintenance workers usually elicited strong approval of this last alternative. For example, it was pointed out that "you get to sit down for twenty to forty minutes both ways" in traveling to and from an executive's home. Beemer saw this as equivalent to "several coffee breaks." Furthermore, the executive's wife "always gives us a lot of good eats." The president of the Milo union local supported the practice and held that it prevented layoffs. Management said essentially the same thing in noting that training costs and turnover were reduced, and at the same time there was no surplus of employees, for many of those "used on odd jobs" had to put in overtime at other periods. As with the machinists called on to service executive cars, those employees sporadically retained for out-plant work with some executive, derived both imponderable and concrete satisfactions. However, some first-line foremen and some workers saw the practice as "dirty," "unfair," and "taking advantage of your authority." And some people will call the practice high-level rationalization or collusion, but as in Chapter 4, it is more likely to be expediency periodically reclothed with new protective fictions.

Theft overlaps with reward-right where lower groups, foremen or workers, draw on plant resources, and higher management knows but dares not interfere, as in the hospital scandal. A European informant tells me of maintenance workers in railroad shops who drive their cars into the plant, rather than park outside as in our cases, and repair each other's cars on company time with company supplies. The cars are few and old and serve as busses as well as private vehicles. The practice is known to all, but since there is no fixed lunch hour, workers give the pretext if questioned that they work on the cars only during their lunch periods. Sometimes five to eight workers will be around one car for two or three hours at a stretch. With a short labor supply, and the practice apparently universal, management may officially protest, but usually looks the other way for fear the workers will seek jobs elsewhere.

The force of materials and services as unofficial incentives—internally for the company and externally for its ties with the community—was clearly visible in the activities of Magnesia's Yacht Club. As we saw in the preceding chapter, at least one hundred and fourteen members of Milo, and an unknown number from Fruhling, were active participants in the Club, at an individual annual fee of $50. Building additions to the Club and maintenance of its plant, as well as of privately owned boats, drew on the stores and services of Milo and Fruhling. Repair work was charged to various orders, which as we saw in Chapter 3 was done with some regular work. Propeller shafts, bushings, fin keels, counterweights, pistons, hand railings, and the like, were made and/or repaired for boat owners among the managers as well as their friends in the community.

All of this was tied in with the prevailing practice here, and throughout industry, of doing "government jobs." These include original, as well as repair, work of many kinds usually done by maintenance forces—with plant materials and equipment on job time—as a "favor" for employees at all levels. At Milo, workers were singled out to aid the Club by doing miscellaneous government jobs. This was a compliment to their skills and a gesture of acceptance by higherups that appealed to the impulse to serve others, however weak this urge is according to cynics, or overpowering according to some theorists. Praise and minor perquisites were accepted as abundant rewards. And for some, inside and across all job divisions, old rifts born in the heat of past emergencies were often healed by shared work on these unofficial assignments. The opportunities offered by such work for exchange of obligations, for establishing warm understandings, and for blurring differences in official reward, needs no comment. Bureaucratic rationality is progressively, if unwittingly, reduced through these invasions by community recreational life. It can be argued that government jobs aid the survival of Maintenance, which is normally at conflict with Operation in their official functions.

We need more study on the ramifications of government jobs* and unofficial services, apart from understood rewards.

The Auditor's Dilemma

Together, theft and socially consumed materials cut into a firm's substance sufficiently to alarm auditors and staffs, committed as they are to compiling the statistics for detection, analysis, and control of all departures from the ideal, and to warrant their own pay.†

Above Milo's divisional level, concern was always shown when inventories turned up losses. The usual reaction was to state that non-supervisory employees were to blame, and to order plant police to be more vigilant in their inspection of lunch buckets, bags, and bulging coats of outgoing personnel at the four gates.

The volume of materials "lost" was not known exactly. But cost analysts totaled and classified all incoming materials, then removed from the compilations all items, about eighty-five per cent of the total,

---

* At least one large company outside this study sees government jobs as a problem unless limited to certain employees and done by specific people during given hours. In this case, only salaried people may take such work to a shop set up for that purpose which operates between 6 P.M. and 10 P.M., Monday through Friday.

† Probably all organizational groups demand the stimulus of extra reward whether it be more of what they are already receiving or a greater share of those things having prestige value. The perquisite of staffs is usually the less material one of late arrival, early departure, and more socializing on the job, though additionally they, too, may participate in small government jobs.

that "could not possibly" be taken from the plant by persons on foot without detection. According to one analyst:

> It's not right on the nose, but about $15,000 of every $100,000 worth of material that *could* be taken out disappear—and never can be accounted for. Books can be juggled on some things but not much on this. Besides it's too damn constant. There's no question that it's carried out. If it's not, where the hell does it go to?

Some of the Milo managers and police suspected each other of carrying out materials or of collusively working with others to that end. Voicing his suspicions, the police chief was notified that his distrust was unfounded and insulting. On its side, management pointed to "statistical evidence" of police laxity. In delivering materials and removing the product, outside truckers had somehow sandwiched in forty-seven of some six hundred motors stored in an empty bay before the theft was discovered by the police. Management suspected some of the guards of bribed collaboration. Hardy set up a plan for unsystematic rotation of police around the circuit of gates. He believed this would prevent collusion between them and outsiders. Rotations were made monthly, but instead of moving all the men from one gate to the next nearest gate, only one man moved at a time and not in any sequence of gates or period of the month. This theory was not based on what had happened, and it was faulty in assuming that the major "nonproductive" consumption of materials was pure theft and was confined to production workers. Both in underestimating the ingenuity of lower ranking employees and in not seeing the nature of human association, the scheme did not prevent production workers from carrying out materials.

First, the theft of motors was accomplished by collusion of a few laborers with the truckers, but was concealed to protect a night supervisor. The suspected laborers were officially laid off for other reasons. The police were not participants. Second, we have seen that the major unofficial consumption of materials was by management itself, and in many cases was not pure theft. Finally, the theory ignored both the backgrounds of the police and the significance of government jobs. The police were not overpaid, and as company watchdogs they were, of course, persons for production workers to stand in well with. But as exworkers, in most cases, the police also knew plant life and had need of government jobs for which they, too, were prepared to exchange favors. For example, when one of the gate guards knew that a friend wished to carry something from the plant, he told the friend which gate he was tending. At the gate, with a guard on each side, the friend making his exit approached his confidant who simulated an inspection and sent him through with a clap on the back.

In Department Stores

The use of internal materials and services as spurs and requitals of course is not confined to factories. Department stores, with their range of commodities, are a rich field for research in the use of implicit rewards.[23] The Rambeau Mart, member of a state chain, was one of the most flourishing department stores in the Mobile Acres area, and probably owed much of its solidarity to its flexible unofficial incentives.

Rambeau had a total of three hundred and seventy employees including the clerical force and three levels of management: the store chief and his assistants, the division heads, and the department heads. The store had the usual official structure—an auditing department with appropriate specialists, a quadruplicate reporting system, explicit rules against personal use of materials and services, and a budget allowance of ten per cent to cover shoplifting. Two store detectives supplemented the controls. They were gatetenders of a kind in seeing that only employees entered the store before opening time, and in checking the parcels of outgoing employees, at quitting time only, to see that they bore sales slips and the signature of a department head. Yet the managers of Rambeau tacitly adapted its resources to individual orientations, and in a showdown clearly approved the practice.

The unofficial incentive system took various forms. When conditions allowed, and within limits, some department heads privately altered the price of merchandise to fit the local market and to satisfy their own needs. Also, department heads aided each other, but in all cases they worked inside the dual requirement of having to show a profit and to pass the scrutiny of an annual audit. The latitude that ingenuity could establish inside these limitations showed that a brand of individual enterprise still exists and is rewarded in organizations that, at least unofficially, accent individual as well as group effort.

A common practice by department heads was to take items they wanted that were "shopworn" or "damaged" and mark them down "reasonably" for their own purchase. Some female heads regularly, but discreetly, gave certain items a "damaged" appearance. Division chiefs unofficially knew of this, and set no limit to the markdown that could be made, other things equal. However, those department heads who shrank from the ambiguities of exercising their authority and asked a division manager the limit for a markdown were usually told "30 per cent."

Heads of the various men's departments usually clothed themselves from each other's stocks at little or no cost. This might be accomplished, for example, by selling a bargain stock of two thousand pairs of socks not at the agreed 59 cents per pair, but at 69 cents, which accumulated to a fund of $200 above profit requirements. A given head could draw from this to cover the suits, shoes, shirts, etc., essential for his proper grooming. The markup, like the kind and volume of stock, might vary.

Normally, merchandise control demanded that each item, even when the stock and price were uniform, have its individual stock number and price tag. But as in the case of the socks, some commodities might be thrown on a table, without their separate labels, under one posted price. This of course allowed inclusion of some lower-priced items of similar quality which, as with the socks, contributed to the private trading fund. Detailed records of what he removed for himself or others in the inter-departmental trading, and careful balancing of the dollar value of total merchandise withdrawn against the dollar value of unofficial markups enabled the department chief to meet the inventory. If emergencies prevented this, he reported his stock as larger than it was at the time of inventory; for instance, he might report thirty suits on hand, when he had only twenty-seven. Help from assistants in the inventory allowed this, but no help could postpone judgment day beyond the next inventory when this particular stock would be double-checked. To prevent abuse of this elastic incentive, there was always the threat that auditors from another unit would be present to assist at some inventory.

Department heads reciprocated in their markdown of items sold to each other. When the transaction had to be written up, the heads sometimes used a fictitious name, or the names of their new employees as customers. This utilized the fact that the employees themselves were as yet still naive, and their names were still strange in the auditing and shipping departments. Obviously intended in part to forestall such practices, the quadruplicate form requiring a name and address meant little in these cases until the employee became widely known. Where the women in these interchanges usually got only clothing, the men fully utilized the system. For example, Joe, in plumbing, wanted furniture, so he talked with Bill, head of furniture, to see what Bill wanted in plumbing of about the same value that could be exchanged. The total of their trades and adjusted records, however, did not prevent them from showing a profit in the annual audit. Where such persons work together for years this becomes simple and so unofficially acceptable that it seems natural.* Like the skeletons in every family closet, these prac-

---

* Favor-trading and adaptation of official procedures are likely to rise above any control. Even the outside organizations called in to assist in guaranteeing a certain conduct among given employees are similarly used by cliques to protect the group and to maintain the informal status of its individual members. For example, Rambeau subscribed to the service of "Willmark," an organization that

tices are not for public consumption but serve to unify the firm, as the skeletons do the family.

However, two department heads were dropped from this unit of Rambeau because of their use of company resources. Officially, one was released because of theft; the other, L. Nevers, because he wanted to transfer to another unit of the firm. The first head flagrantly took money from the tills of his salesmen, so that the following morning their cash and sales tallies did not match. This person was fired outright before he had taken a hundred dollars. But in Nevers' case light is thrown on what the internal use of materials and services meant in the context of incentives.

Nevers followed the procedures we have sketched and added his own refinements. In his accounting he was aided by one of his saleswomen whom he regularly befriended by ringing his sales on her cash drawer. However, her friendly relations with a saleswoman in another department led her to report Nevers' accounting methods and use of merchandise to the store manager and to name it as theft and malfeasance. Nevers' saleswoman, a "rate-buster," had worked with the other woman for years at Rambeau and elsewhere. Her friend's husband, shortly to return from the armed forces, had been head of a Rambeau department before being drafted. However there was uncertainty about his getting his old position back. So his wife, seeing the interpretation that could be made of Nevers' bookkeeping, and the consequences, hoped to have him fired and have her husband succeed him. She persuaded Nevers' saleswoman to report him in as bad a light as possible. The officially ignorant general manager knew roughly of Nevers' techniques and regarded him as "too good a man for the organization to lose." Forced to defend procedural dignity, he simulated a release but gave Nevers his choice of workplace among the statewide units, vigorously recommended him, and aided him in the successful transfer.

Two common merchandising policies encourage the use of goods as a supplementary incentive. First, the department head, as in other organizations, is expected to interpret policy. Second, all items are age-coded and regarded as having an approximate life expectancy. Some

---

checks on the selling behavior of clerks. This is done by confidentially sending representatives to make purchases from employees and then formally scoring and reporting each person's sales behavior to the store office. However, at Rambeau—and doubtless elsewhere—when the "shoppers" registered in the manager's office, an upper member of the grapevine heard of it and whispered the phrase "shoppers today" to an intimate on the selling floor who passed the word. But only insiders were alerted; they in effect commanded deference and aid from new and fringe members of the sales force by tacit threat of not notifying them.

items of women's clothing may be "old" in less than four months, whereas some merchandise in hardware has an indefinite life. The age-code, or purchase date of items, is recorded at inventory. If too old, this advertises both the department head's poor judgment in making the original purchase, and his failure to "move" the goods. Hence in part to escape discredit he marks down older items for disposal among employees. Of course, he simultaneously sets up counter claims. In the phraseology of Rambeau department heads these items were "odds and ends of merchandise lying around in the way that can't be sold anyhow." One of these heads declared that the "paper and handling costs" of storing or returning some items for disposal elsewhere exceeded the worth of the merchandise many times over and were, therefore, a drain on the firm.

The conditions attending demotion of a female department head support the existence of these policies. This person originally gained the post through her brother's office at state headquarters. She "worried the life out of" the division heads because only rarely could she "make decisions on her own." She, too, desired "shopworn" items, including jewelry with chipped stones, but she called on the merchandising chief for judgments on the markdown she should make and was repeatedly given the official "30 per cent." Knowing that others more than doubled this figure, she caused trouble by her gossip and insinuations. She was eventually demoted on the pretext that "store policy" demanded placement of a returning veteran—actually from another unit of Rambeau— and that hers was the logical post. Aware that the conditions of her original employment were contrary to Rambeau's merit system, she offered no resistance and was even "glad to get away from all that crazy paper work."

Thus inside the same unit, officially bureaucratic Rambeau could adjust its incentives to satisfy both its enterprising and its less ambitious managers. But in environments of this kind, the person who fits the ideal of believing that his pay matches or exceeds his worth to the firm becomes a potential isolate and requires special attention, though his contribution is valued and utilized. Higher managers naturally wish to reward this attitude, but since the employee may misinterpret any concrete informal reward as unacceptable "favoritism," the question is how? Rambeau had a female department head of this type. Of all the departments, her inventory came nearest to the expected dollar value. It would have been perfect except for the small surplus from single sales of three-for-a-price items. (The surplus also indicated departmental alertness against shoplifting.) Since she was a known devotee of bureaucratic procedure, her department in effect selected personnel like herself, and acquired a reputation for this. When new heads for the candy counter were required they were drawn from this woman's department because of the likelihood that they would not be "free-loaders," nor tolerant of such people among other employees. The only informal reward that Rambeau chiefs could give this person and her kind was deference, and praise before others.

Rambeau's rule-devotee had a counterpart in one unit of a drugstore chain near Mobile Acres. She managed the drugstore's soda fountain. A problem arose from her consistently having the highest percentage of profits among the chain's soda fountain managers. The matter was an issue among fountain heads in neighboring units of the chain, who were in personal rivalry with her. Her success was officially honored, for the situation was competitive and fountain supervisors received a percentage of profits above a given level. But a typical condition—which some students may mistakenly call "institutionalized theft"—existed among all the other units and worked to adversely interpret her achievement. Volume of business on the fountains was comparable in cities near the same size as was the seating capacity, facilities, and the margin of profits among all but the one fountain. The chief difference between practices in this fountain and the others—covertly charged by the woman and admitted by some of the store managers and pharmacists—was that the other fountain heads gave food and confections free to relatives and close friends, drinks to fountain employees, and variously bartered with nonfountain employees in much the manner of department heads at Rambeau. Unofficial reward, in the form of meals, to fountain employees was, of course, encouraged by the chain's wage rate which, while comparable to that of the local stores, was no higher than the minimum industrial rates. Most of the fountain heads covertly rewarded their "good workers" in this way to hold them.

The practices were engaged in up to the point of maintaining at least a narrow margin of profit for the store if not for the fountain heads. The latter were apparently guided more by concern to show a small profit for the fountain—which they did not share—than by a wish to achieve the higher departmental margin that would allow them a percentage of money profits from the fountain. Prices to the public, set by the chain's state-wide committee, were uniform throughout the system. Excepting the one, all fountain managers discreetly helped themselves to canned foods, dairy products, and meats from the departmental stock, with the knowledge of the store manager who received free meals, and coffee at any time. The one fountain chief allowed no gratis consumption to employees, friends, relatives, or herself. She kept the refrigerators locked and closely supervised the handling of stock. When emergencies prevented her from shopping for her family and she took a loaf of bread from the fountain stock, she deposited the price in the cash register. Married to a farmer-factory worker, she stressed loyalty to the store chief, customer service, and money profits for herself. Her superior could not condemn this, but he was disturbed by her boasting of her standing in the chain, and by the innuendoes from other store managers about her "pencil work." To minimize the woman's behavior, he backed his half-hearted praise of her with the logic that fountains are only a supplement to drug and cosmetic services, and that in total store profits his unit was sometimes second or lower in state rankings. But the resentment of other fountain managers—and of his own non-fountain employees against the woman's opposition to the perquisites usually allowed such personnel—forced him openly to check her records, to imply that she was making errors, and to withhold the praise she obviously craved. Higher chain officials also asked her to explain her unique performance and hinted that she could not be that much superior to other fountain managers. After two years of mounting resentments, she quit the firm. The store manager regarded her as a failure because she did not understand what he could not tell her—that her margin of profits was too high and that some social use of materials, not theft, was expected. In his mind, she was too little concerned with the system's internal harmony, and too devoted to formalities.

These practices at Rambeau and in the drugstore chain are doubtless common in many stores, but they are not made obvious to the students responsible for theory about organizational roles, job structure, resources, and pay. And they mean different things to the people involved.

SUMMARY AND COMMENT

The diversity and range of contributions required of an administrative or functional group cannot be exactly reflected in the official system of rewards. This is an inherent, not a diabolical, shortcoming. It springs largely from (1) the assumption that the total duties and essential skills for a given job are boxed in and paid for, and from (2) the impossibility of officially recognizing some of the extraordinary contributions made by various members—often out of role—during crises.

On the first point, not only must compensation be planned to maintain minimum harmony among personnel, but the limited resources of every firm require it. On the second point, open recognition of some essential contributions would advertise conditions that should not exist, promote rivalries,* hurt official dignity, and encourage disrespect for regulations.

---

* We earlier noted Barnard's analysis of democratic rivalries, and the need in decision making to anticipate and avoid their consequences. In the 1830's an acute French visitor commented on the always smoldering envy among Americans.

Hence recourse is had to semiconfidential use of materials and services as a supplement. This can be both inducement and requital to those who must receive great recognition to do their best, and to those who would move elsewhere without the increment.

Supplementation may be accompanied by abuse to the extent (1) that the reward becomes habitual and is unrelated to contribution; (2) that it is shared by those who make no unusual contribution; or (3) that it expands and becomes coerced theft. The changing line between reward and abuse may be difficult to find and hold, but nothing can be done until the problem is faced. Evading it disposes nonparticipating personnel and the public to label all use of materials and services in this sense as theft. This cynicism cannot be eliminated by allocating ten to fifteen per cent of the budget to cover "shoplifting" by non-supervisory employees and the public. Such allocation may of course enable some managers and subordinates to hide their own theft up to this limit. But it fails to distinguish theft from essential maintenance of the social mechanism. The problem is pervaded by our tradition of political spoils,[24] and our logic that service to the organization must have a one-to-one relation to rank and explicit compensation. We must note that absence of this neat balance induces supplementation, and inflicts moral suffering among members inversely to their capacity for automatic hypocrisy.

It is unlikely that a universally applicable system of informal rewards can be set up, but it is certain that where abuse of the practice develops it will not be eliminated by moral exhortations, elaborate paper forms, or rigid policing. These restraints all help, but as we all know, those who make and apply controls may be like Cellini. If so, their close associates are likely to share their privileges* and echo the general lament of abuse by "others."

Here officially to study our prison system, he remarked that "the hatred which men bear to privileges increases in proportion as privileges become more scarce . . . so that democratic passions . . . seem to burn most fiercely . . . when they have least fuel." Americans, then as now, "dread all violent disturbance . . . and love public tranquillity." But in their mania for equality they attribute the success of an *equal* "mainly to some one of his defects" rather than "to his talents or virtues." For to do otherwise "is tacitly to acknowledge that they are themselves less virtuous and talented." See Alexis de Tocqueville, *Democracy in America* (trans. by Henry Reeve), 2 vols., The Cooperative Publication Society (The Colonial Press), New York, 1900, Vol. 1, p. 229; Vol. 2, pp. 307–308.

* Again speaking timelessly, but referring to earlier Americans, de Tocqueville declared that, "Whatever may be the general endeavor of a community to render its members equal and alike, the personal pride of individuals will always seek to rise above the line, and to form somewhere an inequality to their own advantage." *Op. cit.,* Vol. 2, p. 226.

Admitting the potential disruptiveness of implicit rewards, can we assure the full commitment of all abler members without them? And since we dare not preach what we practice, how do we know that we would have less disturbance and as much or more contribution without supplementation and some abuse? Can we show that the cost of, say 15 per cent, to cover theft and unofficial reward is excessive in lieu of other inducements which also cost? This is not to say that what exists is good, but to say that we do not know how bad it is until we can see it more closely.

Abuse is indefensible, but for the sake of a sharper focus on the issue let us say that as varieties of supplementation and limited abuse sap one brand of company resources, they protect other assets. For example, do they not in many cases also reduce disruptive conflict, break the monotony of routine, allow more personal expression, ease the craving for spontaneity, and to some extent catch up all levels of personnel in a system of mutual claims so that aid can be requested and hardly denied?

However, even with revision of the sheep-or-goat outlook, the problem must mark time until serious students are able in many contexts to at least look at (1) the elusive nature of organization that requires unofficial performances; (2) the relation of reward to informal services given; and (3) the relation of all reward to organizational resources, material and social.

Those who regard this chapter as merely a series of episodes on theft have missed the point. Our study of unofficial rewards is not an attempt to justify internal plunder or to say that theft by membership is inevitable. Both "theft" and "reward" derive their meaning from the social context. To insist that this context is constant—so that we can preserve the admitted convenience of fixed definitions—is to pervert meaning, block the issue, and deny that there are ethics in reward.

To repeat, the aim has been to show that however well defined official tasks may be, and however neatly we think we have fitted our personnel to these roles, the inescapably fluid daily situation distorts expected working conditions. Circumstances require various out-of-role and unplanned actions. Regardless of formal rankings, which are often only nominally based on potential for such action, some personnel more aptly do what is essential than do others. Tacitly or not, both they and their rewarders are aware of who solves problems and sustains the organization. Through time they are compensated as resources and situations allow. The process may seem to overlap with theft, or it may escape control and become theft, but able executives both utilize and contain unofficial rewards.

DOCUMENTARY NOTES

1. S. I. Hayakawa, *Language and Thought in Action,* Harcourt, Brace and Co., New York, 1949, pp. 60–62.

2. Even in the physical sciences there are disputes about the definition, perception, and nature of matter. See the comments of two *physicists:* Martin Johnson, *Art and Scientific Thought,* Columbia University Press, New York, 1949; and J. Bronowski, "Science and Human Values," *The Nation,* 183: 550–566, December 29, 1956, and *The Common Sense of Science,* Wm. Heinemann, Ltd., London, 1951, especially chaps. 6–8. Disputes increase in the biological sciences. For example, because they combine both plant and animal characteristics, we find such organisms as *Euglena viridis* and the slime-fungi studied by both zoologists and botanists. Books from satirical to scientific levels debate the nature of *truth, fact,* and *meaning.* In the opening pages of his *Ethics,* Aristotle notes the difficulty of expecting a mathematician to see facts as *probable,* or a politician to see them as *precise.* For himself he believed that different subject matters admit of different degrees of precision in handling. See also the two works of T. V. Smith, "In Accentuation of the Negative," *The Scientific Monthly,* 63: 463–469, December, 1946 and *The Ethics of Compromise,* Starr King Press, Boston, 1956; and the numerous articles in L. Bryson et al., *Symbols and Values,* Harper and Brothers, New York, 1954, *Symbols and Society,* Harper and Brothers, New York, 1955; Anthony Standen, *Science Is a Sacred Cow,* E. P. Dutton and Co., New York, 1950; S. I. Hayakawa, ed., *Language, Meaning and Maturity,* Harper and Brothers, New York, 1954; H. Hoijer, ed., *Language in Culture,* University of Chicago Press, 1954; E. A. Burtt, *The Metaphysical Foundations of Modern Science,* Doubleday and Co., Garden City, N.Y., 1955; Howard Becker, *Through Values to Social Interpretation,* Duke University Press, Durham, N.C., 1950; Boris B. Bogoslovsky, *The Technique of Controversy,* Harcourt, Brace and Co., New York, 1928, especially chaps. 4–9; Kenneth Burke, *Attitudes Toward History,* 2 vols., The New Republic, New York, 1937, especially Vol. 2, pp. 52–256.

3. See Edwin H. Sutherland, *White Collar Crime,* The Dryden Press, New York, 1949; *The Autobiography of Lincoln Steffens,* Harcourt, Brace and Co., New York, 1931; John T. Flynn, *Graft in Business,* The Vanguard Press, New York, 1931, pp. 103–106.

4. Sumner Slichter, "Report on Current Research: Economics," *Saturday Review,* 36: 24, April 4, 1953; Arthur H. Cole, "An Approach to the Study of Entrepreneurship," *Journal of Economic History* 6, Supplement 1–15 (1946); Robert A. Gordon, *Business Leadership in the Large Organization,* Brookings Institution, Washington, D.C., 1945; Clare E. Griffin, *Enterprise in a Free Society,* R. D. Irwin, Chicago, 1949, chap. 5; John K. Galbraith, *American Capitalism,* Houghton Mifflin, Boston, 1952; Albert Lauterbach, *Man, Motives and Money,* Cornell University Press, Ithaca, New York, 1954; George Katona, *Psychological Analysis of Economic Behavior,* McGraw-Hill Book Co., New York, 1951; *Business Week,* "A Tempo Shapes a Type," April 25, 1953, pp. 56, 58, 60; C. C. Abbott, J. D. Forbes, L. A. Thompson, *The Executive Function and Its Compensation,* Graduate School of Business Administration, The University of Virginia, Charlottesville, 1957.

5. C. I. Barnard, *Functions of the Executive,* Harvard University Press, Cambridge, 1938, pp. 138–160.

6. P. F. Drucker, *The Practice of Management,* Harper and Brothers, New York, 1954, p. 152; Abbott, Forbes, and Thompson, *op. cit.,* pp. 46–55.

7. See also Morris S. Viteles, *Motivation and Morale in Industry,* Norton, New York, 1953; Kornhauser, in Kornhauser, Dubin, and Ross, *op. cit.,* pp. 59–85; W. F. Whyte et al., *Money and Motivation,* Harper and Brothers, New York, 1955.

8. Also see C. I. Barnard, "Functions and Pathology of Status Systems in Formal Organizations" in W. F. Whyte, ed., *Industry and Society,* McGraw-Hill Book Co., New York, 1946, pp. 207–243.

9. The various struggles of Milo and Fruhling with their Offices. Also see Galbraith, *American Capitalism,* Houghton Mifflin, Boston, 1952, p. 28.

10. Barnard, *op. cit.,* pp. 139–160.

11. Griffin, *op. cit.,* chap. 5; Gordon, *op. cit.,* pp. 305–312. Geiger's "free-wheeling" bent is suggested by his remark that "The engineers aren't practical. They want everything to be exact. They can't see that in operation you've got to lie and steal and cheat a little." See also W. H. Knowles, *Personnel Management: A Human Relations Approach,* American Book Co., New York, 1955, p. 130; Robert B. Fetter and Donald C. Johnson, *Compensation and Incentives for Industrial Executives,* Indiana University, Bloomington, 1952, p. 57.

12. Abbott, Forbes, and Thompson, *op. cit.,* p. 41.

13. Lauterbach, *op. cit.,* chap. 1.

14. Katona, *op. cit.,* chap. 9.

15. *Business Week,* April 25, 1953, pp. 56, 58, 60.

16. Will Durant, *The Renaissance,* Simon and Schuster, New York, 1953, p. 401.

17. Article "Aqueducts," *Encyclopaedia Britannica,* Vol. 2, 14th edition, 1932, p. 161.

18. *Newsweek,* "Those Big-Figure Expense Accounts," Vol. 41, No. 20, pp. 87, 90–92, May 20, 1957; Seymour Mintz, "Executive Expense Accounts and Fringe Benefits: A Problem in Management, Morality and Revenue," *Journal of Taxation,* 1: 2–9, June, 1954; Abbott, Forbes, and Thompson, *op. cit.,* p. 41.

19. See various responses (public documents) to form 10-K of the Securities and Exchange Commission, Washington, D.C., for the Fiscal Year ended August 21, 1956.

20. Fred H. Colvin, *The Industrial Triangle,* Columbia Graphs, Columbia, Connecticut, 1955, pp. 95–96; Benjamin Aaron, "Governmental Restraints on Featherbedding," *Stanford Law Review,* 5: 680–721, 1953.

21. See the theory of Abbott, Forbes, and Thompson, *op. cit.,* pp. 34–38.

22. See Havelock Ellis, *The Dance of Life,* The Modern Library, New York, 1923, pp. 89–98, and Robert Dubin, *Human Relations in Administration,* Prentice-Hall, New York, 1951, pp. 336–345.

23. For an intensive study of twenty salesgirls in the setting of a large department store, see George F. F. Lombard, *Behavior in a Selling Group,* Harvard University, Graduate School of Business Administration, Boston, 1955.

24. Walter Lippmann, *A Preface to Politics,* The Macmillan Company, New York, 1913, chap. 1; Charles A. and Mary Beard, *The Rise of American Civilization,* 2 vols. in one, The Macmillan Co., New York, 1937, Vol. 1, pp. 547–557; V. O. Key, Jr., *Politics, Parties, and Pressure Groups,* 2nd edition, Thomas Y. Crowell Co., New York, 1947, pp. 316–339.

CHAPTER **8**

The Interconnections of
Formal and Informal Action

ORGANIZATION AS CONTAINED COUNTER PHASES

In the preceding five chapters we have discussed cases through the device of posing a departmental or organizational façade against the actions behind it. But we have allowed the mass of incidents to obscure the typical and recurrent ways in which the organizations operated. We need now to look at the interdependence of façade and interior, and to discuss the problems of generalizing about their intertwined phases in the organization's ongoing action.

Even pointing to a specific organization is more difficult than appears at first glance. When its personnel are included, the problem of saying *where* and *when* an organization exists is not easy. Its multifarious and interlocking actions and ties with other firms, as well as the community, make it hard to locate precisely. And since it exists unofficially in some form before its formal birth, and after it officially dies, there is more than an academic issue of saying precisely when it exists and when it does not.

Despite its fascinating futility let us avoid metaphysics, and assume that when a planned, or formal, organization initially begins to operate it functions about as expected by its makers. But this is short-lived,

218

for organizations cannot continue to operate solely in terms of their original beliefs, methods, and goals. In a changing world, organizations are rendered obsolete to a degree, and must work with only limited success to catch up.[1] This condition and other factors we have already noted—division of labor, departmental identification, personal ambitions, turnover, etc.—stimulate multiple informal phases in the organization which fluctuate in their distance from the aims and methods of the formal phases. Hence at times the letter of the rule must be violated to preserve the spirit.[2]

For centuries observers and leaders have remarked on the distinctions between expected and unexpected behavior in organizations. The fact that the distinctions continue to be made under various names points to an apparently universal condition. From at least the time of Augustus Caesar,[3] these dissimilarities were recognized and incorporated in the terms *de jure* (by right) and *de facto* (in fact), which are roughly equivalent to *legal* or *official* and *actual* but *unofficial*. In industry and business today one repeatedly hears the same general meaning phrased as "administration versus politics," "theory versus practice," "red tape versus working relations," "fancy versus fact," etc. In other circles the concepts run "ideal–actual," "planned–unplanned," "controlled–spontaneous," "open–covert," "myth–reality," "official–social," "rule–custom," "formal–social," "respectable–*sub rosa*,"[4] "position authority–functional authority,"[5] "manifest structure–latent structure."[6]

Through earlier chapters we have of course used similar paired concepts. For example, "formal–informal," "official–unofficial," with "formal" and "official" meaning that which is planned and agreed on; and "informal" or "unofficial" referring to the spontaneous and flexible ties among members, guided by feelings and personal interests indispensable for the operation of the formal, but too fluid to be entirely contained by it. However, all these expressions distort and oversimplify what occurs. And the great evil is that the terms are often treated as real things, which we too must be guilty of to some extent in this and the next chapter, since space forbids a disquisition on the ultimate reality of the connections and differences between formal and informal action. Such efforts can be a contribution, but unpleasantly often they do little more than satisfy the exceptional student's passion for mental gymnastics, and allow the author to entertain his chosen fraternity with a round of logic-chopping. Certainly analyses of this kind repel those responsible for positive action during emergencies. The latter quickly charge the generalizing researcher with "sailing around on cloud nine," and with being "one of the academic boys who write for each other."

Despite their twitting of the researcher, executives themselves inevitably face and feel our problem when they become concerned with "rule-breaking" and failures in planning. Discounting his loose language and typical error about first-line foremen, Stein (Chapter 6), for example, made a revealing analysis as he lamented the influence of plant dynamics on job descriptions:

> The way things change it would be impossible to have a job description that would be accurate. It would have to be revised daily. Things change too fast. The market changes, your personnel changes, relations with the union are always changing. [The central office] is always reorganizing the setup. Staff people are always racking their brains for improvements of one kind or another. People are always fighting for promotions and when they get them they all handle the same job differently—no two men do a job the same way. There are technological changes going on all the time. That always upsets planning. You can't overemphasize the fact that men don't handle a job in the same way. And a given man on a job changes his ways of handling it. Like everybody else, he's always under pressure to get things done so he's always looking for short cuts. We never get a chance to standardize short cuts because they change too damn fast. Then there's always a lot of undercover stuff going on that the people involved fight like hell to hide. Everybody is looking out for himself and wanting to do things on his own. If he makes a bobble, he covers it up. I come right back to the same point—you can't divorce the job from the man. One man will have a hell of a lot of initiative and will always be trying to get a lot done—he'll try to take more authority than he has a right to. He'll stick his neck out and stick his boss's neck out. Another man can't do a damn thing without running to his boss about it. Take Svendsen, for instance. He runs downstairs to see Hardy about nothing. If he feels that four fans are needed for his department why he runs to Hardy to talk it over. Hell, that's petty. If I had the job and was sure the department needed something, I'd order it! But there you are—no two people'll do the same job alike. Your front-line foreman is about the only man in supervision who has a cut-and-dried job [sic].

Impermanence in general, and the interplay between the obvious and the obscure in human behavior is an ancient problem. One must go back at least to Heracleitus in the sixth century B.C. to give credit for ideas helpful in theorizing about organizations in movement. At least by implication, he speculated on the inherent tie between theory and practice in a way applicable to organizations. He held, for instance, that conflict and strife are indispensable, that harmony is really but a tension of opposites neither of which ever win, but both of which are necessary. He further advanced the principle, supported by modern science, that all things are in a state of flux. Seeing reality as tension and interplay, he would regard permanence more as a condition, or process, than a substance.[7]   Barnard has said much the same about organizations in saying that formal and informal are "interdependent aspects of the same phenomena."[8]

Actual study of organizations and groups in terms of a play between appearances and intent was probably first done by the participant-observer, Thucydides, in his *History of the Peloponnesian War* (between Athens and Sparta and their allies, 431 to 404 B.C.).[9]

In Book 5 of his *Politics*,[10] Aristotle implicitly shows grasp of the bonds between official and unofficial action as he seeks to explain the causes of transitions from one form of government to another, and lists techniques for maintaining a monarchy in power.

Though widely condemned for the amoral overtones of his writings, Machiavelli some 1800 years later dealt with this interplay in Discourse 6, "On Conspiracies," in *The Discourses*.[11]

Also moving in high places with excellent opportunity to participate— and to be caught, fined, imprisoned, and pardoned for his unofficial conduct—Francis Bacon implicitly analyzed the exchange between formal and informal action.   This comes out in his essays, "Of Counsel," "Of Negotiating," and "Of Followers and Friends."

Around 1788, James Madison commented on the interplay by noting the inevitable appearance of faction:

> Theoretic politicians, who have patronized this species of government [pure democracy], have erroneously supposed that by reducing mankind to a perfect equality in their political rights, they would at the same time be perfectly equalized and assimilated in their possessions, their opinions, and their passions. . . . The inference to which we are brought is that the causes of faction cannot be removed, and that relief is only to be sought in the means of controlling its effects.[12]

Of course dozens of literary men before and after Madison have satirized and analyzed social façades and interiors: Lucian, Juvenal, Molière, Voltaire, Swift, Ibsen, Shaw, etc.   In the essay we referred to earlier, "On Patronage and Puffing," William Hazlitt anticipated a favorite theme of Veblen's by nearly a century.   And dying Joyce Cary recently defended the politician's "selected and arranged truth" through an analysis of social fronts and evasions.[13]

FORMAL AND INFORMAL AS TERMS

Systematic focus on the terms "formal" and "informal" as applied to organizations, began with Barnard's theory[14] in 1938, and was fortified with data the next year by Roethlisberger and Dickson,[15] who talked especially of informal activity among workers.   Since then the terms

have been in common use by sociologists and others.[16]   More recent
thought and research have shown, however, that multiple relations, with
continuous interaction and change, become too dynamic to be handled
entirely inside such conceptual walls as "formal–informal."   Students
are increasingly aware that this is the same kind of trap as "form versus
substance," "individualism versus collectivism," "romanticism versus
classicism."   The bare scheme of formal–informal is helpful but inadequate for grappling with all aspects of the behavior we have been
talking about.   Exclusive reliance on this couplet ignores the whole
confused middle ground where there are "mixtures," and where new
formal and informal action are obscurely initiated.   Although this area
may be impossible to deal with concretely, we should at least recognize
that there can be numerous concurrent interplays, interrelated and not,
of varying importance for the organization.

The term *informal* has become especially troublesome in the context
of organizations.   To some it connotes only conspiracy.   And when
used as the counter pole of a couplet there is difficulty in saying where
the informal ends and the *formal* begins.   The term is so broad that
embarrassingly often it requires delimitation and redefinition.   If "informal" is used as "functionally interrelated to the formal," it implies
a complete knowledge of formal expectations by the informal group
under focus.   These points merit enlargement.

Probably in part from the influence of studies on work restriction as
an informal technique implicitly confined to workers, the moral feelings
of some people are inflamed by their experience with the term.   They
think of "work paid for but not done," "failure to fight in the open,"
and the like.   Repeatedly my own students, from various disciplines,
have raised questions about the distinctions between informal, on the
one hand, and intrigue, plotting, frame-ups, "or any other kind of
sneakiness" on the other.   They require correction to see that informal
action may work for many ends: to change and preserve the organization, to protect weak individuals, punish erring ones, reward others, to
recruit new personnel, and to maintain dignity of the formal, as well as,
of course, to carry on power struggles, and to work for ends we would
all frown on.

On the second point, when a clique is recognized, or when grapevines
are known and counted on by all, or when higher management considers
such a clique or practice in its policy making, obviously the informal is
formal for most purposes.   Since it is utilized by all and lacks only
official recognition,[17] it is more correctly called *unofficial* than informal.

On the third point, one can think of informal organization as Barnard
does, as incidental or accidental association without purpose,[18] but this
distinction includes story-telling and small talk of all kinds and confines

the term largely to what we earlier called a "random clique." Such incidental association admittedly can give a basis for later cooperative activity, but always intermingled with the socializers are members who calculatingly participate with additional purposes in mind. So for our aim of stressing the *ties* between formal and informal we need to consider more than what supplies a potential for joint activity; we must talk of the activity itself. This largely conscious action is what we primarily mean by "informal."

Finally, when one uses "informal" as a necessary counterpart of "formal," the implication is that they somehow match and balance each other, that those participating in the informal activity have full knowledge of formal expectations. This oversimplifies the behavior. As we have seen, it is unrealistic to assume that all the managers of a firm have complete knowledge of formal expectations. Since (1) there are varying and inconstant gaps between official and actual influence of members, and (2) the more fully committed members necessarily have secrets not shared by the fringe members; and since (3) some directives are known only by a minority to be for nothing but the record, obviously formal purpose is not shared by all except in the most general way. That is, knowledge of changing policy is often withheld from some subordinates because of belief that they will react unfavorably to the full picture at *this* moment. Then, too, in firms like Milo and Fruhling, procedures, demands by the customer, etc., may change so rapidly that middle and lower officers have only partial knowledge of the formal expectations. Also there is both ignorant and indifferent action in the organization that falls outside this simple scheme.*

These criticisms are not to reject the couplets of "formal–informal," "official–unofficial," etc., but to note their limitations and point the need to study the intervening action.

FORMAL AND INFORMAL AS ASPECTS OF ORGANIZATION

Specialists variously evaluate these two phases of effort. Brief comment on the merits ascribed to each, or to the one that is stressed, will prepare us to talk of how the two interact.

---

* For example, in a large office at Fruhling—apparently typical in terms of nonsupervisory staff skills, interest, and morale—the employees frequently showed fluctuating concern for important procedures. Correction of errors found in the time charged to various departmental accounts required much paper work and checking of all departmental records. Most of this crew, however, merely shuffled the correction cards they received and distributed them equally among members. Each person then divided the total time, on the cards he received, among the accounts *currently* on his desk. To my friendly but unauthorized question about this procedure, they answered, "What difference does it make?"

Dimock thinks of what we usually call the official and unofficial as the engineering versus the psychological approaches.[19] Since the two represent inherent bodies of activity in organizations, he demands more effort to correlate them. Overemphasis on the official, he insists, is likely to engender "psychological quirks" in the individual. When the organization tries to entirely replace discretion with certainty it deserves the popular insult of "bureaucracy." Such "routine is the institutional equivalent of personal introversion."[20]

The sociologist, Tönnies,[21] long ago implicitly denied the possibility of a purely official, or planned, structure, and Urwick ridicules the emphasis placed on "official channels." He admits their necessity but sees them as largely "for the record," except during a change of leaders or the breakdown of "good personal relations." Normally only a simpleton would think that effective collaboration is created simply by setting up formal procedure.[22] The "fiction" that the president "runs" the company, Stryker says in agreement, is built on management's reverence for formally charted relations. Experienced managers know that things get done informally, and that the informal exists in management as its "biggest intangible asset" and "touchiest open secret."[23]

Great emphasis has been placed on the merits of the informal by Donham, Roethlisberger, Mayo, Whitehead, Homans, and others.[24] One executive values the informal because it can be absorbed into the daily routine without official notice. This allows him to win unofficial ends without raising questions.[25]

Like the formal, the informal phases can be overstressed. Some groups are prone to make informal communication an end in itself. Where this occurs, formal procedure may be regarded as not even a necessary evil. The informal takes on such prominence that in-plant luncheons and out-plant socializing become the chief vehicles for communication. Facility in party giving, as the ideal atmosphere for policy making, becomes an informal requirement for acceptance, so that a condition develops comparable to that noted by Willkie.[26]

Some students implicitly stress the formal organization by reluctant admission that "there seems to be a certain minimum amount"[27] of informal activity that remains in organizations whether welcome or not.

Students of bureaucracy as an administrative structure designed scientifically to accelerate movement toward stated goals are, of course, stressing the formal phases.[28] In addition to their evaluations and those of Barnard, Urwick, and Dimock on the subject, the weight of the formal phase in organizational practice is clearly shown by the avoidance of discussion of delegation and by the niceties often attending so-called delegation of authority.

For example, we saw in Chapter 5 how Rees, Milo's Head of Industrial Relations, wished to support first-line foremen by giving them the appearance of being quite independent, while he informally made their decisions. The editors of *Fortune*[29] cite similar cases in large corporations of subtle, "even unconscious" communications between higher and lower executives that enable the latter to make "correct decisions." As the editors see it, the subordinate officers "sustain their egos," by the appearance of authority, while the higherups continue to make the decisions.

The weight of formal organization, even when those in high place seek to share their authority, was shown in an English study. The "Managing Director" of a plant which had long tried to "raise the level of democratic participation" found that subordinate executives were likely to interpret sudden delegation of authority—allowing them to act entirely on their own—as concealed punishment and an attempt by the superior to abdicate his responsibility.[30]

Shartle ironically attributes advantages to excessive formality, as when "red tape" slows action that in the thinking of some department should be delayed, or prevents interference with a fast-moving program.*

These conflicting emphases also show awareness of the potential for varying gaps to develop between formal and informal. Emmerich, however, believes that the two phases "are so closely related that the attempt to isolate [them] can be as misleading as the newer tendency

---

* Shartle, *Executive Performance and Leadership,* Prentice-Hall, Englewood Cliffs, New Jersey, 1956, p. 201. A greater irony appears when Shartle's comment is compared with observations on industry in the U.S.S.R. According to Berliner, his research suggested "that managerial officials count on long bureaucratic delays in helping them avoid detection of irregularities." (See Joseph S. Berliner, *Factory and Manager in the U.S.S.R.,* Harvard University Press, Cambridge, 1957, p. 299.) Evidently, or maybe "obviously," human beings in similar kinds of organizational structure behave somewhat alike in terms of official-unofficial phases, though they may be situated in economies having great cultural and ideological differences.

Though Berliner typically uses the *legal-illegal* framework in discussing his data, there are startling parallels between some of his situations and those in our earlier chapters. For example, compare Berliner, pp. 266 and 319, with some practices in chap. 3; Berliner, pp. 273 (where managers "try to keep off rationalizers and inventors as troublesome people") and 274, with chap. 4; Berliner, bottom p. 208 and top p. 209, to many situations in our preceding five chapters; Berliner, p. 272, where the government expects trade unions "to keep management on its toes," as against Meiner's remark in chap. 5, which indicated that Milo leaders were glad that the "union keeps front-line foremen . . . and department heads . . . on their toes"; Berliner, p. 245 (Malenkov's remarks), with informal selection in chap. 6, etc. These loose ends should be drawn together.

to equate them."[31]   In diverse terms, others see the problem of a breach between formal and informal and propose *integration* in some way.   Urwick, for example, speaks of ceaseless reorganization, or a "continuous evolution," which must be constantly guided by permanent machinery for that purpose.[32]   Van Der Schroeff and Vonk speak essentially the same of "a perpetual state of development."*

THE INTERPLAY OF FORMAL AND INFORMAL

These discussions of official and informal action in the dynamics, development, reorganization, and evolution, of the organization do not, to repeat ourselves, deal explicitly with the interplay of formal and informal.   However difficult, we need to focus more on the inter-connections between formal and unofficial as they draw apart, collide, and/or irregularly perform functions.[33]   Though the action is colored at times with economic, individual, and even chance factors, we have already seen many interplays springing from this orderly disorder.   For example, rise of the FWD at Milo as a response to the developing conflict between Maintenance and Operation; breakdown of the FWD largely as a result of informal evasions and attacks on it; formal action by the Office which was countered and adapted by Milo chiefs; the blocking of Jessup's proposal at Fruhling and his informal perfection of the process which was later adopted; the circumvention of labor agreements by union-management cliques leading to some modification in later contracts; the rise of sinecures and the use of the assistant-to office to soften formal rigidities; the use of unofficial criteria in the selection of new officers; the rise and action of specific clique types to meet recurring situations growing out of formal changes; the informal use of materials and services to supplement formal reward; the endless formal-informal exchanges through Reynolds at Attica; the responses in

---

* H. J. Van Der Schroeff and W. Vonk, "Conditions for an Equilibrium," in H. J. Kruisinga, ed., *The Balance Between Centralization and Decentralization in Managerial Control*, H. E. Stenfert Kroese, N. V., Leiden, 1954, pp. 44–54. For practical purposes, the term "development" is useful in this context, but it has serious theoretical weaknesses.   *Development* implies more of a rational process than can be shown to exist.   The interplay between formal and informal does not inherently move along "progressive" lines.   Failure of Milo's FWD and Milo's adaptation of the Office program and the course of Attica all show, as Urwick implies, that constant alertness and guidance are essential to move the organization in a given direction. The process is not exclusively mechanical, nor are the initially "built in" ends automatically good for the duration.   See C. I. Barnard, *Functions of the Executive,* Harvard University Press, Cambridge, 1938, p. 91.

O'Brien's department to the formal ranking of shifts by their production level; and the whole cluster of interplays between safety regulations and accidents.

Given the functional and random cliques we sketched in Chapter 3, some important steps and mechanisms that connect the formal and informal and enable them to maintain ongoing action are (1) official meetings, (2) command from high levels for unofficial action from below, (3) informal requests from below for the right to engage in specific unofficial actions, (4) transitional roles, (5) recourse to pre-figured justifications, (6) the use of "two-way funnels," and (7) adoption by the formal—acknowledged or not—of unofficial widespread practices that have proved their worth or have become an accomplished fact.

Meetings

As we all know, conferences may be used for more than official purposes. It should be no surprise that the periodic meetings in business and industry are at times much like those of parliamentary gatherings.[34] Because the internal power struggles of business and industry are largely denied and must be cloaked, it is clear that the ferment of unofficial activities may be more intense at times than the frankly parliamentary action.* Right down the hierarchy one finds meetings a stage for exploratory skirmishes; for making authoritative hints to those moving too far in some direction; for study of faces and inflections; for catching slips and checking on premeeting tips, etc. The formal meeting is a gallery of fronts where aimless, deviant, and central currents of action merge for a moment, perfunctorily for some, emotionally for others. All depart with new knowledge to pursue variously altered, but rarely the agreed, courses.

One finds executives called into meetings to solve problems precipitated by their own informal activities, which naturally bind their hands. At the meeting they may learn—as Milo staff forces did by turning luncheons into meetings—how much of their problem is known, and they may pick up helpful leads from responses to guarded questions they raise. Pre- and postmeeting confabs with clique members incorporate these findings. Where the gap between formal and informal phases becomes great, some officers seek to settle issues in meetings and escape the commitment of written statements. We saw this concern in Chapter 5. This allows greater expression to the free-wheelers and tacticians,

---

* Barnard (*Functions of the Executive*), p. 226, notes the limited "overt division on formal issues" that authority can tolerate. Hence the volume of informal activity in both cases.

but inspires fear among the rule-bound.* The existing "balance" of formal-informal action is partially provoked by variants of these two types, and newcomers are in turn selected to some extent in terms of how they will fit into the balance.

Total time spent in meetings can indicate roughly the rate of change and the intensity of interaction between the formal and informal; and also, of course, lack of assurance in making decisions on the part of those calling the meetings. At Milo and Fruhling there were nine to over a dozen different kinds of periodic meetings. Department heads averaged about six hours daily in conferences. General policy, production planning, staff-line, and cost meetings especially reflected the two-way influence. The ostensibly final reports or agreements they brought forth were often tentative. When subject to disapproval and rejection at higher levels or by "powerful" individuals, the reports were officially unofficial for they were often frankly requested to be in pencil—a forewarning that the play of interests would result in revisions and "graphite analyses."

Ordered Unofficial Action

In various emergencies and unusual situations, higherups demand limited unofficial, and even illegal, action by subordinates. The order by Reynolds of Attica (Chapter 5) to flunk certain job examinees is a case in point. However, when the demand embraces too many personnel moral disturbances break out, as at Milo (Chapter 3) when Hardy and his division chiefs forced an adaptation of the Office's program. Restricted demand confined to tested personnel is more common and is more likely to accomplish formal ends without damage to its dignity. Organizationally necessary change introduced in this way gradually blends into ongoing action.

Granted Departures

Where camaraderie is high, so that subordinates do not fear unofficial punishment by superiors, they may ask permission to settle some issues informally. We noted in Chapter 5 the unofficial blanket instructions

---

* For example, E. Flandin, a general foreman and a formalist on procedure, refused to participate in meetings. He remarked, "I just set and listen. You know a damn sight better than to say anything. You're licked before you go in a meeting. If you speak up and make a complaint, you'll have to prove it and you'll make a dozen guys sore. If you make a suggestion there'll be a dozen guys against it because it'll bother them some way or show up their dodges. I'd rather just keep my mouth shut and draw my pay."

to all from above to use containable informal methods. This of course embraced an area of issues crucial to production. In many less important cases formal and informal are similarly bridged without indignities to the formal. For example, the dealing with another department, the rewarding—or even penalizing—of some individual who must be lived with, the handling of some plant-community issue, etc., are all made easier by permission, and sometimes cooperation, from above, though the superior, as in other cases, prefers to remain officially ignorant.*

Both commanded and requested informal actions are likely to be followed by protective official statements, which are "orders for the record" (see p. 231). The intent is of course usually known only to the chosen. An order for the record may be a temporary blind to cover movement toward an end; or it may start as a stopgap and become semi-permanent when conditions show that dropping it would bring greater problems. Orders for the record may also be issued at lower levels to placate threatening formalists or to follow established disciplinary procedure, as when Warren and O'Brien "bawled out" Jackson (Chapter 6).

The Transitional Role

I implied just above that "orders for the record" may induce further complications. Both such orders and the various uses of the office of assistant-to (Chapter 3) are related to the operation of unofficial transitional roles. Typically the accumulated influence of such roles would be little relative to some of the other factors with which they overlap. Usually these roles arise from defective operations, which may have been induced by other informal action, and start as attempts to get the work done and to make loose ends meet. They may be called out by unofficial orders, or start through the voluntary action of some officer who wants to experiment with something new, speed up something underway, or who draws together functions of operation that others have overlooked—or know about and want to avoid. In any case, someone with an official role carries out "temporary" functions (or as Stein said, "sticks his neck out") that become more important than expected. This person may become so expert with these unofficial functions that

---

* Here again, industry and business have no monopoly on unofficial action. In at least one community of a state in which it is illegal for public school students to give presents to their teachers, student cliques sometimes obtain permission from their well-loved principal to give gifts with the proviso that "I know nothing about it."

he must weaken his official contribution. He becomes identified with the function and may be maintained and protected where he is as he is without official changes. If he clamors for reward, he may or not receive it but the function is formalized and someone takes the role.

While this direct interplay of informal and formal can lead to official change, the formal role may merely be enlarged to incorporate informal functions without an official change, according to the abilities of the person playing the role. The role of theft intelligencer (Chapter 7) is a case in point.

Prefigured Justifications

Meetings steer only a part of the course between the formal and informal. The clashes and schisms, the interests of the part and the whole, the action of the bored and the partially committed—all are interwoven by tentative prearranged defenses* that cloak much of the action in and out of meetings.

Since integrity of the formal must be preserved, the gap between it and the informal must be within the tolerance of understood propriety. Where personnel must† depart from expectations, they feel obliged to have ready explanations at hand. The executive who stumbles onto irregularities he did not order, and that uninvolved persons know about, must do something for the record and demand an explanation. He cannot tell *everyone,* "I don't care what you do, but don't let me see you." In many cases he must act on what he knows, or, as we have noted repeatedly, feign ignorance. Because he resents having to take action when his subordinates can easily protect him against action-demanding situations, they typically, as in the vertical symbiotic clique, set up essential appearances.‡ The subordinates of course also have a

---

* As planned alternative courses of action, as concealment of unacceptable but workable methods, as ready and sound reasons for accidents, lapses, etc., the use of defenses at various supervisory levels should be the focus of more research. Defenses are a key to rate of change; to the relative strength of the formal; and, related to this the relative tolerance of originality in the organization. With proper caution against the dangers of overintellectualizing one's inquiry, one could search into how often the same defenses are used, and how defenses are regarded at different levels and in different offices of the firm. Relative weight of the formal would be revealed by the volume of defenses, the kinds that are copied, where defenses are most used, and what issues require defenses. On tolerance, defenses are probably related to the type and age of organization and its traditions.

† That is, voluntary or tacitly coerced departures as compared with commanded or granted departures.

‡ This is the defense we referred to as "nominal surprise" in chap. 3.

general interest in protecting the formal* phases of organization as well as their superior.

Hence from fear of alienating a touchy superior as well as to protect him, they develop logical explanations to cover essential but irregular actions. This is not necessarily defiance of the system. The action may also conceal the spearhead of an embryonic procedure not yet ready for the light. Jessup's covertly perfected process at Fruhling (Chapter 3) was initially such a wedge, though it never precipitated the defense which undoubtedly existed. Defenses may cover a short-cut that saves time, economizes currently limited materials, etc., but one that requires rare judgment in its use and for that reason cannot be adopted as a common practice. Or the justification may screen a forbidden stopgap. In any case, the officer concerned would neither advertise his use of the makeshift nor be disturbed about preparing a justification. If detected and questioned by that kind of chief, his convincing response would save both from embarrassment. Justifications can of course become pretexts† to conceal malfeasance.

Defenses may be offered by an individual or a team. Some superiors openly welcome ideas and constructive departures. But where rivalries for individual credit are strong in the group and the superior "wants no

---

* As Moore notes, the "career man" in a given post of any complex organization, has a real security interest in protecting all aspects of the formal that sustain him. W. E. Moore, *Industrial Relations and the Social Order*, 2nd edition, Macmillan, New York, 1951, p. 93. The formal may even be supported in its *errors* for both social and sound economic reasons. A West Coast manager vouches for an incident (anecdotal variants of which are sometimes only attacks on bureaucratic structure in general) illustrating the logical contradictions that can arise in the large organization with scattered branches. A production worker was paid $250.00 more than he had coming. His check was made out in the distant general office. The man consulted his department head who made some calculations, then advised him to keep the check and say nothing about it, for the cost of sorting, collecting, and sending records, checking through several offices and many people, would be upwards of $2000.00, and would therefore constitute a disservice to the company.

† At some vague point justifications blur with pretexts, or trickery for purely personal reasons. Since this, too, is related to the interplay of official and unofficial action, more research is needed here. Scattered throughout the literature on administration, there are allusions to "orders for the record," "built-in alibis," "hidden outs," etc. In addition to clarifying the exchanges between formal and informal, following these leads might uncover justification-pretexts peculiar to supervisory levels, as well as typical ties between pretexts and the variables of occupation, education, and other common categories. See Clarence E. Redfield, *Communication in Management*, The University of Chicago Press, Chicago, 1953, pp. 31, 52–53; W. H. Whyte, Jr. et al., *Is Anybody Listening?* Simon and Schuster, 1952, p. 52.

complications," the departure, though worthwhile, may be hidden, used privately, and not pushed for development or seriously defended. Where no issue of change or improvement in the firm moves deviants they may instead, as is usually said, "dream up explanations," and "keep a drawerful of right answers." There is comparable behavior when line officers prepare to face the effects of staff reports.[35]

As the area of concern becomes more individual than group, the interplay of formal and informal declines and defenses may become only personal subterfuges, as when the ambitious and demanding subordinate supplies his obliging chief with convincing pretexts to forestall the objections of others to favors he receives. In maintaining harmonious appearances, however, probably all departments and key executives must at times exhaust their justifications and have some recourse to pretexts. Among other things, this arises from the obvious practice in most departments* of camouflaging those of their activities running counter to plant logic. Incomplete knowledge of practices behind the screens of other departments forces a given department to maintain a store of pretexts to meet criticisms, and thus enable it to control other departments to a degree and win their aid when necessary.

The Two-way Funnel

Every firm has its internal combustics fed by policy differences, disputes over "credit due," fear that superiors will covertly punish those who oppose them, and by the blocking of some able people from a voice in decisions because of personality differences.

Such conditions inspire feigned acceptance[36] of directives by malcontents who may limit their cooperation or even resist. In either case, one can—too simply—say that the formal precipitates the informal and counter action begins. But when issues grow large and continue unresolved, both official dignity and communication suffer. Compromises, and the wish to save face, lead to indirect communication.

We noted earlier the anonymous efforts of dissatisfied individuals to communicate supposedly important information by telephone and letter to higher officers. This one-way action may be a part of the ongoing interplay of formal and informal. But usually the device is minor because it is anonymous, and too unreliable an artifice to be used systematically by factions. In the great openly political conflicts involving governments, struggles between organizations, etc., it has immemorially been common to use various go-betweens and intercessors both officially and unofficially, to reestablish workable arrangements.

---

* See the functions of the vertical symbiotic clique, chap. 3.

Always requiring loyal and crafty agents, this role is also used in business and industry as a link between formal and informal action. Certainly Merza of Milo (Chapter 7) was a faction broker of the first rank. But when faces must be saved and situations hidden, there is another role similar in function but more elusive, which is commonly called a "two-way funnel." In general the role functions to communicate things that no one wants to assume responsibility for knowing, doing, or being associated with. The person who fills it is not chosen for loyalty or wiliness, but for almost the reverse—his aptness in "talking out of turn" and in carrying "secrets" to the right people which assures almost predictable communication.

Typically the person who fills this role derives great satisfaction from "knowing everyone," or pretending to, and from having "the inside dope" on all issues. In addition to the personal gratification, or illusion, of having a status that gives entry to places inaccessible to others, these usually low-ranking persons officiously push themselves. They may incidentally do little services, supply information of a kind, and even be welcomed by some higherups for their very attentiveness. But dominant persons in the circles they are able to reach level silent exactions for tolerating this intimacy. When situations seem right, the two-way funnel is given a pseudo-secret, or the equivalent of a proposal, or a projected plan of action by one clique to carry as a feint or a trial balloon to another, or to those who will understand and probably respond in some helpfully revealing way. Naturally there are intended leaks by frustrated higherups who do not utilize the funnel, but the practice is clumsy and dangerous as compared with communication by funnels. Known for what they are by members of all factions, funnels are extremely useful. Unsophisticated rank-and-file members sometimes oversimplify and label the funnel as a stool pigeon. However he is not a decoy, or an informer, as these terms are commonly used, because he is not admitted as a partisan and no explicit promises or commitments are given him. For example, such an informal role as that of theft intelligencer (Chapter 7) calls for fully accepted and committed members who know they will be rewarded. This is not true of the funnel.

Where union-management cross-clique ties were fouled or did not exist at Milo, grievers and managers utilized funnels among production workers as the bridge between their official and unofficial actions. Eager and lower-ranking persons were similarly used in some staff-line communications, as well as in vertical exchanges inside both groups.

In smaller firms, one funnel is typically adequate to span the temporary divisions that arise, but every department in larger concerns may require one as an aid to maintaining its place in the system. Funnels are obviously no more foolproof than the patented communication channels. When the spontaneously delivered messages go astray or backfire, participants usually escape by reminding uninitiated critics that the alleged information, action, or involvements "coming from such a source is only somebody's pipedream." However, the essence of what was meant to be conveyed is clear, so that no one loses face, communication of the officially uncommunicable is made, and understandings are reached. The fog of uncertainty for responsible persons is greatly reduced, while the irresponsible and the peripherally lukewarm do not hinder continuity of action, though they may have something to speculate about as they sift the funnel's talk. The researcher does not have to be on the lookout for funnels: they are usually pointed out to him.

The funnel is most serviceable in the early and intermediate stages of given exchanges between specific formal and informal groups for correction of old, or creation of new, conditions. In the "transition"* from informal to formal over action on an issue, the informal phase becomes a spreading project. As more people are drawn in, supporting defenses evolve and give firmness to the multiplying unofficial agreements. The funnel's importance declines at the stage where the original minority practices have become typical and apparent to all. Certain of the old official procedures have in effect moulted. Even the long-faced formalist among higherups now sees that he must modify the structure to embrace the unofficially incubated and nurtured new practices that have multiplied and shown their worth.†

Of course, in the interplay some person or group may choose, from fear or interest, to flatly oppose the informal by clinging to the official, which does give some protection and is always a semantic bulwark. This spurs the informal to quicken its drive for legitimation through official incorporation of what it represents. But in some cases it will naturally be forced to mark time, or even to "withdraw" indefinitely.

Official acceptance of the informal is more likely to be subtle than

---

* There is, of course, properly no transition *terminal,* since there is rarely a finality, but only a succession of changes, which at times can be in either direction.

† History is rich with cases of "stealing the enemy's thunder," and of documented instances, which are correctly translatable into the scheme of interplay between official and unofficial action, in given organizations. Among well-supported cases are those centering around the conflict between Pope Alexander VI and Savonarola and their followers (Pasquale Villari, *Life and Times of Girolamo Savonarola,* T. Fisher Unwin, London, 1888, pp. 373–480, 517–556). Also the incorporation by Francis and Dominic of techniques to preserve the formal (the Church), which were previously denounced when used by heretics. (*Cambridge Medieval History,* The Macmillan Co., New York, 1929, Vol. 6, pp. 727–742.)

open, for even where higherups are ready to face the accomplished fact, there are obstacles to full and ready recognition. For example, neither the majesty of rank nor the personal contribution of stellar chiefs may be minimized in the process.

Split Vacations

Inseparable as physics and chemistry, the ties between formal and informal come out in the problems arising from executive vacations in many of the middle-sized and larger firms. We saw in Chapter 6 the dread experienced by Perry, the Milo first-line foreman, when he had to replace his vacationing general foreman for a week only. As Perry said, "The least little thing you do, you'll find you've stuck somebody's neck out." When only a worker he "couldn't hardly wait for vacations, but now I hate 'em."

Perry was saying in effect that his chief, and others, regularly operated in a network of unofficial and confidential understandings so that their replacements were confused in following only the official guidelines of the absent officer. Sometimes the interdepartmental working involvements excluded officially close supervisors from knowledge of informal phases. Where informal claims were tied to issues in some critical stage, the executives concerned were reluctant to take their vacations in one stretch. Instead they took only a few days or a week at a time, the better to stay on top of events. And some of those taking an unbroken week maintained telephonic contacts with the plant. From the divisional level down through departmental assistants this was common practice at Milo.* Officially, vacations were split or deferred because the officers were "indispensable" or, in a minority of cases, because vacations overlapped. However, those about to take the recess reflected their concern in remarks that replacements might "gum up the works," "make a miscue," or "do the wrong thing."

Two cases from Milo show the interplay of theory and social demand on vacations. In the first case, Bramwell, an assistant staff head, notified Blanke that the agreed deadline for completion of a project would have to be postponed for two months. Somewhat comparable

---

* W. H. Whyte, Jr. cites and analyzes cases of executive vacation splitting to show the organization's control over the individual. But his evidence seems to support equally well the point we are making (see *The Organization Man,* Simon and Schuster, New York, 1956, pp. 160–161), as well as the thesis (somewhat contrary to Whyte's general emphasis) that some individuals, with informal support, do powerfully influence the organization's operations and use its resources in a way not foreseen or planned, and are therefore not always under the organization's control.

to a case cited in Chapter 4, Bramwell had an agreement with the griever Spencer (Chapter 5) to delay the project so that certain groups of workmen would continue to receive job advantages they were almost certain to lose with the proposed change. To police his pact with Spencer, Bramwell deferred his vacation until expiration of the agreed date. Usually Bramwell's subordinate supervisor, Stokes, replaced him during vacations, but currently there was friction between the two because of Bramwell's alleged unreceptiveness to Stokes' ideas. Hence Bramwell did not want Stokes in a position to know of the agreement for fear it would leak to Blanke.

In the second case, the executive Ruf recently split his vacation because the last week of it extended into a period when his friend, assistant superintendent Scheele of another department, would have a periodic job to be done in one of Ruf's shops. This was an expensive job if all the time for it were charged to Scheele. Ruf regularly saw that Scheele did not have to report the full time. He did not involve his shop foremen, but personally arranged with his staff friends to reduce the time charged to Scheele, and to distribute the difference elsewhere—somewhat in the manner practiced systematically under the FWD.

Vacation splitting as a strain on the formal-informal tie is of course not confined to executives or factories. Though the stakes are naturally much smaller, the sales forces in department stores become similarly involved. In numerous cases at the Rambeau Mart (Chapter 7) male and female clerks were ensnared by their services and promises to customers.* This created problems of coordinating their scheduled vacation period with their private obligations to store patrons, and with finding replacements whom they would trust to know and deal with their commitments in the competitive atmosphere. Splits were a common solution. Vacation time is also naturally influenced by seasonal preferences and rivalries.

SUMMARY

The problem of fusing the open and covert phases of organization is old. Moralists, litterateurs, philosophers, and scientists have variously labeled and debated the phases. Some students have sought to settle the issue by excluding one or other of the phases as a fiction, though to date none has declared this of both. Recognition of the two ex-

---

* As developed in Barnard's theory, customers are also part of the organization. See *Functions of the Executive, op. cit.,* p. 71.

tremes through history indicates that both are essential even though they may be fictions in the philosophic sense.[37]

Granting that they are "real" in a working sense, their interrelations and relative strength in organizational action must be considered. Accepting the terms "formal" and "informal" as helpful labels for the two poles, we saw that they are held together by meetings, unofficially ordered or granted departures from the formal, transitional roles, prefigured justifications, the role of the "two-way funnel," and the eventual formalizing of sound or inescapable practices that may have earlier been taboo.

Our emphasis on the informal as one force in necessary change and supplementation of the formal, and as a protection of individual and group values springing from various social, biological, and cultural "drives," requires a word on minimum functions of the formal.

Beyond its now trite merits of providing correct communication channels and fixing responsibility, the formal is the one sure avenue of exchange between enemies in the organization, as well as the bar to entry of undesirables.

Yet the formal is always subject to pressures to make it so broad and elastic that distinctions between the phases become blurred. This condition obviously increases with the actual participation by members in decisions governing them. Here informal phases often work to prevent clear definitions and planning that threaten to limit freedom to act and to save face. Informalists want liberty to rearrange issues so that neither victory nor defeat, in the maneuvers of contending groups, can damage the organization.[38]

But however irregularly the informal operates to make changes, to check extremes of official—or other informal—action; or however purely evasive or organizationally superfluous the informal may be, the formal restrains it in at least three ways. First, the formal largely orders the direction the informal takes. Second, it consequently shapes the character of defenses created by the informal. And third, whether the formal is brightly or dimly existent in the blur of contradictions, it requires overt conformity to its precepts. Any concern about the state of operations or the trend of organizational events is directly or indirectly concern for the formal, whether it is only understood or is officially explicit. In the ongoing action, however, the formal restructures itself as it seeks to encompass and contain what the formalists regard as evasive activities.

The interplay between formal and informal is of course not always at a high level of intensity, nor is it inherently a "cloak-and-dagger" action as discussion of it usually implies. In rare instances when the phases are fused, the interplay would be negligible or nil. But intensity of the cross movements is subject to many variables, and despite all planning, the reciprocal action leads to personal suffering for some, as we shall see in the next chapter. For others it is "natural" to the extent of being taken for granted.

DOCUMENTARY NOTES

1. This is related to the much more general concept of "Culture Lag." See W. F. Ogburn, *Social Change,* Viking Press, New York, 1922, 1950, pp. 200–280, and H. Hart, "The Hypothesis of Cultural Lag: A Present Day View," in F. R. Allen et al., *Technology and Social Change,* Appleton-Century-Crofts, New York, 1957, pp. 417–434.

2. M. Dalton, "In-Plant Politics at the Executive and Supervisory Levels," *I.R. News,* Institute of Industrial Relations at UCLA, February, 1957, p. 2.

3. From his *lex Julia majestatis,* one of the "Julian" Laws. See Sir William Blackstone, *Commentaries on the Laws of England,* Rees, Welsh and Co., Philadelphia, 1900, Vol. 4, pp. 1481–1482.

4. Thurman W. Arnold, *The Folklore of Capitalism,* Yale University Press, 1937, p. 368. See also chaps. 5, 7, and especially 14, "Some Principles of Political Dynamics."

5. Mary Parker Follett. See H. C. Metcalf and L. Urwick, eds., *Dynamic Administration: The Collected Papers of Mary Parker Follett,* Management Publications Trust, Ltd., London, 1941, pp. 146–160.

6. Marion J. Levy, Jr., *The Structure of Society,* Princeton University Press, 1952, pp. 83–88.

7. *Heracleitus on the Universe* (in *Hippocrates and the Fragments of Heracleitus*), Loeb Classical Library, London, Heinemann Ltd., 4 vols. 1923–1931, Vol. 4, pp. 449–509; *Cambridge Ancient History,* Cambridge University Press, 1939, Vol. 4, p. 38; Bertrand Russell, *A History of Western Philosophy,* Simon and Schuster, New York, 1945, pp. 46–47.

8. C. I. Barnard, *Functions of the Executive,* Harvard University Press, Cambridge, 1938, p. 120. And W. G. Sumner has spoken of "antagonistic cooperation" as "the most productive form of combination in high civilization." See his *Folkways,* Ginn and Company, Boston, 1906, pp. 16–18.

9. The analysis in Book 3, chap. 82, could be applied to many "modern" situations.

10. The Loeb Classical Library, Heinemann Ltd., London, 1932, pp. 459–475.

11. *The Discourses of Machiavelli,* trans. and ed. by Leslie J. Walker, S.J., Yale University Press, New Haven, 1950, 2 vols. See especially Vol. 1, pp. 470–491 and Vol. 2, pp. 154–168.

12. Alexander Hamilton, John Jay, and James Madison, *The Federalist,* Paper Ten.

13. "Political and Personal Morality," *The Saturday Review,* December 31, 1955, pp. 5–6, 31–32. One of the most sophisticated discussions of this problem in professional politics—by a historian who denies it—is that of F. S. Oliver in *The Endless Adventure,* 3 vols., Macmillan and Co., Ltd., London, 1930–1935. See especially Vol. 1, pp. 3–111; Vol. 2, pp. 280–286, 297–302; Vol. 3, pp. 147–178. See also Eugen Ehrlich, *Fundamental Principles of the Sociology of Law,*

Harvard University Press, Cambridge, 1936, chaps. 6–9, and Vilfredo Pareto, *The Mind and Society*, 4 vols., ed. and trans. by A. Livingstone and A. Bongiorno, Harcourt, Brace and Co., New York, 1935, especially the numbered paragraphs 150 ff., 889–990, 991–1088, 1687–2059.

14. Barnard, *op. cit.*, pp. 65–123.

15. F. J. Roethlisberger and J. Dickson, *Management and the Worker*, Harvard University Press, Cambridge, 1939, chaps. 7 and 17.

16. Delbert C. Miller and William H. Form, *Industrial Sociology*, Harper and Brothers, New York, 1951, chaps. 6 and 9; Wilbert E. Moore, *Industrial Relations and the Social Order*, 2nd edition, Macmillan Co., New York, 1951, chap. 12; Robert Dubin, *Human Relations in Administration*, Prentice-Hall, New York, 1951, pp. 47–78; Leonard Broom and Philip Selznick, *Sociology*, Row, Peterson and Co., Evanston, Ill., 1955, pp. 206–216; Robert Bierstedt, *The Social Order*, McGraw-Hill Book Co., New York, 1957, pp. 291–298; John M. Pfiffner, *A Tentative Syllabus for the Study of Informal Organization*, School of Public Administration, University of Southern California, Los Angeles, 1949, and *The Supervision of Personnel: Human Relations in the Management of Men*, Prentice-Hall, New York, 1951, chap. 8; E. Wight Bakke, *The Fusion Process*, Labor and Management Center, Yale University, New Haven, 1953 (This book deals exclusively with formal-informal, status problems, and related items.); Keith Davis, *Human Relations in Business*, McGraw-Hill Book Co., New York, 1957, chap. 6; Peter M. Blau, "Formal Organization: Dimensions of Analysis," *American Journal of Sociology*, 63: 58–69, July, 1957; Reinhard Bendix, "Bureaucracy: The Problem and Its Setting," *American Sociological Review*, 12: 493–507, October, 1947; Chris Argyris, *Personality and Organization*, Harper and Brothers, New York, 1957, pp. 54–75; J. F. Scott and R. P. Lynton, *Three Studies in Management*, Routledge and Kegan Paul, London, 1952, chaps. 5–6.

17. Charles E. Redfield, *Communication in Management*, The University of Chicago Press, 1953, pp. 10–11.

18. Barnard, *op. cit.*, p. 114.

19. M. E. Dimock, *The Executive in Action*, Harper and Brothers, New York, 1945, pp. 9, 156–157, 160, 164, 171–172, and chap. 20.

20. *Ibid.*, p. 240.

21. Rudolph Herberle, "The Sociological System of Ferdinand Tönnies," in H. E. Barnes, ed., *An Introduction to The History of Sociology*, University of Chicago Press, 1948, p. 234.

22. Lyndall Urwick, *Some Notes on the Theory of Organization*, American Management Association, New York, 1952, p. 72, and *The Pattern of Management*, University of Minnesota Press, Minneapolis, 1956, pp. 86–88.

23. Perrin Stryker and the editors of *Fortune*, *A Guide to Modern Management Methods*, McGraw-Hill Book Co., New York, 1954, p. 108.

24. Wallace B. Donham, *Education for Responsible Living*, Harvard University Press, 1944; F. J. Roethlisberger and W. J. Dickson, *Management and the Worker*, *op. cit.*, and Roethlisberger, *Management and Morale*, Harvard University Press, Cambridge, 1947; Elton Mayo, *The Human Problems of an Industrial Civilization*, Macmillan Co., New York, 1933, and *The Social Problems of an Industrial Civilization*, Division of Research, Harvard Graduate School of Business Administration, Boston, 1945; T. N. Whitehead, *Leadership in a Free Society*, Harvard University Press, 1937; W. F. Whyte, *Human Relations in the Restaurant Industry*, McGraw-Hill Book Co., New York, 1948; George C. Homans, *The Human Group*, Harcourt, Brace and Co., New York, 1950.

25. Eli Ginzberg, ed., *What Makes an Executive?* Columbia University Press, New York, 1955, p. 112.

26. H. Frederick Willkie, *A Rebel Yells,* D. Van Nostrand Co., 1946, pp. 186, 188.

27. C. Shartle, *Executive Performance and Leadership,* Prentice-Hall, Englewood Cliffs, N.J., 1956, p. 60.

28. See *From Max Weber: Essays in Sociology,* trans. by H. Gerth and C. Wright Mills, Oxford University Press, New York, 1946, pp. 196–244; Max Weber, *The Theory of Social and Economic Organization,* trans. by A. M. Henderson and T. Parsons, Oxford University Press, New York, 1947; Max Rheinstein, ed., *Max Weber on Law in Economy and Society,* trans. by Edward Shils and Max Rheinstein, Harvard University Press, Cambridge, 1954, especially pp. 349–356; Robert Michels, *Political Parties,* The Free Press, Glencoe, Ill., 1949. For a great range of short discussions on both formal and informal by various specialists, and an extensive bibliography, see R. K. Merton, et al., eds., *Reader in Bureaucracy,* The Free Press, Glencoe, Ill., 1952.

29. See chap. 8, "How Executives Delegate," by Perrin Stryker, in *The Executive Life,* Doubleday and Co., Garden City, N.Y., 1956.

30. Elliott Jaques, *The Changing Culture of a Factory,* The Dryden Press, New York, 1952, pp. 212–213. Also see Chris Argyris, *Personality and Organization,* Harper and Brothers, New York, 1957, p. 205.

31. Herbert Emmerich, "New Bridges between Theory and Practice," in L. D. White, ed., *The State of the Social Sciences,* University of Chicago Press, 1956, p. 385.

32. Lyndall Urwick, *Some Notes on the Theory of Organization,* American Management Association, New York, 1952, p. 16. See also P. Selznick, *TVA and Grass Roots,* University of California Press, 1949, pp. 250–259.

33. Several sociologists who served as American naval officers during the Second World War have made insightful analyses of these interplays involving individuals, and groups of various sizes. See especially, Charles Hunt Page, "Bureaucracy's Other Face," *Social Forces,* 25: 88–94, October, 1946; Ralph H. Turner, "The Navy Disbursing Officer as a Bureaucrat," *American Sociological Review,* 12: 342–348, June, 1947; Arthur K. Davis, "Bureaucratic Patterns in the Navy Officer Corps," *Social Forces,* 27: 143–153, December, 1948. Also see W. F. Whyte, "The Social Structure of the Restaurant," *American Journal of Sociology,* 54: 302–308, January, 1949, and *Human Relations in the Restaurant Industry,* McGraw-Hill Book Co., New York, 1948.

Specialized students will also want to look at Georg Simmel, *Conflict* (trans. by Kurt H. Wolff) and *The Web of Group-Affiliations* (trans. by Reinhard Bendix), The Free Press, Glencoe, Ill., 1955; and Lewis A. Coser, *The Functions of Social Conflict,* The Fress Press, Glencoe, Ill., 1956.

34. See Ginzberg, *op. cit.,* p. 148.

35. See B. B. Gardner and David G. Moore, *Human Relations in Industry,* 3rd edition, R. D. Irwin, Homewood, Ill., 1955, pp. 71–73.

36. Dimock, *op. cit.,* p. 237.

37. Hans Vaihinger, *The Philosophy of As If,* Harcourt, Brace and Co., New York, 1924.

38. In different terms Lyman Bryson touches on this point. See his "Notes on a Theory of Advice," *Political Science Quarterly,* 66: 321–339, September, 1951.

CHAPTER **9**

The Manager Between
Formal and Informal

We have seen managers hurried and hurrying about in various formal and informal groups, but excepting a paragraph in Chapter 6, we have not considered the meaning of this for the individual. To do so now we need first to look quickly at (1) the fundamental clash between the rigorously rational organization and the individual member; (2) the coerced "freedom" of the individual; (3) the moral problems of dealing with ambiguity; and (4) ambiguity as a selective force in separating the "abler" from the "less able" executives.

INDIVIDUAL VERSUS ORGANIZATION[1]

Santayana's observation that "Society is like the air, necessary to breathe but insufficient to live on," essentially reflects the individual's condition in the rational organization, especially those of middle to large size. He lives from the firm, but some of its demands are contrary to his nature and inadequate for his impulses. He may feel so inhibited by it that he combines with others to elude it or to reshape parts of it. We need not repeat the individual victories and defeats, the verbal attacks and ingenious evasions by individuals collaborating or breaking with others, or note the changes they forced in planning as

241

they sought to advance and to protect themselves,[2] or to contain situations threatening parts of the organization essential to them.

Various students and practicing executives have made passing remarks about the effects of organization on the executive, and some students have analyzed the effects on production workers.[3] Though the range of explanations is great and often contradictory, there is general agreement that the individual operates under various stresses. Barnard, for example, cryptically refers to "certain effects of formal organizations which tend to disintegrate the personality."[4] Silberston[5] implies the condition in pointing to "resilience under conditions of adversity" as the vital quality in executives. Roscoe[6] pictures the executive as "confronted with situations complicated by pro and con factors, particularly intangibles. . . ." Stryker[7] talks of executive turnover stemming from a desire to "escape the politics in their companies" as well as the "pressures developed by clashing personalities. . . ." Dimock holds that merely working in large organizations makes many people "neurotic in some way," and that no one is immune.[8] Argyris implies the same problem in a chapter title, "Decreasing the Degree of Incongruence Between the Formal Organization and the Healthy Individual."[9]

The remarks of Barnard and Dimock, particularly, suggest the "dehumanizing" aspects of life in large formal organizations. Such experiences *are* in a sense *unhuman* to the extent that purely rational behavior is demanded. Some students believe that the *distinctively* human thing about man is his capacity to have a socialized feeling and to understand others by sympathetically "taking their roles." And in terms of this capacity they hold that we are not strictly human beings at birth, but are born with only the potential for achieving that condition. We become human beings, they say,[10] only through years of personal, intimate participation from infancy with those who have had similar experiences. They suggest that prolonged discontinuance of such experiences may impair or destroy what was acquired. Hemmed in by necessarily rational and impersonal demands the individual would, therefore, be in an element contrary to his personalizing nature. When requested to neatly separate but *rationally* exercise both aptitudes, he can indeed become distressed.

The editors of *Fortune* quote an executive who hints at how the tightrope between individual and organization should be walked. "The ideal," he says, "is to be an individualist privately and a conformist publicly—if you can pull it off."[11] Since the individual can do relatively little entirely on his own, this executive is really advising—and warning—him that he must learn to square his official with his unofficial actions, which poses another problem.

THE PARADOX OF COERCED FREEDOM

It is fashionable to stress the individual's submergence and loss in the organization. Comparison of pro and con cases for this view quickly pushes discussion to philosophical and infuriatingly unverifiable levels. The case chapters can be used to support either view. But against *total* submergence of the individual—which few in a democracy would admit —there is for many in the organization a kind of unsought freedom that imposes suffering. This is the freedom to choose alternative courses of action, to create new means, official or not, for winning ends, and to devise ways of appearing to conform when practice forbids it. The course and outcome of interplay between official and unofficial are usually uncertain. This itself is a condition of freedom. We saw in Chapter 5 that the individual griever or executive was "free" to follow contract provisions and suffer defeat by those who did not, or to act on his own insofar as he did not embarrass his superiors. This freedom obviously is restricted by his need to be covert, by the state of his informal ties, by unassessable chance factors, and by his moral strictures. This last point must be enlarged.

MORAL ISSUES IN AMBIGUITY[12]

All decisions imply choice and can therefore be regarded as moral acts. But when decisions directly involve others, as in organizations, and are made in an atmosphere of uncertainty, they become acutely moral. Man's peculiar social nature is dependent on certainty in the sense of receiving a flow of gestures of agreement and acceptance from associates. Since he lives by "socially consistent sensation," he is outraged by ambiguity. And he is further tortured by the responsibility, as a formal decision-maker, for transforming it into certainty, and by fear of failure and rejection.

To belabor the point for our situations, his sharpest moral pains grow out of the clash between administrative logic and social demands. The individual decision-maker in line or staff who tries, as he usually must, to match his official and unofficial moralities often finds himself without anchor or guiding precept. However he bears the blame of compromised issues that are never settled to anyone's complete satisfaction and that reverberate endlessly. Any classification of his moral burdens would probably be incomplete and overlap. But the common recurring ones fall into at least four areas: (1) disagreements in the group about "right" and "wrong" decisions as they affect both organizational and individual purposes; (2) moral conflicts that develop in any group from the easy translation of individual preferences, practices, and interests into abstract "rights"; (3) executive entrapment between the organization's ideal and the ethics of his group; (4) decisions and actions in ambiguous situations where new and initially questionable means must be devised. The first three items require but a word; the fourth must be expanded.

Dispute about right and wrong decisions usually arises from failure to match contrary perspectives: the outlook of those who see the situation as essentially fixed and therefore calling for simple, direct action; as against that of those who see it as complex and requiring more dexterous treatment. To express this ancient theme in the ancient manner: whoso here chooses a workable alternative bears the group sin.

On our second point, when clash of interests leads each individual to garb his "rights" in a private moral principle, both the contradiction and the moral load for some superior is obvious.

On point three, the executive who responsibly seeks to correlate his formal with his various changing informal roles is inescapably caught between organizational and group ethics, usually the ethics of several groups. His psychological load is greatest when only he, or a small number of other people in the firm, see the significance of what must be done.

In the fourth category, we have seen many situations confused by intricate and shifting cross-currents of action that the decision-maker, to contain his troubles, must cast into some officially proper mold. This is dealing with the ambiguity of being "an individualist privately and a conformist publicly." To do so effectively calls for moral creativity in finding a solution valid for the agreed ideal, and originality in justifying the solution to those subject to its conditions. Daily the executive sails a "planned" course through a flood of mixed personal and impersonal alternatives and surprises. He must strike some kind of balance between rational and emotional behavior toward his juniors and associates. To survive the clash of logical and personal claims he "must appear to believe in the values of his company" but "be able to ignore them when it serves his purpose."* When he decides in favor of the organization,

---

* From a description by Richard Tynan, cited by W. H. Whyte, Jr., in *The Organization Man,* Simon and Schuster, New York, 1956, p. 165. The essential qualities and strain are implicit in the phrases of practitioners. A West-Coast executive recently advised his collegiate son to "stay out of the business world . . . take something else. . . . You don't have the guile and guts to make a go of it." The late deeply experienced George Eastman characterized his reluctant return home from a safari in 1926 as a move "back to the world of fraud and front."

Also see W. E. Henry, "The Business Executive: The Psychodynamics of a Social Role," *American Journal of Sociology,* 54: 288, January, 1949.

contrary to demands of his group, he is immoral in their eyes. If he follows the group call, and the organization is damaged, he is immoral. Usually he shuns the route of "either-or" and follows the course of "either-and-or," which is compromise, or a third immoral choice to some. To take this path he must penetrate the inscrutable and seize what is useful for the occasion. He must know when and how to use clique ties. And he must improvise and match his departures and defenses and give both the right hue of dogma for powerful formalists who must be lived with.

The word "compromise" has ugly connotations. Against the picture evoked by Chamberlain and Hitler in 1938, we should pose Lincoln's opposition to repeal of the Missouri Compromise, and his request for return to "the spirit of concession and compromise . . . which has never failed us . . . and which may be safely trusted for all the future."*

Compromise may certainly be selfish expediency; and misuse of high principles on occasion seems to have occurred universally. But in any ongoing organization, responsible compromise calls for courage and insight. Courage in facing the complications of *not* fitting absolute meanings to vague situations and shifting commitments; insight† in knowing what items of policy to concede without destroying core principles. To sanctify either formal or informal approaches to the exclusion of the other, when concession is necessary, is immoral and overlooks the fact that the very rules and principles being fought over are products of compromise. Interaction in the large plant, with the mixed and changing rights and obligations of its personnel, mothers both invention and compromise.

Compromise is inescapable‡ when (1) issues are deadlocked and other alternatives are morally and otherwise more expensive; (2) harmony is

---

* Speech, Peoria, Illinois, October 16, 1854. R. C. Davis (*Fundamentals of Top Management,* Harper and Brothers, New York, 1951, p. 147), like one of the executives earlier cited from Ginzberg, believes that the qualities of the "successful politician" apply to any top leadership. He cites James J. Farley as such a politician and quotes him as advocating two essentials, among others: capacity to compromise and to be decisive.

† Max Weber has noted that scientists have no monopoly on insight and creativity. For "the situation is" not "different in a merchant's office from what it is in a laboratory. A merchant or a large-scale industrialist without . . . ideas, brilliant original ideas, remains at best but a clerk or a technician." See "Science as a Vocation," trans. by Edward A. Shils, in *Contemporary Society, Selected Readings* (Social Science 3), University of Chicago Bookstore, 10th edition, 1942, p. 11.

‡ T. V. Smith has pointedly phrased the tie between ideal and action in the context of compromise: "(1) The quantity of compromise required in society varies directly with the area of action; and (2) the quality of ideality surviving

preferable to conflict; (3) the greatest interest is to move ahead; and when (4) powerful associates and superiors (*e.g.,* Milo-Office struggle) are compromising so that those unable to make concessions are forced to accept situations they might have modified more to their liking.

Thus the executive's latitude to choose among workable alternatives is really coercion to find practical means and to resolve his own moral conflicts as well as those of his subordinates.* Although no executive may completely resolve the contradictions, some are more successful than others. Hence the situation operates to select those most able to interweave the moving complex of out-plant and in-plant social, moral, and emotional claims on them with the "logical" demands of higherups.

THE SELECTIVE FORCE OF AMBIGUITY

This selection works ceaselessly throughout the administrative and staff hierarchies. It never operates perfectly, for it is often sidetracked by the cliques; they resist excessive logic, protect certain amiable misfits, and support those who may be weak in their official roles but adept in various informal roles. As with our use of "formal" and "informal," it is helpful for discussion to construct extreme and opposed types that no individual would fit perfectly. But here, too, there are no generally accepted terms for distinguishing the more from the less successful in surviving the tensions we have sketched. One might, as has been done, label them respectively as "goal-oriented" versus "methods-oriented," or "dominant versus submissive," or "entrepreneurial versus bureaucratic," or "rule-creative versus rule-bound," "operative versus rhetorical," etc. However, the presumed objectivity of these phrases obscures other things. If we keep in mind (1) that the types are only models of tendencies that are over-lapped by all practicing executives; and (2) that no moral blame is implied, we can call the more effective *strong,*

---

compromise varies inversely with the size of the collectivity." Combining the two in one formulation, "Quantity and quality of ideality for action vary inversely." See *The Ethics of Compromise,* Starr King Press, Boston, 1956, p. 62, and pp. 64–80; and Georg Simmel, *Conflict,* The Free Press, Glencoe, Ill., 1955, pp. 115–116.

  * See C. I. Barnard, *Functions of the Executive,* Harvard University Press, Cambridge, 1938, especially chaps. 13 and 14 and pp. 272–284, where Barnard argues that executive responsibility correlates with "moral complexity," that leaders fail when gaps develop between their personal and organizational codes and when they exhaust their "moral creativity." Also see Dewey, *Human Nature and Conduct,* Henry Holt and Co., New York, 1922, who analyzes morality as activity, and as "a continuing process not a fixed achievement" (p. 280), and not a "definite sum of accomplishment which will forever stay done" (p. 285).

and the others *weak*. Though usually not, the strong can of course be immoral in the sense of losing sight of organizational and group good to enlarge personal benefits or maliciously use their influence; and the weak may at times show uncommon fiber. Also, the behavior of neither type should be regarded purely as a reflection of convictions, for both the able and the inept are at times forced to act contrary to their feelings —the one in compromising, the other in following reluctantly.

The weak are fearful in conflict situations and absorb aggressions to avoid trouble. Having a low tolerance for conflict, they do not fill their offices. They hesitate to act without consulting superiors, and take refuge in clearly formulated rules whether adequate or not for their footing at the moment. Following their fairy-tale image of the organization as a fixed thing, they suffer from their experience that it is not. This of course aggravates their difficulty in grasping the tacit expectations that associates do not wish to spell out when events are troublesome. When regulations are changed, the weak adjust slowly and often fail to make passable use of the new directives. In their life outside the firm, where conflict is less or different, they may function acceptably, yet fail when trapped among competing claims peculiar to the plant. When they do fall short, they are likely to advertise the fact. In their distress they involve associates in trouble by blunders that disclose departmental secrets. As they seek to escape dilemmas, their unfitness to act outside the haven of understood rules invites aggression from the strong who are searching for shortcuts in the network of official routes.

The strong on the other hand tolerate dilemmas, and even make a game of them. Pulled between official and unofficial claims on themselves, they are less morally disturbed than the weak because they and their followers* variously influence the system and profit from it. They flee neither necessary conflict nor the responsibility for charting new routes. They quickly turn ambiguous situations to their needs. By resolving contrary demands on themselves they aid both superiors and subordinates and thus expand their office. Where the weak look for protection in the letter of rules, the strong find essential meanings in formal precepts by their free and unanswerable interpretations. They

---

* It is only a trifling exaggeration to say that even in bureaucracies the strong always have amiable adherents. These followers must have a certain minimum aptitude to do some of the formally necessary things. Meeting that condition are numerous persons, including some of the weak, who in the roles of quip-artist and applauder ease tensions and cheer the scene, and at times serve as convenient butts. They are in effect variants of the medieval court jester. There is no necessity that these persons reflect the glory of the strong to the extent of being the "yes-men" described by Willkie, *A Rebel Yells*, D. Van Nostrand Co., New York, 1946, pp. 186, 188.

know when to avoid decisions, and they are able to mark time and wait for developments with minor frustration. More able to anticipate and interpret developments, they are more likely to have the reserve which enables them to meet the situation, and to refrain from driving subordinates toward some abstract end they are fearful of missing. If they fail to adjust quickly to reorganization, they at least meet change with minimum distress for themselves and plant goals. They use failures to reorient themselves in the maze of events.

In short, the weak are prone to lose sight of goals in concentrating on procedures. Hence in unstable situations not yet covered by rules, or where rules are outdated or will never be detailed, they cannot improvise. Against this, the strong are so unconcerned with procedure —except when it is a clear aid or can be interpreted to their advantage or is a necessary symbol—and so accustomed to moving directly toward goals that they readily devise new methods in doubtful situations.

The two types are spontaneously identified by associates and subordinates. In general, the weak are spoken of as being "unable to cut the buck," being a "foul ball," as having "no guts," "no savvy," and as being "boneheads," etc. The strong, as "a guy you can count on," or "who won't let you down," as having "a lot on the ball," as "doing what's necessary," as being "on the beam," as one who "really stacks up," "a damn good man," etc.

These sketches of clash between individual and organization, of the individual's coerced freedom, of his moral dilemma, and of the type most likely to survive must be drawn together. This can be done by a summary of typical pressures on the department head and his ways of meeting them. Then we must speak of how the incorrectly or partially conditioned newcomer to the administrative scene learns to deal with situations. Finally we need to rephrase the clash between individual and organization in terms of fitting planned offices (or roles) into the organization, or role system.

THE DEPARTMENT HEAD AS A CLAIMS ADJUSTOR

The Claims

Though all figures in the management hierarchy are subject to pressures, the department head, as a "middle manager," bears the most inconsistent burdens. He must reconcile the complex outlooks and compromising techniques of his superiors with the relatively direct and uncompromising approaches of his juniors. As the claims of each mount on him, he shares their respective burdens. This forces him into the nebulous role of liaison semanticist: he translates the irregularities below him into decorous reports for his chiefs (Chapter 3), and liberally interprets their directives to his subordinates.

Abstracting from Chapters 3 through 6 we see that the department head must be prepared to meet certain recurring situational and personal demands. For instance, he has at least to (1) show that his relations with the union are good but not too good; (2) defeat the ambitions of those seeking his position; (3) meet the cost pressures of higher management, and (4) protect himself against the poaching and intrigues of other departments; (5) oppose stratagems of the union without offending superiors or revealing his techniques and pacts to other departments; (6) aid the advancement of clamoring subordinates, while considering the effect on his own position and the department as well as the organization if he allows able people to quit the firm; and weigh the ego-problems in his department when he sponsors a man; (7) avoid complications with staff groups; and finally, (8) to advance his own career.

The Adjustments

Item 1. The chief who gets a hint from above that his relations with the union are "causing trouble" in other departments, points to his grievance record as proof of his "good relations." If he is then told that the formal record is "O.K.," but that rumors say all is not in the record, he knows that his pacts with grievance committeemen are less secret than he thought. He takes steps to plug leaks and to reformulate arrangements.

Item 2. Learning that others are deviously busy to unseat him,* he sets about improving relations with his superiors and discrediting the individual or clique threatening him. Through persuasive economy, he strengthens his position upstairs. He pares operation costs by reducing overtime, cutting his use of lubricants for short-run savings, and the like. In the same motion he warms up his staff contacts and makes new ones among those who process his records. He reanimates the department by tightening certain formal controls and giving more personal attention to the able but relatively meek supervisors he has shortchanged in submitting to the more aggressive. He gives more attention to screening all reports from below and tries to spend more time at their source. He checks on informal arrangements that could be troublesome. In a word, he redirects his attention from the currently less hazardous to the more hazardous in his ambit of alternatives.

---

* Unlike the positions in many other bureaucracies, the business executive usually does not have the explicit security of tenure. Tenure too, of course, may involve much that is not seen.

His discredit of a rival is, of course, influenced by whether or not
the man is in the same department.   If in, he diminishes the man by
giving information to higherups that puts him in disfavor, by withholding knowledge essential for him to function, or by a prudent
frame up.   If he originally sponsored the rival, he must naturally back
his change of heart with the sharpest casuistry.   If his opponent is in
another department, the executive must call on friends and horizontal
clique members for aid and then proceed more complexly to release or
distort personal knowledge of the rival, and to alter interlinked work
procedures so that he involves himself in trouble and advertises his
unfitness.

Items 3 and 4.   To meet cost pressures from above, and to protect
himself against other departments, the unit chief first cements understandings between himself and central maintenance.   Next he of course
resorts to some of the same maneuvering essential in checking rivals, for
economy is eventually the bugbear on every front.   But in addition he
makes special effort to contain subordinates who are disposed to bait
the accounting, auditing, and inspection staffs, all of whom can—on the
strength of good will and cooperation—soften, reinterpret, and delay
reports.   If as a general tactic this is unsuccessful, as it often is, he seeks
aid from some individual staff member who is, or can be made, indebted
to him.   And now of all times he works for harmonious give-and-take
between his own production and clerical crews.

Item 5.   In meeting union stratagems he goes through the usual routine
of consulting with associates, and he seems to adopt the group wisdom.
But he usually ends by developing barter systems with the individual
griever, or shop steward, or informal shop leader.   Since their actions,
like his, are both group and individual, open and covert, he has the
problem of matching variables.   Oftener than not he finds his best
solutions by bartering as part of a union-management clique.

Item 6.   The department chief meets the career demands of his juniors
by devices adapted to the particular officer.   Where the subordinate's
situation is ideal—a good man in his current post but burdened with
years, limited job prospects elsewhere, indebtedness, heavy family
responsibilities, etc., consolations and promises are usually enough to quiet
him.   But the able, aggressive subordinate with fewer shackles needs
fatherly attention.   The chief usually allows him to get into a compromising situation from which he saves him and claims his gratitude.   Or
by revision of duties he makes the man's current job more desirable
and freer of conflict than the one he seeks.   Where others in the department are on the same job level this device may lead to conflict.   In
such cases the chief may work to get the man a confidential salary

increase. In a few cases he succeeds in getting him a promotion. If unsuccessful, and the person's contributions warrant the complications, he may variously use the role of assistant-to (Chapter 3) as a way out.

Item 7. The line department head must deal with some staff on nearly every front of his official work. As we just saw in items 2, 3, and 4, he must call on various staffs for informal aid. However, he has a general approach toward all staffs in maintaining himself. Behind his easy cooperation with them, as well as during the coldly polite intervals, he is alert to block staff people playing the role of monitor to top line. This he does by leaking misinformation, and by appropriately concealing or coloring events and conditions. At the same time, during the round of meetings he must attend, he filters gossip, rumor, and confidences to learn of higher staff-line arrangements. On the basis of earlier events and this daily gleaning he maintains a set of tentative defenses to meet both developing and existing policy.

Knowing the symbol hunger of staff people, when he needs their aid he plays his role of authority by giving them favors of little consequence to him—lunch together outside the plant, personal rather than delegated attention to simple staff requests, proffered use of line subordinates, readiness to meet with the staff in *their* offices. And at all times he is alert to single out staff malcontents and "eager beavers" for experimental wooing by implied agreements, intimated aid, small talk on possible contacts to make, etc. If successful in this, he lays on claims.

Item 8. In meeting these seven general claims the unit chief naturally makes each of his adjustments with some thought of the eighth claim on his attention: his personal advantage.* As did both Higgins and Gilter in their clash over maintenance work (Chapter 3), he picks some consolatory contribution to the firm from every struggle in which he engages. And whether fanciful or real, he lays them by to garb rhetorically and present at the right time.

In the meantime he dominates his departmental clique. This is of course far from being purely a matter of authority. He persuades those of his formalist juniors to share his compromises. To do this he frequently withholds some information about his involvements in meeting other claims to avoid arousing adverse ethical judgments that would limit their cooperation. Hence on the basis of his knowledge of their outlooks, he strikes some kind of equilibrium among his commanded and granted informal actions, his orders for the record, and his inescapable

---

* See Ralph Currier Davis, *Fundamentals of Top Management,* Harper and Brothers, New York, 1951, p. 468, in which the author frankly states that "Everyone is interested in the well-being of the organization, but only after he gets what he wants."

horizontal clique entanglements. Ignoring the chance factors over which he has no control, his claims for a career thus equate roughly with his success in maintaining a departmental clique that permits him to function as necessary in horizontal cliques. And in adjusting the claims on him, his formal role—whether recognized or not—becomes little more than a dressing room where he prepares to act out his changing repertory of informal roles. His office is thus both a directive and a disguise.

Describing the system as a force in selecting those most able to deal with confusion, calls for some analysis of how this is unofficially learned.

LEARNING TO LIVE IN AMBIGUITY

In Chapter 6 we touched on the transfer potential of incidental conditioning which individuals might receive from life in certain kinds of families, and from their college experiences under some conditions. The generalizations sociologists have made about social class may apply too. For example persons coming from middle classes strive toward high job goals, channel their impulses to that end, manipulate associates as necessary, and wear the proper urbane mask.[13] One entering the executive role with this bent obviously would have a running start over persons from lower classes who often lack foresight, and are impulsive and outspoken.[14] The latter would be like the Milo foremen who denounced their superiors as "liars" and "hypocrites." Since the cases show the successful executive as one guarded in his talk and controlled in his aggressions, the newcomers and subordinates who expect all their interpersonal relations to be fixed and repetitive, and who delight in speaking their minds, are at a disadvantage. They would have to undergo great change to acquire the constant alertness and calculation necessary for success.

To oversimplify the problem, let's assume that regardless of what the incoming, or upcoming, executive brings to the job in the way of "resilience under conditions of adversity," he still has things to learn about managing confusion. Let's say he knows that appearances can be deceptive—from intent as well as chance. If so, he knows he must interpret the *meaning* of what he sees for what he wants to do. Unless he fanatically compartmentalizes his knowledge, he also knows, or is learning, that though situations are in theory subject to rules, rules become less rigid when following them is likely to thwart powerful superiors whose responsible interpretations cannot be strongly opposed without fear of disguised retaliation. If the aspirant balks at this, he has failed to see that action in the ongoing firm is often experimental and that rules commonly are neither complete nor up-to-date. Aware of this condition, responsible figures build a wider latitude for action than some of their associates like. The climber who makes an issue of this discretion has not yet moved from the simple ethic of the small group to that of the complex group; he will accordingly suffer and possibly check his growth for successful action.

This certain uncertainty occasionally provokes even the mature executive to fear personal failure, and to reflect that the informal behavior he and his associates engage in to overmatch each other may be dressed legitimately to block him as he has seen others blocked. Hence the executive combines his drive for success with vigilant search for what the biologist calls "protective coloration." Competing with all for individual credit, and with astute informalists for aid and protection in cliques, thus puts a premium on constructive dominance, alertness, rapid adjustment, mastery of the mobile face, engineering of events and associates, and sound judgment in appraising and interweaving new and obsolescent procedures.

Again, no executive in the very nature of things could fill this bill, but some will more nearly contain the confusion they help make than will others. And some will learn more readily than others. Probably the best body of general theory for explaining the individual's submergence, contributions, and inadequacies in these conflicts of movement in and out of formal and informal groups, is that of G. H. Mead.[15] Limited space and forbidding terms force us to shamefully abridge and interpret his ideas.

Mead held that the individual is largely a product of his experiences in groups, but *not* a completely finished product since he has potential for considerable change. At birth he is little more than a bundle of random reflexes. He has no attitudes or power to organize his action. However, the group into which he is born has these. And from his experiences there he acquires attitudes by the process of "taking roles." In time this enables him to view himself as the group sees him. That is, he takes over ("internalizes") the group's outlook on the world. This is done in a series of steps covering the first twelve years or so of the individual's life. When he is able to organize and guide his behavior acceptably through reference to the groups in which he has lived, he has, as Mead says, acquired a "self," or personality. This "self" is not a simple, inert "thing," but a process consisting of two phases that interact complexly. One is the individual's "me," or conscience; the other is the "I," or the impulse to engage in any new activity. Conscience and impulse interact during waking hours. When the individual wants to do something, the conscience shortly enters to guide the activity if it is proper as defined by his training, or to check it if it is not. If in the interplay the conscience, or "me," fails to control the "I," or impulse, the tug of war is of course being won by the impulse.

The impulses of the person reared in a small stable community would normally be under the thumb of the "me." That is, his experiences, however intense, are with people like himself. His awareness of himself is largely limited to the reflections they give him; his store of justifications is circumscribed by their relatively fixed outlooks fashioned by repetitive experiences in relatively constant situations. But in changing and loosely knit larger areas, where there is dispute about what is "right," impulses often elude the "me" for a time. Escaping the conscience, they may lead it for a merry chase in some forbidden direction. If these new experiences prove satisfying and helpful, the "me" is reshaped, and the "self" in time acquires a variety of "me's." That is, in the interaction between conscience and impulse, the conscience is modified or, as we say, the person's code of conduct is broadened.

In a sense, the individual is now able to pick and choose justifications for a greater range of behaviors. Becoming more complex morally does not of course mean that he has lost his conscience! It means rather that he has become able to consider and deal with all the conflicting interests and values around him. He has in effect become a plurality under one skin. Inconsistency is less of a hobgoblin to him. He is able to find meaning in what is confusion for others, and to act decisively.

Having a "self" of this kind enables the executive to control his behavior to a greater extent. He is limited by the formal organization and by his official role, but inside these boundaries the variety of workable devices he can employ to escape pressures and win ends seems unlimited. And he may reshape the formal restrictions, especially as he is able to influence others to aid him. His behavior is increasingly based more on what he anticipates than on what he has been.

The incoming executive aspirant with a simple "me" would of course initially be guided by that in situations dominated by persons with varied and complex "me's." Hence he would make blunders in terms of what was expected. His frustration would lead him to search for new ways. Hints from associates would accelerate his changing perceptions. As his old "me's" softened he would, so to speak, emerge with a revised code for plant conduct and probably for community life. He would experience less anguish in "living with himself." He would begin to justify workable departures and experiments, check verbal outbursts, and wear appropriate faces. This does not mean that the veteran executive is without some internal conflict. If he were, in Mead's terms his "I" and "me" would be fused—he would be doing precisely what he wanted to do, which is rare. And presumably his behavior would harmonize perfectly with that of his groups, and associates. But even where there is seeming conformity, we know that some, or much, of it is appearance and not based on convictions and preferences. The typical resentments, evasive intrigues, retaliations, and unofficial efforts to control people allow hardly any other interpretation.

The gap between the outlooks of foremen and higher managers is clarified by Mead's theory. Foremen originating in the work group have few and simple "me's" fashioned by narrow experiences. Their codes are so sharp and resistant to experiment that they view change and expediency in dealing with it as immoral. Almost the opposite is true of higherups who, through their job conflicts, personal ambitions, and multiple community activities, have become adept at solving dilemmas by introducing new and advantageous meanings into issues. They survive in given official roles, and move beyond them, only as they are able easily to play contradictory as well as complementary informal roles. This ability grows with and reflects their numerous and complex "me's." The condition is natural to membership in a variety of often conflicting plant and community groups where no one set of rules is adequate for action in all. This enables them to justify given actions by reference to some one group, though another group might regard the behavior as contradictory or even immoral. Typically it is the higherups—quick to change methods, to distinguish minor from major issues, and to compromise on the lesser to preserve the greater, to dress old principles in new symbols—who are among the "strong." On the other hand, the foremen who *remain* at that level are stymied by their scanty and meager alternatives. Their inability to find solutions reflects their limited and inflexible groups, or "me's," and, of course, in some part mental incapacity and lack of training. However, some foremen may have "human skills" and technical competence and still lack the moral complexity and "courage" essential for making some of the decisions and compromises that higherups make at relatively small cost to their nervous systems. The foremen who are left behind are shaped more by what they have been than by what they anticipate becoming. Using Mead's terms, one can say overneatly that the executives are "I"-dominated and the foremen "me"-dominated.

ROLE AND ORGANIZATION

Any systematic look at the place of a planned role in an organization, or the interplay between an office and the person in it (role and role occupant) becomes unreal if treated apart from the interfusion of official and informal acts. Here, we can only sketch some of the conditions that complicate the ideal fitting together of role and person.[16]

Every student knows that role and actor never coincide, and no one seriously expects an invariant decimal answer as to how much they influence each other. Not a student of such matters, Milo's Stein nevertheless pointed the issue for industry (Chapter 8). As factors hampering role fulfilment he clearly listed technological change, market variation, turnover of personnel, intrusion and shake-ups by the Central Office, union-management conflict, individual differences, work pressures and search for short-cuts, rivalries for promotion, staff experiments, and a "lot of undercover stuff." This last of course refers to cliques, but Stein does not see their function or appreciate the influence of personal sentiments.

Planned roles in all organizations must be altered to fit the limitations of available persons.[17] And as we saw in Chapter 6, the aspirant to higher roles commonly conceals unfitness as he probes to discover what is wanted and professes to have it. It is also possible for the person to fit objective role criteria and still be unable to function because significant subjective items were not included. An instance noted earlier is the inherent gap between role and actor in those organizations logically unable to assess the potential of incoming candidates to manage the power struggles that are not supposed to occur.

Role functions are variously distorted by personal ties and sentiments.* These work, for example, to conceal and/or support those who are failing in a role. We saw this in the protective demotions and transfers to less demanding roles: movement of broken line officers to staff roles for which they had no particular qualification; the existence of sinecures which, like the role of assistant-to, may really support the system by giving it flexibility; retention of persons on the payroll in an office they no longer fill (Chapter 5), and so on.

The system of roles, *and* the intrusion of sentiments, sometimes requires manipulation of roles in terms of what the crisis is, and of who plays the role. We saw the forced resignation of the president of the union local at Fruhling because he wished to adhere to a formal role— or as some students would say, because his image of the role was false. Clique actions, both the functional and the corrective, strain formal roles in protecting them, and in creating new roles. The same is true when officers are "lent" to other departments for varying periods where they continue with the same title but different functions, or different title and same functions, or when the formal role is used to disguise an unofficial function, or to conceal the inclusion of an additional function. It is

---

* Mead's picture of the "self" is defective in failing to consider the force of sentiments, which is central to Cooley's thought. See his *Human Nature and the Social Order,* Charles Scribner's Sons, New York, 1922, especially chaps. 3–4.

well, too, to remember that, as was done by Jessup of Fruhling (Chapter 3), formal roles may be created and function without occupants in order to serve the present illegal, but eventually legitimate and praiseworthy, needs of a higher role.

Though indispensable the role system does not, of course, assure that a specific role mirrors the occupant's personality. Since few if any formal roles can function without embracing supplemental informal ones,* there is the attendant problem of dealing with the differential capacity of individuals to take informal roles.† In many connections we saw the ethical obstacle reflected in clashes between formalists and informalists over when and how far to depart from a formal role. We need to know how the social, and possibly the physiological, factor relates to capacity for playing the informal roles necessary to elude or correct the system.

The specific role is so powerful in orienting the occupant that enduring and famous roles shape those who aspire to fill them. Lincoln's long dream of what he would do about slavery if he ever got the chance is a famous example. But once the aspirant takes the position he learns of role involvements, how his office interlocks with other imperfectly functioning roles. Now his formal role sensitizes him to what appearances he must maintain, what masks he must wear, and what justifications he must have on hand to preserve *core consistency* of the role as it changes. But his awareness of this becomes self-defeating when his sensitivity jells to the point where he fails to fit his role to its neighbors and allows his defenses to become cries of blatant vested interest.

---

* Some students see some formal roles as requiring certain complementary informal roles, or role-segments. For example, Dimock sees the executive as having to be a tactician, a philosopher, a statesman, a "responsible manipulator," and a psychiatrist (*The Executive in Action,* Harper and Brothers, New York, 1945, pp. 4–5, 8, 65–66, 157). Quincy Wright believes the social scientist must "combine the methods of the scientist, the philosopher, the humanist, and the historian." ("The Application of Scientific Method to Social Problems," Appendix 25 in *A Study of War,* 2 vols., University of Chicago Press, 1942, Vol. 2, pp. 1358, 1355–1364.)

† Research might show that even professional role-taking, with all its rewards and manifest operations, imposes a strain reflected in the lives of actors. They meet the rational expectation of filling multiple formal, if "unreal," roles and in that exhausting process they are further involved with informal roles that intrude into both their professional and private lives. The result in probably a significant number of cases is that their living becomes "unconventional," "bohemian," "avant-garde," and certainly experimental. Informal roles lead to new formal ones. Whether born in diplomatic intrigue, organizational life, or in the work of professional dramatists and actors, we need to know more of role-making and role-taking. The intensity of making and pursuing multiple images obviously exhausts creativity whether formal roles are involved or not.

To avoid this he must expand his official role to embrace a variety of informal ones.   If he plays a transitional role, he may need to keep his fitness for the formal office at high level, and resist the growing pull of the embryonic position.   The burden of also being sensitive to the informal roles (clique activities, etc.) others are playing is increased by our ethical tradition of fixity, and by the public relations front of "stability," "reliability," and "predictability," set up to meet this larger ethic and to conceal "bad" internal dynamics.

Whatever the limiting factors, executives of the "strong" type most aptly play multiple roles from the formal position, while they interpret, assess, and cross-reference the role repertories of associates.

Oversimplifying, one can say that ceaseless reorganization of the system hinders the matching of roles and occupants.   This arises in part from the system's inconsistent, and usually unavoidable, excess of demands over returns to occupants, who respond by initiating corrective counter claims.   In *qualifiedly* accomplishing its rational ends, the system unwittingly coerces its occupants to *qualifiedly* realize the personalizing urges innate to them.   In the process extreme formalists and informalists are pained at the compromise of their respective ideals.

SUMMARY

The individual manager is caught in a scheme of rational, emotional, social, and ethical claims.   Whatever his responses, he cannot escape some measure of internal conflict.   Initially seeking to reconcile what he does not know is irreconcilable, he moves or is pushed, according to his resourcefulness, through various stages of grappling with elusive certainties.

If his methods are few and fixed, and he cannot devise more suitable ones, he becomes noticeably neurotic.   The system forces an uncertain freedom on him in the sense that he may supplement and adapt existing official methods, or, where these are inadequate, add new ones that square with organizational propriety (or seem to with his artful help). But his liberty is curtailed by his agreements with similarly free associates.   Hence he finds that his power of choice can be a tacit command to compromise.   If he regards compromise as immoral concession, and fears a harmony that brings certain side commitments with uncertain complications, he withdraws to his formal shelter, and watches others find their way through ambiguity to dominate policy and take higher roles.   Ambiguity thus selects those most able to absorb, or resolve and utilize, conflict for personal and organizational ends.   As types, the more effective can be called "strong"; the others, "weak."

Competence in mastering confusion is less a formal learning process and more a vague reworking of perspectives, influenced by background experiences, that stem from critical interpersonal involvements. Obtuse outlooks are tortuously refined to craft in dealing with subtle meanings and anticipated actions.

Organizations are systems of formal roles that direct and shape role occupants. Roles never coincide perfectly with players. At times the system must alter roles and manipulate occupants to preserve itself. Personal sentiments encourage and maintain distortions. While appearing to respect the ethics of his group and of the organization, the occupant must be able to take multiple informal roles, and to deal with those of others while preserving the essentials of his charted role. Through personal endowment and aid from others, the strong occupant shapes his role as it guides him, as against the weak occupant who offers only minimum aid to his role.

In variously compromising its ends, the organization forces role occupants to assert, but compromise, their innately human purposes.

DOCUMENTARY NOTES

1. There is an immense literature on the shaping influences of organizations and groups on the individual—both theoretical and remedial, general and specific. See John Dewey, *Human Nature and Conduct,* Henry Holt and Co., New York, 1922; A. R. Lindesmith and A. L. Strauss, *Social Psychology,* Dryden, New York, 1949; G. H. Mead, *Mind, Self, and Society,* University of Chicago Press, Chicago, 1934; C. H. Cooley, *Human Nature and the Social Order,* Charles Scribner's Sons, 2nd edition, New York, 1922; Gardner Murphy, *Personality: A Biosocial Approach to Origins and Structure,* Harper and Brothers, New York, 1947; M. Sherif and M. O. Wilson, eds., *Group Relations at the Crossroads,* Harper and Brothers, New York, 1953; E. Wight Bakke, *Organization and the Individual,* Yale University, Labor and Management Center, New Haven, 1952; and by the same author and publisher, *The Fusion Process,* 1953, and *Bonds of Organization,* 1950; G. H. Allen, ed., *Individual Initiative in Business,* Harvard University Press, Cambridge, 1950; R. K. Merton, "Bureaucratic Structure and Personality," *Social Forces,* 18: 560–568, May, 1940; A. Zaleznik, *Foreman Training in a Growing Enterprise,* Harvard University, Graduate School of Business Administration, Boston, 1951.

2. See the individual cases, or the involvements, of Springer, Hardy, Ames, Blanke, Geiger, Peters, Revere, Taylor, Jessup, Whymper, Gilter, Higgins, Bingham, Boesel, Miller, Wheeler, and Haller in chap. 3; Jones, Haupt, Jefferson, Hampton, Donovan, Hancock, Dillard, Fitzhugh, Neilson, Tirpitz, Wohler, and the Fruhling chemist, in chap. 4; Reynolds, Phelps, Kincaid, Brady, Beemer, Dicke, Spencer, Randall, Kustis, McGovern, Keeley, Kissel, and Bailey in chap. 5; Bennett, Trimble, Evans, Cunningham, Wilkins, Stein, Gregg, Jackson, Warren, Schwann, Clancy, etc., in chap. 6; Berger, Speier, Merza, and Nevers in chap. 7.

3. See Argyris, *Personality and Organization*, Harper and Brothers, New York, 1957, for a discussion of literature on the subject.

4. C. I. Barnard, *Functions of the Executive*, Harvard University Press, Cambridge, 1938, p. 122.

5. Aubrey Silberston, *Education and Training for Industrial Management*, Management Publications Ltd., The Millbrook Press Ltd., London, 1955, p. 6.

6. E. S. Roscoe, *Organization for Production*, Richard D. Irwin, Homewood, Ill., 1955, pp. 402–403.

7. P. Stryker, *A Guide to Modern Management Methods*, McGraw-Hill Book Co., New York, 1956, pp. 250, 261. See also Shartle, *Executive Performance and Leadership*, Prentice-Hall, Englewood Cliffs, N.J., 1956, p. 178.

8. Dimock, *The Executive in Action*, Harper and Brothers, New York, 1945, pp. 156–157.

9. Argyris, *op. cit.*, chap. 7.

10. C. H. Cooley, *Social Organization*, Charles Scribner's Sons, New York, 1909, pp. 28–31, 62–65, 419; and *Human Nature and the Social Order, op. cit.*, chaps. 1–6, 10–11; René A. Spitz, "Hospitalism" in *The Psychoanalytic Study of the Child*, International Universities Press, New York, 1: 53–72, 1945, and "Hospitalism: A Follow-Up Report," *The Psychoanalytic Study of the Child*, 2: 113–117, 1946; R. E. L. Faris, *Social Psychology*, The Ronald Press Co., New York, 1952, pp. 250–280, 338–349. See some interesting data and speculations around this point in Charles Darwin, *The Descent of Man*, 2 vols., D. Appleton and Co., New York, 1871, Vol. 1, chaps. 2–3.

11. *Fortune*, The Editors of, *The Executive Life*, Doubleday and Co., Garden City, N.Y., 1956, p. 76.

12. P. B. Rice, *On the Knowledge of Good and Evil*, Random House, New York, 1955, especially the Introduction and chaps. 13 and 14. On the "truth" in such matters see T. V. Smith, *The Ethics of Compromise, op. cit.*, pp. 87–103. Also chap. 2 in H. W. Schneider, *Three Dimensions of Public Morality*, Indiana University Press, Bloomington, 1956; G. H. Mead, *Mind, Self and Society, op. cit.*, pp. 379–389; Cooley, *Human Nature and the Social Order, op. cit.*, chaps. 10–12.

13. A. W. Green, "Sociological Analysis of Horney and Fromm," *American Journal of Sociology*, 51: 538–539, May, 1946.

14. Lucio Mendieta y Nunez, "The Social Classes," *American Sociological Review*, 11: 175, pp. 166–176, April, 1946.

15. George H. Mead, *Mind, Self and Society*, The University of Chicago Press, 1934, especially pp. 135–226; *The Philosophy of the Act*, University of Chicago Press, 1938; *The Philosophy of the Present*, Open Court Publishing Co., New York, 1932, pp. 184–195; "The Social Self," *The Journal of Philosophy*, 10: 374–380, 1913; "A Behavioristic Account of the Significant Symbol," *The Journal of Philosophy*, 19: 157–163, 1922. The books, largely prepared by Mead's students from lecture notes, are repetitious and obscure in places, but are exciting and very worthwhile. Also see P. E. Pfuetz, *The Social Self*, Bookman Associates, New York, 1954, pp. 37–116, for a very readable commentary.

16. For a study focussed on the relations between observed and expected behavior see R. M. Stogdill, E. L. Scott, and W. E. Jaynes, *Leadership and Role Expectations*, The Ohio State University, Bureau of Business Research, Research Monograph 86, Columbus, 1956. For various research reports, summaries, and analyses of related topics see H. Goldhamer, "Recent Developments in Personality Studies," *American Sociological Review*, 13: 555–565, October, 1948; R. T. Morris

and M. Seeman, "The Problem of Leadership: An Interdisciplinary Approach," *American Journal of Sociology*, 56: 149–155, September, 1950; R. K. Merton and Alice Kitt, "Contributions to the Theory of Reference Group Behavior," in R. K. Merton and P. F. Lazarsfeld, eds., *Continuities in Social Research*, The Free Press, Glencoe, Ill., 1950, pp. 86–95; M. Seeman, "Role Conflict and Ambivalence in Leadership," *American Sociological Review*, 18: 370–380, August, 1953; R. Tannenbaum and F. Massarik, "Leadership: A Frame of Reference," *Management Science*, 4 (No. 1): 1–19, October, 1957; H. L. Wilensky, *Intellectuals in Labor Unions*, The Free Press, Glencoe, Ill., 1956; R. H. Turner, "Role-Taking, Role Standpoint, and Reference-Group Behavior," *The American Journal of Sociology*, 61: 316–328, January, 1956; T. M. Newcomb, *Social Psychology*, The Dryden Press, New York, 1950, chaps. 13 and 15; M. Sherif, "The Concept of Reference Groups in Human Relations," in M. Sherif and M. O. Wilson, eds., *Group Relations at the Crossroads*, Harper and Brothers, New York, 1953, pp. 203–231, and in the same work, Herbert Blumer, "Psychological Import of the Human Group," pp. 185–202. See also Blumer's "Attitudes and the Social Act," *Social Problems*, 3: 59–65, October, 1955; Argyris, *Personality and Organization, op. cit.*, chaps. 4 and 7; C. Wright Mills, *White Collar*, Oxford University Press, New York, 1951, chaps. 4–9.

17. Barnard, *Organization and Management*, Harvard University Press, Cambridge, 1948, pp. 39–47.

CHAPTER **10**

Conclusions

Larger meanings of our inquiry can be sketched under the topics of (1) typicality, (2) positive aspects of conflict, (3) bureaucratic theory and American society, (4) the firm in the community, (5) conformity, and (6) a recurring issue.

TYPICALITY

All the firms we have described were normal. All were economically sound, and none have been involved in public scandals or have been the target of whispering campaigns. Possibly two of the firms were somewhat "above average," since they have been classified, with other plants, by some students as models in terms of managerial and personnel practices, and good public relations. This fits our argument that personnel practices in the firms were not abnormally "bad" as they may seem to those who regard unofficial action as necessarily pathological. We stress this point because these common practices should be the basis for analysis and the raising of questions by students and higher management, rather than, as now, something to be obscured as "corrupt." We appreciate the fact that certain internal affairs must be confidential and even "sacred" in organizations, as in the home, but we would not include behavior that is commonplace to practitioners in organizations regarded as legal and honorable. If part of these practices should be above discussion by managers and students, we can avoid that part only by knowing it.

In its community relations the Attica plant obviously may not be representative of all firms of its size and kind. And, not all department stores are as successful as Rambeau in terms of profits and general harmony. As we observed earlier, members of a given managerial level sometimes regard their immediate superiors—or even the organization itself—as pathological, and consequently move elsewhere only to repeat their experiences. The recurrence of this and related problems is suggested by executives who declare that the major gain of attending management conferences is finding that "we're all having the same troubles."

POSITIVE ASPECTS OF CONFLICT

If our cases are typical, then conflict is typical. Failing to assess its price objectively, we must at least counter its widely appreciated negative effects—personal and economic frustrations, turnover of malcontents, "dragging of feet"—with a few positive remarks. Conflict fluctuates around some balance of the constructive and disruptive. Inevitably there must be constructive conflict as responsible officers and close associates work with varying success to adapt parts of the structure to changing conditions and personnel, while others for various reasons resist corrective changes. We are currently so busy hiding conflict that we quake when we must simultaneously deal with it and pretend it does not exist.

As suggested earlier, some executives see the competition of interdepartmental rivalries as a game. Others, though, so fear the possibility that unrestrained conflict will destroy more than it creates that they slight its merit in clearing the air and permitting the incorporation of desired changes and findings. Even personal conflict,* such as that between Jessup and his chief (Chapter 3), may stimulate experiments leading to new methods.

Without some conflict growing out of rivalries peculiar to the social nature of man the organization would become an organism, with the

---

* This is not a brief for animosity, but personal conflict can be productive even in the fine arts. Michelangelo's work on the Sistine vault was precipitated, against his violent resistance, by the intrigues of Bramante and others with Pope Julius II, and fed by antipathies as it was executed over a period of four and a half years. An equally rancorous conflict spurred and attended Brunelleschi's erection of the cupola at Florence. See G. Vasari, *The Lives of the Painters, Sculptors and Architects,* 4 vols. (trans. A. B. Hinds), E. P. Dutton and Co., New York, 1927.

social life of members on the same level as that in the beehive. This might of course eliminate moral suffering, nervous breakdown, and neurotic behavior—a gain with more losses than many people would accept. But *with* conflict, some members must momentarily feed it as they inventively channel it to preserve the organization.

In limits, we are all challenged by interpersonal conflict and thrill in exercising our faculties whether or not explicit rewards hang in the balance. The mastery or compromise of one conflict merely launches us into another. These are life-giving skirmishes essential to repel tedium. They become harmful as they exceed our ingenuity. Contained conflict in industry gets the job done, brings recognition to those who blend the official and unofficial, and speeds personal growth to bear responsibilities. In and out of industry, man against man, and man against the organization is a condition unlikely to end until our species evolves to something different. Perpetual harmony is alien to all life. This does not mean that conflict always equates with personal creativity or general progress. But conflict and cooperation are usually inter-mingled in all advances, especially in democracies. Hence the current blanket censure of conflict may obscure some of the steps in supposedly perfect cooperation. Creativity, development, and movement in any new direction can be only partially subject to rules, and are never bound by rigid formulas drawn from summaries of ideal conditions set up by those who crave everlasting order. With its larger blessings partici-pative organization embraces some disorder.

BUREAUCRATIC THEORY

Though American commerce and industry utilize bureaucratic struc-ture to deal with problems of size, complexity, and communication, they streamline the framework in typical American fashion. The operation is fueled by our inherent resistance to the theory of bureaucracy as a society of unequals. Our tradition is against rather than for impersonal selection and treatment. This is not strange, where "all men are created equal," where "that government is best which governs least," and where practically everyone contends that he is "as good as the best and better than most." The theory of bureaucracy hangs much better on the more stratified and disciplined European societies, as it did also on the earlier Persian and Roman monarchies. In America the theory operates chiefly to buttress compromises, channel conflicts, and give dignity to the organization as it yields to the push for careers, and bends to conceal shortcuts and absorb personal relations.

Bureaucratic theory naturally assumes that members of the organization are relatively inert and ready to follow the intent of rules. Yet the active seeking nature of man, his ancient and obvious tendency to twist the world to his interests and to select as well as respond to parts of his environment, erodes the preaching of parents and superiors.

The theory also slights the fact that in the larger organizations, local and personal demands take precedence in most cases. This applies not only to the nationwide units of a corporation, but to the internal structure of the units, where the "organization" is first the department, next the division, then the local plant. In the great surface conformity to higher expectations, some actions are hidden in each section. Tendencies develop that are not detected and incorporated in higher decisions. Hence top action often becomes progressively "unbureaucratic" as new controls are developed for wrong reasons.

Bureaucratic theorists and responsible but wishful-thinking planners often underrate the ingenuity of subordinates and their will and capacity to collaborate in adapting directives. Planners too often regard intelligence as necessarily synonymous with volume of specialized formal education, when in some cases "uneducated" but hard-pressed subordinates ably analyze the motivations of higherups and utilize their directives for unintended purposes.

The iron law of American bureaucratic practice echoes in the refrain, "There's always a way to get around the rule—look for it!" Contempt for formalization grows with emphasis on training and the implication that some hierarchy or branch is an elite group. This goes against the American belief that one man's opinion is as good as another's on administrative matters, and the great dislike of superiors who behave as superiors. The names applied to staff personnel and to "brain-trusters" in government and the charges that neither "could meet a payroll or production deadline," nor "run a peanut stand and stay out of the red," indicate the common attitude toward literal adherence to bureaucratic procedure. Each level does indeed favor bureaucratic control—for its subordinates, and each department or division for the other.

In the expanding and/or larger organization, there are always the warring extremes of democratic versus autocratic action that clash with bureaucratic theory. Some members want limited responsibility with no voice in decisions, and prefer to be told. Arousing initiative in these people may require autocratic action. There are those who crave democratic participation, but become arbitrary and autocratic as they genuflect to democratic form for years on the way up. And typically, of course, there are some managers who variously combine autocratic and democratic practice. In these differentials of identification and influence, bureaucracy's technical aim to recruit personnel impersonally and to contain individuals in well-defined roles is variously compromised. Barnard has realistically noted that democratic administration must be alloyed with occasional autocratic behavior, and that " 'a silent democracy of behavior' determines all systems of government, public or private." But even the most democratic executive knows that he cannot share all plans of his office. He must be autocratic in maintaining certain secrets for a time because he knows some subordinates may "unbureaucratically" use the information for personal reasons, or that morale will be damaged by a leak to extreme formalists and informalists.

Similarly, dynamic situations arise that no "leader" alone can deal with, that only an "oligarchical" group or clique can handle. These too, as we stressed, can get out of control like anything that men of varying pliability put their hands to. They in turn are corrected by comparable unplanned cliques.

THE FIRM IN THE COMMUNITY

Organizational planning limited to the standard aspects of production, profits, recruitment of personnel, and public relations is unrealistic if not irrational. Unplanned political, economic, social, ethnic, and recreational influences of the community play on the firm to modify its rationalization, reinterpret and utilize its goals, supplement its interests, and draw on its resources, as the managers in turn variously color community life. Like the Sabbath, rationality inescapably compromises with social demands.

Through legal fictions the organization exists as an entity. However, in practice its lines are blurred by the extralegal activities of members, by the reciprocal ties between plant and community, and by persons who—with followers—are powerful in both places. We have seen workmen conduct lotteries for political purposes under the company roof with the noncollusive aid of management. We saw Attica develop unofficial policies to exist in the community. And we saw how community recreational activities are in part sustained by company skills and materials. Other less obvious forces spread a personalizing web through the plant. Workmen, clerical personnel, staff and some line managers, and some working wives, perform part-time community jobs in the plant on a scale beyond the minimum that makes it widely forbidden. They sell insurance and gadgets of various kinds and act as representatives of many community organizations, including loan shops and gambling syndicates. Increasingly, employees from any level may be part-time farmers who sell dairy and poultry products on schedule throughout the hierarchy with the smiling aid of gate tenders. During wartime various managers are drawn on to act as members and chairmen of draft boards. Here they are subject to personal approaches by community parents who are their brethren in clubs, churches, associations, and other firms. Manager-draft officers are aided by the community in exposing "slackers." The managers' work colleagues give the same help in the plant and concomitantly focus on "undesirable" persons of military age in staffs, lower line, and among production workers. In the joint effort of plant and community to serve the greater bureaucracy, local personal enemies officially classified as indispensable to the war effort of firm or community, are frequently caught in the process and then found, too late, to have been "drafted by mistake."

Managers are further tied to the community through membership in chambers of commerce, park boards, local trade associations, school boards, joint civic and business sponsored events, management political activities in the community, management sponsored or maintained athletic fields used by the community, management participation in charity drives, and partial or total sponsorship of art, music, and other cultural activities. There are also binding trades and understandings between local tax assessors and management, which are interwoven with the other connections.

Though these cross-ties are all natural in that they represent sundry interests in action and are common and unquestioned by most participants, including those who must officially pronounce some of them illegal, they are outside the formal theory of the firm. Their major function in effect if not intent is to realize and to preserve what is peculiar and ineradicable in man. These practices unintentionally exercise and conserve "human nature" as defined in Chapter 9. A voluminous literature[1] implicitly or directly holds industry responsible for "impoverishing the social existence" of man. The point is made that industry, or its managers, has an ethical obligation to the community to restore and protect the social and moral life of the community now endangered by intrusion of industry's disruptively rational organizations.

We cannot debate the issue. We must argue, though, that the extralegal and extraproductive practices cited above are natural activities which prevent the "dehumanization" of man. These adaptive and functionally spontaneous approaches to the world ease the impersonally wrought tensions more effectively than could any planned spontaneity. The allegedly desocializing pressures are not confined to production workers, but extend into the hierarchy where the too rational hopes of top managers are similarly compromised at lower levels. As a normal expression, the departures simultaneously preserve the nucleus of rational policy and win the organization's goals by mixed personal and impersonal, planned and unplanned means. In the process, the "bureaucratic" firm becomes more or less an extension of the community, which fortifies the relation unofficially as well as formally.

CONFORMITY

The storm today for and against the individual's conformity to the larger society and to his career organizations bears on our study. We can indicate the connection under (1) conformity as a means, and (2) conditions promoting conformity.

Conformity as a Means

The individual is a product of groups. In his development from infancy, he conforms to major demands of his group, or seems to when he cannot. If he fails he is punished. Over the years he is shaped by conformity to ever mounting expectations. As a responsible adult he continues to be punished for nonconformity. In the role of say, production worker, he observes output standards, or is excluded as a "rate-buster," an ostracism few can tolerate. As a staff functionary, he must either curb his "free-wheeling" impulses or reduce his career hopes. G. H. Mead makes the point that much human behavior is built up internally and covertly before it reaches overt expression, which it often does not. This is exploratory conformity which, when the individual learns that his fermenting actions will be unacceptable, enables him obligingly to seem to conform. Obviously weariness with the battle, a limitation of every nervous system and habit structure, also forces a measure of conformity.

Thus we need not be confirmed cynics to admit that much conformity is purposeful—though some of it may be an end in itself. We profess to be individualists but find it wise to observe proprieties for the sake of reward. This is an ancient practice. To preserve order and ease of control in the sphere of government, for example, individualistic monarchs from Antiochus IV through Augustus and Lorenzo the Magnificent have clothed their force by seeming conformity to democratic processes. Maturing societies increasingly demand more conformity and control of feelings as a mark of "good-breeding." Other pressures for another kind of conformity are tritely obvious when such societies are also, as with ours, assuming a larger and more dangerous role in world affairs.

The spread of bureaucratic structures requires increasing conformity. This pressure reaches its highest form where corps of specialists are developed to uncover deviations and maintain records of merit and demerit. Here executives with festering egos demand superficial obeisance, if not a clear "yes." As all covertly battle for the enlarged package of honors and rewards that come at each higher level, seeming conformity is saintly and overt individualism is madness.

Conditions Promoting Conformity

In the larger society conformity has become a medium of exchange. Life demands that we be aware of neighbors with whom we are unlikely ever to be intimate because of the rapid events and superficial experiences in which we are all caught up. We know our mobile neighbors are different, but the distractions of our *"ersatz* diversion and synthetic excitement" keep us from knowing how different. In our touch-and-go life we necessarily base many of our actions on flimsy impressions. Denied full knowledge, our inconstant relations only spur us to wear a better disguise before those who are stranger than strangers. For even where relations have a pseudo-permanence, we find that many of those with whom we must live are intentionally elusive. Bound to them by an interest, and having to take positions toward things we cannot keep up with, we cooperate to support the front we share. We have no choice but to don a protective coloration as we dip and sample here and there.

In earlier days, before transportation and communication devices shrank our physical world and enlarged our social universe, our organizations were different and our individualism more exposed. Today there are no means of pinning the personality down to one organization. Shifting and tangential society and organizations are increasingly based on front and prefigured defenses. The social façade covers name-changing, religion-changing and the hiding of one's past, which gears, as Stein noted (Chapter 6), with the necessity in large organizations that status-givers reward in part on the basis of surmises about candidates.* Capability is measured more by fugitive impressions than by testing, because the essential survival abilities are often overlooked as aspirants prepare relevant impressions to fit the irrelevant criteria they must meet.

To deal with the world, the organization must present an inviting exterior and a promise of superior execution. Swamped in doubts, the leader must have assurance of internal loyalty when he acts. Conformity

* To my suggestion that he refine his personnel forms for recruitment of staff people, a West Coast executive declared that he had "no time to check on people, and besides they don't put down the facts. I don't mind people lying about their past—we all lie [looking at me challengingly]. I just want them to be able to do what they say they can."

is one assurance he rewards. As T. H. Huxley noted in a famous letter to Herbert Spencer on the question of whether the remains of unconventional George Eliot should rest in Westminster Abbey, "Those who elect to be free in thought and deed must not hanker after the rewards . . . which the world offers to those who put up with its fetters."

In today's vast systems of rationality the individual conforms as he evades their schemes of detection. Some members find room for personal choice and ingenuity as they strain and thrill in meeting appearances. Others conform to avoid conflict and to maintain the demanded tranquillity and uniformity which de Tocqueville saw as the passion of people and government alike in all democratic countries. Such conformity is especially characteristic of American middle class groups today. But many individual managers and workers do "fight the organization" and there are "individual dynamics" as we saw in the anonymous communications, deliberate misinterpretation of rules for personal, protective, and constructive reasons; the unofficial use of materials and services to reward differential contributions, to cement essential relations; the adaptation of labor contracts; and the "agreements between gentlemen," which allow each "to assume that the other is acting honorably even if he is morally certain that he is not."[2]

The typical firm is thus a shifting set of contained disruptions, powered and guided by differentially skilled and committed persons. Its unofficial aspects bulk large but are shrouded in a bureaucratic cloak. To satisfy our eternal urge toward consistency we may call this conformity hypocritical, but we must not hypocritically refuse to recognize its protective function for what it is and denounce as hypocrites those executives who do. Conformity in this sense has a function similar to the built-in but unconscious false appearances among other animals, which biologists call "protective mimicry." The individual in the large organization or mobile society, like the uncalculating animals, is also a defenseless creature who calculatingly practices deception for safety's sake against the invisible threats around him.* Since only isolated fanatics spurn such protective coloration, most of those who attack the practice do so to camouflage their own interests.

---

* These threats are too widely known and believed to be entirely fanciful, and they have long had a function in systems of authority and responsibility. Over four centuries ago a diplomat-historian confidentially advised a practice that is more possible now than then: "When one in authority desires to chastise or revenge himself on an inferior, let him not act hastily, but await time and occasion. For if only he go warily, an opportunity will surely come when, without displaying rancour or passion, he may satisfy his desire either wholly or in part." Francesco Guicciardini, *Ricordi*, S. F. Vanni, New York, 1949, p. 21.

A RECURRING ISSUE

The battle between impersonal organization and the personalizing individual is old. That does not sanctify the condition or mean that its recurrence is always the same, or say that the struggle cannot be constructively channeled in various ways. However, recognizing the timeless element allows a better appraisal of the individual's part in the conflict. Today's tempo is faster, but the underlying process is the same. And it may be that the rapid pace is less painful than the strain between appearance and being for individuals who exhaust themselves maintaining unassailable fronts.

In any case, as one looks at the recurring exaltations of rural life through Western history one suspects that a digger of data could show a direct relation between the matched complexity and impersonal regulations of urban life on the one hand, and the cry to escape the city and the frenzies of commerce and politics on the other. The complications of progress in civilization bring size, intricacy, instability—and bureaucracy to order the disorder.

Devised by the few to control the many, impersonal controls provoke a condition of frustration and resistive intrigue that intellectuals have immemorially denounced in cries for a return to nature.[3] At least as early as the fifth century B.C., Athenians were yearning to escape urban conflicts. From the later Republic through the Western Empire wealthy Romans and their intellectuals attacked and fled the city's restrictive irritations; Augustus even sought to recapture the earlier simplicity by legal means. In the fourteenth century Ibn Khaldun condemned urban complexities by lauding rural people as morally superior because "their habits and actions are relatively simple" and "they are nearer to the natural state." Even in "individualistic" Renaissance Italy, Leo Alberti fled to the country when he could, while Leonardo, smothered by hangers-on, felt he was his own only when alone. Cosimo de Medici lamented his inability to escape the group: "I can take care of my enemies, but God preserve me from my friends." In France Montaigne reluctantly served four years as Mayor of Bordeaux, but wished to resist those who would "drive us out of ourselves into the street for the benefit of public society." He was willing only to "take the affairs of men on my shoulders, not incorporate them into me; to be concerned over them, yes; to be impassioned over them, never. I look to them, but I do not brood over them . . . We never conduct well the thing that possesses and conducts us."

During the French "Enlightenment," Rousseau preached a movement back to nature that stirred even Marie Antoinette. In 1824 Goethe declared that the "last two shabby centuries" had produced no one "with strength to be true and to show himself as he is." Emerson and Thoreau were among our own critics who exemplified their preaching.

Today our Green Belt and Garden City planners lead the return to nature as Germany did a century ago around the Krupp Works. We symbolize the return by ranch houses, rustic cabins and furniture, boating, camping, and the growing mania for gardening. As a substitute or supplement to these marks of the simple life, we imaginatively flee oppressive intangibles to the eternal affections of rural and frontier song, and the clear roles and sharp justice of frontier drama.

With more resources to draw on and in more explicit language, demands are now made that the individual not flee but stand and assert himself in his daily life. These pleas—in various veins by H. F. Willkie, W. H. Whyte, Jr., D. Riesman, and Orwell—are focussing too much on the visible. We have seen that the problem is less one of the individual's being himself than it is of his being free to show himself as he is. With higher managers approving departures that bow to the code, no commentary is needed on the volume of individual and collaborative "freewheeling" existing at all levels.

Those who mistake surface conformity in organizations for *total* conformity and the death of originality, should refocus to concern themselves with the ethics of protective coloration among thinking animals.

DOCUMENTARY NOTES

1. Oliver Sheldon, *The Philosophy of Management,* Pitman and Sons, London, 1924, chap. 3; T. N. Whitehead, *Leadership in a Free Society,* Harvard University Press, Cambridge, 1937, chap. 12, and pp. 253–259; C. P. Loomis, *Fundamental Concepts of Sociology* (a trans. and supplementation of Ferdinand Tönnies' *Gemeinschaft und Gesellschaft*), American Book Company, New York, 1940; etc.

2. Lyndall Urwick, *Some Notes on the Theory of Organization,* American Management Association, New York, 1952, p. 23.

3. See some related comments in P. A. Sorokin, C. C. Zimmerman, and C. J. Galpin, *A Systematic Source Book in Rural Sociology,* 3 vols., The University of Minnesota Press, Minneapolis, 1930, Vol. 1, chaps. 1–4; *The Cambridge Ancient History,* Cambridge University Press, Cambridge, England, Vol. 5, pp. 105–110, 141–144, and Vol. 10, pp. 456–459; *Juvenal's Satires,* Satire XI, E. P. Dutton and Co., New York, 1954; *The Complete Works of Montaigne,* trans. by Donald M. Frame, Stanford University Press, Stanford, Calif., 1948, 1957, essay, "Of Husbanding your Will," a plea for resistance to the group; *Conversations of Eckermann with Goethe,* entries for Jan. 2, 1824 and March 12, 1828.

CHAPTER **11**

Appendix on Method

Influenced by the dogmatism of nineteenth century science* research methodology in the social and psychological sciences is now more cock-sure than in the increasingly humble physical sciences. Even in the nineteenth century, celebrated discoveries were often achieved enigmatically. Kekule tortuously arrived at his theory of the benzene molecule; Davy blundered onto the anesthetic properties of nitrous oxide; Perkin's failure to produce synthetic quinine circuitously revealed aniline dyes; and Ehrlich tried 606 times before he succeeded in compounding salvarsan in 1910.

Today a mathematical biologist declares that "no scientist follows any cut-and-dried procedure. Intuition and idiosyncrasies probably play as important a part in the work of the scientist as they do in the work of the artist."[1]

Seeing the physicist's first task as one of establishing universal elementary laws, Einstein declares that "there is no logical path to these laws; only intuition, resting on sympathetic understanding of experience, can reach them. . . . There is no logical bridge between phenomena and their theoretical principles."[2]

---

* J. Bronowski, *The Common Sense of Science*, Wm. Heinemann, Ltd., London, 1955, pp. 124–127. As a physicist, Bronowski notes that "in the strict sense there are no exact sciences. There is science, and there is common sense; and both must learn to assimilate into their methods and basic ideas the underlying uncertainties of all knowledge" (p. 128).

This is not to attack method as such—and certainly it is not to say that unsupported "intuition" is *the* route—but to caution against letting method be a tail that wags the dog.[3] When treated as a fixed set of procedures, method ignores or obscures the researcher's frequent groping, fumbling, and setbacks. In current practice, the listing of fears, mistakes, and interpersonal problems in collecting data is likely to seem unorthodox and to be interpreted as a mark of ineptness. Yet these are accompaniments, and they may greatly influence what is seen, and how it is handled.

In the present research no explicit hypotheses were set up in advance but, as indicated in the Introduction, occupational involvements* usually preceded questions and consciousness of problems to be studied.

Many questions and hunches originating in the experience at Milo and Fruhling were cross-fertilized by concurrent contacts at Attica and Rambeau. Since no simultaneous systematic study could be made of all, and as Milo was the most accessible, that firm became the nucleus of inquiries and the continuing point of major effort. However, general questions and interpretations were increasingly influenced by study of the other firms, especially the factories. Common processes and similar recurring situations evoked interlocking questions which led to establishment of the problem areas. For example, why did grievers and managers form cross-cliques? Why were staff personnel ambivalent toward line officers? Why was there disruptive conflict between Maintenance and Operation? If people were awarded posts because of specific fitness, why the disparity between their given and exercised influence? Why, among executives on the same formal level, were some distressed and some not? And why were there such sharp differences in viewpoint and moral concern about given events? What was the meaning of double talk about success as dependent on knowing people rather than on possessing administrative skills? Why and how were "control" staffs and official guardians variously compromised? What was behind the contradictory policy and practices associated with the use of company materials and services? Thus the guiding question embracing all others was: what orders the schisms and ties between official and unofficial action?

Steps in getting answers to these and other changing questions can be discussed under (*a*) intimates, (*b*) techniques and sources of data, and (*c*) special problems.   •

---

* In the main, I followed the guiding bias that "a subject becomes scientific not by beginning with facts, with hypotheses, or with some pet theory brought in *a priori*, but by beginning with the peculiar character of its particular problems." F. S. C. Northrop, *The Logic of the Sciences and the Humanities,* The Macmillan Co., New York, 1947, p. 274.

INTIMATES

In no case did I make a formal approach to the top management of any of the firms to get approval or support for the research. Several times I have seen other researchers do this and have watched higher managers set the scene and limit the inquiry to specific areas—outside management proper—as though the problem existed in a vacuum. The findings in some cases were then regarded as "controlled experiments," which in final form made impressive reading. But the smiles and delighted manipulation of researchers by guarded personnel, the assessments made of researchers and their findings, and the frequently trivial areas to which alerted and fearful officers guided the inquiry—all raised questions about who controlled the experiments. This approach was not suited to my purposes. Rather, by building on personal knowledge, I furthered the research through intimates—those who gave information and aid that, if generally known, would have jeopardized their careers. Though they knew of my general interest, I made no detailed statement of what I sought, and in all cases I indicated that my interest was broad information on "all kinds of personnel problems" from as many firms as possible. I usually supported this by asking informants questions about their earlier experiences. I hoped this would allay fear that *their* firm, or department, was of special interest. In some cases the procedure stimulated informants to insist on giving local details and drawing parallels with their earlier experiences (*e.g.,* Kincaid, Chapter 5), which gave me leads and information.

The number and rank of intimates naturally varied in different firms.* At Fruhling, for example, where most of my attention was on a division of 3500, I was on close terms with 33 people, including Jessup and 18 other line personnel (13 foremen and 5 production workers), and 14 staff people.

Milo intimates totaled 81. Eleven were workmen, including 3 grievers; 24 first-line foremen; 14 general foremen; 6 line superintendents; 8 staff heads or assistants, and 18 staff supervisors or specialists. I directly or nondirectively interviewed 113 other persons in the Milo sample, and 27 hourly-paid foremen outside the sample.

Reynolds at Attica was merely a speaking acquaintance. However, I had the confidence of one of his secretaries,† two members of the

---

* Number is of course less important than the individual person's reliability and knowledge, and the rapport achieved with him. More time was given to Milo and to cultivation of its personnel, hence the greater number of intimates in, and references to, that firm.

† Several female secretaries and clerks were helpful in the research. The potential contribution of persons in these roles is usually unappreciated. Several

grievance committee, and an engineer whom I had known earlier at Fruhling. I knew two of Reynolds' community intimates, and five former Milo workmen in the plant who supplemented my information about Attica's racial problems.

At Rambeau, I had but three associates—Nevers; the husband of one of Reynolds' secretaries; and the secretary herself, who was formerly employed there full time but now worked only during the evenings that Rambeau was open. Her friendship with the bureaucratic female department head (Chapter 7) was most helpful.

At Marathon Research Company my only informant was the chemist whom I had known earlier at Milo. At Argo Transit the top manager and three persons in his office supplied me with more information than I needed. The X-ray technician (Chapter 7) was my sole contact at his hospital. Four people whom I had earlier known at Fruhling gave me details of their activities under piece-rate work at the unnamed cabinet factory (Chapter 7).

Intimates were invaluable not only as sources of information but for help in the research situation. Especially at Milo and Fruhling they occasionally served as what chemists would call "catalytic agents," because they accelerated reactions. In effect they sometimes initiated and pushed uncontrolled experiments for me. In the staff groups particularly, as well as in any situation where discussion was taking place and I knew in advance that I could be present and seemingly occupied with work, they introduced agreed topics and questions into the conversation. These stimuli were typically on issues in the problem areas. Usually "busy" over in a corner of the room, I was observing and taking notes on the remarks of one or more people. Some intimates developed

---

things fit them to aid research of this kind. They are probably more status conscious than males in the same roles, and quicker to note symbols of rank, differences in influence, and to spot certain of the factors involved. They are also more interested in events and social details and probably remember them better. Having this orientation and access to records and events, they are likely to possess considerable knowledge of unofficial activities and developing policy. Where his personal bent is a hindrance to clique participation, or his clique ties are fouled and he feels isolated, a manager confides more to his secretaries than to others and even relies on their judgment. (Research on the marriages of secretaries to their bosses in all walks of life would probably show that much more than physical proximity and sex attraction is involved.) It is trite to note that women have long played secondary formal roles, have had to use indirect approaches to win ends and have resented the condition. However, this may be relevant for the researcher. For where female secretaries are treated as intellectual menials, they are disposed to be communicative with those who show awareness of their insights and knowledge of affairs. At least this was true at Fruhling, Milo, and Attica.

an interest in this kind of study, and sketched events and conversations they thought relevant for me in my absence. These data were naturally evaluated before use. Such experimentation is of course regarded in some circles as "unethical," and would not be accepted as a "technique." But without note taking and careful assessment, this is a common and legitimate link in the fluid interchanges between the official and unofficial phases of organizational events. It seems no more unethical than the use of "visiting shoppers" in business or "projective techniques" in psychological research.

TECHNIQUES AND SOURCES OF DATA

Though often overlapping, because I expediently used any method that did not endanger the firm or personnel, my core efforts can be discussed under formal interviewing, work diaries, participant-observation, and socializing.

Formal Interviews

I did little formal interviewing because of the obvious problem of explaining what I was doing, and the inadequacy of the approach for getting at unofficial activities—especially when other means were safer and more effective. In interviewing, I normally did not take notes,* but listened with relaxed intentness and then reconstructed the interview as soon as possible after it ended. This was done by first setting up a skeleton of key items remembered and then expanding by association to other parts and reworking until it seemed to be a facsimile. The results were relatively complete on topics covered and apparently accurate on grammar and speech mannerisms—judged by the occasional read-backs I made to intimates of some of our discussions, and the checking of my notes with "catalysts" against what they believed had been said in group discussions involving people whose expressions and idioms they knew better than I did.

In the process of reconstructing interviews, I noted down emphases made, facial expressions, marks of concern and relief, and other gestures —aware that they could mislead—as possible clues to more basic things. When note-taking was essential and I could not keep up, I used abbreviations, *ad hoc* symbols, trade terms, or jargon as quickly decipherable recall crutches. The aim of such interviewing was usually to get a clear official statement, with as many rewarding slips as possible.

---

* Cowper (Chapter 6) however, in a tone indicating he had something of great weight to reveal, commanded me to take notes by asking, "Aren't you going to take any notes?" and handing me a pad.

Work Diaries

Through much of the period at Fruhling and Milo I recorded events, biographical information, gossip, and initial hypotheses in loose-leaf notebooks. For example, I outlined and dated "unusual" incidents (which in a flow of deviations might include a return to "usual" practices); questions to ask certain people; possible ties among events; signs of developing cliques; activities of cliques; out-of-role behavior; additions to biographical data; the search for and use of precedents by individuals and groups; contrary interpretations made of regulations with notes on who made them and leads to follow; overheard remarks made by people about each other—complimentary and not; threats and accusations in arguments; joking remarks that seemed to bear on events; provocative statistics and irregularities in reports as leads to follow or as related to established data; and marginal notes by various departments on work analysis sheets. Tentative answers were later incorporated with the questions; some questions were rephrased or dropped, and others introduced. Materials were later detached and grouped into logical categories. Periodically I sifted and reclassified data as accumulating evidence exposed errors of interpretation and emphasis. The "miscellaneous" category waxed and waned with progress, and with refinement of categories. Concern to miss nothing significant and knowledge that I was missing some things, obviously meant an accumulation of "irrelevant" data for the categories and problems settled on as most meaningful.

Participant-observation[4]

My formal roles at Milo and Fruhling cannot be named without danger of exposing intimates to their superiors there. In both cases I was a member of staff groups which gave me—even required—great freedom of movement and wide contacts without raising questions.

This technique allowed me to spot and, aping line chiefs, utilize malcontents. These included members among first, my staff associates, then Catholics, minority ethnic groups, first-line foremen in general, and various individuals wherever I met them. Such persons were disposed to trust me and to speak more freely than were other initially nonintimates. Their information on past and developing events was most helpful, and constituted solid data once corrected for emotional distortions, such as the Catholic cry at Milo that "ninety-five per cent of management are Masons" and Sarto's allegation that no Italian could enter the hierarchy (Chapter 6). As fringe members of their groups, malcontents may distort from both ignorance and bias.

Of course, (1) the carrying out of *line* assignments to find errors in inventories and the labeling and classification of raw materials; (2) the attendance of safety, union-management (low level), and other meetings; (3) the study and compilation of reports—including those that involved "government jobs" and "graphite analyses," job descriptions, and personnel assessments; and (4) the carrying out of unofficial assignments under an official title, were all important in getting at the similar activities of others and for judging the interplay and interconnections of official and unofficial action; for gaining access to personnel files, and for learning what records were reliable as against those only "for the record."

Such functional intimacies naturally helped me to follow relations between Milo and the Office after the demise of the FWD. Lacking personal communication with the Office, I remained near the interplay by associating with (1) the few visiting representatives that I could; (2) some of the Milo personnel who had formerly been in the Office and continued to communicate with friends there; (3) a few Milo managers who made occasional trips to the Office; and (4) intimates who were critically involved in meeting expectations of the Office.

Grievance records reported for Fruhling (grouped with those of Attica and Milo) were compiled by the president of the local; those for Milo by the grievers themselves. The grievance steps, the grievances, and the decisions at Attica were transcribed by one of Reynolds' secretaries and confirmed by the grievance committee.

Access to Milo personnel files was arranged by two departments who were disputing about the merits of certain tests given to incoming personnel. It was decided that my academic training fitted me to extract "related information" from personnel files that a "clerk" might have trouble doing. Since some of the personnel who had taken the tests were managers and some were not, a powerful intimate in one of the staffs supported my suggestion that it would be helpful to examine the management file for the records of those who had taken the tests. Knowing vaguely of my intent, he cut me short, when I started to explain what I wanted and why, with the statement, "I trust you to be discreet, so I don't care what you plan to do, and I don't want to know anything about it!" In studying the files, I naturally extracted the data presented statistically in Chapter 6.

The subject of Masonry was so touchy at Milo that even some intimates shrank from having a hand in establishing precise membership and the number of Catholics who had become Masons. What seemed like a simple thing to accomplish, aroused fears, and alienated some of my fringe acquaintances whom I had mistakenly counted on for help, and whom I now saw as themselves worthy of more study. These people now avoided me and aroused my fear for success of the research. I learned later that they feared to aid me and feared not to, lest some of my intimates cause them trouble. (What should the researcher do when he disturbs the situation he would like to hold still?) Since the Masons were distributed among numerous lodges, to confirm membership I eventually had to submit lists of doubtful officers to seventeen intimates among the Masons.

Very close to people in Milo's FWD for over a year, I heard gossip from members who had been in various levels and divisions of the hierarchy; received an orientation to events of the preceding five years; studied mechanics of the FWD, and heard members analyze the department's interplay with line executives as I concurrently followed some developments in the shops. Later as a staff representative in the shops, in a role apart from the FWD, I was able to study events more connectedly while maintaining unofficial contacts with the FWD to learn of defenses that line chiefs were presenting there—without, of course, reporting anything but trivia of either side to the other.

Finally, participant-observation allowed what may be called conversational "interviewing." These efforts were verbal interaction, but not interviews in the usual sense. Since my relations with intimates often were already structured at the start of the research, any straining toward a detached manner, or pursuit of points with uncommon persistence would—and did until I learned better—defeat the purpose. Hence conversations dealing with an intimate's view of things were often broken and incomplete. In some cases utterances over a series of exchanges are tied together as one statement. The characteristic thing about them is that they were precipitated by events involving the intimate; they were "situation-centered" and often unguarded. Though most reported utterances were prompted by a question from me, or by an informal aide, some were parts of "noncatalytic" exchanges between others that I overheard in a shop or office. In other instances, comments were made as asides to me, in the shops, over an incident of the moment.

Some statements, such as the long outpourings by Geiger and Evans, in Chapters 4 and 6 respectively, were made at one time and without interruption by me. Geiger's remarks were in response to my question, "How did things go?," with reference to an exasperating cost meeting he had just left.

Usually expecting guarded talk, I sought when possible to catch men in or near critical situations, and to learn in advance when important meetings were coming up and what bearing they would have on the unofficial aspects of various issues. Experiences with reneging informants (below) prompted me to get comments or gestures of some kind from certain people before their feelings cooled or they became wary. In "interviewing" I usually had in mind a schedule of points to follow. But when the respondent's talk uncovered events of seeming greater importance, I omitted or adapted my prepared questions. Then, or at a later meeting, when I had exhausted the planned questions for a given part of the research, and was sure of the intimate, I asked loaded questions in various directions and followed promising responses.

Socializing

Out-plant socializing enabled me to study activities at the Magnesia Yacht Club, which involved the community and leaders from many firms; to develop closer relations with the managers during their periods of relaxation; to attend the installation exercises for Masonic officers and to personally verify the membership of some of the managers; to continue contacts with people at Attica and Rambeau, and at Fruhling when I was no longer employed there.

In-plant socializing, especially on my days off, allowed the cultivation of foreign born and minority groups. Seen by these as one of the majority group, my initial approach was to talk with the foreign born about a topic unforgettable to them—their country of origin. Having a strong interest in European history and culture, I found this an easy way to establish rapport with natives of Britain, Germany, Poland, Italy, Spain, Greece, the Slovak and Baltic countries. Such ethnics were pleasantly surprised to find one of the usually condescending Americans interested in and having a small knowledge of the geography, show places, heroes, artists of various kinds, current political figures and interests, and accomplishments—including culinary skills—of their native countries, and wanting to know more. These persons cleared me with suspicious first-generation Americans. It was but a step from such pleasant beginnings to knowledge of (1) name-changing and associated attitudes, (2) leads to internal plant events that I could not possibly cover in person, (3) information not contained (or distorted) in the personnel records, etc. Since many of these persons, workers and managers, at Milo and Fruhling were Catholics, they also supplied leads and valid information on the Catholic-Masonic struggle in Milo and repercussions in the community. Some of the foreign born introduced me to the priests in Magnesia who helped me with additional details.

Discussions of sports, politics, and sex usually broke the ice with the American born.

SPECIAL PROBLEMS

These include (1) the obstacle of reneging informants; (2) the question of objectivity in covert research; (3) the researcher's predicament of knowing too much for his official role; and (4) the puzzle of escaping identification with any of the key groups under study.

Reneging Informants

Obviously this is a chronic threat in every grapple with the unofficial. Moving in guarded areas, the researcher expediently seizes promising incidents and words, and comes to count on some informants more than others. But the play of events may dispose any informant to talk hot and cold. For example, a currently cooperative informant, caught in a troublesome situation, may fill a sympathetic ear today; but in a changed condition next week be cool, regret what he said, and indicate to the insensitive researcher that the latter's follow-up is in the wrong direction because he "misinterpreted" last week's remarks, etc. Since he hopes to conceal his withdrawal, this reneger offers no explanations. Presumably he thinks the researcher is too obtuse to detect the changed behavior, or he sees him as manageable or as one unable to or above taking reprisal. In dealing with such an informant a second researcher would probably get a different initial response from the first, and the first could not duplicate his earlier results.

In such cases I sought to hide my awareness of the change and my disappointment, and continued friendly relations to avoid arousing fears. However I used the informant's new stance as a clue to his probably changed involvements, and without discussing him I checked with others for possible hints of factors in his change. Drawing on these I naturally followed consistent leads, and utilized what had earlier seemed like contradictory data as they became consistent with the developing actions of this person's group or clique.

Renegers who openly withdraw as the inquiry deepens, threaten the research. Like the other type, they fear they will be labeled by their groups as persons who "talk out of turn," or that they will be punished. Apparently they fear the researcher less than their groups or other personnel, for they excuse the withdrawal, whether they explain fully or not.

Sometimes the researcher must assume blame for not having detected the informant's limits, for not more carefully preparing him and for having moved too rapidly. As with the other type of reneger, I continued on good terms. To reject the reneger is self-defeating and ignores the fact that he can feel friendship for the social analyst and still fear the larger network of ties in which both are caught. Attempts to understand the reneger are usually rewarding. He may add new angles, reveal disturbances he shares with others, and expose misinformation they have given. Though possibly shifting from the role of confidant, he continues as a subject for analysis, and a key to some areas of group feeling and action.

Objectivity in Covert Research

Such situations obviously require careful and intimate contact. Studying them at a distance the investigator may be so "objective" that he misses his subject matter and cannot say just what he is objective about. Better, he alternately immerses himself in the areas he must know, steps out in the role of critic, reorients himself and re-enters. My greatest problem in these immersions and retreats was to distinguish purely official behavior (written or understood) from the more elusive and exciting unofficial phases. Since informalists were more successful in terms of reaching ends, escaping trouble, and maintaining relative poise, my impulse frequently was to slight the formal and to forget its guiding influence on the unofficial. Repeatedly I caught myself moralizing in terms of *my* definition of formal codes which were to others, as I saw later, implicit or so vague as not to fully warrant the meaning I was reading into some informal activities. For over a year, for example, I saw all unofficial use of materials and services (Chapter 7) purely as theft. It was only after developing close relations with Merza and Berger of Milo and Nevers of Rambeau, and after long reflection on the web of incidents which bound them to others, that I saw the oversimplification I was making and shifted from an interpretation of the too rigid and exclusive categories to a more realistic judgment about the whole.

Knowing Too Much

The volume of unofficial activities, the revealing concealments to maintain essential appearances, and the official images personnel have of each other's roles—all can be brought out in time by the inquirer who labors from the screen of his formal (nonresearch) role. However, in his speculative prowling he is almost certain at times to forget that nonintimates see his formal function as embracing only a limited knowledge of unofficial events. Eager to learn more, he alarms some persons, even his fringe intimates, by accidentally disclosing bits of unofficial information they think it strange that he should have. Variously committed people misinterpret his slip, magnify what he knows, and fear that he will imprudently compromise them, or—in the changing scene— use his information for personal ends. In any case they are likely to treat him as a red light and to alert others.

Here the veiled scrutineer of things unofficial must map the total role knowledge and defenses peculiar to the different levels and functions of prospective informants. As he sensitizes himself to the role fronts of nonintimates and adapts his methods to them, he never forgets that he must simultaneously remain close to their view of his own role. Though his indirect actions are suspiciously similar to the "undercover" work of espionage agents, he is not that. He does not collect evidence to report to a control body in terms of a legal-illegal standard, nor does he seek to subvert or destroy any group. He is interested in feelings, motivations, and behavior as scientific, not criminal evidence. He does not regard his subjects as enemies of some norm he represents, and he conceals rather than reports identities. He observes to reach generalizations, not to fix moral responsibility.

Avoiding Obstructive Identifications

Randall and others at Milo, and Jessup at Fruhling, were Masons who gave me valuable aid. In our conversations some of my actions were interpreted as showing a wish to affiliate with the Order. After I attended installation exercises at Randall's lodge, he specifically said, "You talk a good fight. Maybe you'd find out a lot more if you'd get to knowing how we do things." Taking such remarks as hints for more proof of where I stood, I feared that failure to respond to cues for closer identification might be interpreted as deliberate and thus endanger the inquiry. On the other hand I knew that entering the Order would alienate helpful Catholics. By chance I avoided the problem.

Escaping overidentification with any one group while maintaining some intimacy with all groups central to unofficial issues is a prime puzzle for the masquerading researcher. My own "solution" of minimum involvement for maximum findings was a compromise that undoubtedly restricted some specific data as the price for broader information. Knowing the deeper feelings of Masons who entered the Order for career purposes—and of members who were formerly Catholics—might have given important sidelights. The compromise assumes that this additional knowledge was not vital for the study as a whole, and that the cost of acquiring it probably would have hurt the research in other ways.

DOCUMENTARY NOTES

1. Anatol Rapoport, *Operational Philosophy,* Harper and Brothers, New York, 1954, p. 48.

2. "Principles of Research," in *Essays in Science,* trans. by Alan Harris, Philosophical Library, New York, 1933, 1934, p. 4. See the similar but more

elaborate remarks of another physicist, Harold K. Schilling, "A Human Enterprise," *Science,* 127 (No. 3310): 1324–1327, June 6, 1958.

3. Among the minority of people in the psychological and social sciences who give attention to the problem, see A. H. Maslow, "Problem-Centering vs. Means-Centering in Science," *Philosophy of Science,* 13: 326–331, October, 1946; Jessie Bernard, "The Art of Science," *American Journal of Sociology,* 55: 1–9, July, 1949.

4. See recent assessments of this controversial technique: John P. Dean, "Participant Observation and Interviewing," in John T. Doby, et al., *An Introduction to Social Research,* The Stackpole Co., Harrisburg, Pennsylvania, 1954, pp. 225–252; Morris Schwartz and Charlotte Green Schwartz, "Problems in Participant Observation," *American Journal of Sociology,* 60: 343–353, January, 1955; A. J. Vidich, "Participant Observation and the Collection and Interpretation of Data," *Ibid.,* 354–360; Jiri Kolaja, "A Contribution to the Theory of Participant Observation," *Social Forces,* 35: 159–163, December, 1956; Howard S. Becker and Blanche Geer, "Participant Observation and Interviewing: A Comparison," *Human Organization,* 16 (No. 3): 28–32, Fall, 1957, and Martin Trow, "Comment," *Ibid.,* pp. 33–35; Raymond L. Gold, "Roles in Sociological Field Observations," *Social Forces,* 36: 217–223, March, 1958.

Bibliography

This list of writings is confined to items mentioned in the text and notes.

Aaron, Benjamin, "Governmental Restraints on Featherbedding," *Stanford Law Review,* 5: 680–721, July, 1953.

Abbott, C. C., J. D. Forbes, and L. A. Thompson, *The Executive Function and Its Compensation,* Charlottesville: Graduate School of Business Administration, The University of Virginia, 1957.

Allen, Francis R., et al., *Technology and Social Change,* New York: Appleton-Century-Crofts, 1957.

Allen, G. H., ed., *Individual Initiative in Business,* Cambridge: Harvard University Press, 1950.

Argyris, Chris, *Executive Leadership,* New York: Harper and Brothers, 1953.

———, *Personality and Organization,* New York: Harper and Brothers, 1957.

Aristotle, *The Nicomachean Ethics,* trans. by D. P. Chase, New York: E. P. Dutton and Co., 1911.

———, *The Politics,* trans. by H. Rackham, London: Loeb Classical Library, Heinemann, Ltd., 1932.

Arnold, Thurman W., *The Folklore of Capitalism,* New Haven: Yale University Press, 1937.

Bacon, Francis, *Essays, Civil and Moral,* in Vol. 3, Harvard Classics, New York: P. F. Collier and Sons Co., 1909.

Baker, A. W., and R. C. Davis, *Ratios of Staff to Line Employees and Stages of Differentiation of Staff Functions,* Columbus: Ohio State University Press, 1954.

Bakke, E. Wight, *Bonds of Organization,* New Haven: Yale University Labor and Management Center, 1950.

——, *Organization and the Individual,* New Haven: Yale University Labor and Management Center, 1952.

——, *The Fusion Process,* New Haven: Yale University Labor and Management Center, 1953.

Barbash, Jack, "Ideology and the Unions," *American Economic Review,* 33: 868–876, December, 1943.

——, *Labor Unions in Action,* New York: Harper and Brothers, 1948.

——, *The Practice of Unionism,* New York: Harper and Brothers, 1956.

Barnard, Chester I., *Functions of the Executive,* Cambridge: Harvard University Press, 1938.

——, "Education for Executives," *The Journal of Business of the University of Chicago,* 18: 175–182, October, 1945.

——, "Functions and Pathology of Status Systems in Formal Organizations," in W. F. Whyte, ed., *Industry and Society,* New York: McGraw-Hill Book Co., 1946, pp. 207–243.

——, *Organization and Management,* Cambridge: Harvard University Press, 1948.

Beard, Charles A., and Mary Beard, *The Rise of American Civilization,* 2 vols., New York: The Macmillan Co., 1937.

Becker, Howard, *Through Values to Social Interpretation,* Durham, North Carolina: Duke University Press, 1950.

Becker, Howard S., and Blanche Geer, "Participant Observation and Interviewing: A Comparison," *Human Organization,* 16 (no. 3): 28–32, Fall, 1957.

Bendix, Reinhard, "Bureaucracy: The Problem and Its Setting," *American Sociological Review,* 12: 493–507, October, 1947.

——, *Work and Authority in Industry,* New York: John Wiley and Sons, 1956.

Berliner, Joseph S., *Factory and Manager in the U.S.S.R.,* Cambridge: Harvard University Press, 1957.

Bernard, Jessie, "The Art of Science," *American Journal of Sociology,* 55: 1–9, July, 1949.

Bethel, Lawrence L., et al., *Industrial Organization and Management,* New York: McGraw-Hill Book Co., 1945.

Bierstedt, Robert, "An Analysis of Social Power," *American Sociological Review,* 15: 730–736, December, 1950.

——, *The Social Order,* New York: McGraw-Hill Book Co., 1957.

Blackstone, Sir William, *Commentaries on the Laws of England,* 4 vols., Philadelphia: Rees, Welsh and Co., 1900.

Blau, Peter, *The Dynamics of Bureaucracy,* Chicago: University of Chicago Press, 1954.

——, "Formal Organizations: Dimensions of Analysis," *American Journal of Sociology,* 63: 58–69, July, 1957.

Blumer, Herbert, "Group Tensions and Interest Organizations," in Milton Derber, ed., *Proceedings of the Second Annual Meeting, Industrial Relations Research Association,* Champaign, Ill., 1950, pp. 150–164.

——, "Psychological Import of the Human Group," in M. Sherif and M. O. Wilson, eds., *Group Relations at the Crossroads,* New York: Harper and Brothers, 1953, pp. 185–202.

——, "Social Structure and Power Conflict," in A. Kornhauser, R. Dubin, and A. M. Ross, eds., *Industrial Conflict,* New York: McGraw-Hill Book Co., 1954, pp. 232–239.

———, "Attitudes and the Social Act," *Social Problems,* 3: 59–65, October, 1955.

Bogoslovsky, Boris B., *The Technique of Controversy,* New York: Harcourt, Brace and Co., 1928.

Bronowski, J., *The Common Sense of Science,* London: Wm. Heinemann, Ltd., 1951.

———, "Science and Human Values," *The Nation,* 183: 550–566, December 29, 1956.

Broom, Leonard, and Philip Selznick, *Sociology: A Text with Adapted Readings,* second edition, Evanston, Ill., Row, Peterson and Co., 1958.

Bryson, Lyman, "Notes on a Theory of Advice," *Political Science Quarterly,* 66: 321–339, September, 1951.

Bryson, L., L. Finkelstein, R. M. MacIver, and R. McKeon, eds., *Symbols and Values,* New York: Harper and Brothers, 1954.

Bryson, L., L. Finkelstein, H. Hoagland, and R. M. MacIver, eds., *Symbols and Society,* New York: Harper and Brothers, 1955.

Burke, Kenneth, *Permanence and Change,* New York: New Republic, 1936.

———, *Attitudes Toward History,* 2 vols., New York: New Republic, 1937.

Burtt, E. A., *The Metaphysical Foundations of Modern Science,* Garden City, New York: Doubleday and Co., 1955.

Business Week, "A Tempo Shapes a Type," No. 1234: 56, 58, 60, April 25, 1953.

Butterfield, H., *The Statecraft of Machiavelli,* New York: Macmillan, 1956.

Cabe, J. Carl, *Foremen's Unions,* Urbana: University of Illinois, Bureau of Economic and Business Research, Bulletin 65, 1947.

Cambridge Ancient History, 12 vols., Cambridge, England: Cambridge University Press, Vol. 5, *Athens, 478–401* B.C., 1953; Vol. 10, *The Augustan Empire, 44* B.C.–A.D. *70,* 1952; Vol. 12, *The Imperial Crisis and Recovery,* A.D. *193–324,* 1939.

Cambridge Medieval History, 8 vols., Cambridge, England: Cambridge University Press, Vol. 6, *Victory of the Papacy,* 1929.

Cary, Joyce, "Political and Personal Morality," *Saturday Review,* 38 (53): 5–6, 31–32, December 31, 1955.

Chinoy, Eli, *Automobile Workers and the American Dream,* Garden City, New York: Doubleday and Co., 1955.

Clapp, Gordon R., "The Social Scientist and the Administrative Art," in L. D. White, ed., *The State of the Social Sciences,* Chicago: University of Chicago Press, 1956, pp. 393–397.

Coates, Charles H., and Roland J. Pellegrin, "Executives and Supervisors: Informal Factors in Differential Bureaucratic Promotion," *Administrative Science Quarterly,* 2 (2): 201–215, September, 1957.

Cole, Arthur H., "An Approach to the Study of Entrepreneurship," in *The Tasks of Economic History,* Supplement 6 to the *Journal of Economic History,* September, 1946, pp. 1–15.

Collins, Orvis, "Ethnic Behavior in Industry: Sponsorship and Rejection in a New England Factory," *American Journal of Sociology,* 51: 293–298, January, 1946.

Colvin, Fred H., *The Industrial Triangle,* Columbia, Connecticut: Columbia Graphs, 1955.

Cooley, Charles H., *Social Organization,* New York: Charles Scribner's Sons, 1909.

————, *Human Nature and the Social Order,* second edition, New York: Charles Scribner's Sons, 1922.

Cort, David, "World's Most Valuable Men," *The Nation,* 183: 497–500, December 8, 1956.

Coser, Lewis A., *The Function of Social Conflict,* Glencoe, Illinois: The Free Press, 1956.

Dalton, M., "Worker Response and Social Background," *Journal of Political Economy,* 55: 323–332, August, 1947.

————, "The Industrial Rate-Buster: A Characterization," *Applied Anthropology,* 7: 5–18, 1948.

————, "In-Plant Politics at the Executive and Supervisory Levels," *I R News,* Institute of Industrial Relations at UCLA, February, 1957, p. 2.

Darwin, Charles, *The Descent of Man,* 2 vols., New York: D. Appleton and Co., 1871.

Davis, Arthur K., "Bureaucratic Patterns in the Navy Officer Corps," *Social Forces,* 27: 143–153, December, 1948.

Davis, Keith, *Human Relations in Business,* New York: McGraw-Hill Book Co., 1957.

Davis, Ralph Currier, *Fundamentals of Top Management,* New York: Harper and Brothers, 1951.

Dean, John P., "Participant Observation and Interviewing," in John T. Doby, et al., *An Introduction to Social Research,* Harrisburg, Pennsylvania: The Stackpole Company, 1954, pp. 225–252.

Dewey, John, *Human Nature and Conduct,* New York: Henry Holt and Co., 1922.

Dimock, Marshall E., *The Executive in Action,* New York: Harper and Brothers, 1945.

Dobrée, Bonamy, ed., *The Letters of Philip Dormer Stanhope* (*Lord Chesterfield*), 6 vols., New York: Viking Press, 1932.

Donham, Wallace B., *Education for Responsible Living,* Cambridge: Harvard University Press, 1944.

Dorn, W. S., "Prussian Bureaucracy in the 18th Century," *Political Science Quarterly,* 46: 403–423, September, 1931; 47: 75–94, March, 1932; 47: 259–273, June, 1932.

Drucker, Peter F., *The Practice of Management,* New York: Harper and Brothers, 1954.

Dubin, Robert, *Human Relations in Administration,* New York: Prentice-Hall, 1951.

Durant, Will, *The Renaissance,* New York: Simon and Schuster, 1953.

Eckermann, J. P., *Conversations of Goethe with Eckermann,* trans. by John Oxenford, New York: E. P. Dutton and Co., 1930.

Ehrlich, Eugen, *Fundamental Principles of the Sociology of Law,* Cambridge: Harvard University Press, 1936.

Einstein, Albert, *Essays in Science,* trans. by Alan Harris, New York: Philosophical Library, 1933, 1934.

Ellis, Havelock, *The Dance of Life,* New York: The Modern Library, 1923.

Emmerich, Herbert, "New Bridges between Theory and Practice," in L. D. White, ed., *The State of the Social Sciences,* Chicago: University of Chicago Press, 1956, pp. 384–392.

Encyclopaedia Britannica, 14th edition, 1932, Vol. 2, Article, "Aqueducts."

Faris, R. E. L., *Social Psychology,* New York: The Ronald Press Co., 1952.

Fetter, Robert B., and Donald C. Johnson, *Compensation and Incentives for Industrial Executives*, Bloomington: Indiana University Press, 1952.

Flynn, John T., *Graft in Business*, New York: The Vanguard Press, 1931.

Fortune, "The Nine Hundred," *Fortune*, 42 (5): 132–135, November, 1952.

Fortune, editors of, *The Executive Life*, Garden City, New York: Doubleday and Co., 1956.

Francis, R. G., and R. C. Stone, *Service and Procedure in Bureaucracy*, Minneapolis: University of Minnesota Press, 1956.

Galbraith, John K., *American Capitalism*, Boston: Houghton Mifflin, 1952.

Gardner, B. B., and D. G. Moore, *Human Relations in Industry*, third edition, Homewood, Illinois: R. D. Irwin, 1955.

Ginzberg, Eli, ed., *What Makes an Executive?*, New York: Columbia University Press, 1955.

Gold, Raymond L., "Roles in Sociological Field Observations," *Social Forces*, 36: 217–223, March, 1958.

Goldhamer, Herbert, "Recent Developments in Personality Studies," *American Sociological Review*, 13: 555–565, October, 1948.

Gordon, Robert A., *Business Leadership in the Large Organization*, Washington, D. C.: Brookings Institution, 1945.

Gouldner, Alvin, ed., *Studies in Leadership*, New York: Harper and Brothers, 1950.

———, "Red Tape as a Social Problem," in R. K. Merton, et al., *Reader in Bureaucracy*, Glencoe, Illinois: The Free Press, 1952.

Green, Arnold W., "Sociological Analysis of Horney and Fromm," *American Journal of Sociology*, 51: 533–540, May, 1946.

Griffin, Clare E., *Enterprise in a Free Society*, Chicago: R. D. Irwin, 1949.

Gross, E., "Symbiosis and Consensus as Integrative Factors in Small Groups," *American Sociological Review*, 21: 174–179, April, 1956.

Guicciardini, Francesco, *Ricordi*, trans. by Ninian Hill Thomson, New York: S. F. Vanni, 1949.

Gulick, Luther, and L. Urwick, eds., *Papers on the Science of Administration*, New York: Institute of Public Administration, Columbia University, 1937.

Hamilton, Alexander, John Jay, and James Madison, *The Federalist*, New York: The Colonial Press, 1901.

Hayakawa, S. I., *Language and Thought in Action*, New York: Harcourt, Brace and Co., 1949.

Hayakawa, S. I., ed., *Language, Meaning and Maturity*, New York: Harper and Brothers, 1954.

Hazlitt, William, *Table Talk, or Original Essays*, New York: E. P. Dutton and Co., 1908.

Heberle, Rudolph, "The Sociological System of Ferdinand Tönnies: 'Community' and 'Society,'" in H. E. Barnes, ed., *An Introduction to the History of Sociology*, Chicago: University of Chicago Press, 1948, pp. 227–248.

Hegner, R. W., *College Zoology*, 5th edition, New York: The Macmillan Co., 1942.

Henry, W. E., "The Business Executive: The Psychodynamics of a Social Role," *American Journal of Sociology*, 54: 286–291, January, 1949.

Heraclitus on the Universe (in *Hippocrates and The Fragments of Heraclitus*), 4 vols., trans. by W. H. S. Jones, London: Loeb Classical Library, Heinemann Ltd., Vol. 4, pp. 471–509, 1923–1931.

Hertzler, J. O., *Society in Action*, New York: The Dryden Press, 1954.

Hoijer, Harry, ed., *Language in Culture*, Chicago: University of Chicago Press, 1954.

Homans, George C., *The Human Group*, New York: Harcourt, Brace and Co., 1950.

Hughes, Everett C., "Queries Concerning Industry and Society Growing Out of Study of Ethnic Relations in Industry," *American Sociological Review*, 14: 211–220, April, 1949.

———, and Helen M. Hughes, *Where Peoples Meet*, Glencoe, Illinois: The Free Press, 1952.

Hunter, Floyd, *Community Power Structure*, Chapel Hill: University of North Carolina Press, 1953.

———, "The Decision-Makers," *The Nation*, 179: 148–150, August 21, 1954.

Jacques, Elliot, *Measurement of Responsibility*, London: Tavistock Publications Ltd., 1956.

———, *The Changing Culture of a Factory*, New York: The Dryden Press, 1952.

Jameson, Samuel Haig, "Principles of Social Interaction," *American Sociological Review*, 10: 6–10, February, 1945.

Johnson, Martin, *Art and Scientific Thought*, New York: Columbia University Press, 1949.

Juvenal's Satires, trans. by William Gifford; revised and annotated by J. Warrington, New York: E. P. Dutton and Co., 1954.

Katona, George, *Psychological Analysis of Economic Behavior*, New York: McGraw-Hill Book Co., 1951.

Keller, Suzanne I., "Social Origins and Career Lines of Three Generations of American Business Leaders," Ph.D. Thesis, New York: Columbia University, 1954.

Kennedy, Van D., "Grievance Negotiation," in A. Kornhauser, R. Dubin, and A. M. Ross, eds., *Industrial Conflict*, New York: McGraw-Hill Book Co., 1954, pp. 280–291.

Key, Jr., V. O., *Politics, Parties, and Pressure Groups*, second edition, New York: Thomas Y. Crowell Co., 1947.

Khaldun, Ibn, *An Arab Philosophy of History: Selections from the Prolegomena of Ibn Khaldun*, trans. and arranged by Charles Issawi, London: Butler and Tanner Ltd., 1950.

Knowles, W. H., *Personnel Management: A Human Relations Approach*, New York: American Book Co., 1955.

Kolaja, Jiri, "A Contribution to the Theory of Participant Observation," *Social Forces*, 35: 159–163, December, 1956.

Kornhauser, A. W., "Analysis of 'Class' Structure of Contemporary American Society—Psychological Bases of Class Divisions," in G. W. Hartman, and T. Newcomb, eds., *Industrial Conflict* (First Yearbook of the Society for the Psychological Study of Social Issues), New York: The Cordon Co., 1939, chap. 11.

Kornhauser, A., R. Dubin, and A. M. Ross, eds., *Industrial Conflict*, New York: McGraw-Hill Book Co., Inc., 1954.

Kruisinga, H. J., ed., *The Balance Between Centralization and Decentralization in Managerial Control*, Leiden: H. E. Stenfert Kroese, N.V., 1954.

Laski, H. J., "The Limitations of the Expert," *Harper's Magazine*, 162: 102–106, December, 1930.

Lauterbach, Albert, *Man, Motives and Money,* Ithaca, New York: Cornell University Press, 1954.

Learned, E. P., D. N. Ulrich, and D. R. Booz, *Executive Action,* Boston: Division of Research, Graduate School of Business Administration, Harvard University, 1951.

Lepawsky, Albert, *Administration,* New York: A. A. Knopf, 1949.

Levine, Solomon B., "Management and Industrial Relations in Postwar Japan," Institute of Labor and Industrial Relations, University of Illinois, Reprint Series No. 42, from *The Far Eastern Quarterly,* 15 (1): 57–75, November, 1955.

Levy, Marion J., Jr., *The Structure of Society,* Princeton, New Jersey: Princeton University Press, 1952.

Lewis, Gordon F., and C. Arnold Anderson, "Social Origins and Social Mobility of Business Men in an American City," *Transactions of the Third World Congress of Sociology,* 3: 253–266, 1956.

Lindesmith, A. R., and A. L. Strauss, *Social Psychology,* New York: The Dryden Press, 1949.

Lippmann, Walter, *A Preface to Politics,* New York: The Macmillan Co., 1913.

Lombard, George F. F., *Behavior in a Selling Group,* Boston: Harvard University, Graduate School of Business Administration, 1955.

Lytle, C. W., *Wage Incentive Methods,* New York: The Ronald Press Co., 1942.

MacIver, R. M., and C. H. Page, *Society: An Introductory Analysis,* New York: Rinehart and Co., 1949.

McCormick, T. C., *Elementary Social Statistics,* New York: McGraw-Hill Book Co., 1941.

Machiavelli, Niccolo, The Discourses of, 2 vols., trans. and edited by Leslie J. Walker, S.J., New Haven: Yale University Press, 1950.

Marriott, R., *Incentive Payment Systems,* London: Staples Press Ltd., 1957.

Maslow, W. H., "Problem-Centering vs. Means-Centering in Science," *Philosophy of Science,* 13: 326–331, October, 1946.

Mayo, Elton, *The Human Problems of an Industrial Civilization,* New York: The Macmillan Co., 1933.

———, *The Social Problems of an Industrial Civilization,* Boston: Division of Research, Harvard Graduate School of Business Administration, 1945.

Mead, George Herbert, "The Social Self," *The Journal of Philosophy,* 10: 374–380, July 3, 1913.

———, "A Behavioristic Account of the Significant Symbol," *The Journal of Philosophy,* 19: 157–163, March 16, 1922.

———, *The Philosophy of the Present,* edited by Arthur E. Murphy, New York: Open Court Publishing Co., 1932.

———, *Mind, Self, and Society,* edited by Charles W. Morris, Chicago: University of Chicago Press, 1934.

———, *The Philosophy of the Act,* edited by Charles W. Morris, Chicago: University of Chicago Press, 1938.

Mendieta y Nunez, Lucio, "The Social Classes," *American Sociological Review,* 11: 166–176, April, 1946.

Merton, Robert K., "The Unanticipated Consequences of Purposive Social Action," *American Sociological Review,* 1: 894–904, December, 1936.

———, "Bureaucratic Structure and Personality," *Social Forces,* 18: 560–568, May, 1940.

————, "The Machine, the Worker, and the Engineer," *Science*, 105: 78–81, January 24, 1947.

Merton, Robert K., and Alice Kitt, "Contributions to the Theory of Reference Group Behavior," in R. K. Merton and P. F. Lazarsfeld, eds., *Continuities in Social Research*, Glencoe, Illinois: The Free Press, 1950, pp. 86–95.

Merton, Robert K., A. P. Gray, Barbara Hockey, and H. C. Selvin, *Reader in Bureaucracy*, Glencoe, Illinois: The Free Press, 1952.

Metcalf, H. C., and L. Urwick, eds., *Dynamic Administration: The Collected Papers of Mary Park Follett*, London: Management Publications Trust, Ltd., 1941.

Michels, Robert, *Political Parties*, trans. by Eden and Cedar Paul, Glencoe, Illinois: The Free Press, 1949.

Miller, Delbert C., and W. H. Form, *Industrial Sociology*, New York: Harper and Brothers, 1951.

Miller, Delbert C., "The Seattle Business Leader," *Pacific Northwest Business*, Seattle: College of Business Administration, University of Washington, 15: (5)5–12, February, 1956.

Miller, William, ed., *Men in Business: Essays in the History of Entrepreneurship*, Cambridge: Harvard University Press, 1952.

Mills, John, *The Engineer in Society*, New York: D. Van Nostrand Co., 1946.

Mills, C. Wright, "The American Business Elite: A Collective Portrait," in *The Tasks of Economic History*, Supplement 5 to *The Journal of Economic History*, December, 1945, pp. 20–44.

————, *White Collar*, New York: Oxford University Press, 1951.

————, *The Power Elite*, New York: Oxford University Press, 1956.

Mintz, Seymour, "Executive Expense Accounts and Fringe Benefits: A Problem in Management, Morality and Revenue," *Journal of Taxation*, 1: 2–9, June, 1954.

Montaigne, Michel de, *Complete Works of*, trans. by Donald M. Frame, Stanford, California: Stanford University Press, 1948, 1957.

Moore, Harriet B., and Sidney J. Levy, "Artful Contrivers: A Study of Engineers," *Personnel*, 28: 148–153, September, 1951.

Moore, Wilbert E., *Industrial Relations and the Social Order*, revised edition, New York: The Macmillan Co., 1951.

Morris, Richard T., and M. Seeman, "The Problem of Leadership: an Interdisciplinary Approach," *American Journal of Sociology*, 56: 149–155, September, 1950.

Murphy, Gardner, *Personality: A Biosocial Approach to Origins and Structure*, New York: Harper and Brothers, 1947.

Myers, Charles A., and John G. Turnbull, "Line and Staff in Industrial Relations," *Harvard Business Review*, 34: 113–124, July–August, 1956.

Newcomb, T. M., *Social Psychology*, New York: The Dryden Press, 1950.

Newcomer, Mabel, *The Big Business Executive*, New York: Columbia University Press, 1955.

Newsweek, "Should Companies Give?" 48: 59–60, December 24, 1956.

————, "Those Big-Figure Expense Accounts," 49:87, 90–92, May 20, 1957.

Nightingale, Florence, *Notes on Hospitals*, New York: Longmans, 1863.

Northrop, F. S. C., *The Logic of the Sciences and the Humanities*, New York: The Macmillan Co., 1947.

Ogburn, William F., *Social Change*, New York: Viking Press, 1922, 1950.

Oliver, F. S., *The Endless Adventure*, 3 vols., London: Macmillan and Co., Ltd., 1930–1935.

Orwell, George, *Nineteen Eighty-Four*, New York: Harcourt, Brace and Co., 1949.

Page, Charles Hunt, "Bureaucracy's Other Face," *Social Forces*, 25: 88–94, October, 1946.

Pareto, Vilfredo, *The Mind and Society*, 4 vols., edited and trans. by A. Livingstone and A. Bongiorno, New York: Harcourt, Brace and Co., 1935.

Park, Robert E., "Symbiosis and Socialization: A Frame of Reference for the Study of Society," *American Journal of Sociology*, 45: 1–25, July, 1939.

Parkinson, C. Northcote, *Parkinson's Law*, Boston: Houghton Mifflin Co., 1957.

Perry, Ralph Barton, *Realms of Value*, Cambridge: Harvard University Press, 1954.

Person, H. S., ed., *Scientific Management in American Industry*, New York: Harper and Brothers, 1929.

Pfiffner, John M., *A Tentative Syllabus for the Study of Informal Organization*, Los Angeles: School of Public Administration, University of Southern California, 1949.

———, *The Supervision of Personnel: Human Relations in the Management of Men*, New York: Prentice-Hall, 1951.

Pfuetz, P. E., *The Social Self*, New York: Bookman Associates, 1954.

Quinn, T. K., *Giant Business: Threat to Democracy*, New York: Exposition Press, 1953.

———, "Sovereign State of G.M.," *The Nation*, 182: 447–448, May 26, 1956.

Rapoport, Anatol, *Operational Philosophy*, New York: Harper and Brothers, 1954.

Redfield, Charles E., *Communication in Management*, Chicago: The University of Chicago Press, 1953.

Reissman, Leonard, "A Study of Role Conceptions in Bureaucracy," *Social Forces*, 27: 305–310, March, 1949.

Rice, P. B., *On The Knowledge of Good and Evil*, New York: Random House, 1955.

Riegel, John W., *Administration of Salaries and Intangible Rewards for Engineers and Scientists*, Ann Arbor: Bureau of Industrial Relations, University of Michigan, 1958.

Riesman, David, N. Glazer, and R. Denney, *The Lonely Crowd*, New Haven: Yale University Press, 1950.

Roethlisberger, F. J., and J. Dickson, *Management and the Worker*, Cambridge: Harvard University Press, 1939.

Roethlisberger, F. J., *Management and Morale*, Cambridge: Harvard University Press, 1941.

———, "The Foreman: Master and Victim of Double Talk," *Harvard Business Review*, 23: 285–294, Spring, 1945.

Ronken, Harriet O., and Paul R. Lawrence, *Administering Changes*, Boston: Harvard University, Graduate School of Business Administration, 1952.

Roscoe, E. S., *Organization for Production*, Homewood, Illinois: Richard D. Irwin, 1955.

Ross, E. A., *Principles of Sociology*, New York: D. Appleton-Century Co., 1938.

Russell, Bertrand, *A History of Western Philosophy*, New York: Simon and Schuster, 1945.

Sampson, Robert C., *The Staff Role in Management*, New York: Harper and Brothers, 1955.

Santayana, George, *The Life of Reason*, 5 vols., New York: Charles Scribner's Sons, 1905–1906.

Sayles, Leonard R., and George Strauss, *The Local Union*, New York: Harper and Brothers, 1953.

Schilling, Harold K., "A Human Enterprise," *Science*, 127 (no. 3310): 1324–1327, June 6, 1958.

Schleh, Edward C., *Successful Executive Action*, Englewood Cliffs, New Jersey: Prentice-Hall, 1955.

Schneider, H. W., *Three Dimensions of Public Morality*, Bloomington: Indiana University Press, 1956.

Schwartz, Morris, and Charlotte Green Schwartz, "Problems in Participant Observation," *American Journal of Sociology*, 60: 343–353, January, 1955.

Scott, Jerome F., and R. P. Lynton, *Three Studies in Management*, London: Routledge and Kegan Paul, Ltd., 1952.

Seeman, Melvin, "Role Conflict and Ambivalence in Leadership," *American Sociological Review*, 18: 370–380, August, 1953.

Selznick, Philip, "An Approach to a Theory of Bureaucracy," *American Sociological Review*, 8: 51–54, February, 1943.

———, *TVA and the Grass Roots*, Berkeley and Los Angeles: University of California Press, 1949.

Shartle, C. L., *Executive Performance and Leadership*, Englewood Cliffs, New Jersey: Prentice-Hall, 1956.

Sheldon, Oliver, *The Philosophy of Management*, London: Pitman and Sons, 1924.

Sherif, Muzafer, "The Concept of Reference Groups in Human Relations," in M. Sherif and M. O. Wilson, eds., *Group Relations at the Crossroads*, New York: Harper and Brothers, 1953, pp. 203–231.

Siegel, Abraham J., "The Economic Environment in Human Relations Research," in *Research in Industrial Human Relations*, Publication 17 of the Industrial Relations Research Association, New York: Harper and Brothers, 1957, pp. 86–99.

Silberston, Aubrey, *Education and Training for Industrial Management*, London: Management Publications Limited, The Millbrook Press, Ltd., 1955.

Simmel, Georg, *Conflict*, and *The Web of Group Affiliations*, trans. respectively by Kurt H. Wolff and Reinhard Bendix, Glencoe Illinois: The Free Press, 1955.

Simon, Herbert A., *Administrative Behavior*, first edition, New York: The Macmillan Co., 1948.

Slichter, Sumner, "Report on Current Research: Economics," *Saturday Review*, 36: 24–25, 53–55, April 4, 1953.

Smith, T. V., "In Accentuation of the Negative," *The Scientific Monthly*, 63: 463–469, December, 1946.

———, *The Ethics of Compromise*, Boston: Starr King Press, 1956.

Sorokin, Pitirim A., *Social Mobility*, New York: Harper and Brothers, 1927.

Sorokin, P., C. C. Zimmerman, and C. J. Galpin, *A Systematic Source Book in Rural Sociology*, 3 vols., Minneapolis: The University of Minnesota Press, 1930.

Spitz, René A., "Hospitalism," in *The Psychoanalytic Study of the Child, Vol. 1*, New York: International Universities Press, 1945, pp. 53–72.

————, "Hospitalism: A Follow-Up Report," in *The Psychoanalytic Study of the Child*, Vol. 2, New York: International Universities Press, 1946, pp. 113–117.

Standen, Anthony, *Science is a Sacred Cow*, New York: E. P. Dutton, 1950.

Starch, D., "An Analysis of the Careers of 150 Executives," *Psychological Bulletin*, 39: 435, July, 1942. A summary of a study presented at the Fiftieth Anniversary Meeting of the American Psychological Association.

Steffens, Lincoln, *The Autobiography of*, New York: Harcourt, Brace and Co., 1931.

Stogdill, R. M., E. L. Scott, and W. E. Jaynes, *Leadership and Role Expectations*, Columbus: The Ohio State University, Bureau of Business Research, Research Monograph 86, 1956.

Stryker, Perrin, and the Editors of *Fortune, A Guide to Modern Management Methods*, New York, McGraw-Hill Book Co., 1954.

Stryker, Perrin, "How Executives Delegate," in the Editors of *Fortune, The Executive Life*, Garden City, New York: Doubleday and Co., 1956, pp. 135–148.

Sumner, William Graham, *Folkways*, Boston: Ginn and Co., 1906.

Super, Donald E., *The Psychology of Careers*, New York: Harper and Brothers, 1957.

Sutherland, Edwin H., *White Collar Crime*, New York: The Dryden Press, 1949.

Tacitus, *Historical Works*, 2 vols., Vol. 1, *The Annals*, trans. by Arthur Murray, New York: E. P. Dutton and Co., no date.

Tannenbaum, Robert, and Fred Massarik, "Leadership: A Frame of Reference," *Management Science*, 4 (No. 1) 1–19, October, 1957.

Tannenbaum, Robert, V. Kallejian, and Irving R. Weschler, "Training Managers for Leadership," *Personnel*, 30 (4) 2–8, January, 1954.

Taussig, F. W., and C. S. Joslyn, *American Business Leaders: A Study in Social Origins and Social Stratification*, New York: The Macmillan Co., 1932.

Tead, Ordway, *The Art of Administration*, New York: McGraw-Hill Book Co., 1951.

Thompson, James D., "Authority and Power in Identical Organizations," *American Journal of Sociology*, 62: 290–301, November, 1956.

Thucydides, *History of the Peloponnesian War*, trans. by R. Crawley, New York: E. P. Dutton and Co., 1910.

Tocqueville, Alexis de, *Democracy in America*, 2 vols., trans. by Henry Reeve, New York: The Colonial Press, 1900.

Tönnies, Ferdinand, *Fundamental Concepts of Sociology*, trans. and supplemented by C. P. Loomis, New York: The American Book Co., 1940.

Trow, Martin, "Comment" (on Becker and Geer, 'Participant Observation and Interviewing: A Comparison' in the same issue), *Human Organization*, 16 (no. 3): 33–35, Fall, 1957.

Turner, Ralph H., "The Navy Disbursing Officer as a Bureaucrat," *American Sociological Review*, 12: 342–348, June, 1947.

————, "Role-Taking, Role Standpoint, and Reference-Group Behavior," *American Journal of Sociology*, 61: 316–328, January, 1956.

UAW–CIO, *How to Win for the Union*, Handbook for Stewards and Committeemen, seventh edition, 1945.

United States, Security and Exchange Commission, Washington, D.C.: *Public Documents, Form 10–K*, Fiscal Year ending August 21, 1956.

Urwick, Lyndall F., *Some Notes on the Theory of Organization*, New York: American Management Association, 1952.

——, *The Pattern of Management*, Minneapolis: University of Minnesota Press, 1956.

Urwick, Lyndall F., and E. Dale, "Profitably Using the General Staff Position in Business," *General Management Series*, no. 165, New York: American Management Association, 1953.

Vaihinger, Hans, *The Philosophy of As If*, trans. by C. K. Ogden, New York: Harcourt, Brace and Co., 1924.

Van Der Schroeff, H. J., and W. Vonk, "Conditions for an Equilibrium," in Kruisinga, H. J., ed., *The Balance Between Centralization and Decentralization in Managerial Control*, Leiden: H. E. Stenfert Kroese, N.V., 1954, pp. 44–54.

Vasari, Giorgio, *The Lives of the Painters, Sculptors, and Architects*, 4 vols., trans. by A. B. Hinds, New York: E. P. Dutton and Co., 1927.

Vidich, A. J., "Participant Observation and the Collection and Interpretation of Data," *American Journal of Sociology*, 60: 354–360, January, 1955.

Villari, Pasquale, *Life and Times of Girolamo Savonarola*, trans. by Linda Villari, London: T. Fisher Unwin, 1888.

Viteles, Morris S., *Motivation and Morale in Industry*, New York: W. W. Norton and Co., 1954.

Warner, W. Lloyd, and J. C. Abegglen, *Occupational Mobility in American Business and Industry*, Minneapolis: University of Minnesota Press, 1955.

——, *Big Business Leaders in America*, New York: Harper and Brothers, 1955.

Warner, W. Lloyd, and Leo Srole, *The Social Systems of American Ethnic Groups*, New Haven: Yale University Press, 1947.

Weber, Max, "Science as a Vocation," trans. by Edward A. Shils, in *Contemporary Society, Selected Readings* (Social Science 3), tenth edition, Chicago: University of Chicago Bookstore, 1942.

——, *From Max Weber: Essays in Sociology*, trans. by H. Gerth and C. Wright Mills, New York: Oxford University Press, 1946.

——, *The Theory of Social and Economic Organization*, trans. by A. M. Henderson and T. Parsons, New York: Oxford University Press, 1947.

——, *On Law and Economy in Society*, ed. by Max Rheinstein, trans. by Edward Shils and Max Rheinstein, Cambridge: Harvard University Press, 1954.

Whisler, T. L., "The Assistant-To: The Man in Motley," *The Journal of Business of the University of Chicago*, 29: 274–279, October, 1956.

White, Leonard D., ed., *The State of the Social Sciences*, Chicago: University of Chicago Press, 1956.

Whitehead, A. N., *Science and the Modern World*, New York: The Macmillan Co., 1925.

Whitehead, T. N., *Leadership in a Free Society*, Cambridge: Harvard University Press, 1937.

Whyte, William F., ed., *Industry and Society*, New York: McGraw-Hill Book Co., 1946.

——, *Human Relations in the Restaurant Industry*, New York: McGraw-Hill Book Co., 1948.

——, "The Social Structure of the Restaurant," *American Journal of Sociology*, 54: 302–308, January, 1949.

——, et al, *Money and Motivation*, New York: Harper and Brothers, 1955.

Whyte, William H., Jr., *Is Anybody Listening?* New York: Simon and Schuster, Inc., 1952.

———, *The Organization Man,* New York: Simon and Schuster, 1956.

Wilensky, Harold L., *Intellectuals in Labor Unions,* Glencoe, Illinois, The Free Press, 1956.

Willkie, H. Frederick, *A Rebel Yells,* New York: D. Van Nostrand Co., 1946.

Wray, Donald E., "Marginal Men of Industry: The Foremen," *American Journal of Sociology,* 54: 298–301, January, 1949.

Wright, Quincy, *A Study of War,* 2 vols., Chicago: University of Chicago Press, 1942.

Zaleznik, A., *Foreman Training in a Growing Enterprise,* Boston: Harvard University, Graduate School of Business Administration, 1951.

Name Index

301

Subject Index

Specific managers and workers in the study are listed by their italicized surnames, and indexed in terms of their activities and comments.